Bare-Knuckle Britons
and Fighting Irish

Bare-Knuckle Britons and Fighting Irish

Boxing, Race, Religion and Nationality in the 18th and 19th Centuries

ADAM CHILL

McFarland & Company, Inc., Publishers
Jefferson, North Carolina

ISBN (print) 978-1-4766-6330-2
ISBN (ebook) 978-1-4766-3028-1

Library of Congress cataloguing data are available

British Library cataloguing data are available

Front cover photograph courtesy Library of Congress

Printed in the United States of America

McFarland & Company, Inc., Publishers
Box 611, Jefferson, North Carolina 28640
www.mcfarlandpub.com

To Niamh, Sam, and Mary

Table of Contents

Acknowledgments

I have accumulated many debts during the long journey since my interest in Georgian-era bare-knuckle boxing was first sparked in the Burns Library at Boston College. Archivists and staff at the Burns, the British Library, the British Museum, the National Archives, and the Houghton Library at Harvard were very helpful as I gathered the evidence on which this book is based. I am especially grateful to the British Library newspaper archive at Colindale, which is now sadly closed. Much of its collection is digitized but an online database can never replace the kind and patient assistance I received from the staff there. I am also thankful to the Irish Studies program at Boston College for awarding me the Adele Dalsimer Fellowship, which enabled me travel to London. In Ireland, Denis Harte generously showed me around the Curragh, helped me find Donnelly's Hollow, and took me on my first (but certainly not last) trip to Croke Park.

At Boston College many faculty mentors were a critical part of my development as a scholar. Among many others, Paul Breines, Robin Fleming, Kevin Kenny, and Prasannan Parthasarathi were particularly important. My dissertation committee—Kevin O'Neill, Peter Weiler, and Deborah Valenze—read my work carefully and gave invaluable advice at every stage. I also benefitted (and continue to benefit) from a great group of friends and colleagues at Boston College, especially Laura Baines-Walsh, Jill Bender, Jen Cote, Mimi Cowan, Jason Cavallari, Andrew Finstuen, Bethany Jay, Meredith Volker, and Greg Walsh. The Irish History Reading Group—Anthony Daly, Mark Doyle, Meaghan Dwyer, and Ely Janis—read all of my chapters in draft and offered crucial criticism and encouragement. Kevin Creehan, Babette Faehmel, and Ted Petro have been great friends and supporters as well.

Since moving to Vermont, I have had the good fortune to be surrounded by generous and supportive colleagues. Andre Fleche, Trish van der Spuy, Carrie Waara, Rich Clark, Melisse Pinto, Judy Robinson, and Scott Roper have all listened to me talk about the historical importance of prizefighting. I am lucky to be part of an engaging and vibrant intellectual community at

Castleton University. Sue Generazzo, Charlotte Gerstein, Marybeth Lennox, Melinda Mills, Matt Moriarty, Lauren Olewnik, Tony Peffer, Kathryn Sperry, Jonathan Spiro, Michael Talbott and many others have been great colleagues and friends. In Rutland, I worked on this project at the Rutland Free Library and at Speakeasy Café. I am thankful to the staff of both for allowing me to sit for hours, staring at a computer screen.

Small parts of this book were published elsewhere. I wish to thank the Department of Hebrew and Jewish Studies at University College London as well as editors Michael Berkowitz and Ruti Ungar for granting me permission to use some material from my essay for the collection *Fighting Back? Jewish and Black Boxers in Britain*. I would also like to thank the *Journal of the Study of British Cultures* for permitting the use of material from my article "Ireland Forever! Irish Boxers and Britishness in the Early Nineteenth Century."

My biggest debt is to my family. Mary Irene Steele was my inspiration to study history and I always benefited from her favoritism. I wish she were here to read this book. Bill Bergmann has been my closest friend and an honorary family member for years and I have relied on his advice and support more than he knows. John and Mary Lynch have welcomed me into their family and have helped in innumerable ways, both big and small. My parents Patricia Henkel and Michael Chill always believed in me and encouraged me, even when I wanted to go far away. Sam and Mary keep things in perspective and made it all worthwhile. Finally, none of this would have been possible without my wife Niamh Lynch. She read and commented on multiple drafts, always kept me focused, listened to me talk about boxing for countless hours, and let me be away for long stretches to work on this book. Although any errors are my own, this work is hers as much as mine.

Preface

This book is about bare-knuckle prizefighting in Britain and Ireland in the eighteenth and nineteenth centuries. While the fortunes of the sport ebbed and flowed, it was one of the most popular phenomena of the era. Thousands of spectators attended important matches, often walking or riding many miles to do so. Members of the royal family patronized boxers, leading literary figures wrote about them, and MPs debated the merits of boxing in the House of Commons. Small fortunes were won and lost on the outcome of prizefights and, in some cases, fighters from humble backgrounds won riches themselves. In far fewer instances, they were able to maintain their new wealth after the ends of their careers. Allusions to boxing appeared in literature, popular prints, and political speeches. The sport was symbolically powerful as well. For proponents, it represented the timeless strength of British character while, to opponents, its popularity signaled the moral decay of the country.

The prominence of bare-knuckle prizefighting in the eighteenth and nineteenth centuries makes it a worthy object of study. It is also particularly important, however, for what it can tell us about identity in this critical period of British and Irish history. A central premise of this book is that the sport's popularity was not preordained but, rather, was actively cultivated by a variety of characters: especially patrons, journalists, and boxers. A critical way they did so was by exploiting national, ethnic, religious, and racial identities. The use of identities by fighters, journalists, patrons, and many others is a central theme in the pages that follow.

While this book offers a detailed survey of many of the people involved in bare-knuckle prizefighting and the culture they created in and around their sport, it is not intended to be exhaustive. Because of my central theme—and because their importance has often been underappreciated—I particularly highlight the many Irish, Jewish, and black boxers who participated in the sport. The best white, Christian, English fighters are part of the story too but do not figure as prominently as they might in other works on this topic.

The book also focuses less on the relationship of the sport to literature (a topic that has been well studied in recent years) and more on the social and cultural aspects of the sport itself. The reader will thus find more publicans than poets here.

The focus of this book has also shaped the sources on which it is based. Journalists, boxers, and publicans from the eighteenth and nineteenth centuries left behind very little correspondence or other unpublished material, while the aristocrats and other members of the wealthy elite who were involved in the sport rarely wrote privately about it. The book therefore relies to a great extent on newspapers, which are often the only window (or sometimes keyhole) we have to glimpse the world of prizefighting. These sources can be problematic, of course, but if used with care can reveal much about the experience of boxers and their world. Newspapers are now much more accessible than when I undertook the research for the dissertation that was the genesis of this work. Then, I spent long months at the now-shuttered British Library newspaper archive in Colindale. Now, many of its newspapers have been digitized and are available (for a fee) on a searchable online database. This has enabled me to examine them from New England in the past few years.

Before the mass digitization that made possible such peripatetic research, this work began life as a dissertation. I was interested in the relationship between Britishness and other identities in Britain and Ireland when I chanced upon nineteenth-century journalist Pierce Egan's magisterial *Boxiana* in the Burns Library archive at Boston College. This source piqued my interest in boxing, especially as a way to understand national, religious, and racial identities and my dissertation highlighted the languages that writers used to describe identity in the sport between 1780 and 1830. In the years that followed, I became more interested in how fighters and other participants in the sport used identities. As this book began to take shape I sought to shift the center of my focus, as much as possible, to the boxers and their world. This change also prompted me to broaden the chronological scope of this work to incorporate the whole of the bare-knuckle boxing era, from its genesis in the early eighteenth century to its demise in the late nineteenth century. As we will see below, extending the story into the Victorian era helps us understand that bare-knuckle prizefighting was an important cultural phenomenon even when most aristocratic patrons had abandoned it.

This book is arranged chronologically. Its periodization is determined in part by the internal dynamics of the sport but, as the sport reflected and was shaped by the world beyond it, the chapters are also framed by the critical events of the period. Thus, for example, the two phases of conflict with revolutionary and Napoleonic France provide the backdrop for chapters three and four, while the reforms of the early 1830s divide chapters seven and eight. Because much of the popularity of the sport was derived from the belief that it was a symbol of the health and strength of the nation, I argue, it needs to be understood in this larger context. Although the limitations of space mean that not every connection can be pursued here, I have endeavored to put bare-knuckle prizefighting in the frame that contemporaries understood it.

The era of bare-knuckle prizefighting is a deeply interesting and important chapter in British and Irish history and boxing that can tell us a great deal about wider society in the period. Demonstrating this requires a certain amount of engagement with scholarly literature but I have tried to balance this by giving equal time to the fascinating stories of the pugilists and their world. The book will thus be of interest not only to scholars but also to those who wish to know more about the bare-knuckle era and the colorful men and women who populated it. It is my hope that both groups will find something of value in this book.

Introduction

Since the late nineteenth century, nationalism has heightened interest in sporting contests. The Olympics, the World Cup, the Davis Cup, the Six Nations, and many other tournaments pit one country's side against another and encourage spectators to see individual athletes or teams as representative of their nation.[1] As we shall see, the roots of this phenomenon lay in an earlier time, in the immensely popular sport of prizefighting in Britain and Ireland in the eighteenth and nineteenth centuries. Pugilists, promoters, and other supporters tried to attract spectators—and defend their sport against its many critics—by claiming that prizefighters embodied the best qualities of the (male) nation. In addition to highlighting nationalism, modern sports competitions have also been sites of resistance. In perhaps the most famous example, African American medalists Tommie Smith and John Carlos famously raised their fists in a black power salute during the 1968 Olympic games. This subversion of nationalism in sport also had a precedent in bare-knuckle prizefighting. The Irish, Jewish, and black pugilists who often were the opponents of Protestant English prizefighters fashioned their own identities in and out of the boxing ring, (unlike Smith and Carlos) in an effort to improve their own fortunes. The competing identities promoted by bare-knuckle prizefighters, their patrons, and many others are the focus of this book.

Prizefighting advocates' frequent and unabashed evocations of English/British nationalism are consistent with the influential conclusions of Linda Colley and others, that a militant Protestant British identity had great purchase in the eighteenth and early nineteenth centuries.[2] Especially in the late eighteenth century, many Britons believed that aristocratic corruption and various foreign influences were, as Kathleen Wilson has argued, "corroding both national manners and martial might." These nefarious forces could only be kept at bay by promoting "English virtue"—exactly what the supporters of bare-knuckle prizefighting claimed that their sport did.[3] They defended it by endlessly repeating the English values that they claimed boxing promoted—fair play and courage chief among them—and the foreign vices that it kept at bay; the stiletto-wielding Portuguese or Italian was a stock villain and counterpoint of virtuous English pugilists in much boxing writing of the period. Not surprisingly, the high points of bare-knuckle prizefighting's popularity (the 1740s, the 1780s, and the 1810s) coincided with periods of war or threatened war with Catholic foes on the continent.

In reality, English boxers' opponents were very rarely from the continent. Instead, pugilists from minority[4] groups *within* Britain were often their antagonists. Irish, Jewish, and black pugilists were seen as foils for Britishness as (usually) embodied by English fighters and, as we shall see, they frequently encountered hostile spectators and, in some cases, were clearly cheated of victory. This also supports the claims of historians who have suggested that hostility toward Irish and Jewish people has been as important in the construction of Britishness as attitudes to Catholics on the continent.[5] Moments at which the Irish Catholic or Jewish populations were believed to be on the verge of gaining greater rights provoked strong and bloody responses, as in public reaction to the so-called "Jew Bill of 1753" and in the anti–Catholic Gordon riots of 1780.[6] The black community in Britain, never large enough in this period to be perceived as a threat, was nevertheless subject to condescension and ridicule.[7] English crowds were thus primed to see minority pugilists as fundamentally different than—and even antagonistic to—white English Protestants.

Minority prizefighters were not simply passive foils, however. Many of them took an active role in shaping their public images. From the 1780s, the Jewish and Irish communities in Britain publicly supported Jewish and Irish pugilists, who used words and symbols to encourage them to do so. Prizefighting thus became a means for Jewish and Irish people to express solidarity and pride in their respective communities, even as the sport in which they participated (as combatants, spectators, or patrons) loudly proclaimed its Englishness. In this way, minority fighters and their supporters not only played a role in the culture of prizefighting but also worked to redefine themselves in the process. A similar dynamic was at work in ethnic performances beyond the prize ring. Caricatures of "ethnic, colonial, and provincial character types" that proliferated on the theater stage and in print both reinforced and subverted Englishness. Audience members also sometimes challenged negative depictions.[8] The same was true of Jewish and Irish boxing spectators, who occasionally intervened in matches when foul play was suspected.

Through these kinds of activities, minority fighters and their communities played an important role in shaping the representation of identity in and out of the boxing ring. Despite the confident pronouncements of its defenders, the sport therefore reflected the divided and contested nature of the United Kingdom much more than it did a unified and timeless national identity.[9] Indeed, a number of prominent sporting journalists and other writers claimed that Jewish, black, or Irish boxers demonstrated courage and a sense of fair play by participating in prizefights. On this view, pugilists' willingness and ability to fight set them above continental men and possibly even on the same footing as Protestant Englishmen. Many minority prizefighters, on the other hand, publicly defended the national importance of their sport and the values it promoted. Since these values were usually imagined to be English, minority pugilists thereby included themselves in an identity from which some sought to exclude them.

Whatever their differences, the various advocates for boxing in Britain and Ireland all agreed that prizefighters embodied manhood. Although women contested some bare-knuckle prizefights and attended many more, proponents conceived of the sport as a contest of men for the edification of other men.[10] Physical courage, fair play, and a lack of refinement defined an English man and set him apart from his continental rivals. When left to his own devices, it was imagined, this man would settle disputes with a simple and fair boxing match. The wealth and cosmopolitanism that came with the ever-expanding empire (often equated with "effeminacy"), however, introduced forces that threatened to transform the humble John Bull and, with him, the nation.[11] Watching prizefights, the argument went, provided an antidote to this dangerous contagion by reminding spectators of the basic principles that made English men and their nation great. As Kasia Boddy has written, supporters of boxing could thus feel "in touch with an older, and somehow more authentic, England."[12] Despite this narrow focus on Englishness, however, the importance ascribed to the manliness of prizefighters ironically also led some writers to consider Irish, Jewish, and black pugilists on the same plane as Protestant Englishmen. At the very least, they were elevated above supposedly effeminate men from the continent.

These ideas about the essential manliness of bare-knuckle prizefighting were linked to a popular belief, shaped by the wars of the eighteenth century, that certain "manly qualities" were at the core of Englishness. As a number of historians have shown, the often-reckless physical courage of a number of military commanders was the subject of public veneration during the long eighteenth century.[13] Fears of effeminacy, which became more pronounced during the 1780s, were the other side of the coin. Defeat in the war against the American colonies, anxieties about the political and cultural influence of fabulously wealthy "nabobs" from India and planters from the West Indies, and political conflict in Britain and Ireland conspired to produce a feeling of crisis.[14] Not coincidentally, bare-knuckle prizefighting also became a craze in the 1780s, especially among young military officers and aristocrats, who patronized prizefighters and trained behind closed doors to prove that they had not succumbed to effeminacy. The equation of prizefighting and manly courage continued into the nineteenth century. During the wars with revolutionary France and Napoleon, many politicians fretted about the lack of "military spirit" among the populace and made attempts to encourage it.[15] Some of them—most notably William Windham—publicly argued that boxing was an important means to do so.

Alternative notions of masculinity had long existed (not least among the moral reformers who attacked prizefighting) but, in the decades after the end of the war, "bourgeois" masculinity became entrenched in British society. As John Tosh has argued, this cross-class ideal emphasized the importance of domesticity and the avoidance of physical violence.[16] The spread of bourgeois masculinity in the 1820s and 1830s undoubtedly undermined support for prizefights, which were increasingly denied elite patronage and broken up by police. The raucous environment of a match, with its valorization of bloody combat, seemed out of step with the times. Nevertheless, the sport endured into the 1860s. Perhaps more importantly, the values that underpinned it—including physical courage, endurance, and decisiveness—never totally disappeared. They lived on in imperial spaces, where domesticity could often not be practiced to the same extent as in Britain.[17] They also reemerged in public schools and universities in the second half of the nineteenth century, albeit in a revised form emphasizing the connection between strong male bodies and pure minds.[18]

In its focus on the use of identities and values to promote prizefighting, this book differs from other studies of the sport. A number of recent works have described bare-knuckle boxing's nationalist culture but these have often relied heavily on literary sources and thus can tell us less about how the organizers of and participants in the sport used identities to generate interest in individual boxers or fights.[19] Dennis Brailsford's influential *Bareknuckles: A Social History of Prize-Fighting*, on the other hand, uses contemporary newspapers extensively to provide a thorough examination of the mechanics, social background, and geography of the sport but largely avoids questions of identity.[20] This book follows Brailsford in mining newspapers for information about boxers, matches, sparring exhibitions, and other associated phenomena but, unlike Brailsford, focuses on boxers from minority groups.

From the early eighteenth century to the late nineteenth century, bare-knuckle boxing was a phenomenally popular sport in Britain and Ireland. In this book, I argue that a critical reason for this popularity was that pugilists came to be seen as symbols of something larger than themselves. Prizefighters and other advocates of the sport encouraged spectators, newspaper readers, and others to identify with pugilists on the basis of gender, race, religion, or nation and, to a large extent, their public took them up on it. This relationship between pugilism and its public not only illuminates the early history of sport and identity. It can also give us an important glimpse at a motley collection of Britons negotiating, understanding, and contesting a variety of identities over the better part of two centuries.

Chapter One

Blood Sport, Identity and the Making of Bare-Knuckle Prizefighting, c. 1660–1770

Bare-knuckle prizefighting originated in the early eighteenth century.[1] Throughout its nearly 150-year history, promoters and defenders of the sport claimed that boxing was a lofty "noble art" and that it promoted timeless, authentic, and manly English characteristics, such as courage and fair play. These arguments sought to obscure the importance of commercialism, gambling, and bloodlust to the development of prizefighting. In fact, claims about the importance of the sport were themselves the result of early fighting promoters' attempts to attract paying spectators and to defend their product against the attacks of the many reformers who sought to ban it. The owners of fighting booths and theaters enticed customers by encouraging them to think about boxers not just as individual men but as representatives of a place or a people. To watch a boxing match, from this perspective, was about more than the grim excitement of witnessing a bloody spectacle or the fleeting thrill of gambling. It was about seeing the mettle of one place or people tested and, often, about witnessing "British spirit" on display. Especially from the 1740s, such claims were particularly attractive to a public increasingly accustomed to cultural displays of nationalism. Non-English fighters, often from the burgeoning Irish population of the metropolis, offered one way to test "British spirit" and so played a disproportionate role in the sport from the start. After bare-knuckle prizefighting was forbidden at indoor locations in London and was driven to rural locations, Irish fighters played an even larger part.

This chapter argues that the association between boxing and nationalism, which remained a critical part of the culture of bare-knuckle prizefighting throughout its history, developed alongside the sport itself in the second quarter of the eighteenth century. This association was made by proprietors of fighting booths and theaters, who were anxious both to differentiate their product from the seedy world from which it had sprung and to heighten the interest of paying customers. When boxing was forced out-of-doors from the 1750s, its many defenders and promoters continued to make this connection.

Bare-knuckle prizefighting evolved from the rowdy world of amusements characteristic of late seventeenth and early eighteenth-century London. Among the more popular of these were bull and bear-baiting, which involved staged fights between a chained bull or bear and several trained dogs. Both sports had roots in medieval England but were enjoyed by different groups; bear-baiting was an amusement of the nobility while bull-baiting was generally for commoners. Bear and bull-baiting both fell into disrepute during the reign of the first two Stuart Kings and remained so during the Cromwellian period. Once the austerity of the Puritan Commonwealth was safely in the past, however, bull-baiting enjoyed a resurgence in the provinces as did bear-baiting in the metropolis. By the eighteenth century, bull-baiting was a largely plebeian and non-commercial recreation in which commoners took control of public spaces in the center of towns for the purpose. In London, in contrast, the "bear gardens" where bear-baiting had traditionally been conducted became increasingly commercial enterprises, with admission charged and seating organized by class. Bear-baiting events were often accompanied by combat of various kinds between two or more people.[2]

Despite the divergence between the practice of these two activities, bull and bear-baiting were often conflated. A number of writers associated both practices with an idea of traditional England. As population growth and economic change were transforming London they seemed to be shelters of Englishness in the midst of the storm of changing times. Advertisements for the bear gardens of London eagerly took up these ideas and associated human combat, which was often part of the entertainment, with supposedly timeless English values as well. Such claims contributed to a perception that a love of fighting was at the core of Englishness. The French Huguenot refugee Maximillian Mission, for example, observed the popularity of various kinds of combat in England, writing in 1698 that "Tout ce qui s'appelle *Fighting* … est une chose délicieuse à un Anglois" (All that is called fighting … is a delicious thing to an Englishman).[3] Many in England would have proudly agreed with this assessment and, in fact, many happily quoted it. In this way, bear-baiting and human combat in London were ironically both increasingly commercialized and considered representative of a traditional and authentic England. This association had a profound influence on the culture of bare-knuckle prizefighting.

The bear gardens of the metropolis, with their array of blood sports on display, were very popular but also controversial. The tremendous growth of newspapers and other printed material in the early eighteenth century publicized the gory details of events at venues such as the infamous Hockley-in-the-Hole Bear Garden. At Hockley, a large indoor arena on the banks of the Fleet Ditch that had replaced an older bear garden of Elizabethean vintage, swordsmen battled, boxers and wrestlers grappled, and dogs baited bulls and bears (and even, on occasion, leopards or lions). Handbills and newspaper advertisements highlighted the drama and danger of combat to draw paying customers. Advertisements for combat between men or women typically took the form of a challenge and answer and referred to the "noble science of self-defence" and the courage of the combatants.

Although the violence was bounded and controlled, the danger inherent in such pursuits was part of the product. The perils of Hockley were made evident in 1709 when proprietor Christopher Preston was killed and his body devoured by one of his bears. This prompted a sermon denouncing the bear garden by high-profile reformer the Rev. Deuel Pead at St. James' in Clerkenwell, which was published later in the year.[4] Pead was just one of a number of moral reformers who decried the cruel treatment of animals and the sinful nature of bear gardens. Political and military authorities also worried about such places, especially the gambling and criminality that accompanied them. Hockley-in-the-Hole survived until the middle of the century but was often denounced. Owners of bear gardens and, later, booths and theaters for fighting felt compelled to defend their enterprises, often with reference to the courage of humans or animals on display. John Gay captured both the grandiose claims of defenders of Hockley and its growing disrepute in his 1726 satirical ballad opera "The Beggar's Opera" by having one of his main characters—the wife of a criminal—tell another character that "you should go to Hockley-in-the-Hole ... to learn valour."[5]

Partly as a result of criticism of the bear gardens—and also sensing an opportunity—some successful fighters sought to strike out on their own with performances focused solely on human combat. The most famous of these was James Figg, who opened his so-called "amphitheater" on the Oxford Road in 1719. Dennis Brailsford describes this venue as "a hybrid structure, a cross between a large fairground booth and a theatre, similar to Astley's riding theatres in London and Birmingham."[6] Figg and others performed all manner of combat as individuals and in groups, but animal baiting was not included. He and his imitators reached out to the wealthy young bucks of London, for many of whom wagering large sums on fighters and taking lessons in "the art of self-defense" became fashionable. Fighters offered lessons and exhibited their skills in less seedy and more comfortable surrounds than the bear garden; an advertisement for Figg's booth at the Southwark Fair (which he maintained even after the opening of the amphitheater) announced that it was "fitted up in a most commodious manner for the better reception of gentlemen."[7] The amphitheater provided an even more attractive space for wealthy patrons. Admission prices for the amphitheater were over two shillings, well out of the reach of the laboring poor.[8]

For those who could afford entry, the new fighting venues promised dramatic confrontations between skilled fighters. Colorful challenges and responses printed in newspapers and handbills enticed potential customers. While the fair booths and amphitheaters sought to create a different atmosphere to the rowdy world of the bear garden, this mode of attracting paying spectators owed much to advertising for Hockley-in-the-Hole. The formula of providing a more respectable place to witness dramatic and bloody spectacles proved quite successful. By the 1730s, combatants might collect as much as £100 in entrance money for their efforts.[9]

As the new venues focused exclusively on the drama of combat between people, fighters developed new ways to promote their battles. Reference to a

James Figg's booth at the Southwark Fair offered demonstrations of many different forms of combat. William Hogarth, "Southwark Fair" (1734), from Miles, *Pugilistica*, vol. 1.

fighter's place of origin, made resonant by the increasingly cosmopolitan experiences of many eighteenth-century Londoners, became an important means to do this. Innovations in commerce, transportation, and manufacturing were changing England dramatically in the eighteenth century, as were the ideas of reformers determined to remake towns around the country. In the midst of this transformation, however, was an increased emphasis on local identity, of which a surge in the publication of local histories is an example.[10] In this context, fighters began to emphasize their connection to a place. Figg—who hailed from Thame—was often called "the Oxfordshire Champion," for example. This advertising tactic aimed to promote fighters as representatives of the place associated with them, rather than simply as individuals. Thus, even if a potential spectator knew nothing about a fighter, he or she might be drawn to a match by the prospect of seeing one place—represented by a fighter from that place—matched against another. By the 1730s, unknown fighters began to appear with known commodities like Figg and others in order to add excitement.[11] Combatants from outside the metropolis offered an intriguing challenge for an established fighter, or at least so it was hoped. Spectators—and gamblers—might be drawn to the dramatic twist offered by the prospect of a provincial novice defeating an established Londoner.

In addition to local identity, national identity also increasingly factored into the promotion of performances at the amphitheaters. By the early 1700s, London

An advertisement for James Figg's amphitheater on the Oxford Road. From Miles, *Pugilistica*, vol. 1.

had become the center of a global trading empire and knowledge of and commerce with the wider world were transforming the metropolis. Partly in response to this, many English people were particularly eager to stress the uniqueness of their island nation.[12] Ideas about gender were a critical element of this national identity. In particular, the notion that England was defined in part by its sturdy and courageous men that never turned away from a fight was an important element of the national mythology; for many, "aggressive masculinity" became a "touchstone of Englishness."[13]

The bear gardens and fighting amphitheaters and booths increasingly took advantage of this and, therefore, challengers from beyond the shores of England were particularly enticing. A famous example involved a man known only as "the Venetian gondolier." The Venetian was apparently notorious in London because of his loud boasting about his prowess as a fist fighter as well as his claim that he would break the jaw of any who fought him. According to Captain John Godfrey—a former student of Figg's who wrote a treatise about the "useful science of defense" in 1747—Figg responded that, while the Venetian might be able to break the jaws of other Italians, he would put forward a English boxer whose jaw could not be broken "with a sledgehammer." With interest thus piqued, a "Gentleman of an advanced Station" made a match between the Venetian and Bob Whitaker at Old Slaughter's coffeehouse.[14] *The London Journal* reported that the fight "looks like a national concern."[15] When the bout was contested at Figg's amphitheater, the Venetian had an early advantage until Whitaker hit him with, as Godfrey put it, "one *English* Peg in the stomach (quite a new thing to foreigners)" and won the bout.[16]

Although the match between Whitaker and the Venetian was one of the most famous of the era, Irish fighters were a much more common site in the amphitheaters and fighting booths than the occasional continental visitor. Irish migrants and immigrants had long come to London, of course, but it was only in the eighteenth century that the Irish population of London became, in the words of nineteenth-century historian John Denvir, "tolerably numerous." Poor Irish migrants came to bring in the English harvest, middling Irish to study at the Inns of Court and for commercial opportunities, and aristocrats to be at the epicenter of power and society. The discriminatory Penal laws certainly hindered them and the bloody events of the seventeenth century were a not too distant memory but, as John Bergin has shown, all but the poorest Irish Catholics could find success in the metropolis.[17] As more Irish appeared in the streets of London than ever before, stereotypes about them became more prevalent. To be sure, negative depictions of Ireland by the English dated to at least Gerald of Wales in the early thirteenth century.

Still, the comical "stage Irishman" became a fixture of the eighteenth-century London theater. Given the visibility of Irish—both Catholic and Protestant—on the street and in stereotype, it is perhaps not surprising that, throughout this period Irish challengers were by far the most frequent non–English opponents of established London fighters.

In the fighting world, this combination of difference and accessibility translated into possibility. James Figg, in particular, was regularly matched against Irish fighters. Recognizing Figg's reputation for beating Irishmen, one contemporary wag suggested that his motto should be "A Fig for the Irish." A public challenge issued to Figg and Edward Sutton by Irishmen William Holmes and Felix MacGuire provides an example of the way in which Irish fighters were employed to add excitement. Figg and Sutton, who frequently battled one another at Figg's, were now allied against the Irish newcomers who, according to the notice, were "the two first and most profound Swordsmen in the Kingdom of Ireland, whom in combat the Universe never yet could parallel, being requested to return to our native country, are determined to make our departure ever memorable to Great Britain, by taking our solemn public leave of the renowned Mr. Figg and Mr. Sutton, at the time and place appointed; to which we hereby invite them, in order to prove we can maintain our titles, and claim a preference in the list of Worthies." The indication that Holmes and MacGuire had the "titles" of best swordsmen in Ireland cast them as representatives of Ireland and thus particularly intriguing opponents. While Figg and Sutton's response reminded readers that the two men were English, it did not mark Holmes and MacGuire as wholly different. Figg and Sutton's answer compared their Irish adversaries to Admirals Benbow and Carter, two naval commanders of the War of Spanish Succession who had lost limbs in battle. Though this macabre comparison suggested that Holmes and MacGuire would lose appendages in the fight, the comparison to the two admirals marked them as part of the British tradition. Significantly, the historical reference was not to the Williamite wars in Ireland but to a moment of British heroism abroad. Holmes and MacGuire, who were almost certainly Protestants considering that facility with weapons that were legally denied to Catholics was an obvious necessity, represented Ascendancy Ireland.[18]

Later public challenges dropped the ambiguity and cast fighters from England and Ireland as representatives of two antagonistic people. Thus, when Irishman Francis Sherlock challenged Figg's former collaborator Sutton to fight with swords in 1736, Sutton responded that he would "not fail meeting this Hibernian bravado with the same resolution as I always had for the honour of my country." Further, he noted that "there have been several battles fought between the English and Irish [and] I desire this may be a decisive battle, and doubt not but to end it to the honour of Old England."[19] Unlike Figg and Sutton's response to MacGuire and Holmes of a few years earlier, this answer clearly positioned Sutton as the representative of England and Sherlock as that of Ireland. Spectators were made aware that the "honour" of each place was at stake in the battle.

Although the importance accorded to the honor of place in challenges came to be associated with manhood, staged fights of the 1720s and 1730s were not as exclusively associated with men as they would become and, in fact, many women participated. Indeed, one later (and hostile) commentator wrote that there "was evidently a recognised band of these hardy women" in the 1730s.[20] It was therefore no novelty when, in 1733, Felix MacGuire—announcing himself as the "Fencing master from Dublin"—came to England with his wife Letitia, who battled the most well-known woman fighter of the era: Elizabeth Stokes (neé Wilkinson).[21] Stokes had been active for at least a decade before fighting Letitia MacGuire. Her first known fight (as Elizabeth Wilkinson) was at Hockley-in-the-Hole in 1722 against Hannah Hyfield and, a few years later, she and her husband James Stokes opened an amphitheater to compete with Figg. Elizabeth Stokes fought a number of women in the 1720s and 1730s at the Stokes amphitheater. Like her male counterparts, she relied on dramatic advertisements to draw paying spectators to her amphitheater. In 1728, for example, the *Daily Post* printed Ann Fields's challenge to Stokes. In her reply, Stokes noted that "the blows which I shall present her with will be more difficult for her to digest than any she ever gave her asses." In this public notice as in others, Stokes was styled the "European Championess." She, like Figg and others, also recognized the draw of a match involving an Irish fighter. As the "city championess," Stokes challenged a woman called the "Hibernian Heroine" to a match.[22]

Despite the evident skill and successes of Stokes and other women fighters, their presence in the sport was always ambiguous. A print from 1766 titled "Sal Dab Giving Monsieur a Receipt in Full" shows a topless English woman beating a bewigged French man, but the woman's appearance suggests that the print was meant to skewer the supposed effeminacy of the Frenchman rather than highlight the heroism of the English woman. In addition, the main focus of reports of fights between women was on what they wore and, more importantly, what they did not.[23] So, even though women appeared in the amphitheaters, fighting booths, and bear gardens, they were more often considered novelties or sexual objects than anything else. Women continued to fight organized boxing matches through the eighteenth and early nineteenth centuries, but such matches seem to have been much more rare than in the 1720s and 1730s and, when they did occur, occasioned derisive comment from male commentators.

The decline in combat between women coincided with an increasing reference to manhood in public challenges and other promotions. Figg died in 1734 and, by 1740, the fighter George "the Barber" Taylor had assumed control of his amphitheater. Fist fighting took precedence under Taylor's leadership and advertisements for matches became much more dramatic. The style of these advertisements strongly influenced later boxing journalism.[24] Although the advertisements typically took the form of a challenge from one boxer to another, the fighters almost certainly did not write them. It is not clear who actually did, but the *Gentlemen's and London Magazine* later claimed that Taylor employed well-known actor and author Theophilus Cibber for the job.[25] In any case, advertisements for matches at Taylor's amphitheater (commonly called the "Great Booth") also explicitly invoked manhood. Near the end of April 1742, a match between "The Fighting Quaker" William Willis and Thomas Smallwood at Taylor's, for example, was described as a "trial of manhood." Willis's challenge belittled Smallwood, claiming that "the weak attempts of a few Irishmen and boys that have of late fought him for a minute or two, makes him think himself inconquerable." Smallwood's response reminded readers that he was known for "intrepid manhood on and off the stage" and promised that he would silence the "puffing Quaker." Smallwood won the match on April 28 and, with it, the prize of £100.[26]

Advertisements for matches at Taylor's also exploited national feeling to attract paying spectators. As in Figg's time, Irishmen were the most readily available non–English fighters and hostility toward Irish migrants and immigrants helped fuel interest. Outside the ring, competition between Irish and English workers periodically led to violence, as in the anti–Irish riots of the summer of 1736 and hostility among English tradesmen toward Irish migrants only heightened the excitement for a match involving an Irishman.[27] At the same time, because boxing does not require advanced skill with a weapon, it was easier for more Irish people—including Catholics who were denied access to weapons by the Penal laws—to participate. It is not surprising, then, that Irish-born Patrick Henley was a regular performer at Taylor's.[28] In May 1742, Taylor's amphitheater publicized a "trial of manhood" between Henley and an Englishman named John "the Jumping Soldier" Francis. Francis's challenge referred to an earlier match between he and Henley (won by Henley) before announcing that Francis was not "ashamed to mount the stage when my manhood is called in question by an Irish Braggadocia." Henley responded by threatening Francis with "one of my bothering blows, which will convince him of his ignorance in the art of boxing."[29] On May 5, Henley again defeated

Francis. Such exchanges show the increasing importance of appeals to manhood and place in boxing advertisements.

One of the most resonant themes in advertisements of the era had to do with national feeling. This was in line with an increasingly powerful popular sense of Britishness in the eighteenth century. From 1739 and 1815, as H.V. Bowen reminds us, "war was a semi-permanent feature on the historical landscape."[30] The expansion of trade and empire continued apace as well. During this long period of war and empire-building, continental enemies embodied treachery and duplicity in the popular imagination. In contrast, military heroes such as Admiral Edward Vernon or General James Wolfe were believed to personify all that was best about British men.[31] This formulation imagined the nation to be embodied by an ideal type of man, whose key traits included courage, stamina, and fair play.

For many Britons a structured fight relying only on fists offered a clear demonstration of ideal manhood. A probably apocryphal story in Scottish sailor Alexander Hamilton's *A New Account of the East Indies* illustrates how boxing skill, manhood, and national feeling were intertwined in this period. In the story, an English sailor carrying a keg of arrack in Amoy (Xiamen) refused to leave the street when a Mandarin and his servants appeared. One of the Mandarin's men struck the English sailor, who then hit him back. The group of servants attacked the sailor but the Mandarin ordered them to stop and called for an interpreter. Asked what had happened, the sailor said that he had been unjustly assaulted. Then he produced a Spanish dollar and told the Mandarin that he would fight him and all of his men. After laughing, the Mandarin called for an enormous Tartar "famous for boxing" to fight the sailor. The seaman agreed and the two set to fighting. At first the Tartar kicked, but the sailor easily knocked him down. The Tartar then asked to have "a fair Bout of Boxing." The sailor, of course, drubbed the Tartar, who was "forc'd to yield to old *England*."[32] As the last line reveals, the sailor's victory was not simply proof of his own fighting prowess. The headstrong seaman's thrashing of the Tartar champion demonstrated—for Hamilton anyway—the superiority of England to China.

Supporters of boxing and other forms of combat suggested that these important elements of British strength needed to be encouraged, especially as Britain fought foreign wars and sought to expand its empire. Because the amphitheaters and fighting booths had always offered fighting lessons as well, it was a short step to claim that boxing served a broader pedagogical purpose: to teach spectators to emulate the traits personified by boxers and thereby to make them better men and soldiers of the Empire. For some, the connection between war, boxing (and other forms of human combat), and nation were clear. Captain John Godfrey, a soldier and sword-fighter trained by James Figg, wrote the *Treatise on the Useful Science of Self-Defence* in 1747 in part to highlight this link. Godfrey dedicated his treatise to the Duke of Cumberland and claimed that boxing and other forms of organized fighting "inure the common People to Bravery; and to encourage that truly *British* Spirit."[33] Godfrey's dedication was timely. The Duke, the king's younger son, was the commander of the forces that crushed the Jacobite rebellion and was well regarded (by Whigs at least) when Godfrey published in 1747.

The Duke of Cumberland was also the main patron of Jack Broughton, the most famous boxer of the eighteenth century. A former boatman on the Thames, Broughton captured the attention of the public when he entered and won a boat race that had been organized by the Dublin-born actor Thomas Doggett. A large and talented athlete, Broughton began to train as a fighter with James Figg and by the time of Figg's death in 1734, he was one of the best in London. As fist-fighting began to become the central attraction at the amphitheater—now under George Taylor's management—Broughton became the star performer. The amphitheater continued to flourish under Taylor's leadership; as seen above, his vivid advertisements upped the ante from Figg's time and drew more customers than ever before. Broughton could expect to pocket as much as £50 in a day, much more than the annual income of a craftsman and certainly an enormous sum for a former boatman.[34]

In 1743, Broughton determined to build his own amphitheater, which would be larger and more elaborate than Taylor's venue. Cumberland, soon to be commanding troops against a French army at the Battle of Dettingen, supplied some of the funding for the new structure. Modeled after the new theaters of the era, Broughton's amphitheater was meant to cater to a diverse clientele, with boxes, a pit, and a gallery to allow his wealthy patrons—who had helped pay for the structure via a subscription—and their friends to sit apart from the meaner class of spectator. Broughton immediately took aim at his old master George Taylor by lowering ticket prices; the advertisement for the new venue announced that no one would pay more than one shilling for entry. Broughton built his structure on the Oxford Road, directly behind Taylor's amphitheater on the Tottenham Court Road and opened on March 13, 1743, the same night that Taylor had planned a major fight. Taylor denounced Broughton's timing in a public advertisement addressed to "all Encouragers of the manly art of Boxing" and even challenged his former employee to a fight for £100 a side (Broughton did not answer).[35] Broughton was a better fighter with more important backers, however, and soon Taylor closed his amphitheater. He and his stable of performers went to work for Broughton.[36]

With the support and patronage of the Duke of Cumberland, Captain Godfrey, and other wealthy young military men, Broughton enjoyed tremendous success throughout the 1740s. In 1747, he advertised the opening of an "academy" at his house in Haymarket for instruction in "the majesty of boxing ... that truly British art." To prevent injuries to lofty personages, he introduced the use of padded gloves for training. Long after bare-knuckle prizefights were forbidden indoors in England, boxers took the stage with these "mufflers" for paid exhibitions.[37] He contested prizefights at his amphitheater as well, defeating all comers (without mufflers of course), including all of the leading fighters of the era. Spectators were amused by novelties like Broughton or one of his stable of boxers fighting several other men at once.[38] The former boatman was widely admired and thought invincible. In his 1747 treatise, Godfrey rhapsodized about Broughton's "manly merit" and suggested that he would never be defeated.[39]

Broughton was also an important innovator in the sport. To provide a greater sense of order to the proceedings at the amphitheater, especially for the benefit of gamblers, he established a set of seven rules for boxing. The rules were extraordinarily influential and were widely used in Britain and Ireland until the middle of the nineteenth century. Most of the rules concern the beginning and end of what came to be called "rounds" and the end of a fight. The first rule stipulated that a "square of a yard be chalked in the middle of the stage." A round began when each fighter returned to the side of the square facing the other. If a boxer could not make it to this spot before thirty seconds had elapsed, the match was to be ended and that fighter considered beaten. The fight could also be ended by a pugilist's second (a position borrowed from the duel). A bout was to be temporarily stopped if either fighter fell to the ground; the seventh rule forbade hitting an opponent on the ground, pulling hair, or hitting below the waist. Nevertheless, wrestling moves remained an important part of the sport. Rounds often ended with a grapple and a throw, such as the "cross-buttock." Other rules clarified the portion of money to be allocated to each fighter and the choosing of umpires to ensure compliance.[40]

The seven years after Broughton opened his amphitheater were a critical moment in the development of the culture of bare-knuckle prizefighting as well. His relationship with his patron Cumberland brought the worlds of war and boxing closer together than ever before. He accompanied the Duke to Germany for the peace negotiations that concluded the War of Austrian Succession in 1748 and to the court of Frederick the Great. In a probably apocryphal but oft-repeated story, Broughton told Cumberland that he could fight an entire regiment of Prussian grenadiers if the Duke "would only be kind enough to allow me a breakfast between each battle."[41] Whether or not Broughton actually made this quip, it demonstrates the blurring of the boundary between soldiers and boxers that was central to the promotion of boxing. For the supporters of the sport, Broughton's willingness (and, his backers would argue, ability) to defeat an entire regiment of elite enemy soldiers was proof of the superiority of British men to Prussian men and thus of Britain to Prussia. Boxing's defenders often repeated this story because it neatly expressed the sport's raison d'être: pugilism showcased Britain's martial strength and the superiority of its men to their counterparts on the continent.

Much as Broughton's backers wanted to believe that he was an invincible symbol of British strength, he was nearing fifty years of age by the end of the decade and fighting much less frequently. In early April 1750, he attended the Hounslow Races and there had a row with a fighter named Jack Slack, a butcher from Norwich who had been a performer in the boxing amphitheaters for several years. Broughton apparently threatened Slack, prompting Slack to challenge him to a fight.[42] Broughton accepted the challenge and, though he had not fought in some time, did not consider Slack a serious threat. Broughton even gave Slack ten guineas to ensure that he would turn up for the fight. Slack then wagered ten guineas that he would win at 10 to 1 odds. Many others put their money on Broughton, including Cumberland. Broughton justified their confidence early in the match but after a few minutes of fighting Slack blinded Broughton with a punch between the eyes. Broughton gamely contested the fight for another ten minutes but, deprived of his sight, was forced to admit defeat.[43]

Broughton's loss in this match was a turning point in the history of bare-knuckle prizefighting. By all accounts, Cumberland and others in his circle lost large sums on the match and the Duke subsequently discontinued his patronage of the great boxer. Broughton never fought again and his amphitheater ultimately closed. Although he lived on for nearly forty years, the shuttering of his famous venue and the failure of imitators to survive were a turning point for the sport he helped create.[44] From Figg and George Taylor to Broughton, bare-knuckle prizefighting had evolved in closed spaces catering to paying customers. While indoor prizefighting in London survived for another decade, the landscape for pugilists would not be the same again.

Early historians of the sport claimed that Cumberland, feeling that he had fallen victim to a fixed match, caused Broughton's amphitheater to be closed by "the interference of the Legislature."[45] More recently, finding no mention of pugilism in parliamentary records of the era, Dennis Brailsford has argued that the Duke simply pressured authorities to close Broughton's amphitheater "using their considerable and ill-defined powers."[46] While Brailsford's claim that no Act of Parliament explicitly closed Broughton's amphitheater is accurate, it would have had to receive a license under the Disorderly Houses Act of 1751 as a place of "public entertainment." The Act made exception for the theatres royal in Covent Garden, Drury Lane, and the Haymarket but not for fighting amphitheaters. Later commentators claimed that the Act was intended to suppress bull-baiting (among other practices) and it is likely that a license would have been withheld from any would-be successor to Broughton who might seek it as well. In fact, Thomas Higginson, the proprietor of the Tennis Court near the Haymarket where indoor prizefights were sometimes held, was indicted in February 1761 "for keeping a disorderly house, permitting cock-fighting, cudgel-playing, and boxing."[47] It is unlikely that the Duke caused the Disorderly Houses Act to be passed—it seems to have been prompted by Henry Fielding's pamphlet "An Inquiry into the Causes of the Late Increase in Robberies"—but clearly the tide of official opinion in London had turned against such amusements.[48]

Still, Broughton's amphitheater was not closed for some time and there is evidence that boxing matches continued to attract crowds there after the famous boxer's disastrous defeat. In early May 1751, Broughton's old master George Taylor defeated Thomas Smallwood in around 30 minutes at the amphitheater.[49] On April 13, 1752, two years after his great victory, Slack fought and defeated Tom Faulkner "the cricket player from Kent" there as well. Faulkner was a veteran fighter and a packed house saw an exciting contest with the advantage shifting between the two men before Slack prevailed. A sum of £300 in admission money was collected.[50] It seems clear, however, that the venue was closed by 1754. Advertisements no longer appeared and Broughton's fighters were dispersed. The satirical journal, *The Connoisseur* claimed in that year that the amphitheater had become a Methodist meetinghouse. Whether or not the journal invented this ironic fate, Broughton's house was no more by the middle of the decade.

The closing of the amphitheater did not end the careers of the boxers who performed there. Many of them brought their sport to the provinces, recreating the amphitheater scene outside. For example, Slack met a Frenchman named Pettit on a stage in Harleston in Slack's home county of Norfolk in July 1754. A contemporary newspaper account reported that Pettit tried to strangle Slack and, when Slack broke this hold, Pettit ran at him and tackled him by the legs. He also threw Slack over the rails and off the stage. Soon, however, Slack recovered his strength and kept near Pettit, where he used punches to wear Pettit down. After about 25 minutes, Pettit had enough and walked off the stage without "saying anything to any person." The account noted that Slack, as the victor, "drew the first ten guineas out of the box." Although this was a much smaller sum than Slack might have commanded at Broughton's house, it does suggest that admission was charged. This and the fact that the match was fought on a stage suggest that there was an attempt to maintain the forms of the amphitheater.[51] The choice of a novice Frenchmen as an opponent as war with France loomed shows that the culture of the amphitheater endured as well.

For the remainder of the decade, it was possible to see Broughton's fighters perform, provided one was willing to take a long walk outside of London or to travel to the provinces.[52] In early 1755, Slack twice defeated a local collier named Cornelius Harris in Bristol and, in February, he beat Harris in about six minutes. The two fought again in Bristol in March for 100 guineas and Harris performed better (lasting for twenty minutes) but Slack won after beating his opponent nearly to death.[53] Two years later, in July 1757, two other veterans of the amphitheater, Edward Hunt and Thomas Smallwood, fought on a stage much nearer the City, in Hounslow. With Slack and George Taylor as their seconds, the two men boxed for fifty minutes before Smallwood won the match and 150 guineas with it. In August 1758, Taylor and Tom Faulkener contested a match in Hertfordshire for 200 guineas and the admission fees. After more than an hour of violent boxing, Faulkener was declared the winner. The following year Faulkener fought Joe James, the brother of one of Broughton's roster of boxers, for £100 in Putney. The two battled for ten minutes outside on a specially constructed stage but James walked off the stage to boos and hissing after taking a hard punch from Faulkener. In February 1760, Bill Stevens (known as "The Nailer") fought Jacob Taplin at a natural amphitheater at Marylebone basin. Nearly three thousand spectators saw him badly maul Taplin.[54] Many of Broughton's boxers continued to fight in the prize ring, but the certainties of the amphitheater for boxers and spectators were slipping away. Competition could no longer be as effectively guaranteed and, for fighters, gate money could not always be collected—especially in an open field.

The final end of the old amphitheater culture came at a moment when its glory days seemed on the verge of being recaptured. In June 1760, Slack fought Bill Stevens on an indoor stage, at a venue called the Tennis Court in the Haymarket. This was the first time an indoor prizefight had been contested in London since the closure of the amphitheater. More important than the site of the match was the fact that royal patronage had returned; the Duke of Cumberland backed Slack while his brother the Duke of York was Stevens's patron. Slack had the early advantage, but Stevens eventually won the fight with an effective defense and by tripping Slack. He won 90 guineas for his efforts. Although Stevens's winnings still depended on stakes placed for the fight rather than admission fees, the fight raised the possibility that regular indoor prizefighting might return to London.[55]

Any such hopes were dashed at the beginning of March 1761, when Stevens met a Bristol collier named George Meggs at the Tennis Court. The fight was hotly anticipated and generated extraordinary interest. The *London Chronicle* reported that, though seats were priced from a crown to a half guinea—considerably more than the 2s 6d admission at Broughton's amphitheater—twice as many people were turned away than saw the match. Thomas Smallwood seconded Meggs, who had been trained by Slack, and Tom Faulkener was Stevens's second. Unfortunately for the paying spectators, the gamblers, and the boxing community, Stevens accepted 50 guineas to lose the match. At the outset of the fight, he swung and missed Meggs and then fell. The two avoided one another for another 17 minutes before Stevens quit the stage.[56] Large sums were lost on the clearly fixed bout. A few months later Thomas Higginson, the proprietor of the Tennis Court, was tried and found guilty of keeping a disorderly house.[57] Indoor prizefighting was finished.

The long-term consequence of the fiasco at the Tennis Court was that prizefighting became an outlaw endeavor; henceforth matches were contested outside in remote rural locations. The location of matches could not be advertised in advance, though public challenges were issued much as before. For boxers, this meant a more precarious existence than in the days of Broughton, Taylor, and Figg. The owners of amphitheaters collected admission fees and divided them among the fighters, who could thus rely on an income. Gifts and money thrown on stage were part of a fighter's take at the amphitheater but not the only (or even main) compensation. Advertising for matches was arranged as well. In short, amphitheaters provided a center of gravity for boxing, which provided structure and ensured basic standards for boxer and spectator alike.[58] After the suppression of amphitheaters, boxers' livelihood was much more tenuous and they had to be more entrepreneurial. They had to rely much more directly on patrons and, as individuals, had to pursue strategies that would bring them fame and therefore money. These realities shaped the culture of the sport for the next century.

In 1760, just before the final demise of indoor prizefighting in London, many new boxers appeared on the scene. They were, according to *The Art of Boxing* (a history of and manual about boxing written nearly 30 years later), "for the most part, a set of drunken, dissipated, idle fellows." Many of them were also Irish. *The Art of Boxing* named an Irishman named O'Neal one of the "best masters and sportsmen this time afforded," though he is not mentioned in other sources. More typical perhaps of the Irish boxers in this era was James Doyle, a chairman who, though possessing "no knowledge of the art," had abundant strength and stamina. Another Irishman named Nicholas Grady was also a less than skillful boxer and was beaten by a much smaller fighter for £200. Grady's patron was Dennis O'Kelly, who later achieved fame as the owner of the famous racehorse Eclipse. Only recently out of debtor's prison, O'Kelly reportedly lost £600 on the match.[59] Such a substantial loss did not deter O'Kelly, who offered patronage to many Irish boxers later in his career.

The influx of Irish boxers from the 1760s was likely a result of surge of popularity of boxing in Ireland in the 1740s and 1750s. The first boxing match in which the names of the fighters was recorded occurred in December 1749 in County Dublin. More significantly, some London fighters held an exhibition in Dublin in January 1753. At a house in the Ormond Market, Martin Ochy defeated both Dan Dugan, "a famous jaw-bone breaker" from London, as well as the ubiquitous Tom Smallwood. This was only the first example in which London boxers traveled to Dublin and other destinations in Ireland to showcase their talents for paying crowds. English fighters would continue the practice well into the nineteenth century. Such exhibitions helped stimulate interest in prize fighting in Ireland among both spectators and would-be pugilists. Certainly the periodic efforts of Dublin authorities to crack down on assemblies for boxing matches suggests that the sport "had taken root in the plebeian culture of the city" in the 1750s.[60] Many of the increasing numbers of Irish boxers active in England from the 1760s would have had at least some knowledge of the rules and norms of London prizefighting even before crossing the Irish Sea.

The influx of Irish boxers and, as we will see in the next chapter Jewish fighters, was one consequence of the ways in which prize fighting changed after the demise of the London fighting amphitheaters and booths. Their end had eliminated any central organizing structure that might have developed in boxing. At the same time, however, this development meant that Broughton and his small circle of patrons would not control who would appear on the stage. Henceforth, the most important criteria (in addition to some boxing skill) was the ability to engage the interest of patrons, gamblers, and the rest of the public that supported boxing. As the growing number of Irish boxers suggested, "ethnic conflict" was becoming an important way in which to excite boxing supporters.[61] When the sport emerged from the doldrums in the 1770s and 1780s, ethnicity was a critical element in the exploding boxing publicity of that period.

Chapter Two

Britishness, Minorities and the Revival of Prizefighting, 1770–1790

By 1771, bare-knuckle prizefighting had reached a low point. Broughton's amphitheater was gone and the transition to outdoor prizefighting in the countryside had not been smooth. Corruption was rampant and consistent patronage difficult for boxers to find. Public challenges were much more rare than in earlier years and newspapers did not regularly report matches. When they did comment on boxing, it was usually to denounce the sport and call for its suppression. In October 1771, for example, the *London Evening Post* printed part of a letter in which one of its readers asked why magistrates did not do more to prevent prearranged matches.[1] Nineteenth-century historians of prizefighting looked back at this period as a "dark age."[2] Fifteen years later, however, the story was almost entirely different. Newspapers widely reported matches and some of the leading men of the kingdom attended them. Prints and other ephemera depicting boxers and bouts sold briskly and huge crowds came to the most important fights. In 1786, the Prince of Wales attended a match on which £30,000 was reportedly wagered.[3]

This dramatic change owed much to the staging of boxing matches at races. Race meetings organized by elites were becoming ever more popular in the second half of the century and their guaranteed crowds and gambling infrastructure were a critical part of the success of many boxing matches that were contested in the 1770s and 1780s.[4] The change in the fortunes of boxing was also, however, a product of a shifting public mood that was a consequence of the loss of the American colonies, political disquiet in Ireland, and growing unrest at home. In this context, old arguments about prizefighters as the embodiment of a pure and timeless English masculinity found a receptive audience among the aristocracy and gentry, many of whom were already inclined to enjoy rakish pastimes. Partly because of this focus on the Englishness of boxing, matches involving Irish and Jewish opponents—fights in which English masculinity was imagined to be tested—were popular. The most famous matches of the era pitted Jewish boxer Daniel Mendoza against the Christian English fighter Richard Humphries. Humphries was often depicted in popular prints and other cultural products as the strong and solid embodiment of Englishness. The flamboyant Mendoza, on the other hand, was no passive heel. As a number of scholars have shown, he was a skillful pugilist and self-promoter who understood the terms of engagement and used them to his advantage.[5] He pioneered an aggressive persona that—for love, hate, or something in between—drew spectators to his matches and influenced many minority boxers in the years to come.

This chapter examines the careers of Mendoza and other minority pugilists of the 1770s and 1780s. It argues that Mendoza was a pivotal figure in the development of bare-knuckle prizefighting. His fearless responses to verbal and physical attacks endeared him to his fellow London Jews, while his showmanship and public persona helped captivate a much broader audience. Mendoza both charted a course for later minority boxers and was critical to the evolution of bare-knuckle prizefighting from a hobby of wealthy young bucks to a popular phenomenon. For all of Mendoza's talents as a fighter and a showman, however, he was not a lone pioneer. This chapter also shows that some other minority boxers and their patrons sought to take advantage of the opportunities that arose in the nationalist boxing culture of the late eighteenth century. While Mendoza is deservedly the most famous minority boxer of the period, a number of other Jewish and Irish fighters achieved some manner of success as well.

During the "dark age" of boxing, Irish fighters began to play a larger role than ever before. In 1771, a London correspondent for a Dublin newspaper wrote that dueling had come to such "an amazing pitch" in London "that the lowliest order of Hibernians have dropt boxing, and taken to sword and pistol."[6] This was, of course, a satirical comment on the increase in dueling (the poorest London Irish were certainly not dueling), but it was also an indication that the Irish were widely associated with boxing. The involvement of poor Irish in prizefighting is perhaps surprising as many of them were Irish speakers and as a consequence lived in a relatively insular community.[7] As the capital grew larger and more cosmopolitan, however, the London Irish were becoming ever more integrated into its culture.[8] This included involvement in prizefighting. Not surprisingly, the epicenter of Irish boxing was the parish of St. Giles, the most important area of settlement for poorer Irish in eighteenth-century London. While this group has long been the focus of research on the Irish in the capital, recent scholarship has highlighted the burgeoning middle strata of lawyers, merchants, and physicians. This group was connected by a shared sense of Irishness that often crossed confessional lines. In addition, some of the middling London Irish forged links with their poorer countrymen.[9] The shared bond of Irishness also extended to boxing. Indeed, a critical element in the success of Irish boxers in the late eighteenth century and the early nineteenth century was the support of middle-class Irish patrons. This enabled them to depend less on the fickle tastes of English gentlemen.

The most successful Irish boxer of the eighteenth century, the controversial Peter Corcoran, owed much to the support of an Irish patron: the racehorse owner and gambler Dennis O'Kelly. An obituary for O'Kelly in the *Edinburgh Magazine* detailed his rise from a peasant childhood in Connaught to become a wealthy landholder in England. O'Kelly was very likely born a Catholic and probably converted either just before or after immigrating to England; he joined the Westminster militia in 1760 and later rose to the rank of Lieutenant-Colonel, which would have been denied him had he been a Catholic. When not fulfilling his annual military commitment, O'Kelly was an extraordinarily successful gambler. His winnings ultimately enabled him to buy the famous racehorse Eclipse, which had been bred by the Duke of Cumberland. Despite his immersion in English life, his Irishness seemed to have remained important to him. He maintained ties with Ireland and supported his Irish relatives.[10] He also used his winnings to back Irish boxers. As we saw above, he lost £600 betting on his relatively untalented client Nicholas Grady in September 1761.[11]

O'Kelly had more success as the patron of Corcoran, who he claimed to have "imported," at the end of the decade.[12] With the help of O'Kelly and with a reputation as a defiant Irish Catholic fighter, Corcoran enjoyed a period of fame in the 1770s. He was a native of County Kildare and immigrated to England as a young man. He followed a circuitous path to the prize ring, traveling first to Birmingham, where he fought and defeated a well-known local boxer. He then went to London to work as a laborer before a "trifling dispute" caused him to be pressed into the navy. He was a client of a Captain Perceval while serving and gained some minor celebrity after an incident in which he supposedly broke the sword of his Lieutenant over the officer's head. This event became an important part of Corcoran's image as a defiant Catholic Irishman and may have helped bring him to the attention of O'Kelly. After being discharged from the navy, Corcoran became the proprietor of the Black Horse Inn in St. Giles and a well-known figure among the Irish there. He also began to fight matches as O'Kelly's client.[13] While he lost his first recorded match against a veteran boxer named Turner near the new British Museum in Bloomsbury Fields in September 1769, his fortunes soon changed and he defeated two fighters, one of them an Irishman, at the same place.[14]

Corcoran's victories in Bloomsbury led to bigger things. In May 1771, O'Kelly organized a match between Corcoran and a former dyer from Bath named Bill Darts, who many considered to be the English Champion. As with other important matches of the 1770s and 1780s, the fight took place during a race meeting. Corcoran and Darts met at Epsom on a purpose built stage near a spot where O'Kelly had recently acquired property. The fight was brief; Corcoran knocked Darts into the rails in the first few minutes and Darts quit. Rumors circulated that O'Kelly had fixed the match so that an Irishman could claim the title and he could win a fortune in the process. There has long been considerable disagreement about this rumor; most nineteenth-century histories of the sport repeated it (though some dissented), while more recent sources often identify Corcoran as "the first Irish champion."[15] Whatever the merits of Corcoran's claim to the title, there is little dispute that O'Kelly—the organizer of the match and Corcoran's patron—wanted an Irishman to be champion. For O'Kelly as for many others at the time and much later the national identity of the winning fighter was important, especially given that the title was at stake.

The Irish of St. Giles believed Corcoran defeated Darts even if many others did not. This was important because their support was as critical to Corcoran's success in the 1770s as was the patronage of O'Kelly. The London Irish, some of whom he trained to fight, helped make Corcoran's Black Horse Inn a popular spot for much of the decade. This support had to be maintained by cultivating an image, however. While evidence for Corcoran's career outside the ring is particularly sparse, an anecdote described by journalist Pierce Egan several decades later (and which he may have heard growing up in St. Giles in the 1780s) is suggestive of how the Irish champion was perceived. The story was that one of his students, an enormous Newgate turnkey called "Big Pitt," encountered Corcoran at another Irish fighter's pub. Drinking and bragging, Big Pitt stood and announced that some pupils could defeat their masters. Corcoran immediately rose to his feet and challenged Pitt to back his words with his fists. Predictably, Corcoran pummeled Pitt and forced him to admit his mistake.[16] Whether true or not, the anecdote circulated among the Irish of St. Giles and the tale of the skilled Irish pugilist easily besting his insolent English student must have been particularly satisfying to them.

Stories about Corcoran's fighting prowess were not enough to maintain his reputation, though. Prizefights were considered the only real test of a boxer. If won, they not only reaffirmed a pugilist's fame, they also lined his pockets; a winner could expect a gratuity in addition to the prize money. As a result, after three years out of the ring, Corcoran fought again. On Monday, September 12, 1774, he faced Sam Peters for a prize of 100 guineas in a "long expected" match at Waltham Abbey.[17] Peters, a gunsmith who had won fame in Birmingham before coming to London, had contested three other prize-fights in the capital, all of them against Irishmen.[18] Contemporary accounts of the match are sparse and so it is difficult to determine the extent to which it was presented or interpreted as a battle between an Irishman and an Englishman. Still, the fact that Peters had made a name fighting Irish pugilists and that Corcoran's reputation was in part built on the idea that he was a defiant Irishman suggests that national identity played at least some role in bringing a "great number" of people to Waltham Abbey.[19] Corcoran's victory in a little over six minutes helped maintain his position among the Irish of St. Giles, where he kept the Black Horse for another two years.

The great Irish fighter's career came to an abrupt end in 1776 in another controversial match, this time against sawyer Harry Sellers for 100 guineas. Sellers worked for the Blackwall timber merchant Thomas Weston and had not contested a major prizefight previous to his match with Corcoran. Despite Sellers's lack of experience, the match was highly anticipated—probably at least in part because of Corcoran's reputation and the national feelings that it encouraged. Sellers won a coin toss to determine the location of the fight and chose Staines "because he had a number of acquaintances" there. The White Lion Inn hosted the match and a stage was built outside. A crowd of thousands came from London "in coaches, landaus, post and single horse chaises, and on foot." The spectators were charged for admission and around £60 was collected. More than 100 people luckily escaped injury when the roof of a nearby barn they had climbed for a better view (and to avoid paying the fee) collapsed. Thousands in wagers depended on the outcome of the match and one gambler reportedly lost £1800. When the fight concluded, carrier pigeons delivered the news to London. Sellers won the match—and around £110 in prize and door money—when, after about twenty minutes, he landed a punch that "cut [Corcoran's] cheek bare to the bone from the top of the jaw bone to the neck."[20]

This dramatic and unexpected conclusion ruined Corcoran's reputation and his career. Despite the gruesome injury he suffered at the end of the match, rumors circulated that he had been paid to lose. Writing in 1812, Pierce Egan claimed that Corcoran had been threatened with eviction from the Black Horse and that he had no liquor to serve on the eve of the match. A few days after the fight, according to the story, Corcoran's house was "flowing with spirits, filled with new dishware, and covered in fresh paint." Egan also wrote that Corcoran was playing at skittles the day after the match and generally behaving as though he had not recently been in the ring. It is difficult to imagine that Corcoran was doing anything of the sort with a massive fresh laceration on his face and neck, but the fact that the sympathetic Egan repeated the tale suggests that most people believed it. Whatever the reason for his defeat, Corcoran's many Irish supporters lost large sums on the outcome. He lost the Black Horse and ultimately died penniless. A subscription collected after his death saved him from a pauper's burial.[21]

During Corcoran's high profile career, some enterprising Englishmen discovered that the feelings aroused by the Irish champion could create opportunities. Sam Peters, later to be defeated by Corcoran, exploited the publicity surrounding Corcoran's victory over Bill Darts at Epsom, fighting three matches against Irish fighters as controversy swirled about whether Dennis O'Kelly had bought the championship for Ireland. The first of these was for £20 in early June against an experienced Irish fighter named Trainer. Peters won after about thirty minutes. The following month, Peters fought Rossemus Gregory in the Epping Forest. This match ended in controversy when Bill Darts, who acted as Gregory's second, interfered on Gregory's behalf and Peters stopped in protest. Peters and Gregory met again in September and the match garnered enough interest that the Three Hats Riding School in Islington risked mounting an indoor match on a stage.[22] The Three Hats, which usually showcased horsemanship, was struggling in 1771 and so took chances to try to boost attendance; in addition to the Gregory and Peters fight, the owners brought in swordsmen and other acts. The gamble paid off for The Three Hats and for Peters when he defeated Gregory before a large crowd.[23] The controversial Irishmen, O'Kelly and Corcoran, thus helped make money for Englishmen as well.

Irish boxers also profited from the growing interest in matches between Englishmen and Irishmen. Despite the lowly state of the sport in that decade, several fought for large prizes in the 1770s. In early April 1773, a hatter named Joyce fought and was defeated by a farm laborer called Nicholls for 100 guineas in Hendon. Joyce was the favorite, but Nicholls broke his jaw with an early punch.[24] As we have seen, Peter Corcoran defeated Sam Peters for £100 near Waltham Abbey in 1774. Unfortunately, the available evidence does not reveal how the spectators responded to these matches or what (if any) attempts were made to stoke national feelings among them. Rossemus Gregory and Peters did have a dispute when they each acted as seconds for a match in 1773. Although the conflict may have had nothing to do with Gregory being Irish, the man Peters seconded—Joe Hood—was matched against Irishman Dennis Kellyhorn for a £50 prize in 1775. It is possible that Hood and Peters passed remarks about Ireland during the dispute and that Hood (or his patron) saw a reaction from the crowd and sought to capitalize on it. Whatever his motives, Hood defeated the "famous Irish bruiser" Kellyhorn.[25]

The sparse accounts of matches in the 1770s limits what can be known about how Irish boxers, their opponents, and the patrons of both sought to exploit national feeling, but some anecdotes from the period suggest that the London Irish community strongly identified with Irish fighters. Pierce Egan claimed that, after his victory over Corcoran in 1776, Harry Sellers regularly taunted the many Irish people who were upset that "their champion" had been defeated.[26] A story recorded by the German Anglophile J.W. von Archenholtz provides more detail about the reaction of some in the Irish community to Corcoran's great defeat. Archenholtz wrote that the "disgrace was severely felt by a number of his countrymen," until a boatswain named Feirns challenged and easily defeated Sellers to restore Ireland's honor. Feirns then, according to the story, theatrically "offered to vindicate the superiority of his country in gymnastic excellence, by defying all England to the combat." To do so, he proceeded to St. James's Palace and asked one of the guards to convey his offer to the King.[27] It seems clear that many in the London Irish community saw Corcoran as their champion and took pride in his accomplishments, though it is difficult to know the extent to which Corcoran sought to cultivate this feeling. His reputation even extended to Ireland; an Irish boxer announced that he was Corcoran's pupil when challenging all comers behind St. Mark's in Dublin in 1787.[28]

Although they were less numerous than Irish boxers, some Jewish boxers were active in the 1770s as well. They tended to receive less support from their community in that decade, however. The Jewish community, which was centered in London, had gradually grown since the mid-seventeenth century. The building of the Bevis Marks synagogue at the beginning of the eighteenth century demonstrated its increasing size and influence. Seven or eight thousand Jews lived in England in the 1750s and the population probably doubled by the early nineteenth century; most were poor, but a wealthy minority actively sought greater rights.[29] These efforts culminated in the so-called "Jew Bill" of 1753, in which Parliament sought to make naturalization somewhat easier. Despite the relatively modest reforms of the bill, it unleashed a firestorm of controversy. This episode and other instances of anti–Semitism throughout the eighteenth century suggest that Jews were considered one of the "others" against which Britishness was contrasted.[30] As Dana Rabin has argued, the "violent, militant, and sexually dangerous nature attributed to Jews suggests a physical threat to the nation."[31] Because of this, Jewish leaders were particularly concerned with an upswing in crime among poor Jews. This surge happened in the 1760s and 1770s, just as the first recorded Jewish prizefighters appeared. The two phenomena were probably not unrelated. In any case, more wealthy Jews considered them to be and so stayed away from boxing in the 1770s.[32]

Despite this lack of support, Jewish pugilists became an important part of the sport. As we have seen, the strong national feelings surrounding boxing helped open opportunities for Irish boxers. The same was true for Jewish pugilists, who started to appear in records of prizefights in the late 1760s. Like most early Irish boxers, Jewish fighters were considered easy victories for Christian English fighters. The first two bouts involving Jewish combatants that are recorded in most sources were in 1769, when the London plasterer Jack Lamb defeated Abraham da Costa and Isaac Mousha.[33] Perhaps more representative—at least for those who associated Jewish boxers with criminality—were two fights reported in the early 1770s involving a pickpocket known as the "fighting Jew." Twice in 1766, "the famous fighting Jew" was caught stealing only to avoid detention when members of his gang came to his rescue.[34] Several years later, in January 1772, the "noted fighting Jew" was matched to fight a Whitechapel butcher in Stepney Fields when a Justice of the Peace arrived and broke up the crowd.[35] In October of the following year, thousands appeared in the same spot to watch "the fighting Jew" battle an Irish coalheaver for several hundred pounds. The same JP attempted to break up the crowd, this time with a few constables, but only succeeded when he read the Riot Act.[36]

Few Jewish boxers—apart from notorious ones—appeared in newspaper accounts, but boxing according to the "Broughtonian" system was becoming a part of life in the Jewish community in London. In his memoirs, the famous Jewish champion Daniel Mendoza described his "first pitched battle" in 1780 at the age of sixteen. At that time, Mendoza worked for a tea dealer and a dispute arose with a porter making a delivery. When the porter challenged Mendoza's employer to a boxing match, the future Jewish champion agreed to fight him instead. The two men went outside the shop, where a ring was made and seconds chosen for each fighter. Mendoza did not specify if the match adhered strictly to the Broughton rules, but the forming of a ring and the choosing of seconds suggests at least some familiarity with them. Some of the spectators who witnessed the match were linked to the prizefighting scene. One of them, identified by Mendoza as a friend, arranged for the future champion to participate in his first prizefight. There is no direct evidence that the fight maker was Jewish but, as Mendoza moved mostly within the Jewish community in his youth, it is a strong possibility that the man was his co-religionist.[37] Whatever the case, it is clear that, by the time that Mendoza fought his first several prizefights in the early 1780s, boxing was a part of the Jewish community in London.

While Mendoza was fighting his first matches and Duggan Feirns was defeating Harry Sellers, the stage was being set for gambling on, reading about, and watching prizefights to become a fashionable aristocratic pastime. In part, this had to do with the tremendous popularity of horseracing in the 1770s. Not only were a number of boxing matches fought at race meetings, but also a gambling infrastructure emerged that facilitated wagering on horses and other sporting contests. This infrastructure owed much to the horse dealer Richard Tattersall who, with patronage from Lord Grosvenor, established a house near Hyde Park corner that included a tavern, a coffee shop, two rooms for the Jockey Club, and another room for gamblers.[38] This provided a more respectable setting for making and betting on boxing matches (among many other things) that helped make pugilism palatable to the less rakish of young aristocratic men.

The appearance of a more organized gambling infrastructure facilitated but did not create the national popularity of boxing in the 1780s, though; Tattersall established his house in 1766, when the sport remained in the wilderness. Rather, the rapid rise in the popularity of boxing in the 1780s had much to do with the question of British identity in the wake of the defeat in North America in 1783. This was a moment when, as Kathleen Wilson has argued, many Britons believed that the values that helped create the British Empire were on the verge of collapse. Not only had American colonists rejected their British identity, but newcomers to the island seemed to be destabilizing it from within as well.[39] As a letter to the *Public Advertiser* put it in April 1786, "the British Lion, ignominiously driven into a corner of his vast dominions, soon lost all courage, energy, and exertion; grown the scorn of his enemies, and the despair of his friends."[40] The 1760s and 1770s had seen political radicalism in England, revolt in America, nationalism in Ireland, and corruption in India. The Gordon Riots of 1780 were but one (if particularly dramatic) response to profound anxieties about change and disruption in London.[41] For many, fears about a transforming Britain were connected to ideas about manhood. Some worried in particular that the solid John Bull manhood of an earlier age was being eroded by foreign-inspired effeminacy. Too much softening the "rough and brutal, ungracious, rugged" Englishmen, the argument went, risked transforming the nation into a collection of weak and servile Frenchmen.[42]

While many were undoubtedly drawn to boxing matches in the 1780s simply to gamble on something fashionable, others gravitated to boxing because it appeared to be a powerful tonic for what ailed the nation. For its supporters a boxing match was a simple, physical contest between two men outside the boundaries of polite society; fighters did not best one another with verbal barbs but with displays of strength and stamina. Their courage and honor seemed a clear rebuff to disorder and effeminacy and a powerful reassertion of the uncomplicated and timeless values of the solid Englishman. The presence of Irish and Jewish boxers—increasing since the 1760s—amplified the symbolic importance of many of these contests by offering a test of Protestant English manhood and by bringing the representatives of change and difference to life. In some of the most popular fights of the 1780s and 1790s, the public performance of manhood was a central concern for both boxers and spectators, helping to draw crowds. This was particularly true in matches involving Jewish or Irish fighters.

The fight that was widely regarded as a turning point for the sport did not involve a Jewish or Irish boxer, however. It was contested on May 3, 1786, at the Newmarket race meeting between the Bath butcher Sam Martin and Richard Humphries, an established London boxer who had trained Mendoza. The match was a spectacle that was widely covered in newspapers, discussed in drawing rooms, and witnessed (and wagered on) by some of the leading men of the Kingdom. The Anglo-Irish army officer George Hanger arranged the bout at Tattersall's in April. The pugnacious Hanger, a friend of the Prince of Wales, was a veteran of the American war who tried to embody the values of the ring—an acquaintance later claimed he was a weapons expert and that he carried a massive club to intimidate would-be attackers.[43] The Prince of Wales, then under intense scrutiny for his profligate spending, let it be known that he approved of the match. He and the Duke of York both attended. The Duc d'Orleans (father of the future French King Louis Phillipe), the Duc de Lauzun, and other members of the French aristocracy witnessed the fight as well.[44] A stage of nineteen square feet was erected and one guinea charged for spots nearest to it. In all, £320 was collected for the winner. The well-heeled spectators wagered around £30,000 on the outcome, which was a victory for Humphries after fifty-five minutes of fighting.[45] The Martin and Humphries match signaled the arrival of boxing as a national phenomenon. Journalist John Badcock later claimed that the tremendous interest of aristocrats in this match spawned the new term, "The Fancy," which described supporters of the sport through the 1820s.[46]

The success of the fight was a happy one for those who sought in pugilism an antidote to the condition of Britain in the 1780s. Some elements in the newspaper press, which had been almost uniformly hostile to boxing since the 1750s, began to repeat the arguments of boxing supporters. A summary of the Martin-Humphries match in the *Morning Post* concluded with the remark that "there is a good political reason" for prizefights because they inspired "the lower order of people with an ardour, intrepidity, and courage

Satirical print showing Richard Humphries training some gentlemen. In the back, an artist applies "artificial bloody noses and black eyes." "School for Boxing" (1788), from Library of Congress, digital ID cph 3c32988//hdl.loc.gov/loc.pnp/cph.3c32988).

... in engagements more important to national honour."[47] Several months later, the *Cambridge Chronicle* noted the "good effects attending the practice of boxing among gentlemen" and recounted the story of a coachman attempting to defraud "a well-dressed man." The gentleman challenged the coachman to a boxing match and "beat him handsomely in less than ten minutes." The *Chronicle* considered this exemplary and honorable behavior.[48] This was the argument pedaled by promoters of the sport since the days of Broughton's amphitheater. For many, the reassuring message of these stories was that boxing could help restore British strength abroad and proper order at home.

Richard Humphries, the conqueror of Martin, was considered a particularly effective ambassador of the virtues of boxing. Humphries, whose father had worked in the household of one of the Clapham Sect, was known as the "gentleman boxer" and widely regarded as the "epitome of English manliness."[49] A contemporary print depicted a manful Humphries in his fighting stance facing a ridiculous-looking fop. Long after his death, training manuals lauded his stance as the essence of manliness.[50] He was also considered a model of conduct outside the ring. The friends of his patron, Wilson Bradyll, found him "obliging" and "modest" while, in an obituary for him in 1799, *The Sporting Magazine* noted that he had "manners the most civil and obliging to everyone."[51] Like Broughton in the 1740s he also trained some of the leading sporting gentlemen of the day, including Bradyll and George Hanger.[52] Powerful in the ring and well-mannered out of it, Humphries was widely regarded as the embodiment of the values of British boxing. Because of his status as the leading Christian English exponent of pugilism, Humphries three famous fights with the great Jewish boxer Daniel Mendoza in 1788, 1789, and 1790 became a cultural phenomenon. As Pierce Egan later noted, London was overrun in this period with pamphlets, newspaper stories, prints, and other cultural ephemera depicting the two fighters.[53]

Mendoza had a rather different background to the "gentleman boxer." He was born in 1764 into the small Jewish middling class, received an education in a Jewish school, and was apprenticed to a glasscutter at thirteen. As we saw above, he fought his first bout in 1780. Mendoza quickly gained a reputation among the Fancy, winning a number of minor bouts in the early 1780s. Humphries trained him in these years and, in March 1787, Humphries's patron Bradyll organized a match between Mendoza and Sam Martin.[54] The first attempt to stage the fight at Shepherd's Bush was interrupted by the magistrates—who asked the Prince of Wales to leave before reading the Riot Act and destroying the stage—but the second attempt further afield at Barnet was successful. Mendoza beat his opponent badly and Martin quit the match after twenty-eight minutes. For his troubles, Mendoza received £500 from

Bradyll and several hundred more from the Prince of Wales. In all, he earned more than £1,000.[55]

Bradyll and others rewarded Mendoza handsomely because they had won large sums wagering on him and because they were interested in promoting boxing. They organized the match without Mendoza's knowledge (as was often the case in this era), staged it, and then paid Mendoza for his successful performance. Despite this, fights and their aftermath were never entirely in the control of the gamblers of Tattersall's; unlike horses, boxers could not simply be sent back to the stable. This was especially true of the charismatic Mendoza. When he was declared the winner of his match with Martin, Mendoza immediately jumped on top of the railing on the side of the stage to present himself to the crowd.[56] Many members of the Jewish community celebrated his victory with him. After the conclusion of the festivities at Barnet, Jewish spectators organized a procession with torches and music for the twelve-mile trek back to the City. When the crowd arrived in Houndsditch that evening, the people of the area came out to greet them. The singing and festivities continued into the night and many shops closed the next day.[57] Claims that boxing represented a timeless Protestant English manhood were a critical element of the newfound popularity of the sport. Many in the Jewish community seem to have accepted the symbolic importance of boxing and, in the aftermath of Mendoza's great victory, celebrated it as a triumph for themselves. As Michael Ragussis has argued for the Georgian theater, a cultural product that trafficked in ethnic performance could become "a site of resistance" for minority groups to defy negative stereotypes.[58]

Portrait of Jewish Champion Daniel Mendoza. From Egan, *Boxiana*, vol. 1.

Predictably, some in the Christian English community took umbrage at Mendoza's great victory and looked forward to his defeat. During the summer of 1787 these hopes came to rest on the "gentleman boxer," Richard Humphries.

While real antagonism likely existed between Humphries and Mendoza—Mendoza implied in his memoirs that it originated in his failure to follow Humphries's training advice before an important fight—the conflict between them was amplified by the newspaper press and helped build anticipation for a showdown between Christian and Jew. The bad feelings between the two men were apparent immediately after Mendoza's victory over Martin. Mendoza later recalled that, on the road to London, his great procession encountered Humphries, who disparaged Mendoza as a boxer. Humphries's companion, Colonel Glover, responded that Humphries should "depend upon it, one day or other he will beat you." The two met and insulted one another in public several times in the following months.[59] The building conflict culminated in an encounter at an inn in Epping, where the "gentleman boxer" again insulted and perhaps struck Mendoza. The innkeeper organized an impromptu match between the two men in the adjacent yard and there they fought for several minutes before being interrupted by magistrates. Details about punches and injuries were meticulously reported in the newspaper press.[60]

Throughout the autumn of 1787, public negotiations to arrange a prizefight between the two boxers took place. Reports in the newspaper press generally blamed Mendoza for the delay in organizing a match, hinting at a failure of his nerve. When Mendoza and Humphries met after a prizefight between Kellyhorn and Savage in October, negotiations broke down on the issue of a stage. According to *The World and Fashionable Advertiser*, Humphries "very properly objected" to Mendoza's demand that the fight occur on the turf because "it is a common practice with the Jews to break the ring, when they find their champion is in danger of being beaten." When Mendoza did not immediately accept Humphries's "very fair and honourable" counterproposal, the newspaper suggested that the "champion of the Israelites" did not have the courage to face him.[61] Two days later, the same newspaper compared Mendoza unfavorably to Shylock for demanding too much of a Christian.[62] The match was finally made in an exchange of public letters on October 19 and the rules for it agreed at a subsequent meeting in a house in the City on December 5. The *Whitehall Evening Post* noted that Humphries agreed to the proposed terms "instantly" and "without the smallest alteration."[63] In the months before the fight, a narrative had taken shape that cast Humphries as a courageous Englishman ready to fight for honor alone and that depicted Mendoza as a calculating and cowardly Jew eager to find and exploit an unfair advantage.

The match between Humphries and Mendoza, which the *Morning Post* claimed was more anticipated than the "memorable *bout* between ACHILLES and HECTOR," took place on a wet Sunday morning in early January at Odiham in Hampshire. The stage was erected in a paddock and leading pugilists guarded each entrance. Several hundred spectators paid the half guinea admission fee before a mob broke the gates. The highly partisan crowd included a "prodigious concourse of Jews."[64] A report in the *Cambridge Chronicle* high-mindedly complained about "the distinction made between these two men, as champions for the Christian and the Jewish cause," before remarking on the supposed overriding loyalty of Jews to money.[65] Mendoza dominated much of the match, driving his opponent around the stage, frequently landing punches, and even laughing at Humphries when dodging his blows. Humphries was only saved being knocked into the crowd by the controversial intervention of his second, Thomas Johnson, who caught one of Mendoza's punches when Humphries was crumpled against the rails that bounded the stage. Mendoza later retaliated by pulling on Humphries's nose and grinding his knuckle in his adversary's eye. Ultimately, however, Humphries gained the advantage after switching to worsted stockings and thus improving his footing on the slick surface. A powerful punch to Mendoza's neck and an ankle injury forced him to concede after twenty-eight minutes.[66]

The result of the match generated great excitement; for much of January, it was the talk of London. There were also great opportunities for profit, especially in images of the fighters and of the match. Prints of John Hoppner's famous portrait of Humphries sold briskly for fifteen shillings each in the weeks after the fight. Commissioned by Wilson Bradyll in 1787, the portrait depicted the pugilist alone in a natural setting and solidly planted in a fighting stance. This image of a masculine ideal was very unlike the retreating strategy on which Humphries had relied for much of the match with Mendoza.[67] A number of other prints of the boxers and the fight were peddled in London as well. Large plates and prints from an original drawing of the match were advertised for half a guinea and eight shillings in the *Morning Post* though the newspaper later complained about the quality of the print. At the same time, the availability of another "very *elegant engraving* of this memorable event" was promoted.[68] Despite the result of the match, there was great interest in the Jewish community as well. A theatrical performance of the match with music, dancing, and (it was claimed) technical advice from Mendoza was staged at the Royalty Theatre in Whitechapel at the end of the month.[69]

Almost immediately after his defeat, Mendoza began to lobby for a return match on the grounds that he would have won if he had not unluckily sustained injury. In a series of public letters addressed to Humphries he not only demonstrated, as many scholars have argued, an aptitude for publicity but also an ability to deploy the language of the prize ring for his own ends.[70] In the days and weeks after the fight, discussion about foul play centered on Mendoza's actions rather than Johnson's questionable intervention in catching Mendoza's punch. Commentators considered Humphries's refusal to allow the umpires to consider whether Mendoza's actions constituted foul blows a clear indication that Humphries only cared for an honorable victory.[71] In his first letter after the match, Mendoza addressed the emerging narrative that Humphries was a superior boxer who had won despite numerous attempts at foul play. He claimed that an unlucky fall had injured him and prevented him from fighting effectively and inserted a long letter from a surgeon to support this claim.[72] The implication was clear: if Humphries truly only cared about winning an honorable victory, he would grant Mendoza a return match. In his response, Humphries refused to accept Mendoza's interpretation of events but agreed to fight for five hundred guineas.[73] Mendoza consented to fight for this amount but demanded that neither fighter be permitted to "close" (grapple and deploy legal wrestling throws). The *Morning Post* ridiculed Mendoza for this condition but then conceded Mendoza's point in noting that, if "it could be supposed that the victory was decided by *accident*, the willingness of *Humphreys* to renew the contest, would destroy that doubt."[74]

Mendoza's injury and disagreement about the rules of the match delayed matters and prompted another exchange of letters in which each fighter questioned the courage and manhood of the other. In his letter, Humphries doubted Mendoza's injury and his willingness to fight on fair terms. He also remarked on Mendoza's use of gouging "and other unmanly arts."[75] Mendoza responded in even stronger terms, charging that "Mr. Humphries is afraid; he dare not meet me as a boxer" and that he "meanly shrinks from a public trial of skill."[76] In response to the charge that he was afraid to fight, Humphries hoped that Mendoza "or any of his friends, will be kind enough to tell me so *personally*."[77] A match was not agreed in consequence of this exchange—though Mendoza's boxing school thrived in subsequent months—or when a group of patrons put forward 500 guineas for the two men to fight. Finally, in early July, Humphries went to Mendoza's school and the two engaged in a public argument that ended with strongly worded threats. The *London Chronicle* commented that Humphries had "chosen the most candid and manly way of expressing himself" by appearing at Mendoza's school.[78] The two met in Whitechapel the next month but again could not agree to terms. This prompted another exchange of letters in which each fighter accused the other of cowardice and of a failure to "stand up like a man."[79] In November, a match was finally made for the 1789 Newmarket race meeting.[80] Despite nearly a year of delays after losing the first match of his career—a year during which he was often ill and had (and subsequently lost) his first child—Mendoza had a thriving school and was more famous than ever before. When he appeared to spar on stage with another boxer in January, some in the audience hissed and others applauded.[81] His public verbal combat with Humphries, and his deployment of the language of courage and manhood, had proven a very effective strategy.

After more than a year of build-up, the second match between Mendoza and Humphries finally took place on Wednesday, May 6 near Stilton in Cambridgeshire. The contest was hotly anticipated. A few days before the fight, the *Morning Post* reported that the "beds in and near Stilton, and the horses on the road, are all engaged for the ensuing combat between HUMPHRIES and MENDOZA."[82] Extensive preparations were made to accommodate the crowd. A builder received around £300 to erect an octagonal stand around a forty-eight-foot ring in a paddock owned by local landowner and sportsman Henry Thornton.[83] The stand had ten rows of seating, the highest of which was eighteen feet from the ground. Spectators climbed a ladder to the higher seats and a door was built in the bottom of the structure through which the fighters could enter the ring. Around 2,500 spectators purchased pre-printed tickets for a half guinea. Several London newspapers arranged for reports to be sent the eighty miles from Stilton for publication on Thursday.[84]

The fight justified the excitement and the theatrical language of courage, cowardice, and skill that had figured powerfully in the long public exchanges between the two boxers was a critical part of their encounter in Thornton's paddock. Mendoza again dominated the early part of the match until Humphries fell to the ground in trying to block a punch. Mendoza's supporters, citing the agreement that any fall that was not from a blow would result in forfeiture, claimed Mendoza had won. Mendoza sat on the side of the stage and refused to continue fighting. Humphries's supporters disputed this interpretation and the "gentleman boxer" and his supporters taunted Mendoza and questioned his courage for not continuing the match. As a result, Mendoza was finally persuaded to fight on. When the fight resumed, however, Mendoza turned the tables on Humphries and openly mocked him. Several times, he approached his opponent with his arms folded and "with a look of contempt" before easily blocking Humphries's punches. On the many occasions in which Humphries fell or was knocked to the ground, Mendoza pointed to him and looked at the crowd "with an expressive countenance" that encouraged them to ridicule Humphries as well. Humphries responded to Mendoza by saying, "Very well indeed! Very well!" when approaching him but Mendoza taunted him for this as well. When he knocked Humphries to the ground, he repeated the words and "patted him with an air of mockery."[85]

Mendoza's actions in the ring, while certainly expressive of real outrage toward Humphries during the match, should also be considered an extension of the discourse of manhood and identity that shaped public understanding of the fighters, the match, and its meaning. Before and after the first match, a narrative emerged in the newspaper press, in visual media, and among elite patrons of the ring that cast Humphries as an honorable and courageous fighter and Mendoza as a weak and calculating manipulator. Mendoza sought to subvert this narrative, both with letters to newspapers and through his work with elite "amateur"[86] fighters at his school. His mocking of Humphries during the fight continued his challenge to the strong and solid "gentleman boxer" depicted in Hoppner's famous portrait. It also provides a clear example of how the boxing ring, like the theater, could be a "site of resistance" in which a minority fighter might challenge stereotypes.[87]

The match at Stilton ended when Humphries fell again without receiving a blow and the umpires agreed that Mendoza had won.[88] On May 11, Humphries wrote a public letter defending his first fall and implying that the dispute was a ruse by Mendoza to gain valuable rest that helped him ultimately win the fight. Despite the early reports of the match, which detailed the extent to which Mendoza controlled the match, many London newspapers accepted Humphries interpretation and, as a result, questioned the validity of Mendoza's victory. They also cast doubt on his manhood and deployed anti-Semitic stereotypes. The *Morning Post and Daily Advertiser*, for example, argued that early accounts of the match were false and that Humphries seemed "to have been *jockied* out of the battle by a cunning Jew's trick, when he was on the very eve of victory."[89] This attitude leaked into the authorities' relationship with Mendoza as well. On May 16, *The Whitehall Evening Post* reported that a group of constables with the authority of the Lord Mayor had closed Mendoza's school, which had reopened soon after the fight "with all the insolence of recent triumph."[90] Not surprisingly, given such anti-Semitic vitriol, many in the Jewish community supported Mendoza. *The St. James's Chronicle* groused that the "Jews are grown witty" and were claiming to be superior in both boxing and theology. In some print shops, according to the story, a portrait of Mendoza could be seen with a "curious inscription" that read: "Thus the Jewish pugilist was as superior to the Christian, as David Levi to Dr. Priestley."[91]

Mendoza soon agreed to another match with Humphries but wanted to put off the contest until 1790 as he had already made engagements for the summer months, including exhibiting boxing at the Manchester Theater. He received 75 guineas for a three-night performance.[92] Mendoza used his fame as the great Jewish conqueror of Humphries to create other opportunities for himself throughout 1789. In the summer, he was seen wearing a long shirt with large silver buttons inscribed with the word "Stilton."[93] He also took to appending the letters "P.P." ("Professor of Pugilism") to the end of his signature. *The St. James's Chronicle* sarcastically remarked that this was a "fascinating" title.[94] Such actions were intended to generate publicity not only for his tour but, more especially, for boxing exhibitions in London. In June, the Royal Circus Theater in St. George's Fields engaged Mendoza and Irish boxer Michael Ryan to spar on stage. The entertainments also included displays of horsemanship.[95] Later in the summer Mendoza advertised boxing exhibitions at his own theater, at the Lyceum in the Strand. With box and gallery seating, he claimed that the performances were "divested … of every degree of Brutality" and thus were even safe for ladies to attend.[96] Toward the end of the year, he was in Oxford "delivering some *Lectures on Boxing*" and fighting (and defeating) a much larger local tough.[97]

After several delays, Humphries and Mendoza contested their final match at the Doncaster races in southern Yorkshire on Wednesday, September 29. A stage was again erected in a paddock and half a guinea charged for admission. Several hundred pounds in admission fees were collected. The fight was anticlimactic. Although Humphries knocked Mendoza down in first round, in the second Humphries fell and dislocated his knee. He gamely fought on for over an hour but Mendoza stopped nearly every punch and mangled Humphries face badly with his own blows. By the end, even Humphries supporters urged him to quit. Many reports of the match were brief. *The St. James's Chronicle*, for example, sullenly noted that "the Jew gained another victory over the Gentile" before suggesting the fight was fixed and moving on to other news.[98] Sampson Perry's radical daily *The Argus* was one of the few newspapers to provide an extensive account, providing one of the first round-by-round descriptions of a prizefight. To justify the inclusion of this, the writer argued that other newspapers had "represented the whole affair with a most shameful partiality." The article in *The Argus*, in contrast, sought to avoid every "possible degree of bias or prejudice."[99] Most of the newspaper press did not follow *The Argus's* lead, however, and briefly described the result as an unfortunate accident.

While Mendoza was the most successful and famous minority fighter of this period, he was certainly not the only one. His exploits inspired many other Jewish fighters; while few Jewish boxers were active before Mendoza, many came after him. In April 1788, only a few months after the exchanges of public letters between Mendoza and Humphries following their first fight, a Jewish fighter named Elisha Crabbe faced the veteran pugilist Stephen Oliver. The Prince of Wales, Hanger, and other elite patrons watched Crabbe win the fight. In its report of the match, the *Public Advertiser* noted that Oliver "stood up to his man very honestly, while the Jew shifted."[100] In June, the Prince and the leading boxing amateurs watched Crabbe lose to Robert Watson, who later issued a series of challenges to Mendoza in the summer of 1789 in which he questioned Mendoza's manhood.[101] In August 1789, with Mendoza's great victory at Stilton not far in the past, a huge crowd descended on Chingford Hatch, about 10 miles northeast of London, for a fight between a Jewish boxer named Solomon and the Christian Jack Lee. Solomon was seconded by the great Christian fighter Thomas Johnson and advised by Mendoza. The match ended when Johnson called a blow foul. The *Morning Post* noted that he thus "gained the affection of the Jews."[102] Crabbe fought another well-attended match in early 1790 against Tom Tyne (against whom Mendoza had fought earlier in his career), as anticipation for the final Mendoza and Humphries fight started to build. All of these fights demonstrated that the excitement surrounding Mendoza in the Christian and Jewish communities helped create opportunities for Jewish boxers. Many more would follow Mendoza's example in years to come.

The revival of boxing, with its emphasis on identity, and the popularity of Mendoza, who demonstrated how to win the support of a minority community, also created opportunities for Irish boxers. The most successful of these in the 1780s was former sailor Michael Ryan, who twice fought against the Yorkshire corn porter Thomas Johnson for the Championship of England. Like its neighbor to the east, Ireland experienced an upsurge of interest in pugilism in the final decades of the eighteenth century and Ryan developed his fighting skills there and probably also on a ship on which he served for five years before coming to England in the 1780s. He was most likely Catholic, though contemporary sources were silent on this issue, as they were with most Irish boxers of the period.[103] Before his famous matches against Johnson, Ryan won at least two other bouts: a fight with the well-known pugilist Dunn in Epping forest in late August 1786 and another with a boxer named Fry, who Johnson had also easily defeated.[104] The match with Johnson was first made in August 1787 after attempts to arrange a fight between Johnson and "Big" Ben Bryan failed.[105] Final arrangements were not concluded, however, until the two fighters met at the same house in London where Humphries and Mendoza came to terms.[106]

The match between Johnson and Ryan was fixed for Wednesday, December 19 at Staines, which had last been the scene of a major fight when Sellers defeated Corcoran in 1776. As with many other prizefights in these years, elaborate preparations were made for a large crowd. A stage with seating was erected at the cost of £12 and a multitude of spectators crowded the road from London. Most of the leading amateurs made the journey to Staines, though the Princes of Wales and of York were unable to attend. Unfortunately for the large crowd gathering there, a local magistrate appeared and ordered the stage and the seating destroyed. After some debate about what to do, the organizers of the match determined to move to Wraysbury Common and erect another stage. An "immense column of carriages, horsemen, and pedestrians to the amount of two or three thousand" followed the boxers and paid admission to see the fight. Several carriages were parked just beyond the crowd, with seats atop them sold to those seeking a better view. Houses surrounding the common sold seating as well; a handbill posted on one advertised views from windows for "a fine sighte [of] thee fit between thee Inglishe Man an Irishe Man." This large crowd witnessed Johnson defeat Ryan in thirty-two minutes after cutting his forehead and blackening his left eye.[107]

Although initial reports of the match described a clear and uncontroversial victory for Johnson, Ryan and his supporters complained of foul play. At a critical moment in the fight, after Ryan knocked Johnson senseless with a powerful punch to his temple, Humphries (Johnson's second) caught a second punch that might have ended the bout. Mendoza, who had trained Ryan and was also his bottle-holder, came into the ring to cry foul and was struck by Johnson. Ryan refused to continue the match for some time after the incident.[108] When Ryan's supporters made the charge of foul play in the days after the fight, some newspapers hinted that it might be true. *The World* admitted that Ryan had "been very hardly used" and that there "certainly was a strong partiality shewn in favour of *Johnson*." A few days later, the *Morning Post* also noted that *"many circumstances were unfriendly to"* Ryan in the fight.[109] The "strong partiality" shown by the spectators at the match probably resulted in large measure from Ryan's being Irish. Ethnic and religious identities—and strong feelings and even bigotry about these identities—had long been critical to the success of many fighters and so strong partisanship at the Johnson and Ryan match was no surprise.

Prevented from delivering a potential knockout blow, Ryan had at least as strong an argument about the hostile crowd and foul play as Mendoza had in January 1788. Although he was no Mendoza, Ryan was able to keep himself in the public eye and, ultimately, win another match with Johnson. He was not heard from in the immediate aftermath of the fight but, by late spring, he was active again. In May, he appeared at Mendoza's school for a sparring match with Birmingham champion Fewterel, though his opponent did not arrive. He announced plans to open his own boxing school the following month. This school, at his house in St. Giles, probably relied heavily on the local Irish community of which Ryan was a member. The reputation he gained, along with the controversial end to his first match with Johnson, convinced the champion to fight him again. He was also successful enough in the spring and summer of 1788 to post 100 guineas of his own money for the second fight.[110] Johnson and Ryan met at a house in Fetter lane in November to sign articles of agreement and to make a ten-guinea deposit. Ryan then went to Buckinghamshire to train with Mendoza and a baker named Rolfe, who was his second in the match. Johnson trained in Epping Forest and a group of gentlemen came each Sunday to watch.[111]

The second match between Ryan and Johnson was contested on a cold and wet Wednesday, February 11 and was an even bigger event than the first. A stage was built at the bottom of a gravel pit situated in Rickmansworth on the land of Henry Fotherley Whitfield, the lord of the manor of Rickmansworth, who also prevented the magistrates from stopping the fight. Some six thousand spectators sat on the steeply-sloped sides of the gravel pit and paid a total of £512 in admission fees, which the boxers had agreed to split evenly. Before the fight began, George Hanger walked around with a hat to collect admission from those who had not yet paid. Once the match began, both fighters delivered hard blows but, after thirty rounds in thirty-three minutes, Ryan gave in and Johnson was declared the winner. His supporters placed a hat decorated with blue ribbons on his head and pigeons were released to carry the news to London. Newspaper reports variously blamed Ryan's defeat on his use of the downward-swinging "chopper" blow taught to him by Mendoza and his fighting "in a passion."[112] Pierce Egan later claimed that Ryan's anger resulted from Humphries (who was again Johnson's second) insulting Ireland.[113] Whatever strong feeling was expressed in the ring did not remain after the fight; Johnson claimed that he would back Ryan for 50 guineas against any man in the kingdom.[114]

Both boxers did well after the fight. Johnson's old employer, a corn factor, won a great deal of money on the match and declared his intention to give Johnson £20 a year for the rest of his life.[115] In October, Johnson fought and defeated Isaac Perrins. He received £800 in admission fees and a further £1,000 from a man who had won £20,000 betting on the match. Unfortunately for Johnson, he lost all of his money gambling. He ended his life in Ireland; when he died in 1797, he was teaching boxing in Cork.[116] Ryan, though his face was unrecognizable after the match, eventually recovered and continued to teach boxing at his popular public house in St. Giles. His son, Bill Ryan, was a moderately successful prizefighter in the first decade of the nineteenth century.[117] While Ryan was not nearly as skilled a self-publicist as Mendoza, he nevertheless leveraged his status as a great Irish fighter into a comfortable living amidst the Irish community in St. Giles.

Daniel Mendoza was an uncommonly skilled boxer and publicist whose fights with Richard Humphries helped make the late-Georgian period a golden age of boxing. His success was made possible in part, however, by the culture of bare-knuckle prizefighting that had been developing for much of the eighteenth century. As we have seen, promoting fighters as representatives of their national, ethnic, or religious communities had a long pedigree stretching back to the amphitheaters of Figg and Broughton and these strategies endured during the sport's "dark age" in the 1760s and 1770s. It was the anxiety of the 1780s, though, that renewed interest in bare-knuckle prizefighting and made it more popular than ever before. Uncertainty following the loss of the thirteen colonies combined with concerns about the influence of new men with ill-gotten wealth from India and the Caribbean to make the sport's claims to embody a simple, pure, and timeless particularly attractive. The excitement of the sport and the opportunity to gamble surely played a part as well, but the keenest supporters—men like the club-wielding George Hanger—seem to have been genuinely drawn to the opportunity to put Christian English manhood to the test.

There is little doubt that the great Mendoza's unique talents transformed bare-knuckle prizefighting. His innovative skill as a boxer was matched by his ability as a showman and a promoter; he used anti–Semitic hostility to his benefit, developing a larger-than-life persona that was heroic for some, villainous for others, and very profitable for him. His skillful manipulation of the newspaper press, reliance on symbolism, and encouragement of support from his community offered a model for later minority fighters as well. The opportunities he exploited so successfully, however, existed because his sport had tapped a vein of popular nationalism. The relationship between British and minority identities would help define bare-knuckle prizefighting in the years to come.

Chapter Three

Sport as Symbol

Prizefighting in the Age of the French Revolution, 1790–1802

Although the boxing craze accompanying the Mendoza and Humphries fights did not endure, the sport remained popular in the 1790s. Large crowds continued to travel outside London to see important matches and many newspapers reported details of these fights for their readers. The boxing schools of Mendoza and others thrived, while gentlemen amateurs made extravagant wagers and fêted the best fighters. As the sport continued to have a high profile, moral reformers, who had attacked boxing and other "blood sports" throughout the eighteenth century, became more vocal. Their denunciations of prizefighting had particular resonance as the French Revolution grew ever more radical and many feared the contagion would spread to Britain and Ireland. A letter to the editor of *Lloyd's Evening Post* in the summer of 1791 characteristically warned that the elite patrons of the ring would soon rue their support for an endeavor that "paves the way to anarchy, revolt, and rebellion."[1]

In response to moral reformers, defenders of boxing—including some of the most powerful men in the kingdom—honed their arguments about the importance of the sport. They focused particularly on effeminacy, which they blamed for aristocratic corruption in France and England. Far from encouraging rebellion, the argument went, the timeless values on display in the prize ring were the best guarantor of order at home and British power abroad. Many of those who agreed with these sentiments read about boxing matches (and many other sporting contests) in an embryonic sporting press. Publishers such as John Bell and John Wheble led the way in dramatically expanding the coverage of sport in newspapers and periodicals. This helped create a much wider audience for claims about the importance of pugilism, but it also began the process of shifting the publicizing and organization of the sport away from gentleman gamblers. One consequence of this was to give even greater importance to minority boxers and ethnic spectacles, the popularity of which helped publishers sell their wares. These developments, though still in an early stage at the turn of the century, would help make British and minority identities an even greater part of the sport in the first third of the nineteenth century.

This chapter argues that the 1790s were a critical moment in the development of boxing and, more particularly, the making of the relationship between identity and the sport. The political climate in Britain and the emergence of the sporting press during this period of radicalism, rebellion, and reaction helped bring the claim that boxing represented timeless values to a wider audience and also helped pave the way for the commercialization of minority identities that characterized the culture of pugilism in the 1810s and 1820s.

As the three fights between Mendoza and Humphries brought the popularity of boxing to unprecedented heights in the late 1780s, the sport came under sustained attack as part of a campaign for moral reform, which was an extension of the eighteenth century "luxury debates" in France and Britain. Most of the amateurs of boxing—the wealthy young men such as Wilson Bradyll and George Hanger who sparred and socialized with prizefighters, made matches, and gambled extravagant sums on them—were part of the fast and fashionable set of Whigs centered on the Prince of Wales. Many moral reformers saw this circle as the epitome of a broad problem of "national moral decay." In an effort to counter this perceived moral decline William Wilberforce led an effort (with the acquiescence of Prime Minister William Pitt) to convince the King to reissue the proclamation "for the Encouragement of Piety and Virtue: and for the preventing of Vice, Profaneness and Immorality," which he did in June 1787. The proclamation, and the society formed by Wilberforce to enforce it, emphasized the importance of the elite in providing an example of moral behavior to the rest of society.[2] The very public profligacy of the Prince and his circle, many of whom admired and sparred with plebeian boxers, seemed to set just the wrong sort of example.

With the energy for moral reform building and boxers and their wealthy patrons often in the newspapers, boxing was a natural target for criticism. Anglo-Irish minister and pamphleteer Edward Barry called for parliamentary action against the sport in *A Letter on the Practice of Boxing*, published in 1789. Deploring the "scandalous popularity" of boxing and the patronage offered to it by men of wealth and standing, Barry dismissed the claim that pugilism represented timeless English values necessary to maintain the strength of the nation. He argued that it imposed an unnatural "spirit of savageness" and "barbarism" in those who participated in or observed the sport. Callousness of feeling and dissipation of manners rather than effeminacy were the root cause of "the gradual extinction of that *bravery*" that adorned "the British character." Barry did not simply call on spectators to stop supporting boxing. Following Wilberforce's strategy of seeking official sanction for the reform of morals, Barry addressed his letter to Watkin Lewes, a former Lord Mayor who represented the City in the House of Commons in 1789, and called for parliamentary action.[3] Although there is no record that Lewes or any other person in a position of authority responded to Barry's call, it proved influential among moral reformers concerned about boxing.

The moral reformist attacks on boxing could also be heard in the debating societies of the metropolis. Crowds consisting largely of skilled tradesmen and shopkeepers participated in the "rational entertainment" of debating societies throughout this period.[4] A flurry of debates about boxing occurred at these forums between 1788 and 1790—the years of the three matches between Humphries and Mendoza and the high-water mark of the sport's popularity in the eighteenth century. At the end of January 1788, just weeks after the first Humphries and Mendoza match, the "School of Eloquence," a debating society which met at Carlisle House in Soho Square, took up the topic of boxing. The sport was "was pointedly reprobated by almost every speaker" and the audience agreed with them. Similarly, on April 15, 1789, a few weeks before the second Mendoza and Humphries match, the Westminster Forum considered whether the authorities ought to make every effort to prevent that fight and all future matches. The debate pitted the advocates of "Refinement and Civilization in Society" against those who argued that boxing was "consistent with the naturally bold and hardy Characters of the ancient Race of Britons." In March 1790, the Westminster Forum discussed Edward Barry's treatise, focusing specifically on Barry's claim that boxing was a barbarous practice that did not teach men to be courageous, as its promoters claimed. The audience overwhelmingly supported Barry. This is perhaps not surprising, given that spectators at debating societies chose to spend their money on "rational entertainments." Nevertheless, they helped publicize the moral reformist position that pugilism was part of the problem, not part of the solution.

Some proponents of boxing answered this tide of criticism, reasserting the claim that boxing was a manly activity and questioning the manhood of its opponents. The author of *The Complete Art of Boxing, according to the Modern Method* intemperately noted that many "Frenchified English effeminate scribblers" attempted to denounce "manly exercises" as brutal. The author would "soar above the trifling squibs of cowardly petit maîtres," however.[5] Henry Lemoine's *Modern Manhood; or, the Art and Practice of English Boxing* countered claims about the unnatural brutality of boxing by arguing that it was a quintessentially English and manly activity. In early February 1790, the *Public Advertiser* also claimed that boxing was a laudable English pastime and even suggested that it be exported to the continent. Citing an Italian affinity for the dagger, the newspaper noted that "many useful lives might be annually saved" in Italy if boxing were introduced there. The enthusiasm of some reformers for suppressing boxing, conversely, threatened to "unwittingly cause the substitution of the refined Italian poniard" in England.[6] As the 1790s began, both opponents and proponents of boxing considered the sport to be closely connected with the issues of manhood and public order.

Although manhood and public order continued to be central to discussions of boxing, the outbreak of the French Revolution in the summer of 1789, and especially its increasing radicalization, shifted the ground of debate. Shortly after the second match between Daniel Mendoza and Richard Humphries, Parisians stormed the Bastille and members of the French Third Estate formed the National Assembly. By the time of Mendoza and Humphries's third match in May 1790, civil disabilities for Jews in France had been ended and many other reforms enacted. That summer more radical ideas gained traction. Across the English Channel, debate about the course of events in France inevitably reflected differing ideas about the present and future of British politics and society. In November 1790, Edmund Burke published his influential *Reflections on the Revolution in France* and, a few months later, Thomas Paine responded with *The Rights of Man*. This exchange launched a "pamphlet war" in which loyalists and radicals debated the nature of the British government. Following Paine, many radicals attacked aristocratic rule and associated it with what they considered to be the effeminacy and slavish obedience of the French aristocracy. Loyalists defended what they claimed was the British system of "mixed government," which effectively balanced power and interests. Although loyalist pamphleteers invoked manhood much less frequently than their radical counterparts, they did occasionally claim that Britain's rulers were manly in response to radical attacks.[7]

The earlier criticism that boxing promoted immorality and the dangerous disruption of the social order was reinvigorated by this debate about the French Revolution in the early 1790s, especially because public discussion of the Revolution concerned the nature of British society. Radicals used elite patronage of boxing—along with many other pastimes—as an example of the wickedness of aristocratic rule. The author of the pamphlet *A Dialogue in the Shades, between Mercury, a Nobleman, and a Mechanic* argued that the nobility might be overthrown, as they had been in France, "in consequence of their own indiscretions." In a dialogue with a mechanic, "Mercury" proudly listed his achievements, including heavy drinking, gambling, and having "officiated as bottle-holder at a dozen boxing matches" before his eighteenth birthday. The mechanic responded that, while he could not boast of such accomplishments, he was "that *prejudiced, old-fashioned, ridiculous* being, an HONEST MAN."[8] Upending the pro-boxing argument about the timeless values of pugilism, the pamphleteer suggested that sober hard work was the real "old-fashioned" quality of English men.

Attacks on boxing also came from those who saw in the French Revolution a dangerous attack on the social order. These drew on moral reformist criticisms and tended to see boxing, with its elevation of plebeian manhood and evasion of legal authority, as encouraging revolutionary forces in Britain. *The Morning Post and Daily Advertiser*, for example, ridiculed the Duke of Hamilton for his close association with his "intimate friend" Daniel Mendoza in 1791. The same paper also opined that the reason the Duke of Hamilton elevated Mendoza "into the rank of his *companion*, arises from his admiration of the *French Revolution*, and wishing to set an example of the *Levelling system*."[9] The same year, a letter to the editor of *Lloyd's Evening Post* expressed surprise that nobles and magistrates patronized "that fashionable, though brutal science, Pugilism." The letter-writer argued that this support "paves the way to anarchy, revolt, and rebellion."[10]

The execution of Louis XVI and the start of war between France and Britain in 1793 also helped sharpen the arguments of boxing's proponents. After the commencement of hostilities, Pitt's government increasingly clamped down on dissent at home and sought to pursue an aggressive strategy abroad. This touched off a political realignment: Wilberforce and many moral reformers were uncomfortable with (or opposed outright to) the conduct of the war, while a number of leading Whigs supported it. Led by the Duke of Portland, a group of these broke with Whig leader Charles James Fox and joined the government. One of the most prominent members of the Portland Whigs was William Windham of Norfolk. A disciple of Edmund Burke, Windham was a strong supporter of boxing who sparred with pugilists and attended prizefights. Although he deplored the excesses of many boxing amateurs, he seems to have sincerely believed in the importance of the sport as a proving ground for manly courage and honor. As a young man, he worried in his diary that he would not have the bravery to endure pain in the ring.[11] When he grew older, he became convinced that the sense of fair play fostered by pugilism tempered dangerous passions. In a private letter to James Boswell in 1791, Windham argued that "the manly and honourable spirit of our common people, is in a great measure produced by" boxing matches. Watching or participating in a match helped prevent the spread to Britain of "that rancorous spirit, and thirst for blood, that we see rage with such violence among our neighbours" by reminding Britons that they knew a better and more honorable way to settle differences.[12] For Windham, pugilism inoculated Britain against disorder and violence by nourishing courage and a sense of fair play.

Windham's convictions were in step with many of his Whig allies as well as with the Pitt government's efforts to stamp out radicalism and encourage martial values among potential soldiers.[13] Many pro-war Whigs believed, like Windham, that the war must be fought not only against France but also against the forces of disorder at home. In a letter congratulating him for joining the government, Windham's good friend Charles Burney alluded to this connection, telling him that Britain was being "attacked by an infuriate Enemy abroad; endangered by an insidious enemy, at home."[14] Some members of the government that was formed in 1794 argued that instilling martial values in British men was the key to defeating these enemies and that, therefore, moral reformers (along with political radicals) were sapping the strength of the nation. Secretary of State for War Henry Dundas were central to this effort and "hammered again and again" at the point that there was a "need to inculcate a 'military spirit' among the people." He exchanged letters with Windham on the same theme. Pitt agreed with Dundas about the importance of "military spirit" and both of them sought to institute national conscription partly in order to instill it in British men.[15] For Windham and others, reformers who sought to destroy boxing, which encouraged courage and honor, undermined this goal. War with revolutionary France had hardened the battle lines between pugilism's opponents and its defenders and raised the stakes of the debate about the sport.

Developments in the newspapers and periodical press also had important consequences for boxing and its proponents. By the 1770s, newspapers were widely read and had become politically influential through their relationship with "public opinion." To be profitable and survive, they had to draw readers and many of these wanted immediate news of sporting results. For boxing this was especially true after the Humphries and Martin match in 1786. A number of newspaper editors were happy to oblige them and reports of important bouts sometimes stretched to several paragraphs.[16] Coverage of prizefighting also expanded beyond descriptions of matches. Some newspapers carried information about the making of matches and the activities of boxers outside the ring, often under the heading "Boxing." These included exchanges such as those between Richard Humphries and Daniel Mendoza and challenges between pugilists, to which the language of courage and manliness were central. Even though newspapers usually printed this type of material without comment, its inclusion nevertheless reminded readers of the claim that boxing nourished courage and authentic British manhood.

One of the publishers most responsible for reporting information about boxing in the late eighteenth century—and thus the language of national character associated with it—was the bookseller and publisher John Bell. From the 1780s to the 1820s, his newspapers were one of the most important sources of boxing intelligence, though boxing information was always but a small part of his business as a publisher and bookseller. Born in 1745, he began selling books on the Strand in 1768 and remained in business there for nearly his entire career; he was best known not for boxing journalism but for volumes related to the theater and for a circulating library he founded. In 1772, only a few years after being established on the Strand, he started *The Morning Post* with eleven other shareholders. These included both Richard Tattersall and "the fighting parson," the Reverend Henry Bate, a boxing amateur. If Bell was not yet familiar with the sporting world, his association with these two men certainly introduced him.

Bell's time at the *Morning Post* showed him that boxing news attracted readers, a lesson he acted on in future ventures. Two years after leaving that newspaper in 1786, Bell founded the *World, or Fashionable Gazette* with Captain Edward Topham.[17] This newspaper, which began as a means to advance the career of Topham's mistress, soon became "*the* authority on taste and fashion." It is most known for influential stylistic changes: Bell replaced the old long s, which was easily confused with an f, and left space between paragraphs for a more pleasing appearance. He also made the newspaper the leading source of information about boxing; the correspondence between Mendoza and Humphries was an early draw for readers. He and the wealthier Topham had connections with the young Whigs who then controlled the sport and used them to deliver gossip and other intelligence about it. After a dispute with Topham, however, Bell was forced out and founded *Oracle, or Bell's New World* in 1789. Once again, Bell's paper immediately became a leading source for news of prizefighting. Finally, in 1796, he founded *Bell's Weekly Messenger*, which continued long after his death.[18] Like the other three newspapers, *Bell's Weekly Messenger* was a leading publisher of stories about boxing. While Bell was not himself a patron of the ring, his newspapers helped bring the sport to a much wider audience at a critical moment in its history.

Publisher John Wheble, founder of the popular *Sporting Magazine* in 1792, was another critical figure in early sporting journalism. He had a much more circuitous path to sporting journalism than Bell, however. Wheble came to London in 1758 at the age of twelve and was apprenticed to the publisher and bookseller John Wilkie. He struck out on his own while still quite young, publishing the *Middlesex Journal* in his early twenties. In the summer of 1770, he printed correspondence between the Duke of Cumberland and Lady Grosvenor in order to take advantage of an adultery scandal.[19] This brought him in contact with opposition leaders. In 1771, John Horne Tooke concocted a scheme to challenge the illegality of publishing speeches made in Parliament. The plan involved Wheble printing them, along with Tooke's satirical commentary, in the *Middlesex Journal.* Wilkes saved Wheble from prosecution and then he and his allies used the affair to make precise reporting of debate in the Commons possible. Wheble and two other publishers received a gift of £100 from the "Supporters of the Bill of Rights" in recognition of their efforts.[20] Despite his association with this critical moment in the freedom of the press, Wheble soon fell into financial difficulties. After a long legal dispute regarding a new publication called the *Lady's Magazine*, he was forced to declare bankruptcy at the end of 1772. When he emerged the following year, he continued as a bookseller but soon had to look for another source of income. In May 1776, he offered his services to the public as an auctioneer. He continued in this capacity until at least 1778, when he began a post with the Commissariat that he held until the end of the war in 1783.[21]

Despite the fame he achieved early in his career, Wheble was nearing forty in 1783 and had had to work as an auctioneer and with the Commissariat in order to prevent another slide to bankruptcy. Soon, however, he struck on a new formula that ultimately brought him, according to his friend John Nichols, to a "state of respectable independence."[22] In the mid–1780s, he founded the *County Chronicle*, a weekly newspaper "calculated for the Metropolis and Sixty Miles round it." Shifting from Wheble's earlier focus on politics and society in London, the *Country Chronicle* published information about commerce, agriculture, and other aspects of life in the country.[23] The paper showed Wheble the market for rural news—the *Chronicle* remained a profitable concern until his death in 1820—and encouraged him to explore similar opportunities. According to Nichols, Wheble traveled extensively outside London to gather information for the *County Chronicle.*[24] This put him in contact with sports staged in rural areas such as horse racing and, increasingly, prizefights.

Following his success with the *County Chronicle*, Wheble founded the monthly periodical *Sporting Magazine* in October 1792. The *Sporting Magazine* followed the model of established periodicals such as *The Gentleman's Magazine*, with a mixture of short squibs, some verse, and longer articles. Unlike these others, however, Wheble focused almost exclusively on sport, including news about and discussion of activities as varied as horseracing, running, and cricket. The *Sporting Magazine* was also one of the only publications to print stories about bull baiting and dog fighting. Not surprisingly, it was sharply critical of moral reformers. Readers provided much of the information about sporting events and Wheble encouraged their contributions. He insisted, however, that correspondents provide accurate accounts and personally edited any information in doubt. *The Sporting Magazine* quickly became a leading source of intelligence about boxing, including reports of all major prizefights and two multi-part histories of the sport in the 1790s. The venture proved a tremendous success. By the time of his death in 1820, Wheble's early struggles and bankruptcy were long forgotten. He enjoyed a respectable old age and even served on the London Court of Common Council for sixteen years near the end of his life.[25]

Wheble and John Bell did much to create a journalism of sport—of which boxing was a critical part—in the 1780s and 1790s. As Adrian Harvey has argued, the sporting press transformed sport in this era by generating a body of knowledge, by airing political and social opinions related to sport, and by then selling these to the public.[26] Sporting journalism, in other words, helped make sport a commodity. Perhaps more than other early modern sports, prizefighting was already a commercial enterprise; the bear gardens from which it had emerged advertised their bloody spectacles to the paying public more than a half century before Wheble and Bell were born, as did Broughton's amphitheater in the 1740s. Facts about the sport had certainly been compiled earlier in the century—John Godfrey's *Treatise on the Useful Science of Defense* is perhaps the most famous example—and political and social opinions about pugilism were proclaimed as well, not least by the amphitheaters in their attempts to attract spectators. Still, the emergence of sporting journalism marked a critical shift in the history of bare-knuckle prizefighting. Wheble and Bell helped define boxing as a sport with its own culture, past, and future. They brought it to a readership much larger than the narrow band of fickle gentlemen amateurs that had been the sport's main patrons and consumers. This new audience proved to be keenly interested in seeing pugilism as a showcase of identities in broad brush strokes—the hot-blooded and hard-headed Irishman, the cunning Jew, the stoic and courageous Englishman—and in understanding matches as a contest between these identities. This provided more opportunities for minority boxers than ever before as the claim that boxing represented an authentic Britishness that was critical to wartime success was amplified in the 1790s.

Nearly as skilled a showman as he was a boxer, Daniel Mendoza was particularly well situated to take advantage of these opportunities. Awareness of the affairs of the sport of bare-knuckle prizefighting was growing around

Britain and Ireland, along with the idea that boxing was a quintessentially British sport. In the years after his three matches with Richard Humphries, Mendoza toured the kingdoms, performing at theaters and sparring with locals. His flair for the dramatic, and the fact that he was the Jewish conqueror of the English "gentleman boxer" Humphries, helped attract crowds wherever he went. Mendoza's tours brought commercialized ethnic conflict to the country.

Mendoza's first exhibition tour of England, Scotland, and Ireland occurred in the last three months of 1790, just after his third and final match with Humphries. This was a tremendous success, as the great Jewish champion cashed in on his fame at private clubs, theaters, and fairs. He first traveled to Lancashire and the north to exhibit his skills at several theaters, where he enjoyed "great and unprecedented" success. Next, he and the boxer Fewterell went to Edinburgh, where Mendoza was introduced to the Edinburgh Gymnastic Society. Mendoza sparred with many of the members and they presented him with a gold medal and elected him president. This success probably brought him to the notice of the Duke of Hamilton, a Scot who became his patron. He then moved on to Glasgow, where he again received "a very liberal remuneration" for his exertions.[27] Local advertising played a role in drawing crowds, but his reputation as the great Jewish conqueror of Humphries was already widely known.

After his success in Scotland, Mendoza accepted an invitation to exhibit at Philip Astley's Amphitheatre Royal on Peters Street in Dublin. Astley, a famous trick rider and a pioneer of the modern circus, opened his amphitheater in Dublin for a two-month season each winter in the early 1790s. He showcased a wide variety of acts on his stage and was so well positioned to exploit novel entertainments. Boxing was just such a trend in early 1790s Ireland. Stories about the sport were widely reported in newspapers around the island, so many Irish people knew about Mendoza and his victories over the great "gentleman boxer."[28] The disappointment of English hopes with Humphries's defeat may have made many Irish sympathetic to Mendoza, especially in the context of the rising nationalist tide of the 1790s. Astley's calculation in bringing Mendoza to Dublin proved a lucrative decision. Large crowds appeared to watch the Jewish champion in action. Indeed, when Astley kept Mendoza off stage for one night so that he could have a benefit for his son, the clamor among the audience was so great that the Duke of Leinster had to go backstage and ask Mendoza to appear. Mendoza even claimed that he had to leave the theater in disguise to avoid being accosted by ruffians who recognized him. Astley brought him back for the 1791–92 season and he again proved a great success, partly through his skillful self-promotion. In

February 1792, for example, he "challenged all Ireland" to fight a match for 100 guineas.[29] By 1792, engravings of Mendoza appeared in Dublin newspapers and the phrase "tipped a Mendoza" (to throw a punch) was current in that city.[30]

Mendoza also worked hard to maintain his fame in London. In early 1791, he returned to the metropolis, where he resumed tutoring gentlemen amateurs (often at their own houses) and made several public appearances. In early May, he reopened his boxing school in the Grand Saloon at the Lyceum on the Strand, generating publicity by sparring with other pugilists, including one called "the Celebrated FRENCHMAN."[31] He was even known well enough to have his name invoked in the House of Commons. Matthew Montagu elicited howls of laughter when, during an exchange with Richard Brinsley Sheridan regarding a report from the finance committee, Montagu noted that "in matters of sarcasm, repartee and witticism" Sheridan "was the acknowledged MENDOZA of the House; therefore in this line he would not enter the lists with him."[32] The great Jewish champion was the most recognizable prizefighter in the kingdoms.

In a time when boxing was increasingly under attack by both proponents and opponents of the French Revolution, the success and fame of Mendoza challenged the pro-boxing argument that the sport represented a timeless English and, it was assumed, Christian manhood. Lines in an introduction to a poem written in this period by Peter Pindar (the pseudonym of John Wolcott, one of the chief writers for *The Morning Post*) captured this sentiment. These referred to "the news, the very Antichristian news, of Israel's hero having won the day."[33] While the point of these lines was to beg the reader's indulgence for the verse to come, the reference suggests that such feelings were widely shared. The newspaper press was also unsympathetic to Mendoza, if not usually openly hostile. As described above, *The Morning Post* complained about the Duke of Hamilton's patronage of Mendoza. In May 1792, Mendoza defeated William Ward in unexpectedly easy fashion. Although by virtue of his victory Mendoza was considered the "Champion of England," the match received relatively little mention in the newspaper press. Nevertheless, Mendoza was the most visible symbol of the sport. For many supporters of boxing this undermined the claim that boxers were the epitome of English manhood; for most, a truly English sport needed a Christian champion.

For the Jewish community of London, in contrast, the success and fame that Mendoza achieved had a profound effect. As an outspoken champion who succeeded against long odds and refused to be cowed, Mendoza emboldened many London Jews, particularly young men, to resist abuse. Looking back on his childhood, Francis Place documented the particularly cruel treatment of Jews in the 1770s and 1780s, including spitting, pulling by the beard, and other physical assaults. Jewish victims of this harassment knew that they could not expect protection from the authorities or from bystanders. Mendoza's great victories over Humphries encouraged many young Jewish men to train as boxers and his school provided them an opportunity to do so. As Place noted, this was a critical reason that, after the turn of the century, "it was no longer safe to insult a Jew unless he was an old man and alone."[34] A short report in the *Morning Post* about the magistrates preventing a fight between Mendoza and William Ward also alluded to the pride taken in Mendoza's triumphs, noting sarcastically that the magistrates had "preserved the boast and honour of the synagogue."[35] Jewish boxers proliferated in the next several decades and many in the Jewish community offered financial and moral support for them. In the process, Mendoza and his imitators helped shape both the attitudes of many young Jewish men and also perceptions of them among the broader public.

Despite the great financial success and fame Mendoza enjoyed, his sparring tours and boxing school were not enough to sustain him. The lifestyle necessary to be in the company of wealthy gentleman was costly; he complained in his memoirs that he had "almost unavoidably adopted an expensive mode of living … from the nature of my profession." With a growing family, frequent bouts of ill health, and an income dependent on the whims of his wealthy customers, Mendoza found himself unable to pay his debts and was forced into bankruptcy. He had stints in the oil trade and in the military recruiting service in Scotland in an attempt to pay his creditors, but was drawn to the prize ring again.[36] After an aborted attempt to fight Ward in January 1794, which was arranged by their mutual patron the Duke of Hamilton, the two met in November of the same year. Mendoza won easily but did not make enough money from the match to discharge his debts.[37]

In an effort to remedy his situation, Mendoza agreed to fight a final match against a young boxer named John Jackson. Like Richard Humphries, he came from a more prosperous background than most pugilists and was later known as "Gentleman" John Jackson. He had fought matches earlier in the decade but, as one contemporary report noted, "had never much distinguished himself before either for skill or courage."[38] Still, his large physical size raised hopes that the Jewish champion could finally be beaten. Jackson and Mendoza met at Hornchurch in Essex in early April 1795. Like the second match between Thomas Johnson and Michael Ryan, a stage was built at the bottom of a hollow, with seating on the sloped hillsides for about three thousand spectators. This crowd saw Mendoza fall victim to questionable tactics.

Portrait of "Gentleman" John Jackson. After his triumph over Daniel Mendoza, Jackson retired and became a well-respected leader of the sport. From Egan, *Boxiana*, vol. 1.

In the fifth round, the much larger Jackson "caught hold of Mendoza's hair and gave him several severe body blows, which brought him to the ground." Although Mendoza's supporters "hallooed out foul, foul," the umpires ruled that this was fair. Mendoza fought weakly for a few more rounds and gave in after Jackson threw him to the stage "with astonishing violence."[39] Although rumors swirled that the match was fixed, "Gentleman" John Jackson was considered the winner and new Champion of England.[40]

Jackson retired from the ring after his victory, never to fight again. Of his three prizefights, only his victory over Mendoza was notable. Nevertheless, Jackson became a leading figure in the sport and a symbol of British manhood for more than thirty years. He was an arbiter of disputes, a master of ceremonies, and an ambassador of the sport to men of means. In 1811, journalist Pierce Egan wrote that "JACKSON has *practically* realised the character of a gentleman; equally respected by the rich and poor … ever ready to perform a good action [and] personally known to most of the first characters in the kingdom."[41] Popular prints depicted him in the dress of a gentleman and he was long the standard against which other boxers were measured. When he died in 1845, a memorial stone was constructed for him that was topped with a large British lion. Not all accepted this image of Jackson. Mendoza in particular reminded boxing supporters of the questionable treatment he suffered. He later claimed that, after the match, he had denounced Jackson's "unmanly conduct" and "offered to fight him for 200 guineas [but Jackson] declined fighting under 500 guineas!! Here was courage!"[42] This was a solitary voice, however, and no other leading boxing figures agreed. In fact, by the time Mendoza published his memoirs in 1816, even he claimed Jackson as a friend.[43] Despite having accomplished relatively little in the prize ring—and the fact

A large monument topped by a British Lion was erected for John Jackson after his death. From Miles, *Pugilistica*, vol. 1.

that his most notable triumph was questionable—Jackson was, by the first decade of the new century, a symbol of the sport and, for boxing advocates, of British manhood.

By the turn of the century, and especially after Jackson won the championship of England, the claim that boxers embodied the ideal qualities of British manhood was amplified. This happened even as the involvement of women in the sport was becoming more visible. While men had always been the main producers and consumers of the sport, women had played a small role since the days of the bear gardens. Reports of women attending and participating in prizefights increased in the 1790s, but this might indicate greater hostility to women pugilists than to an actual increase in matches. *The St. James's Chronicle*, for example, reported that "a very great proportion of the spectators" at the Mendoza and Jackson match were women, though it may have done so in order to claim it as evidence of the "influence of French principles in this country."[44] *The Sporting Magazine* described a "pitched battled" fought near Chelmsford between two women in the summer of 1793. This match seems to have been fought according to Broughton's rules and the account described one of the women as "an adept in the science." Still, the report expressed outrage that the victorious boxer's husband had encouraged his "fair rib" to fight.[45] *The Sporting Magazine* also reported a match between Mary Ann Fielding, of Whitechapel, and "a noted Jewes of Wentworth street" in July 1795. Many spectators assembled to watch and, according to the author of the report, both women evinced fighting skill.[46] *The Sporting Magazine* published brief notices about two other matches between women in the 1790s: one prevented by magistrates in Chelmsford in 1796 and another in which Mrs. Ruff defeated Moll Glass in Stepney in August 1799.[47]

The reporting of these matches in the *Sporting Magazine* coincided with a renewed emphasis on manliness in that periodical. The reporter of the match in Chelmsford in 1793 wrote that the victor's husband evinced "a degree of barbarity that would have disgraced a savage" for inducing his wife to fight.[48] For the correspondents of *The Sporting Magazine*, upon whom John Wheble relied for much of his content, boxing was a manly activity. Letter writers underscored this later in the decade. One wrote that the decline in support for boxing in the 1790s helped to produce the "present race of spindle-shanked beaus," who would "rather close with an orange wench at the playhouse, than engage in a bye-battle on the stage."[49] Another letter writer, calling himself "Bob Boxer," suggested that the British and French soldiers should lay down their arms and fight with their fists. This mode of resolving conflict was preferable to that involving firearms, "which reduce the manly and effeminate to a level." The letter writer was confident of victory in any battle with the French because boxing was becoming popular in Britain again. In contrast, defeat in the "last disgraceful war" (the war against the American colonies) was the "the regular and inevitable consequence" of the neglect of the sport in the 1760s and 1770s.[50]

Jackson's victory over Mendoza was one of a number of developments that set the stage for a new era of popularity. The success of the *Sporting Magazine* and, a few years later, *Bell's Weekly Messenger* assured that the fortunes of boxers were no longer entirely dependent on the whims of unpredictable young gentleman. Instead, following the example of Mendoza, pugilists might hope to win fortune and fame by attracting the attention of a broader public. At the same time, the increasing prominence of boxing supporters—most notably William Windham—and the government's emphasis on inculcating martial spirit among British men from the second half of the 1790s brought the long-standing rhetoric of boxing advocates in line with the wishes of the powerful. As this happened, the victory of Jackson over Mendoza removed the ambiguity of a Jewish champion and elevated one whose manliness seemed unassailable. Journalists seized on this and began to market the British identity of the sport more zealously than ever. At the same time, minority boxers and their communities sought to recapture Mendoza's glory.

Those who sought to replicate Mendoza's accomplishments included a strong contingent of fighters from Ireland. The "sister kingdom" had experienced great upheaval in the 1790s, with important consequences for boxing. The rising of 1798 was brutally crushed and, two years later, William Pitt engineered a union of the kingdoms of Great Britain and Ireland. Catholic hopes for equal rights in the new United Kingdom were dashed, undermining the claim that the Act of Union would benefit the Irish, a large majority of who were Catholics. With the bloody repression of 1798 having temporarily closed the door on political nationalism, opportunities to challenge the Union or Britain were few. In this context, in the early 1800s, boxing became an important vehicle to express Irish identity. Stories about prizefighting, which often included claims that boxing demonstrated the superiority of English manhood, had been reported in Irish newspapers throughout the 1790s. Thanks in part to Mendoza's successes (and his exhibitions in Dublin), many Irish in Ireland and Britain understood that the sport could be a vehicle to challenge this superiority. After the failure of the rising and the Act of Union, prizefighting could be seen as a way for Irish boxers to demonstrate the manly mettle of their national community. Although this was not a new idea—Peter Corcoran's popularity with the people of St. Giles in the early 1770s had something to do with his having defeated English fighters—the transformed political situation and the rise of sporting journalism made it much more important after the turn of the century.

As the Act of Union moved through the House of Commons in 1800, a relatively unknown Irish boxer named Andrew Gamble enjoyed a meteoric rise to fame. A stonemason from the Liberties in Dublin, Gamble was well known as a boxer in that city and, for some time, gave sparring exhibitions in the Phoenix Park.[51] He had his first major prizefight in England on October 5, 1792, against Benjamin Stanyard, an established English boxer. The result was disputed and the match was considered a draw, but the combatants fought with great skill. One report noted that the fighters had "exhibited as great a display of knowledge in the art, as was ever shewn upon the stage in this, or any other kingdom."[52] Gamble may have gone back to Dublin after the match, for he did not contest a major prizefight in England again for eight years. He returned to the English prize ring at the beginning of July 1800, just as the Act of Union was passed in the House of Commons, fighting a former Horse Guardsman from Cheshire named Noah Jones for 100 guineas. Gamble brutally beat Jones, breaking his nose, jaw, collarbone, and breastbone in thirty-one bloody rounds before many of which Jones vomited large quantities of blood. *The Dublin Journal* added the comment that Gamble had "displayed an uncommon degree of science and coolness throughout the whole affair" to its report. The Cheshire boxer was close enough to death that Gamble visited his bedside and made his wife a gift of money.[53]

The match between Gamble and Jones was well attended and had large sums wagered on its outcome. It was probably arranged by amateurs, some of whom were Anglo-Irish, as a result of their own interest in the Union and, but for the outcome of the match, it likely would not have created much interest.[54] Unlike Peter Corcoran, Gamble does not seem to have been a fixture of the London Irish community. His impressive victory over Jones, however, took place in the context of the impending political union between Britain and Ireland (and, in fact, on the day that the bill received royal assent). Although the Union was intended to bring Britain and Ireland together—or so it was claimed—Gamble's triumph provided an outlet for the strong feelings that continued to simmer below the surface of the new political reality. As newspapers reported Gamble's triumph over Jones, they also announced that Gamble would fight one of the best boxers in Britain, Jem Belcher. The *Whitehall Evening Post* added that the match would "ascertain whether England or Ireland be the most capable of supplying, at this time, the best pugilist!" The *Sporting Magazine* repeated this claim in its July number.[55]

The battle between the symbols of England and Ireland was more hotly anticipated than any match since Jackson's defeat of Mendoza in 1795. The fight took place on the morning of Monday, December 22, 1800. Large crowds trekked to Wimbledon Common to witness the event; more than sixty coaches were hired for the journey, while the "number of light carts, horsemen, and pedestrians, were ... *incalculable*."[56] Gamblers wagered huge sums on the outcome, led by the Prince of Wales and his brother, who purportedly won £3,000 wagering on Belcher.[57] With the Act of Union between Britain and Ireland due to become law on January 1, strong feelings about it provided an important context for this excitement. In the evening after the match, opponents of the Union interrupted a performance at the Theatre Royal in Covent Garden because they objected to the inclusion of "an allegorical groupe of three figures representing THE UNION." Uproar from the audience also prevented "an air in honour of the event from being sung."[58] Similar feelings shaped perceptions of the match between Belcher and Gamble. *The Times* claimed that the sedan carriers of London—who were disproportionately Irish—called the fight "the *Union-battle*."[59] Other newspapers picked up on this theme in their accounts of the match. *The Star* compared the match to the iconic family feud in *Romeo and Juliet*, noting that Belcher and Gamble were "two Gentlemen—not of Verona—but of England and Ireland."[60]

The London Irish seem to have been particularly interested in the outcome of the match. Irishmen helped organize the fight and gambled heavily on the result. A greengrocer named Kelly held the stakes in the ring and lost 70 guineas when Gamble was defeated. After Belcher defeated Gamble, Belcher's brother fought an Irish shoemaker called Kelly in the same ring.[61] Large numbers of Irish traveled to Wimbledon for the match, including some who crossed the Irish Sea. *The Morning Post* reported that there were "thousands ... of the lower orders of the people," many of who were Irish.[62] *The Times* claimed that "a triumphal entry into the metropolis" was planned in the event that Gamble won.[63] In the tense political environment of 1800, the large crowd put the government on alert. According to *The Morning Post*, "the guards were put under arms" and the authorities made other military preparations in the event of an insurrection.[64] There were other indications that boxers and spectators considered the fight to be a test of English manhood. Significantly, Daniel Mendoza was Gamble's second. After the fight concluded, Belcher challenged Mendoza. After defeating the "Irish champion," Gamble hoped to beat the "Jewish champion" as well. Mendoza, now thirty-six, demurred. His old antagonist John Jackson was not directly involved in the match but won £100 wagering on Belcher.[65]

Unfortunately for those who hoped he might strike a blow for the Irish and for those who hoped for a well-contested match, Gamble lacked the skill of Mendoza. The talented Belcher humbled him in nine brutal minutes and, for many boxing advocates, sent an unambiguous message about the superiority of English manhood. The match seemed to confirm stereotypes that were becoming central to the narrative of boxing as well: the cool and highly skilled Englishman was seen to have easily dispatched the hardheaded but less proficient Irishman. Many accounts of the match noted that Belcher was a descendant of Jack Slack, the conqueror of Broughton, thus encouraging readers to see Belcher as heir to a long tradition of English fighters. In contrast, expectations for Gamble among the London Irish had run so high and he had performed so poorly that rumors spread that the match was fixed.[66] Despite his dismal showing, all was not lost for Gamble. A year later, he received three guineas a week to spar with Belcher at a local theater.[67] The broader appeal of boxing, made possible by the changes of the 1780s and 1790s, assured that life after a major defeat was far different for Gamble than it had been for Peter Corcoran twenty-five years earlier.

The excitement generated by Gamble's fight against Jem Belcher created opportunities for other Irish boxers, as Mendoza's fights against Humphries had done for Jewish fighters in early 1790s. Jack O'Donnell, an eighteen-year-old Irish immigrant, was an early beneficiary. In September 1802 O'Donnell was matched against Belcher's brother-in-law, Pardo Wilson at Wormwood Scrubs. Several thousand attended the match, including many London Irish. As the popularity of boxing broadened, many of the spectators at matches had not attended a prizefight before and were unaware of—or refused to abide by—older rules of decorum at matches. The construction of expensive stages, which were liable to be torn down by interfering magistrates, was much more rare as well. As a consequence, pugilists had to use "thick sticks" to clear an area for the ring. Once this had been done, the match began and O'Donnell defeated Wilson in ten rounds. His supporters carried O'Donnell to a coach and planned to celebrate the victory in St. Giles.[68] Two months later, on November 15, O'Donnell fought a shoemaker named James Smith at the same location. Once again, "a vast concourse of pedestrians" attended and, this time, a boxer named Caleb Baldwin used a whip to clear spectators from the ring.[69] After O'Donnell defeated Smith, "much rejoicing took place among the Irish visitors," who "threw up their hats and flourished their sticks."[70] O'Donnell's supporters escorted him back to St. Giles, accompanied by "huzzas, so as to deafen the ears of the spectators."[71] A concourse of Irish supporters greeted him along the way while, according to one account, an aged blind fiddler played "See the Conquering Hero Comes."[72] The growing popular appeal of boxing—fueled by ever expanding newspaper coverage of the sport—along with the claim that prize fights were symbolic contests between different religious, ethnic, or racial groups helped create opportunities for minority boxers like O'Donnell and changed the nature of the crowds that supported them.

As Gamble and O'Donnell involved the Irish of St. Giles in boxing as never before, the public dispute between boxing advocates and moral reformers resurfaced, this time on the floor of the House of Commons. Once again, the relationship between manhood and nation was at issue. Although the debate was initiated by a reformist attempt to ban bull baiting, boxing—a similarly controversial and far more popular sport—lurked in the background.

On April 2, 1800, Scottish MP William Johnstone Pulteney, prompted by moral reformers, introduced a bill to make bull baiting illegal.[73] The bill sought to assess a penalty of between 20 shillings and £5, depending on the severity of the offense. After some preliminary discussion in Committee, debate was scheduled for April 4. When it commenced, Pulteney told the House that bull baiting ought to be banned both because of its cruelty and because it prevented men from "earning subsistence for themselves and families."[74] In Pulteney's view, bull baiting was a problem because it kept men from fulfilling their role as providers. William Windham (now Minister for War) dominated the subsequent debate, assuring the House that he would put all of his considerable influence against the bill because he considered it the thin end of a wedge to ban other sports. In language similar to that he had used in his letter to James Boswell seven years earlier, Windham told the House that the people's amusements were "composed of athletic, manly, and hardy exertions" that afforded "trials of their courage."[75] He claimed that he would always resist the efforts of reformers because "sports of a people went a great way to form their national character."[76]

Windham's opposition successfully killed the bill, but its proponents continued their campaign, challenging his association between sport, manhood, and nation. Two weeks after the debate in the House of Commons, one of the bill's supporters published a letter claiming that support for bull baiting invited comparison with the Spanish and "the *driveling* disposition of that cowardly people." The writer feigned wonder at "the bewitching efficacy of cruelty to inspire manliness and martial courage." In reality, the writer argued, bull baiting simply encouraged men to "leave their wives and children penniless, whilst they themselves are murdering their time" at the alehouse.[77] Many others disagreed, however, and saw heroism in Windham's defense of boxing. In a letter to Hannah More, William Wilberforce described an incident in which Surrey magistrates were accosted by spectators at a prizefight, who threw their hats in the air and called out "Windham and Liberty" when the magistrates attempted to prevent a match.[78]

Undaunted by Windham's success, reformers made a second attempt to pass a bill to make bull baiting illegal in the spring of 1802. The matter came before the House just as the peace treaty with France was being debated and so the issue of war and peace provided critical context. Prime Minister Henry Addington and William Pitt had backed the peace largely because of public pressure in favor of it, but Addington's position pushed Windham and other like-minded colleagues into opposition; Windham melodramatically exclaimed, "We are a conquered people!" in Parliament.[79] In late April, Sir Richard Hill, a member of the Clapham Sect who had seconded the first bull-baiting bill in 1800, presented a petition against bull baiting and asked the House to take action.[80] John Dent introduced a bill on May 4 after agreeing to postpone doing so to permit discussion of the peace.[81] When debate commenced, Windham was again the leader of opposition to it. Supporters of the bill used his hostility to the peace—which was publicly popular—to argue that Windham was a bloodthirsty warmonger. Hill mockingly found it strange that opponents of peace "should be anxious to prevent peace even between the bull and the dog." Similarly, the Foxite Whig Richard Brinsley Sheridan argued that Windham opposed the bill against bull baiting because he was frustrated in his attempts to prevent peace with France. As the war "between the human race" was over, the famous playwright wryly remarked, Windham and other opponents of the bill found "something consoling in the idea that we were still to have a *Bellum internecinem* between bull and dog."[82]

Supporters of the bill also attacked the claim that bull baiting—and, by association, boxing—reinforced the manly national character, contending that proper manhood demanded that a man provide for his family. Hill complained of the "barbarous torments" inflicted on the bull, arguing that the practice was unchristian and "degrading to the character of the nation."[83] William Wilberforce also spoke in favor of the bill, saying that bull baiting "was inconsistent with every manly principle." He contended that domestic tranquility, rather than bull baiting, provided the happiness that "belonged naturally to the people of England" and he urged the members to consider the "wretched family" of the bull baiting spectator "condemned to feel the want of money which he squandered away on such occasions."[84]

The bill's opponents also focused on manliness and national character, but contended that men were properly independent and courageous, not primarily concerned with domestic matters. Sir Thomas Frankland of Yorkshire argued, for example, that national character was "implicated in the present question." For Frankland, the support "given to such manly sports" was essential to this character.[85] Windham agreed and contended that reformers wrongly favored the pastimes of gentlemen, such as horse-racing, over the manly sports of the common people, claiming that in horse-racing, unlike boxing, he "saw no possibility of eliciting one generous feeling or manly sentiment."[86] He also implied that the opinions of the bill's supporters were unmanly, remarking caustically that they "seemed to be influenced by a species of argument dictated by their wives."[87] Once again, Windham's influence won the day and the debate ended with a successful motion to postpone another reading of the bill for three months. The measure died without further debate and bull baiting was not finally made illegal until 1835.

William Windham continued to promote his ideas of manhood and nation until his untimely death in 1810. Plans for an inscription on a "Windham Monument" in Norfolk reflect the importance of these ideals to him. The inscription would show that Windham was "anxious to preserve, untainted, the National character" and that he "laboured to exalt … courage."[88] Sport, manliness, and British military might were closely related in his thought. He countered those who favored peace and the reform of manners by noting that strength, courage, and respect for tradition were the bulwarks of British power abroad and order at home. In the second bull baiting debate, Windham read a petition against the bill from "a body of sober loyal men, who … never meddled in politics." Traditions such as bull baiting, he argued after reading the petition, were crucial to maintain the natural martial ardor of British men; "it was connecting the past with the present," he claimed, "and the present with the future, that genuine patriotism was produced and preserved."[89]

Journalists, who became the main public advocates of boxing in the 1810s and 1820s, often repeated William Windham's powerful words in favor of bull baiting and boxing. By that time, however, boxing was a quite different sport than it had been in Windham's youth. Gentlemen amateurs were still an important part of the sport but, increasingly, boxers and journalists arranged matches and generated publicity for them. Large crowds of spectators crowded to the most important matches, many of which involved fighters from minority groups who relied on support from their communities or at least on their status as foils to white Christian English pugilists.

Much of this altered world had been made possible by the changes of the 1790s. Debates about boxing, echoing broader public discussion of the French Revolution and the nature of British society, amplified claims about the sport's essential Britishness. In response to attacks by reformers, defenders of boxing argued that it helped bolster national spirit and martial values at a critical juncture in the country's history. Such assertions became an ever-increasing part of the language of bare-knuckle prizefighting and were brought to the attention of much larger audiences by John Bell, John Wheble, and other publishers, who sought to sell their newspapers by expanding coverage of the sport. Daniel Mendoza, perhaps the greatest boxer and showman of his generation, fully exploited the opportunities created by this heightened association between boxing and Britishness. Long after the end of his career, Jewish and Irish boxers attempted to emulate his success, benefiting from the support of their communities and from their status as foils of British manhood. A commercial culture and identity politics were a critical part of boxing after the turn of the nineteenth century and cast a long shadow over sport down to the present. Much of what boxing was to become in that age was created in the 1790s.

Chapter Four

National Spirit, Minorities and Prizefighting During the War with Napoleon, 1803–1812

So, huzza for the science of boxing!
It keeps up our courage, you know;
And if the French here sound their tocsin,
We'll give them a *clean knock-down blow.*[1]

The nine years from 1803 to 1812 were a critical period in the struggle with Napoleonic France. When war resumed in late spring 1803, fears of a French invasion galvanized the nation. Displays of loyalism, military volunteering, and preparations for resistance dominated public discourse.[2] Dissent continued in some quarters but, for many, the contentious 1790s were left behind. Boxing continued to be an important focus of efforts to promote "national spirit" and the stepped-up attempts of magistrates to prevent or interrupt prizefights and the ongoing efforts of reformers to ban the sport provided many opportunities for boxing's defenders to proclaim its national significance. As a result, the link between prizefighting and the health of the nation was made more frequently and vociferously than ever before. Pugilists, journalists, and others involved in the sport took full advantage of this surge of national feeling and boxing became more popular than it had been since the 1780s.

The stronger association between boxing and the welfare of Britain that helped undergird this surge in the sport's popularity had important consequences for minority pugilists. More than ever, spectators were encouraged—not least by the proliferation of newspaper coverage of prizefights—to see white Christian English fighters as representative of the fighting prowess of the nation. In the symbolic drama of a prizefight, Jewish, black, and Irish pugilists were cast as foils. This provided opportunities for minority fighters, who were often catapulted from early success into high-stakes, high-profile matches. It also created great challenges for them. The much more aggressive efforts of magistrates to break up boxing matches in the first years after the renewal of war—prompted by fears of invasion—meant that the location of prizefights often had to be changed at the last moment. As a consequence, matches were usually contested on the ground; organizers were less willing to arrange and pay for a stage that might be destroyed by authorities. This put spectators closer to the action and made interference much more common. Rings were often broken when minority fighters seemed on the cusp of winning. The shifting location of fights also made it more difficult for spectators from minority communities, which were concentrated in central London, to travel to matches, thus eliminating a possible check on partisan crowd interference. In response to these challenges, a number of black, Jewish, and Irish fighters acted more aggressively and even outlandishly. Following the example set by Daniel Mendoza, minority boxers challenged perceptions of them as passive "others" against which white Christian English manhood might be measured. They were increasingly active agents in managing their own images, both to encourage support from their own communities and to shape events in and out of the prize ring.

This chapter argues that the resumption of hostilities with France in 1803 raised the profile of boxing, despite the best efforts of authorities to prevent matches. This was in part because the claim that the sport encapsulated the essential qualities of British manhood and the unique spirit of the nation was particularly resonant during this period of heightened national feeling. Spectators and newspaper readers increasingly imagined that prizefights were displays of the fighting prowess of British men and therefore bouts involving minority boxers, who were cast as stand-ins for the nation's enemies, were more popular than ever. While black, Jewish, and Irish boxers faced tremendous hostility, some learned to turn the tables and generate fame and opportunities for themselves.

The Peace of Amiens, signed in March 1802, seemed more like a fragile truce for the fourteen months it was in force. After an anxious year in which Bonaparte continued to interfere in the affairs of several states on the continent in defiance of the treaty, the government of new Prime Minister Henry Addington declared war in May 1803. Britain was, however, without allies on the continent and France was assembling a massive invasion force across the Channel. Fear gripped the country and preparations were made to resist the expected onslaught. Overcoming their own anxieties about arming the lower classes, the Addington government passed the Levee en Masse Act and encouraged military service by nearly all men from 17 to 55. Mass conscription was avoided, however, because the Volunteer forces grew dramatically in size. Henceforth the expanded and increasingly plebeian Volunteers became a focal point of patriotism.[3]

While the Volunteers were controversial because they were raised locally and had much more independence than regular army units, many political leaders embraced them because they provided needed manpower and because they were believed to spread patriotic feelings among the populace. Richard Brinsley Sheridan, a formerly anti-war Whig who had needled Windham for opposing peace in 1802, now joined the St. James's Volunteer corps. In August 1803, he wrote to Addington and urged him to support the Volunteers, arguing that Parliament ought to "appeal … to the spirit and loyalty of every individual Man in the Country" and encouraging Addington to repeat the refrain "One and all" around the country. This was consistent with the ideas held since the 1790s by Henry Dundas, William Windham, and William Pitt. Dundas in particular was a long-time advocate of the need to inculcate "military spirit" and "patriotic feelings."[4] The argument that national spirit must be cultivated among British men, a claim made by promoters of boxing since the days of Broughton, was more widely accepted than ever.

Despite such strong support for a position long advocated by the defenders of boxing, prizefights in this period were frequently prevented or stopped by magistrates. Matches were considered potentially riotous assemblies and worrying threats to public order in these anxious years. In response to the more aggressive efforts of authorities to interfere with the sport, a number of writers and activists defended prizefighting on the grounds that it was particularly useful in encouraging the spread of national spirit. If boxing were suppressed, the argument went, Britons would become more cowardly and continental. Journalist William Cobbett wrote to his mentor Windham in November 1803 expressing just this sentiment. Enclosing a copy of the *Times*, he referred Windham to a report of a stabbing, "precisely of that sort which has arisen out of the disuse of boxing." The assault, in Cobbett's view, was the product of foreign influence, "particularly the crying, canting … cut-throat Italians."[5] The following year, Cobbett wrote Windham to voice concern about a bill before Parliament, which, "under disguise, is intended to eradicate boxing [and] bullbaiting." Once again, Cobbett warned, reformers put a bill forward that "goes to the rearing of puritanism as a system."[6] The significance was clear. As Windham had argued in the second bull baiting debate, puritanism was an attempt to change the "manners upon which the security of the Constitution and the Country materially depended" by depriving the country of practices that produced "manly sentiment."[7] Windham and Cobbett agreed that Britain depended on the "manly sentiment" produced in the boxing ring.

Cobbett also promoted this cause publicly. In 1802, he had founded the *Political Register,* which at that time supported the New Opposition, a label used to describe Windham and other opponents of the peace who believed in the necessity of fighting Bonaparte (and to distinguish them from the Foxite "Old Opposition"). In the pages of the *Political Register*, Cobbett sought to promote the national spirit that many in the New Opposition thought was critical to this battle. Defending boxing, as he did in his letters to Windham, was an important tool to do so. In an August 1805 article, Cobbett highlighted a "political view" of the sport. He argued that attempts to ban boxing would ultimately lead to "submission to a foreign yoke" because Britain was undergoing a process of "national degradation" in which its men were becoming effeminate. The clearest sign of this was "a change from athletic and hardy sports or exercises to those requiring less bodily strength." The answer to this problem was to promote British sports and thereby assure that British men were superior to French men. In an echo of his 1803 letter Cobbett argued that, whereas the men of France and other continental enemies were "cutters and stabbers and poisoners," British boxing matches "make the people bold: they produce a communication of notions of hardihood; they serve to remind men of the importance of bodily strength."[8] Cobbett's language was hyperbolic but his message was clear: national spirit must be cultivated to defeat Napoleonic France and boxing was a critical means to do so.

Other defenders of boxing evoked the feared French invasion. *The Sporting Magazine* printed some lines of verse on this theme in March 1804: "So, huzza for the science of boxing! It keeps up our courage, you know; And if the French here sound their tocsin, We'll give them a *clean knock-down blow.*"[9] Pamphleteer and activist John Thomas Barber Beaumont also connected support for boxing with effective resistance to invasion. A painter and founder of an insurance company, Barber was a particularly energetic advocate of national preparedness. He raised a rifle corps, argued that British men should be trained as sharpshooters (even holding a demonstration in Hyde Park), and penned two pamphlets describing his ideas about national defense. A later writer described him as characteristic of his age in his "hatred of the French Emperor [and] in his love of boxing."[10] Barber linked these two passions in a pamphlet printed in 1805, arguing that "*the radical means of ensuring a nation's safety is the preservation of a vigorous and patriotic character throughout its population.*" In a footnote, he contended that the "policy of fastidious humanity, which endeavours to suppress the national practice of boxing, is very questionable," because it might undermine the vigorous character of the male population. The practice of boxing, he wrote, was the chief reason for "the Englishman's superiority of courage, in fighting with foreigners."[11]

Barber expanded on these arguments in a multi-night debate at the British Forum in April 1806. On Friday, April 11 the debating society considered the question "Ought Boxing to be reprobated as a vulgar and brutal Practice, or countenanced as tending to inspire a Contempt of Danger, and promote personal Courage and national Independence?" The debate attracted so much attention that the British Forum decided to continue the discussion the following Friday.[12] Although there is no transcript, philologist William P. Russel, an ardent opponent of boxing, published a speech that he intended to give on the second night. This publication quoted some of those who spoke on April 11, including Barber. According to Russel, Barber had argued that boxing was "useful to promote national courage" because it required "deeds committed in a bold manly way." Moreover, boxing encouraged direct confrontation between two men, who "come out fairly opposed, man to man, on open ground," unlike the "acts of the bravo or assassin, armed with a stiletto in the dark, (as in Italy and other parts of the continent)."[13] Much like Windham and Cobbett, Barber defended boxing because he considered it a bulwark of "national courage" and manliness against the threat from foreign influence.

Russel attempted to refute these arguments in his speech—which he decided not to deliver at the British Forum on April 18—by arguing for a different form of manliness. First, he disputed the notion that any action was acceptable as long as done in a "manly way," arguing, for example, that highway robbery might be made legal if done in the daylight. Indeed, he regretted that "Mr. Windham did not hit upon this excellent method … for making us a nation of heroic men." Much as Richard Brinsley Sheridan had in the second debate about bull baiting, Russel equated support for violent sports with promotion of violence more generally, contending that Windham's system of manhood was only necessary "so long as the system of war and carnage is preferred to the system of peace and commerce." The "system of war and carnage" elevated physical over mental powers and was therefore "derogatory to the *intellectual dignity* of MAN." To bolster this point, Russel cited Edward Barry's, *Letter on the Practice of Boxing*, highlighting Barry's claim that boxing was not necessary as a proof of courage to promote "the bravery of Englishmen." Instead, Russel agreed, courage was "a virtue of the mind."[14]

Despite Russel's efforts (he sold copies of the speech from his home) such views enjoyed much less support in the militarized environment of 1806 than they had in 1789 and many defenders of boxing countered in language similar to that used by Cobbett and others. A letter to the *Sporting Magazine* in August 1806 argued that boxing offered "a proof … of national spirit, rather than national barbarity." Calling opponents effeminate, the author claimed that eliminating boxing would "bring us upon a par of degeneracy with the Italians, and disgrace us as a nation of cut-throats."[15] Another letter in the same issue called attention to a paper written by Dr. Samuel Argent Bardsley for the Philosophical Society of Manchester called "The Use and Abuse of Popular Sports and Exercises." Bardsley argued that barbarism prevailed in places where boxing was not practiced. As a result, he advocated the teaching of pugilism in public schools and in large factories.[16] Two years later, the second volume of a biography of the Prince of Wales began with an extended defense of boxing. This included the now-familiar claims that boxing promoted "a manly and courageous spirit" and that it therefore prevented the spread of the continental customs of dueling or knife fighting.[17]

The emphasis on the importance of fostering courage and national spirit among men in wartime had as its corollary a belief that women should be passive receivers of male protection and admirers of men's courage. Sporting journalist Vincent Dowling later put it very simply: "We would have men, men; and women, women."[18] Windham articulated such sentiments in a debate about Pitt's scheme to transform the British military in 1804. Opposing the plan, Windham argued that the best way to bolster the "military spirit" of the nation was emphatically not to make every man a soldier. In fact, he claimed, civilians maintained military spirit among the general population much more than soldiers. This was consistent with Windham's position that popular sports were a critical element in bolstering national morale. Some men, of course, needed to be soldiers, and Britain needed women to encourage them to serve. Women's love of soldiers, Windham claimed, was "the greatest inducement [for men] to undertake military enterprise." It was this approval that "excited men to run the risks and endure the toils of military life."[19] Cobbett had a similar view of women's purpose. In *Advice to Young Men*, he counseled unmarried men about "The Qualities to Look for in a Wife." A critical quality was "female beauty," which was of "great practical advantage" as it assured that a man would be "*pleased with his bargain*."[20]

Sporting journalists and boxing amateurs shared Windham and Cobbett's ideas about men and women. These were most apparent in comments about women boxers; as we saw above, letters and reports in the *Sporting Magazine* frequently attacked them. Matches between women continued to occur, but they were subject to ridicule at best and denunciation at worst. In October 1802, for example, the *Sporting Magazine* reported that some gentlemen amateurs had arranged a match between two "well-known" women near Whitechapel. The short account noted that the women were known as "*Farthing Rush-light*" and "*The Walking Tun*" because of their difference in size. The author then remarked that the latter lost the match because she was "deficient in breath."[21] The amateurs who arranged the bout seem to have done so because they considered it an outlandish spectacle. A few years later, the *Sporting Magazine* reported "a ludicrous affair": a boxing match between two women. The "modern Amazons," the article continued, fought until one combatant shed tears and began "a furious attack" without regard to Broughton's rules. Finally, the indulgent crowd intervened "to prevent serious mischief."[22] While, given the dismissive tone of such reports, it is difficult to determine the actual events in these matches, it seems clear that they were fought using Broughton's rules and that they were organized in the same fashion as small-scale prizefights between men. Nevertheless, reports of women's bouts increasingly cast them as an absurdity or a perversion of the manly sport of boxing. Fears of invasion—which did not abate until the crushing defeat of the combined Spanish and French fleet at Trafalgar in October 1805—and the expansion of the British military lent support to a narrow definition of men and women. Proponents of boxing argued that, in addition to soldiering, their sport best displayed the courageous British manhood that was critical to national survival. As they did, the manliness of boxing was even more narrowly defined.

While women boxers came under attack, men's prizefighting experienced a revival. John Jackson's refusal to fight after his victory over Daniel Mendoza and Mendoza's own retirement had left a void in the late 1790s. In response to a reader's question in its September 1798 number, John Wheble's *Sporting Magazine* admitted that it could not name the leading pugilist of the day.[23] By 1800, however, the emergence of the "dashing, genteel" Jem Belcher placed a Christian Englishman (and a descendant of Jack Slack) in the forefront of the sport again.[24] Belcher enjoyed a successful run as the Champion of England until he lost an eye after being struck by a ball in the summer of 1803. He was the first of a line of champions from Bristol that lasted until 1820. Henry Pearce, known as "the Game Chicken," claimed the title after Belcher's accident and fought several matches culminating in a victory over the now one-eyed Belcher in December 1805. Pearce retained the championship until 1808, when he retired (he died of consumption in 1809) and the title passed to Bristolian and future MP John Gully. The three pugilists were widely regarded as exemplary characters and stories circulated that seemed to demonstrate their courage and selflessness.[25]

The sport continued to evolve while these popular figures were champions. Newspapers printed extensive descriptions of their matches, their heroic deeds, and their other activities for an eager public. Many publishers saw this enthusiasm and, recognizing the potential of the burgeoning interest in boxing, made sporting intelligence an important part of new publications.

These included John Bell's *Bell's Weekly Messenger* and *Bell's Weekly Dispatch*, founded by Robert Bell in 1801.[26] Established newspapers began to include more regular reports as well, including some in Ireland. The greater visibility of the sport, however, along with the anxious mood of the country, prompted magistrates to step up their efforts to prevent the staging of prizefights. The increase in "magisterial interference" (as it was called by boxing supporters) had important consequences for the organization of prizefights. Because the location of fights was rarely known in advance and often shifted at the last moment, stages were constructed much less frequently than in the 1780s and 1790s. Most matches were now fought on the turf, with crowds much closer to (and thus able to influence) the action. Last-minute changes to fight locations also meant that it was more difficult for pedestrians from London to make it to the site of a match and so locals often made up a large part of the crowd at prizefights.[27]

The decline in stage matches and the necessity of shifting the scene of prizefights created particular problems for minority pugilists, who often found themselves uncomfortably close to hostile crowds. These changes occurred just as public utterances about the relationship between boxing and national spirit created more opportunities (and greater enmity) for minority fighters, who could supposedly test English manhood in the ring. Fights cast as a battle between Christian and Jew were particularly popular in the first few years of the new century. The association of Jews with the continent along with stereotypes about them as untrustworthy made Jewish prizefighters particularly potent emblems of "otherness." These ideas were not new, of course, but the renewed war with France and reinvigorated them. In the midst of a patriotic speech to grand jurors in Cardiff in autumn 1803, for example, Justice George Hardinge claimed that Bonaparte was grateful for the curse that Jews had put on Britain.[28] Bonaparte's call in 1799 for Jews to reestablish their homeland in Palestine prompted many English commentators to associate Jews with the French enemy as well.[29]

Such perceptions of Jewish "otherness" and association with Bonapartist France provided opportunities for Jewish boxers but it also left them vulnerable to foul play at the hands of hostile crowds. This was the case in December 1802 at a battle between Isaac Pitton and George Maddox. A large and diverse group of spectators assembled at Wormwood Scrubbs to see the bout but, unfortunately for the crowd, constables arrived to stop it. After several hours of confusion and miscommunication, the two fighters met at Wimbledon Common in front of a significantly smaller group of spectators. Pitton had the better of Maddox and was on the verge of winning when Maddox's brother and "a strong body of friends" broke the ring. A bloody melee ensued and, when it was finally stopped, the fight was ended and declared a draw.[30] Pitton had a similar experience in July 1804 in a match against Bill Ward. According to the *British Press*, the match was hotly anticipated as a battle between Christian and Jew and thousands depended on the outcome.[31] Pitton gained the advantage after twenty-five difficult rounds, but a raucous and hostile crowd "determined that the Jew should not win the battle" and broke the ring. When the match resumed spectators continued to interfere, nearly causing Pitton to lose. Finally several gentlemen amateurs used their horses to clear the ring and, after several more rounds, Ward quit the match.[32]

Not surprisingly, given this energetic hostility, some Christian pugilists sought to capitalize by challenging Jewish fighters. As he tried to advance his claim to the championship in January 1804, Henry Pearce challenged Pitton for two hundred guineas.[33] The much smaller Pitton wisely refused the match. In November 1804 Joe Bourke, another aspirant for the championship, "offered to fight any Jew in England for 100 guineas, at a week's notice."[34] The challenge went unanswered. After winning an easy victory in April 1805 and then watching Jewish fighter "Dutch" Sam Elias defeat Bristolian Tom Britton, Pearce "challenged any Jew in England to fight him within the space of one month from that time."[35] *The Sun* claimed that "the Jews decided" not to accept this challenge because they thought "it more prudent to match their champion against another man." Their champion was a fighter named Heakapeake who, unlike Pitton and Elias, was big enough to face the larger Christian boxers. Heakapeake fought newcomer Tom Cribb at Blackheath in May 1805. Using the retreating tactics for which Jewish fighters were often criticized—the *Morning Post* claimed that he "studiously avoided standing to his man"—Cribb won the match. While several accounts criticized him for his defensive style, the victory launched his career. Three years later Cribb was the champion.

Hostility to Jewish fighters was an important element of the popularity of boxing in the first few decades of the new century but Jews were not passive in the face of enmity. This was true in other cultural spheres as well; the theater was an important site of contestation about the definition of the nation as Britain became more cosmopolitan. Jewish spectators (as did their Irish counterparts) attempted to control the portrayal of Jews on the stage. Reaction to negative depictions of Jews on the stage continued into the nineteenth century. Jewish spectators shouted down performances of the comic opera *Family Quarrels* at the Covent Garden Theater for three days in December 1802, for example. A song called "I courted Miss Levy," sung in a mocking dialect, was the subject of the audience's ire.[36] The same was true for boxing. Jewish crowds attempted to defend Jewish boxers against charges of foul play (often framed in anti–Semitic language) and supported their co-religionists in other ways, such as attending banquets or offering patronage. When Isaac Pitton (seconded by Mendoza) defeated Tom Jones on Wimbledon Common in July 1801, for example, a number of Jewish spectators were on hand, "exalting in their brother's prowess."[37] Conversely, the worst instances of foul play suffered by Jewish boxers often occurred when the location of a match was shifted at the last moment because of the threat of magisterial interference, as was the case when the crowd broke the ring at Pitton's match with George Maddox.

The most successful Jewish boxer to navigate the troubled waters of this era was "Dutch" Sam Elias. As he made his name early in his career, Elias earned praise for his skill as well as for his conduct in the ring. The *Sporting Magazine* noted that the "science was never better displayed" at one of his earliest matches in the summer of 1801.[38] Several years later, in August 1804, Elias won the support of many in the crowd in a match against Caleb Baldwin by not hitting his opponent as he fell, a gesture that "was loudly applauded." The crowd was fickle, however. A few rounds later, when Elias struck Baldwin as his opponent began to fall, some spectators shouted "foul" and broke the ring to prevent Elias from winning the match. Fortunately for Elias, the referees disagreed and awarded him the victory.[39] Journalists could be capricious as well. Of his victory over Tom Britton in April 1805, the *Sun* commented that "a more gallant battle" had not been fought "in the Annals of Pugilism."[40] When Elias defeated the popular Tom Belcher—brother of Jem Belcher and a very popular figure in his own right—in February 1806, however, reports suggested that he had only defeated Belcher because he was the bigger man.[41]

Portrait of "Dutch" Sam, the most skilled Jewish prizefighter of the early nineteenth century. From Miles, *Pugilistica*, vol. 1.

Perhaps in response to the fickle public, Elias soon began to take on a new persona in the ring. Mendoza, his mentor, provided inspiration. One month after Elias's first battle with Belcher, the aging Jewish champion contested his final prizefight. The bout originated in a dispute between Mendoza and Harry Lee, another fighter in middle age, regarding a bail given by Mendoza and his brother for Lee.[42] A massive collection of spectators traveled to Grindstead Green, near Bromley to see Mendoza enter the ring once more; *The Morning Chronicle* described the size of the crowd as "almost incredible." Although Lee was a skillful pugilist, Mendoza beat him badly and, reminiscent of his battles with Humphries, laughed at Lee in several rounds.[43] Even after his long absence from the prize ring, he retained his skill as a performer.

Mendoza's flair for the dramatic was an important influence for Elias. The child of Dutch immigrants, Elias had been born at the home of Mendoza's father and the great champion served as his second early in his career. Newspapers often compared Elias to his mentor and commented that Elias fought in a style similar to Mendoza.[44] Elias also adopted a similar persona, especially Mendoza's flair for showmanship. This was clear in Elias's early match with Tom Britton in April 1805. It was rumored that the fight with Britton—a Bristolian who had nearly beaten Jem Belcher before Belcher lost his eye—was a trap or "plant" to defeat the Jewish boxer. Elias dominated the fight, however, repeatedly knocking Britton to the ground. Several times, he knelt next to the fallen Britton smiling and exclaiming, "you are a plant, are you?... I'll soon plant you!" Later in the fight, Elias treated Britton "with the utmost contempt" by throwing up his hands when Britton rushed him and telling the spectators "see, see, this plant wants to kiss me!"[45]

As his career advanced, Elias became known for this brash style. At a large gathering for a sparring exhibition in June 1807, Elias "vauntingly" told the crowd that he could beat Tom Belcher "without a scratched face."[46] After some failed attempts to arrange a match, Elias and Belcher finally fought again in July 1807 at Moulsey Hurst. In the match, a dispute arose following a blow from Elias that Belcher's backers argued was foul and the fight was ended. Although John Jackson declared the blow fair, Elias did not receive the stakes.[47] Because of the dispute the two men fought again, this time near Crawley on August 14. After severe fighting, a badly beaten Belcher tried to draw a foul blow by purposely falling. Elias "held up his hands and laughed at" his opponent lying on the ground. Other reports noted his look of "contempt" for Belcher.[48] In later bouts, he derisively mimicked the pain of his opponent or patted the cheek of a fallen adversary, assuring him that he was beaten.[49]

Elias's persona made him both tremendously popular and notorious. *The Morning Post* noted that the final fight between Elias and Belcher, before which Elias had promised to defeat Belcher without a scratch, prompted "universal anxiety, which has been on its full stretch amongst all classes." The spectators were so numerous that the ring had to be moved to accommodate them. Some gentlemen amateurs even insisted that fights be staged further from London to prevent such large crowds attending future bouts.[50] *The Sporting Magazine* reported that people came from all districts of London to view the match and that "the Sandman, the Jew, and Gentile vied with each other for superiority in pace" en route.[51] Many Jewish people rewarded Elias's aggressive behavior and success with their support. Elias was reputedly always able to find "Jewish money" to back him.[52] Many Jewish spectators aided Elias in other ways, seeing him as a powerful symbol of Jewish defiance. At his last fight, a group of Jews broke into the ring and stopped the match for a time when he seemed on the verge of defeat.[53] Although many London newspapers perpetuated the stereotype that Jews cared more about their money than supporting a Jewish boxer, they continually reported the large groups of Jewish spectators present at Elias' fights. Similarly, a popular print produced by George Cruikshank mockingly depicted the disappointment among the numerous Jewish spectators after Elias's only defeat.[54]

Despite his success, Elias died in poverty. After the only defeat of his career in 1814, he never contested a prizefight again. A nearly twenty-year boxing career had taken its toll on his body, as had excessive drinking, and his health soon deteriorated. Without the money he earned boxing, he sank into poverty and spent his last days at a workhouse in London. He had few remaining friends when his body was buried without ceremony.[55] Elias's rapid impoverishment was partly the result of his failure in the ring; his success depended on his ability to perform as an aggressive Jewish boxer and to win fights. Like Mendoza, he generated excitement for his bouts—and made large sums of money—by acting as a foil for Christian boxers and as a symbol of the subversion of stereotypes about Jews. He and Mendoza had helped fashion an image of young Jewish men as ruffians rather than victims of oppression, an image bolstered during the Old Price Riots of 1809. When the Theatre Royal in Covent Garden re-opened with higher prices after a fire, the manager hired Mendoza, Elias, and other Jewish fighters to maintain order. In response, rioters shouting anti–Jewish slogans started a number of brawls. Shortly after the riots, the *New Newgate Calendar* noted that Jewish men had recently become "the bullies of the people of London" and that the "disgraceful practice of pugilism" had "greatly increased … their audacity."[56] "Dutch Sam" died in obscure poverty but his career had a powerful influence on boxing and the Jewish community.

Irish boxers had less success than their Jewish counterparts in the first

Satirical print about the Old Price Riots in 1809. The Old Price Theatre hired Jewish boxers, including Daniel Mendoza, to keep order after prices were raised. Many patrons hurled anti-Semitic insults at the pugilists. "The Set-To Between Old Price and Spangle Jack the Shewman (1809)," from Library of Congress, digital ID cph 3g06455 //hdl.loc.gov/loc.pnp/cph.3g06455.

decade of the nineteenth century. No Irish pugilist of the caliber of "Dutch Sam" Elias appeared and bouts involving Irish fighters did not create the same interest as did fights between "Jew and Christian" in this period. They also did not receive the same support from Irish London as did Jewish boxers from their community during the war. Irish crowds had strongly supported their countrymen Andrew Gamble in 1800 and Jack O'Donnell in 1802—a strong communal identity and continuing hostility from the English population encouraged support for an Irish boxing champion—but the difficulty of traveling to matches dampened Irish enthusiasm for Irish boxers for the remainder of the war. This lack of support put Irish prizefighters in a relatively vulnerable and disadvantageous position. Without strong backing from their community, they struggled to make matches, faced hostile crowds, and frequently suffered from foul play.

As we saw above, many London Irish celebrated Jack O'Donnell's victories in 1802 in grand style. The story was very different, however, when he fought the experienced Caleb Baldwin for 50 guineas on Wimbledon Common in October of 1803. Because of worries about the magistrates, the site of the match was shifted and a relatively small crowd of several hundred people witnessed the contest. The large body of Irish supporters that had attended O'Donnell's earlier matches did not appear to see him fight Baldwin. Throughout much of the bout, the two boxers were evenly matched but, in the seventh round, Baldwin landed a punch on O'Donnell's kidney, producing a "horrid ghastly smile" on O'Donnell's face and effectively ending the fight. A report in the *Sporting Magazine* bemoaned the fact that O'Donnell's backers had left him in a hackney coach "for two hours, without any assistance." Journalist Pierce Egan later complained that, after O'Donnell's defeat, he was simply laid "to groan" in the coach without "*shoulders offered to support the drooping hero!*"[57] His backers were clearly only interested in O'Donnell for the purposes of their wagers. When he did not win them money, they abandoned him to watch (and presumably bet on) the next bout.

O'Donnell may have been unlucky in his match against Baldwin but, despite his evident skill as a boxer, he was not able to make another prizefight for two years. While his patrons claimed that the bout had been fixed and arranged for him to fight Baldwin again for 100 guineas, this match never occurred.[58] In fact, O'Donnell did not enter the prize ring again until the end of April 1805, when he faced Tom Belcher on Shepperton Common for twenty guineas. O'Donnell ended the bout after the fifteenth round and rumors circulated that he had been paid to lose.[59]

The ignoble conclusion to this match put O'Donnell's career in an even more precarious state; the *Sporting Magazine* reported that he had "lost his fighting fame, and consequently could not get backed for a large sum." Not long after his loss to Belcher, and while O'Donnell was ill, a plasterer named Emery challenged and defeated him. The two fought again in December 1805, and this time O'Donnell won easily, prompting the *Sporting Magazine* to opine "he has always been considered one of the most skilful little men of the day."[60] The following May, O'Donnell again easily defeated a novice, this time a Spitalfields dyer named Wasdell, for twenty guineas. After O'Donnell dispatched his opponent even Wasdell's backers recognized "the folly of matching an unskilful man against such a man as *O'Donnel*."[61] In June, he won another match against an inferior opponent.[62] It was clear that only untrained or untalented fighters would face him. Despite his popularity with the London Irish in 1802 and the fact that he had improved as a boxer, by 1806 O'Donnell continually fought inferior opponents for relatively small amounts of money.

A few months after his victory over Wasdell, O'Donnell—who was still only twenty-two—suffered much greater misfortune. In August he and three accomplices were arrested for robbing the owner of the Worcester coffeehouse on the Oxford road. According to testimony at trial, O'Donnell, apparently a well-know customer, "began to jump about the place, and kick up a noise, he sang a song, and broke a pipe" to distract the owner while the other two men stole fifty guineas from his bureau.[63] All four suspects were found guilty and sentenced to death, though the jury recommended mercy for O'Donnell and two of the others because "it appeared the witness Cuddeford had seduced them to commit the crime."[64] While O'Donnell was on trial for this offense, a man named Luke Codgell accused him of highway robbery. In his defense, O'Donnell claimed that the charge was a fiction and that Codgell "knew my person only from happening to see me at prize fights." The jury agreed and found him innocent.[65] Still, O'Donnell's days as a prizefighter were over.

Other talented Irish boxers were active in this period and, while not enduring as dramatic a fall as O'Donnell, similarly suffered because of hostile crowds and foul play. Bill Ryan, the son of pugilist Michael Ryan, fought several matches between 1804 and 1806 before descending into alcoholism and dying young. His first prizefight of note was against Tom Belcher at the end of November 1804. The crowd strongly supported Belcher and roared when he cheekily threw his hat over their heads and into the ring with Ryan. When the fight ended with Ryan seemingly victorious, spectators broke the ring and claimed that Ryan had struck a foul blow. Only the intervention of Belcher's patron ended the dispute and awarded the purse to Ryan. Although newspaper reports described a large and socially diverse crowd, no mention was made of an Irish presence.[66] The two boxers fought again the following June at Shepperton Common and Belcher defeated Ryan in 30 rounds. *Bell's Weekly Messenger* reported that "the ground was unusually thin of the lower orders, from the great distance from town."[67] In August, Ryan fought Caleb Baldwin (who had defeated O'Donnell in 1803) at Blackheath. The location was changed shortly before the fight and so relatively few spectators attended. Ryan defeated Baldwin in 27 rounds but the crowd broke the ring claiming that he had struck a foul blow. As the gentlemen amateurs present were trying to resolve the dispute, a unit of Woolwich artillery arrived and attempted to disperse the crowd. One man was reportedly killed in the melee that followed.[68] Like O'Donnell, Ryan was acknowledged by most observers to be a talented fighter but, also like his younger countryman, the dearth of Irish spectators in these years meant that he was at a distinct disadvantage. Ryan had another minor fight and sparred with other leading boxers at benefits but died shortly thereafter as a consequence of alcoholism.[69]

As the careers of O'Donnell and Ryan came to sorry ends, Dan Dogherty began his. Active in England between 1806 and 1812, Dogherty's early experiences mirrored those of his fellow Irishmen. A few months before Jack O'Donnell's conviction in 1806, Dogherty fought his first match, in which he defeated a Jewish boxer.[70] In June he won again, this time beating a fighter named Wall in a "clumsy and unskilful business." Ryan's last prizefight—a hard-fought victory over a novice named Clark—followed.[71] In August 1807, Dogherty defeated Dick Hall, described by the *Star* as "a man used up in his profession" for a subscription purse. This type of prize, usually raised by passing a hat at the match, was reserved for the lowliest of prizefighters.[72] Like O'Donnell and Ryan, Dogherty also toiled before small and partisan crowds; Irish spectators still did not attend matches in large numbers. A very small crowd, who were mostly "of the better order," attended his match with Hall, for example.[73] On the way home from his match with Hall, Dogherty fought with Jack Ward following a dispute "about their respective attainments in the pugilistic art."[74] In February of the following year Dogherty easily defeated George Cribb, brother to future champion Tom Cribb, at Highgate Common for another subscription purse.

Without the support of his community, Dogherty depended on the whims of gentlemen amateurs. In 1808, he attracted the attention of the young Lord Byron who, along with other members of his circle at Cambridge, had become interested in prizefighting. Dogherty sparred with one of these young men at Byron's lodgings and the poet matched and backed him against Tom Belcher for fifty guineas in April 1808.[75] On a hill near Epsom Downs, Belcher out-fought Dogherty and defeated the Irishman with a right hand to the jaw.[76] The loss again relegated Dogherty to matches against inferior fighters. In June, he fought a Scottish baker named Pentiken. Unlike many of Dogherty's other matches, stakes were posted in advance but the patrons thought so little of Pentiken that he was only backed for 20 guineas against Dogherty's 40. Although Dogherty was out of shape, he easily won the match.[77] In February 1809 he fought another novice for a subscription after two other matches at Epsom Downs. In May 1810, he performed at a dinner for eighty "gentlemen Amateurs" for a subscription purse.[78] The following year, however, the hard-working Dogherty's fortunes revived. He faced a fighter named Silverthorne for 100 guineas near Kingston in January. Despite losing to Silverthorne, he was matched against and defeated Tom Hall outside Portsmouth in November.[79] Although Dogherty was by most accounts less skilled than either O'Donnell or Ryan, his willingness to fight often and for subscription purses helped him maintain a longer career. Nevertheless, he was dependent on the whims of gentlemen amateurs. Probably as a result of this, he undertook sparring exhibitions "not only in various parts of the kingdom, but also in the sister country." He opened a boxing school in Dublin in 1812 and never fought in England again.[80]

In addition to Jewish and Irish pugilists, black boxers came to prominence for the first time in the first decade of the nineteenth century. There had been pugilists of color before: one of the first recorded bouts involving a black prizefighter occurred in June 1791, when a pugilist of African descent defeated a white fighter named Treadaway.[81] The first black boxer to have a successful career, however, was an African American named Bill Richmond. Richmond had an extraordinary life that began as a slave in the household of the Reverend Richard Charlton, the rector of St. Andrew's parish on Staten Island in New York. In the summer of 1776, his loyalist owner gave him to Brigadier General Hugh Percy (the future Duke of Northumberland), an opponent of slavery who was leading the British forces then occupying Staten Island. Percy took Richmond with him to his next post in Rhode Island and then to Northumberland when Percy left the war after a dispute with his commander, General William Howe. In England, Richmond received a basic education and an apprenticeship with a York cabinet-maker. After completing his apprenticeship, Richmond married and moved with his new wife to London. Around the turn of the century, he entered the service of Lord Camelford, a prominent (and notorious) gentleman amateur. Although Richmond had fought boxing matches in York, it was through his connection with Camelford that he was introduced to the London prizefighting scene.[82]

A former slave from Staten Island, Richmond became the first great black boxer. He trained and supported many other black prizefighters in the 1810s and 1820s, including Tom Molineaux. From Miles, *Pugilistica*, vol. 1.

As a black boxer, Richmond faced far greater hardships than either Irish or Jewish fighters; the black population of London, though not insignificant, was for the most part small, poor, and transient. Exceptional figures such as Ignatius Sancho, Ottobah Cugoano, and Olaudah Equiano might have formed the nucleus of a black community, but their experiences and connections reflected the concerns and preoccupations of the middling classes much more than those who made up the vast majority of London's roughly five thousand black residents. The Corporation of London had forbidden the apprenticing of blacks since 1731, and so men of color were overrepresented as seamen and servants and dramatically underrepresented as tradesmen and craftsmen; with a particularly high status trade as a cabinetmaker, Richmond was unusual among black Londoners. Transient seamen and servants of uncertain status were not typically in a position to attend boxing matches, let alone offer patronage or other support. At the same time, high profile black figures would have been highly unlikely to offer a pugilist like Richmond any backing given their close connections with the anti-slavery movement, the members of which were among the strongest opponents of boxing.[83]

Without a community of support, Richmond was more dependent on white gentlemen patrons than were other boxers and often experienced profound hostility. In a biographical sketch, journalist Pierce Egan described the "taunts and insults" that Richmond faced (and usually had to ignore) in both York and London.[84] His first prizefight was in Wimbledon Common in late January 1804 when a novice boxer quickly gave up against a strong fighter named Maddox and Richmond—described by the *Star* as Lord Camelford's servant—was prevailed upon to enter the ring with Maddox. Many in the crowd were openly hostile to him. As *Blackwood's Magazine* later explained, "the yelling of the mob" caused Richmond to quit in the fourth round despite fighting well.[85] A report in *The Star* added that "the indignation of the women was roused at seeing a black man fight a white."[86] Richmond also experienced the ire of the crowd at his next match in May 1805 against the Jewish boxer Youssop. This fight followed Cribb's defeat of Heakapeake and so many Jewish spectators were on hand. The presence of Richmond in the ring, however, united the diverse crowd; as the *Courier* reported, "the crowd, both Jew and Gentile, were very clamorous against the Black."[87]

Richmond's skill and his novelty as a black boxer brought him to the attention of the gentlemen amateurs and rapidly created more opportunities for him. Lord Camelford had died following a duel in March 1804 but, after Richmond defeated Youssop, leading amateur Fletcher Reid became his patron.[88] Reid backed Richmond against Jack Holmes in July 1805 and Richmond won relatively easily in less than forty minutes.[89] This victory brought Richmond more acclaim and, a few months later, Reid and another gentleman amateur organized a match with Tom Cribb, even though Cribb was at least forty pounds heavier than Richmond. Unlike "Dutch Sam" Elias or Isaac Pitton, both of whom resisted attempts to match them against much larger Christian fighters, Richmond had little choice but to enter the ring with the future champion if he hoped to maintain the support of his patrons. When the two met after a championship match between Henry Pearce and John Gully on October 8, Richmond understandably fought defensively and tried to avoid Cribb for as long as possible. Newspaper accounts ridiculed Richmond for his retreating tactics but made no mention of the vast size difference between the two men. After an hour and a half, Cribb was declared the winner. Richmond did not fight again for several years.[90]

Lacking the support of a community put Richmond in a more vulnerable position than Jewish or Irish fighters, but he became adept at performing for boxing audiences. His often-outlandish performances drew both on long-held stereotypes casting black people as entertainers and on the precedents established by other minority boxers, especially Daniel Mendoza. Several years after Richmond's match with Cribb, writer William Oxberry described Richmond's retreating style in that bout. According to Oxberry, Richmond "hopped and danced about the ring, sometimes falling down, at others jigging round somewhat in the style of an Otaheitan [Tahitian] dance."[91] At his next match in April 1808, against a boxer identified only as "a West-countryman, who was a candidate for the list of pugilists," Richmond amazingly "got his adversary on the ropes [and] went over him in a summerset." John Wilson of *Blackwood's Magazine* later wrote that he had never seen the like of this stunt and that it "caused much merriment." The West-countryman laughed at Richmond and tried to play to the crowd but grew tired from this "bravado" and lost the match.[92]

Richmond used his skill and fame to provide the assistance and community to other black boxers that he had lacked. He made available economic support, training, and used his experience as a performer to advance their careers. The most famous of these was another black immigrant from the United States named Tom Molineaux. Likely born a slave, Molineaux worked as a freeman on the docks in New York in the first years of the nineteenth century and probably participated in boxing matches with American and British seamen there. In 1809, Molineaux traveled to England and sought out Richmond. The two men were quite different. Richmond was twenty years older than Molineaux, had a family, and had a disciplined temperament that reflected his education and apprenticeship. Molineaux, in contrast, was uneducated, came from the rowdy world of the New York docks, and was much more powerfully built than Richmond. Nevertheless, after the two men met, Richmond offered Molineaux patronage and training.[93] Only a year after

Molineaux's arrival in England, Richmond had helped him make a match against the English Champion, Tom Cribb.

The speed with which Molineaux accomplished this feat illustrates both Richmond's skill as a promoter and the value of a talented black boxer to gamblers looking for large wagers, white boxers looking for high stakes and publicity, and spectators and journalists eager for a spectacle. In July of 1810, after a few months of training with Richmond, Molineaux fought for the first time in Britain against Jack Burrows of Bristol. The match "excited more than usual interest," in part because Cribb was present and acted as the Bristolian's second. He and Richmond helped to draw over a thousand spectators to the match by sparring after the prizefight. Molineaux badly beat the untalented Burrows.[94] Molineaux's success captured the public imagination and, a few weeks later, he was matched against Tom Blake (often known as Tom Tough), another Bristolian who had nearly defeated Cribb several years earlier. Despite Molineaux's lack of experience, the two men fought for the large sum of 100 guineas and gambling odds only favored Blake 5 to 4.[95] The match was staged on the Kentish coast near Margate and was therefore "more ... respectably attended than the ordinary exhibitions." Blake was driven to the ring with Cribb in a Baronet's coach. Richmond addressed the crowd, introduced Molineaux to them, and acted as his pupil's second in the bout.[96] Molineaux defeated Blake relatively easily, utilizing a combination of power and speed. Contemporary accounts credited Richmond's training as well. After the match, Molineaux challenged

An unheralded fighter early in his career, Tom Cribb became one of the best-known pugilists of the era after defeating African American Tom Molineaux in two fights in 1810 and 1811. From Egan, *Boxiana*, vol. 1.

Cribb. *Bell's Weekly Messenger* reported that the "Black, who is 26 years of age, threatens to *mill* the whole race of fighters of the day."[97] Not since Mendoza's fights with Humphries had a match of such symbolic importance been staged.

Cribb was a somewhat unlikely representative of English manhood in 1810, though he was acknowledged as champion. He had experienced a dramatic rise since his uninspiring victories over Heakapeake and Richmond in 1805. Journalists had often complained about his defensive style in these early matches. The *Morning Post* commented about his victory over Heakapeake that, despite winning, Cribb had "shewed himself to be a complete shifter."[98] Two years later, when Cribb fought Jem Belcher, the *Morning Post* again disparaged Cribb's talents, noting that he owed his victory to Belcher's lack of an eye and declaring that, before Belcher's accident, "it would have been farcical to have matched *Crib* against him." The paper claimed that Cribb had "but humble pretensions to the character of a skilful boxer," largely because his mode of fighting was "that of falling back."[99] Indeed, many considered this method of fighting "unmanly," because of its association with retreat, though a number of successful boxers practiced it.[100] When Cribb won the championship in a match against Bob Gregson in 1808 the *Post* commented that the bout was one of "most remarkable specimens of skill and courage that stand recorded," but Cribb was considered fortunate to have won. Many still thought him an unworthy champion and not the equal of his predecessors Belcher, Pearce, and Gully.[101]

The discontent with Cribb among boxing enthusiasts paralleled a general malaise about the course of the war and a related flagging of "national spirit" among the populace. Although the battle of Trafalgar in October 1805 ended the immediate threat of French invasion, it brought Britain no closer to defeating Napoleon. In December, Napoleon crushed the Austrian army at Austerlitz and, in October 1806, the Prussians at Jena. The situation seemed to improve in 1808 with British intervention in Spain, but early failures quickly turned public opinion against the expedition. When government deception about the Convention of Cintra, a truce with French forces in Spain that was widely perceived as an unnecessary capitulation to France, became known "popular disenchantment with the Peninsula" was complete.[102] The passivity of the British army in Spain ran counter to the (often-reckless) aggression of earlier British commanders and undermined confidence in the war effort. For many, Cribb's "falling back" fighting style was uncomfortably close to the failures of the Peninsular Campaign.

Opinions of the governing class were souring as well. The public attitude toward the Portland and, from October 1809, Perceval governments worsened with the disclosure of the "Duke of York Affair," which involved the King's second son (the commander-in-chief of the armed forces) permitting his mistress Mary Anne Clarke to take bribes from military leaders in exchange for advancement. In 1809, she appeared before the House of Commons and revealed the sordid details. As Anna Clark has argued, the scandal "undermined the patriotic consensus that had seemed to unite Britons at a time of war."[103] If heroism and courage were the bases of British military strength, why were men not promoted on the basis of merit instead of at the whim of a Duke's mistress? If British men (and especially military commanders) were brave and heroic, why did they perform so poorly in Spain? For many Britons, the answers were not apparent in 1809. 1810 proved to be an even more unsettling year. Napoleon finally destroyed the power of the regular Spanish resistance in January, forcing British forces to fall back in Portugal. Although the Duke of Wellington defeated a French attack at the end of the summer, he was unable to exploit his victory, prompting disappointment in Britain. In addition, the British economy entered a severe recession in the summer of 1810. Finally, the King succumbed to illness in October, precipitating a political crisis that lasted until the end of the year.[104]

It was in this context that Molineaux and Cribb fought for the championship on December 18. A few years later, journalist Pierce Egan described the "lively interest" in the fight and the fact that, even those who normally ignored boxing, "felt for the honour of their country."[105] Ten thousand "Lords, Nobles, and Commoners" traveled to East Grinstead, Sussex in a chilling December rain to attend the match. These travelers choked the roads the morning of the match and the inns could not accommodate half of those seeking a room. The path to the site of the match was a knee-deep morass of clay because of torrential rain and the enormous traffic.[106] Although the events surrounding the Regency bill dominated the news, most London papers carried substantial stories about the fight.

The rain-soaked crowd was rewarded with a brutal spectacle. Following the now customary practice, the match was contested on the ground. John Jackson, acting as "Master of the Ceremonies" organized the "outer ring" of carriages and the planting of stakes and ropes to surround a twenty-four-foot square fighting ring at the side of a hill. In the first part of the bout, Cribb determined to change his style and to continually advance at Molineaux. He was on the verge of losing when, in the twentieth round, he and Molineaux became entangled in the ropes. At this point, the crowd broke the ring and the fight was temporarily stopped. While contemporary accounts of this event differ, it is clear that the spectators were hostile to Molineaux and that their actions hindered his performance. Shortly thereafter, Cribb adopted his customary defensive mode of fighting and gained momentum. After falling on his head, Molineaux was dazed and, when he was deemed to have fallen without a blow, Cribb was declared the victor.[107]

Cribb had won the match and retained the championship, but the nature of his victory raised uncomfortable questions for those who argued that boxing illustrated the superiority of white British manhood. The hostility of the crowd and Cribb's resort to defensive tactics cast doubt on the legitimacy of his victory. A letter written in Molineaux's name shortly after the bout made a plea for a rematch and expressed the hope that "the circumstances of my being of a different colour ... will not in any way operate to my prejudice."[108] Cribb's performance also helped to generate uncertainty about the meaning of his victory. His mode of fighting through retreat evoked memories of the tactics of the Duke of Wellington in the recent Battle of Bussaco, which had raised the hopes of many Britons in September. In this battle, the Duke defeated a French army in Portugal before withdrawing to safety. Initial hopes for a heroic and tide-turning triumph were thus disappointed.[109] Cribb's victory seemed similarly marred by retreat, undermining what would have been considered a strong statement about the superiority of his country.

Although reports of the bout in the London newspapers highlighted Cribb's courage, his "retreating" tactic stood in marked contrast to depictions of Molineaux. *Bell's Weekly Messenger*, for example, commented that Molineaux was "as good a man as ever entered a ring."[110] A contemporary poem recorded similar feelings about Molineaux: "Tho' beat, he prov'd a man, my boys, what more could a man do."[111] The well-respected pugilist Bill Gibbons claimed that "MOLINEAUX only wanted an 'English heart.'"[112] Other reports noted Molineaux's strength and resiliency and implicitly contrasted his courage with Cribb's defensive style. To many, courage and aggressiveness were preferable even in defeat.

As a result both of the popularity of the first match and the questions about its outcome, Cribb and his patrons organized another bout the following year. This time they worked to eliminate any ambiguity or doubt about the outcome. Molineaux had difficulty procuring patronage and spent most of the ten months between the two matches on an arduous tour of England, staging exhibition bouts for money. Cribb rarely sparred publicly during the same period, enjoying generous patronage to offset the time and expense of readying himself for the rematch. A contemporary treatise gives some sense of what was expected of a championship-caliber pugilist in training. Among other things, it described a daily regimen of very particular foods, including "stewed veal (without rice)" and "well-fed fowls ... boiled to a jelly."[113] In September, nearly two months before his second bout with Molineaux, Cribb traveled to Ury in Scotland to engage in a rigorous nine-week training regimen with one of the most famous athletes of the day, the "pedestrian" Robert Barclay Allardice.[114] Cribb walked eighteen to twenty miles daily on Barclay's land, carrying a musket with which to hunt game if the spirit moved him to do so. He twice trod sixty miles to Barclay's hunting lodge in the Highlands. As he trained for the most important match of his life, Cribb enjoyed a mode of living largely unknown to men of his background.[115] Molineaux, in contrast, labored endlessly at exhibitions and did not have the leisure to train effectively.

Drawing of a silver cup given to Tom Cribb in honor of his second victory over Tom Molineaux. From Egan, *Boxiana*, vol. 1.

The hopes of Cribb's patrons were fulfilled in the second match between Cribb and Molineaux in late September 1811. This match seemed to erase the outcome of the first fight and made Tom Cribb a national hero. For weeks, it was "the first and only consideration amongst the sporting world," and received extensive coverage in many newspapers in London and around the country.[116] To remove any doubt about crowd interference, a stage was built five miles from Grantham, Lincolnshire, more than 100 miles from the metropolis. The bout again drew thousands of spectators. Local inns were filled and allegedly no bed was available within twenty miles.[117] When Cribb and Molineaux arrived at the scene of the match, the crowd's allegiance was clear. According to the *Manchester Mercury*, the "prejudice against the black colour seemed to exist as much in the country as in London."[118] No interference from the spectators was necessary this time, however. Molineaux delivered tremendous punishment early in the match but exhausted himself in the process. Cribb broke Molineaux's jaw and, though Molineaux continued the fight for two more rounds, he could no longer offer effective resistance and was beaten in less than nineteen minutes. Newspaper reports of the match reveled in Cribb's victory and dismissed the outcome of the earlier fight,

A monument featuring a British Lion erected for Tom Cribb after his death in 1848. From Miles, *Pugilistica*, vol. 1.

claiming that "Molineaux could have no chance in any combat with him" and that Cribb possessed "heroism never excelled."[119]

In the immediate aftermath of the fight, people in London and around England hailed Cribb as a symbol of the superiority of British manhood. Two days after the match, Cribb traveled back to London, arriving in great style in a coach decorated with blue ribbons. Crowds cheered him along the route and a large assemblage choked the streets around his pub, which was filled throughout the day.[120] The following week, boxer Bob Gregson hosted a dinner in honor of Cribb. After a series of toasts to the King and to the country, a gentleman amateur raised a glass to Cribb, "who has nobly and successfully combated for the laurels of native championship, against a Moor." The next week, Gregson hosted another dinner in Cribb's honor at which the English Champion was presented with a silver tankard commemorating his victory.[121] The inscription proclaimed both the importance of Cribb's victory and of the sport of boxing for Britain.

The excitement surrounding Cribb's victory took place against the back-

A satirical print illustrating a negative response to the Cribb and Molineaux fights. The print shows a boxing match between a British sailor and a black African American opponent amidst a scene of debauchery. "A Milling Match Between Decks" (1812), from Library of Congress digital ID cph 3c12877 //hdl.loc.gov/loc.pnp/cph.3c12877.

drop of an improving situation in Spain. Masséna, the French commander in Spain, gave the order to retreat in March 1811. When news of the withdrawal arrived in London in April, Whigs and Tories united in Parliament to vote thanks to Wellington. Central Spain now seemed open to British armies and the government gave the Duke free rein to pursue the French. In this context, Cribb's victory in October presented an opportunity to highlight British strength and unity at a time when the tide of war seemed to be turning. Newspapers around Britain trumpeted Cribb's victory as an illustration of the superiority of British manhood through the vehicle of boxing. Drawing on the language of martial manhood and British military strength developed in the debates around boxing and other embattled sports in the first years of the century, the rhetoric surrounding the second bout between Tom Cribb and Tom Molineaux presented the fight as a perfect demonstration of this ideal.

The matches between Cribb and Molineaux were the culmination of a decade in which boxing appealed to a much wider audience than ever before. It did so because prizefights had become, in addition to bloody spectacles, contests of national importance. Just as Wellington pushed back French forces in Spain, Cribb symbolically defeated the nation's enemy in his decisive second bout with Molineaux. At the same time, the dramatic rise of Molineaux also demonstrated the possibilities before black, Jewish, and Irish pugilists. Molineaux's success was due as much to his (and Bill Richmond's) skillful publicity campaign as it did to his tremendous boxing skills. Boxers, and the journalists who wrote about them, increasingly shaped the sport. They would become even more important in years to come.

Chapter Five

The Rise of "Boxing's Professionals"

Journalists and Boxers in the Postwar Years, 1812–1823

After Napoleon was finally defeated at Waterloo in June 1815, the United Kingdom stood at the pinnacle of its global power. More than twenty years of nearly uninterrupted warfare were over and many Britons looked forward to a new era of peace, prosperity, and stability. The reality was quite different. The end of wartime demand depressed agricultural prices, causing widespread misery. Old divisions returned too: the reform movement was reignited and nationalist protest reemerged in Ireland. Rather than a return to the status quo ante, Britain and Ireland were dramatically altered in the next twenty years. This spirit of change also shaped the sport of bare-knuckle prizefighting. In these years, boxers and journalists began to take control of the sport from the sporting gentry and aristocrats who had dominated it since the 1780s. High-born gentlemen continued to be a very visible and active presence at prizefights and at benefits, but increasingly the interests of a new breed of popular writers (along with their expanding readership) and a new crop of boxers (and their supporters) organized, publicized, and championed the sport. In doing so, they fashioned a commercial enterprise in which the identities and stories of boxers and the spectacles of prizefights were marketed and sold to the public.[1]

The growing importance of these "professionals" had critical consequences for the culture of the sport and for minority pugilists.[2] Coverage of boxing in newspapers, growing since the 1780s, was greatly expanded after the war. A number of popular histories of the sport appeared as well. These influential publications amplified defenses of pugilism and broadcast them to a growing readership. Claims about the relationship between boxing and national strength continued to provide opportunities for minority boxers, who represented the supposed threats to British manhood. At the same time,

Jewish and Irish boxers in England increasingly solicited financial support and patronage beyond the narrow circle of gentlemen amateurs who had traditionally provided the bulk of it. These fighters managed their images more actively, using words, deeds, and symbols to encourage potential patrons and spectators to see them as a symbol of their communities and to support them. Backing was often forthcoming because pugilists seemed to subvert ethnic caricatures and strike a blow for the community in the ring. Some members of the sporting press also challenged stereotypes despite their full-throated support for the superiority of British manhood.[3] A few—most notably the influential Anglo-Irish journalist Pierce Egan—cast minority fighters as paragons of British manhood. Similarly, even as they traded on their minority status, many Jewish and Irish pugilists and their patrons made a point of publicly embracing the vision of Britishness promoted by the boxing press. Journalists, boxers, and patrons thus not only used identity to highlight difference but also to underscore common values.

This chapter argues that journalists and pugilists increasingly controlled the sport of boxing after the war and accelerated its transformation from a spectacle created by and for the aristocracy and gentry into a commercial enterprise for popular consumption. A critical way in which they did so was by channeling the burgeoning national, ethnic, and religious differences and conflicts of a changing United Kingdom through the relative safety of the ring.

The famous matches between Tom Cribb and Tom Molineaux in 1811 were a critical turning point for bare-knuckle prizefighting. Like the bouts between Richard Humphries and Daniel Mendoza in 1788–90, they were a cultural phenomenon. Unlike the Humphries and Mendoza fights, however, they led to a sustained period of growth for the sport. Popular prints, verse, songs, and material culture joined mushrooming publicity in newspapers and other publications to make the 1810s a decade of "boximania."[4] Some of the leading literary lights of the era—including Lord Byron and William Hazlitt—were fascinated with the sport and reveled in its language and "flash" style. Byron patronized, trained, and dined with boxers. He also peppered his work with allusions to pugilism. Keats even described Byron's *Don Juan* as "a flash poem." Hazlitt similarly used references to boxing in a number of works and penned the influential essay "The Fight," which described the day of a boxing match between Bill Hickman and Bill Neate in 1822.[5] The influential critic John Wilson wrote several long pieces about boxing for *Blackwood's Edinburgh Magazine* using the pseudonym Christopher North. According to Thomas de Quincey, Wilson patronized boxing as well as cockfighting, wrestling, boat racing, and horse-racing. Another friend remarked that he prominently displayed Pierce Egan's *Boxiana*, along with *The Wealth of Nations* and *The Faerie Queen* in his office.[6]

Not surprisingly, the theaters of London tried to capitalize on this enthusiasm. On the night of August 26, about a month before the second of the two Cribb and Molineaux bouts, the Lyceum staged a "new musical farce" written by Samuel Beasley called "The Boarding House; or, Five Hours at Brighton." "The Boarding House" cast popular comedic actor William Oxberry as Christopher Contract, a recent Cambridge graduate who had been "consumed with the fashionable art of boxing." While Oxberry's "pugilistic exertions … produced considerable dissatisfaction" among the audience the play was generally well received, with critics applauding the comedy and music but considering the plot thin and unoriginal.[7] Members of the audience were clearly familiar enough with boxing to know bad form when they saw it.

Oxberry, though primarily an actor, was also a writer. He had been a printer's apprentice as a young man and published throughout his life. A memoir produced shortly after his death noted, "In literature, he was ever for commencing something." While he mostly published on topics related to the stage, he also periodically wrote about sport.[8] Several months after the premiere of "The Boarding House," possibly given the idea by his role in the play, he published an anthology of boxing called *Pancratia*. The book, priced at 12 shillings, presented a detailed chronology of the history of prizefighting. It was the first such work to appear in a decade and far more popular than its predecessors. Starting with Figg's amphitheater in the 1730s, *Pancratia* drew from newspapers, advertisements, the *Sporting Magazine*, and other sources. It offered readers "accurate, empirical information" in a narrative that described the development of the structure, history, and heroes of the sport.[9] The book thus was a critical part of the development of boxing as a sport, with an organization and history that existed independently of individual bouts and fighters.

Pancratia also included an extended introduction that proclaimed the importance of boxing in reinforcing the "character and manners" of the nation.[10] This claim about the political importance of the sport was taken seriously enough that *The Monthly Magazine* placed *Pancratia* under the heading "Politics and Political Economy" (alongside books about currency and Catholic Emancipation) in its listing of new publications for March 1812.[11] The author of the introduction, identified as "J.B.," was almost certainly journalist John Badcock. Little is known about Badcock other than that he published a number of works about sport and other topics in the 1810s and 1820s under the pseudonym "Jon Bee" and that he probably had a connection to Devon.[12] It is a strong possibility, though, that he is the same John Badcock who was identified in bankruptcy proceedings in 1805 and 1813 as a bookseller located on Paternoster Row. Significantly, Badcock (as "Jon Bee") began a period of prolific writing about a year after the last public notice about the bankruptcy.[13]

In his anonymous introduction to *Pancratia*, Badcock borrowed liberally from the many public defenses of the sport during the war. He argued that boxing prepared British men to "resist Slavery at home and Enemies from Abroad" and claimed that watching and participating in boxing matches set Britain apart from its continental neighbors. While Italians and Spaniards resolved disputes with a stiletto driven silently into the back of their enemies, Badcock argued, honorable British men settled their differences with "a manly appeal to boxing, in which the parties are not allowed to take unfair advantage of each other."[14] As much as its thorough coverage of boxing history, these overt appeals to national feeling made *Pancratia* a commercial success. An advertisement for a second edition of the book in 1815 highlighted the book's inclusion of "an argumentative proof, that Pugilism ... demands the admiration and patronage of every free state, being calculated to inspire manly courage."[15]

Oxberry and Badcock's achievement encouraged the production of similar publications. *Boxiana*, published later in 1812, was the most influential of these and ultimately dwarfed *Pancratia* in popularity, becoming an "indispensable part of a sporting gentleman's library."[16] The author, Pierce Egan, was Anglo-Irish—his grandfather Carbery Egan was a vicar in County Cork and his uncle John "Bully" Egan was a prominent barrister and Chairman of the Quarter Sessions for Kilmainham. Bully Egan was also a member of the Irish House of Commons and a fierce opponent of the proposed union between Great Britain and Ireland. Understanding that voting against the bill would deprive him of his position in Kilmainham, he reportedly shouted "Ireland—Ireland forever! and damn Kilmainham!" during the final debate.[17] Florid statements of British nationalism were commonplace in the work of Pierce Egan, but his uncle had been an ardent Irish nationalist.

Pierce Egan was most likely born in Ireland in 1774. His father, a younger son of Carbery Egan, moved the family to London for reasons that are unclear and took work as laborer. Growing up a poor Irishman in the metropolis, Pierce very likely heard about the exploits of the famous Irish fighters Peter Corcoran and Michael Ryan. At the age of twelve or thirteen he became a printer's apprentice. Gradually, he began to write copy himself and, eventually, he served as a Parliamentary reporter.[18] In this capacity, he may have witnessed William Windham's speeches in 1800 and 1802 defending "manly, athletic exercises."[19] Around this time, Egan went to work for George Smeeton, a prominent printer and engraver of materials related to sport. He gained a minor reputation as a "racy reporter," writing about the scandals and pastimes of aristocrats.[20] Since rakish young aristocrats were some of the leading patrons of boxing, Egan would have become closely acquainted with the leading personalities of the sport. When George Smeeton decided to put out a serialized anthology of pugilism, then, he turned to Egan.

The work Egan produced was called *Boxiana*. It was published anonymously and there was some controversy about authorship, but the style is clearly that of Egan. *Boxiana* was priced at twelve shillings (like *Pancratia*) and the publishers also offered it in 22 parts, each costing 6d. Even at this price the volume was out of the reach of most Britons, but nevertheless its public reception quickly established Egan's reputation as an authority on boxing. Such was its influence that *Boxiana*'s brash tone came to infuse boxing coverage in newspapers; many of the slang terms Egan popularized in *Boxiana* began to appear in their accounts of matches. In this way, the work helped open the world of gentleman amateurs to a much wider audience. Egan's "flash" style was a kind of boxing insider's code that made it possible for any reader of a newspaper to feel familiarity with and included in the fashionable prizefighting scene.[21]

Following Badcock's introduction to *Pancratia*, *Boxiana* also broadcast the claim that boxing was not simply a bloody spectacle but a critical element of British national character. In his introduction, for example, Egan noted that Englishmen were "animated by that native spirit, which has been found to originate, in a great measure" from boxing. The effect of this spirit, he continued, could be seen in the "daring intrepidity of the BRITISH SOLDIER in mounting the breach producing those brilliant victories which have reflected so much honour on the English nation."[22] In appending this language to a history of the sport, Egan—like Badcock—was expanding on the mythology of boxing and Britishness. In his telling, the "heroes" of boxing were not poor men pummeling one another for the enjoyment of rakish aristocratic gamblers but instead the purest specimens of manly Britishness. *Boxiana* and *Pancratia* helped develop the literary life of pugilism that tied the sport to a mythical and timeless manly British character.

Reporting of boxing matches in newspapers did not immediately change following the publication of *Boxiana* and *Pancratia*. The rapidly evolving military situation on the continent dominated the news for much of 1813. Some accounts of fights appeared amidst the war coverage but most only offered a short summary of the action. Newspapers also occasionally described the activities of prizefighters outside the ring, including a successful benefit for Tom Cribb in April and an exhibition at Derby in which Tom

Molineaux fought and handily defeated several local brawlers in June.[23] *The Sporting Magazine* was still the most complete source for detailed descriptions of prizefights but the monthly periodical was intended for a wealthier clientele and did not have the same reach as many newspapers. The language and tone of reports in newspapers and periodicals continued much as before and did not yet show the influence of *Boxiana* and *Pancratia*. A description of an eighty-seven-round match between a farmer and a cattle dealer in the *Courier* noting that the two novices evinced "native characteristic bravery" was an exception.[24]

The turn of the calendar to 1814 brought important changes. Napoleon's regime collapsed in the spring and, after a brief resumption of hostilities in spring and summer 1815, the long conflict was finally ended. Critical developments in prizefighting accompanied the return of peace. At the beginning of 1814, a number of leading gentlemen amateurs had agreed to form the Pugilistic Club to bring order to the sport, as the Jockey Club and the Marylebone Cricket Club had done for horse-racing and cricket. At its first public dinner on the evening of May 22 at the Thatched House Tavern in St. James's Street, Lord Yarmouth—a member of the Marylebone Cricket Club and a prominent MP—gave a stirring speech "on the advantages of pugilism in a national point of view," arguing that "the people of England ... owed their present GREATNESS to their generosity and manliness in battle." Members agreed to contribute a subscription and to wear a uniform of blue coats and buff waistcoasts with P.C. inscribed on gilt buttons. The Club maintained ropes and stakes with "P.C." painted on them and decided to fund purses of between 10 and 50 guineas for prizefights. Around fifty men attended this first dinner, including many prominent prizefighters.[25] The Club awarded its first purse of 50 guineas to Bill Richmond for his defeat of a boxer named Davis at Coombe Warren. The P.C. ropes and stakes made their debut as well.[26]

Much as the establishment of the Pugilistic Club seemed a reassertion of the power of gentlemen over the sport, it also formalized the role of pugilists, journalists, and tavern-keepers in the organization and staging of matches. "Gentleman" John Jackson, the conqueror of Mendoza, had served as an unofficial "master of ceremonies" at major fights for nearly a decade. He now became the secretary of the Club and was responsible for the managing of the ring at matches. Jackson held prize money, deliberated in the case of disputes, and oversaw crowd control. Other boxers kept the ring clear of spectators, with horsewhips as a last resort.[27] Although the Pugilistic Club eventually collapsed, it established a precedent of formalized organization that was followed by a number of other groups. As high-born men increasingly withdrew from the sport in the 1820s and 1830s, boxers and journalists took an ever larger role in organizing and staging matches. In 1824, for example, Egan was elected the chairman of the "Partiality Club," which subscribed money to purchase a silver cup for a successful boxer named Joshua Hudson. After the presentation of the cup at a public house in East Smithfield, Egan addressed the crowd and expounded "on the national benefits of pugilism."[28] The prominent position occupied by Egan and other journalists led the Liverpool-based newspaper *Bethell's Life in London* to complain in 1826 about what was, in its judgment, the excessive influence of the newspaper press on the sport.[29]

As journalists became more involved in the organization of the sport after the war, coverage of boxing and other sports in newspapers expanded and became more uniform. Newspapers increasingly repeated the arguments of *Pancratia* and *Boxiana*. An article in the *Morning Chronicle* in September 1814, for example, lambasted a Parisian play about two French servants passing as English boxers. The article reminded readers that "the spirit of justice which it inculcates, the fair play that it enacts, and the *bottom* or courage which it cherishes, have a main influence on the English character."[30] Reports of boxing matches, often included under the heading "Sporting Intelligence," used similar language. They also assumed that their readers would understand the terminology of prizefighting and references to the history of the ring. A report in the *St. James's Chronicle and London Evening Post* in April 1817, for example, described one of the combatants, Jack Randall, as a "scientific Hibernian" ("scientific" was understood to mean skillful) and made an extended comparison between his style and that of "the late O'Donnell," the Irish fighter active more than a decade earlier. The report also mentioned the "Commander-in-Chief," as John Jackson was often described, without using his name.[31]

Pierce Egan was at the forefront of this new sporting journalism in the postwar period. From around 1814 he found a platform at *The Weekly Dispatch*, which became one of the most widely circulated weeklies in London by the early 1820s. In its pages, Egan regularly reminded readers of pugilism's history and that boxing matches were more than individual bloody spectacles but part of a great tradition that perpetuated values—such as fair play, courage, and stamina—that were central to British national greatness. In March 1817, for example, he wrote that the Lord Mayor of London permitted boxing exhibitions in the metropolis because he was "an admirer of true British courage" and in September of the same year he noted that spectators assembling near Molesey Hurst would witness "true British valour" at a boxing match.[32] Egan's editor Robert Bell expressed similar sentiments. In a statement of the paper's philosophy in January 1821, Bell noted that sports like boxing encouraged a "bold, vigorous and manly spirit among the mass of people" and shaped "the national character of Englishmen."[33] By framing boxing in this way, Egan and Bell encouraged their readers to see the sport as a timeless national institution rather than a series of bloody spectacles organized for the vulgar pleasures of dissolute rakes. The literary culture of the sport, which repeated critical words and phrases to emphasize the heroism of pugilism's past and present, sought to draw readers in with this language and make them feel they were part of the boxing scene.

As sporting journalists urged readers to see prizefighting as a higher expression of their national spirit, many also (explicitly or implicitly) suggested that black, Jewish, or Irish boxers could be symbols of British manhood. This did not mean erasing distinctions, however. Rather, they highlighted the (often stereotypical) differences between boxers of dissimilar ethnic or religious backgrounds. In doing so, they imagined—and prompted readers to imagine—a British nation that wove together distinctly different identities.[34] The Anglo-Irishman Egan was a leading promoter of this expansive idea of Britishness. Reflecting on the career of the great eighteenth-century Jewish boxer, Daniel Mendoza, he noted that "true courage is not confined to any particular place, colour, or station." In a story describing black boxer Bill Richmond delivering a thrashing to a man who had attacked him for accompanying a white woman Egan applauded Richmond, remarking that he "soon taught [his antagonist] to acknowledge that it was wrong, and beneath the character of an Englishman, to abuse any individual ... on account of his COUNTRY or his *colour*."[35] In this case Egan sided with the American-born ex-slave even when the volatile issue of miscegenation was implicitly in question, suggesting that Richmond knew better how to behave as "an Englishman" than his white antagonist.

Despite such enlightened sentiments, Egan frequently used stereotypes and derogatory terms such as "Paddy," "Sheenie," and "Massa" to describe Irish, Jewish, and black fighters. Describing the anticipation for an upcoming fight involving a Jewish boxer, for example, Egan wrote that knowledgeable observers considered the Jewish boxer "most *mischievous*." He also noted that Jewish people betted in favor of the underdog Jewish boxer, "nowithstanding [sic] the love of *monish* by the various tribes."[36] Egan did not spare his fellow Irishmen either. He described the "*warm-hearted* attentions of his countrymen" for Irish fighter Dan Donnelly before lamenting the fact that Donnelly had "rather more *spirits* on board, than *cool* judgement to regulate his *steerage*."[37] Egan's use of slang and chummy humor were key elements of his popularity, helping his readers feel part of the boxing scene. Nevertheless, such writing also reveals a more serious vision of Britishness. While many writers used such stereotypes to remind their readers what British men were not, Egan highlighted the courage and manliness of "greedy" Jews and "excitable" Irishmen. They could be British too.

Egan's attitude stands in contrast to John Badcock. Badcock, a competitor and harsh critic of Egan, was either mockingly derisive or explicitly hostile to Irish, Jewish, and black boxers. For him there was no question that such fighters could embody British manliness. In his boxing history *Annals of Sporting and Fancy Gazette*, Badcock described an impromptu match between Bill Richmond and future English champion Tom Cribb in 1805, noting that the "the black hopped and danced round his man … without making a mark upon the steady nob of our hero." Badcock ridiculed the "frolic of blackey," declaring it "mere burlesque" that "ought not to have been tolerated one minute."[38] For Badcock, as for many other Britons, black people were comical or entertaining figures not to be taken seriously. They were inherently incapable of demonstrating something as important as British manhood.

Badcock did not reserve his scorn for black boxers. He complained that the "Israelitish or Hebrew School" of boxing was responsible for "the circumstance of each side hoisting up the stakes to unexampled sums." He also derided Jewish people in general, adding, "To deal with … Jews" to a list of undesirable life situations that included living in prison and having an unattractive wife. Badcock held the Irish in contempt as well. After recounting Tom Belcher's defeat of Irish boxer Jack O'Donnell, Badcock sarcastically remarked that O'Donnell was "christened by his countrymen, as usual, 'Irish hero.'" He also mocked Irish national aspirations, noting that Irish boxer Dan Dogherty chose to face Tom Belcher "*on national grounds*—or rather we might say *provincial*, for Ireland is but a component part of the Empire, let her warm-headed sons say what they will."[39] Unlike many other journalists, Badcock steadfastly refused to leaven such derisive commentary with descriptions of the courage of minority boxers. For him, strength and courage—the pillars of British strength—were the exclusive domain of white English Christians.

Minority boxers did not passively accept such characterizations in print but, rather, shaped their own images more actively, often borrowing the language of sporting journalists. They were able to do so more effectively as they began to exercise greater control of their careers and to find new ways to make money. Sparring exhibitions—indoor performances in which pugilists fought one another on a stage with gloves—were an important way in which they did so. Admission could be charged at these events, they could be advertised in advance, and sparring pugilists did not assume the physical risk involved in a prizefight.[40] The Fives Court in St. Martin's street was the most important venue in London and, by the first decade of the nineteenth century, it was staging monthly exhibitions.[41] As a focal point for boxing in the metropolis, the Fives Court was also where most new fighters made their debut. A successful performance was rewarded by a few coins on the stage and, more importantly, the possibility of attracting patronage. Not surprisingly, the paying spectators exercised a great deal of control over the proceedings, often shouting for unpopular boxers to leave the stage.[42] Stimulating the interest of the fickle crowd of the Fives Court was therefore particularly important for aspiring pugilists.

Partly as a response to the growing power of the Fives Court and partly to cater to the growing number of supporters of boxing outside of the West End, some sparring exhibitions began to migrate to the East End. The Minerva Rooms in Leadenhall Street, were among the first to challenge the influence of the Fives Court. Although not owned or managed by Jews, this venue offered Jewish boxers greater opportunity to perform before Jewish audiences and potential patrons. Veteran Jewish boxer Isaac Bitton and another Jewish fighter named Lazarus, for example, performed at a benefit for Christian boxer Harry Harmer in February 1817. The following year, at a benefit for a

The Fives Court was a focal point of prizefighting in the first three decades of the nineteenth century. Sparring "benefits" and the making of matches often occurred there. From Egan, *Boxiana*, vol. 1.

Christian boxer named Church, the strength of the Jewish presence prompted the *Weekly Dispatch* to quip that the "Jews were so numerous, that some punning occurred respecting their *devotion* to *Church*." Other East End locations also defied the Fives Court's dominance. In July 1817, at the Three Pigeons public house in Houndsditch, Jewish boxer Abraham Belasco and Irish fighter Tom Reynolds announced an upcoming bout for forty guineas. Several years later, Isaac Bitton held a benefit exhibition at the Fishmonger's Arms in Houndsditch. A "new Jew" made his debut at this event.[43]

Jewish boxers also struck out beyond the metropolis on sparring tours, earning money and fame while spreading the culture of prizefighting. Abraham Belasco had a successful tour through England and Scotland with Daniel Mendoza in 1818 and 1819. Belasco had won several prizefights in the immediate postwar years and had received patronage from Jewish backers.[44] Unfortunately, he then lost two closely contested matches in 1817 and many Jewish gamblers surrendered large sums betting on him. He held a benefit exhibition at the Fives Court in October but could not find any financial backing despite being called "the Champion of the Jews."[45] In order to restore his fortunes, he embarked on a tour with Mendoza. The two Jewish pugilists publicized their performances with language about the national importance of boxing popularized by sporting journalists. Handbills invited spectators to their exhibitions, where "a display of the *science* will have a *moral tendency* to prove unnecessary the custom of duelling."[46] Belasco also enhanced the entertainment by fighting local boxers, who may have thought they could easily dispatch the "Champion of the Jews." In the summer of 1818, when the tour reached Gloucestershire, he defeated the "Winchcomb Champion," a much larger man, in twelve minutes. At the end of the year, he fought and easily triumphed over the champion of Coventry, who had confidently bet his watch on the match.[47]

Belasco's exploits were eagerly reported in London newspapers and interest in him was renewed in the metropolis.[48] Shortly after his return, he fought and defeated Philip Sampson for 100 guineas. This success was short-lived, however. Sampson's supporters disagreed with the outcome and frustrated the Jewish fighter's attempts to make further matches. In order to generate a more reliable income, Belasco made a contract with Samuel William Hunt at the end of 1821 to hold regular sparring exhibitions along with his brother and two sisters at the Tennis Court on Great Windmill Street.[49] As part of this arrangement, he performed in the character of the Christian fighter "Gasman" Thomas Hickman in a recreation of Hickman's famous fight against William Neat. Appearing in January 1822, the first advertisement for these exhibitions announced that the performers would show "correctly and minutely every manoeuvre and exertion practised … to decide this tremendous contest."[50]

The performances attracted crowds but also public hostility. A letter to the editor of the *Weekly Dispatch* claimed that the exhibitions were "novelties … the absurdity of which, to say the least of it, is only to be equalled by various duels between cats, birds, and even an oyster."[51] *The Devil Among the Fancy*, a pamphlet attacking the performances, focused on the Jewishness of Belasco and his family. The anonymous author protested that Hunt's "principal, indeed his only scientific, exhibitors were members of a family of the *tribe of Israel*."[52] Further, the author charged that the Belasco family kept a brothel. To make matters worse, *Bell's Life in London* repeated the specious connection with prostitution in May. In response, Belasco wrote a scathing letter to the editor, claiming that he had been "wilfully [sic] misrepresented."[53] The attacks against the Tennis Court and the Belasco family were so damaging that Hunt ultimately sued Robert Bell of the *Weekly Dispatch*. Clearly, London newspapers' sympathy for Jewish boxers had limits.

APPENDIX. 607

A FINE OPPORTUNITY OFFERS
TO THE
LOVERS OF LIFE AND FUN!!!

A. BELASCO

Most respectfully invites the Amateurs from the West and East Ends of the Metropolis, to witness

THE ART OF
SELF-DEFENCE
AT THE
FIVES COURT, St. Martin's Street,
LEICESTER FIELDS,
WHICH WILL BE EXHIBITED FOR
HIS BENEFIT,
On TUESDAY, APRIL 17, 1821.

The *Out-and-Outers* on the Fighting List have promised to lend him a *hand* upon this occasion. The *Game Cocks* want no spurs to do *ABRAHAM* a service. The *Big* and *Little Coves* are all ready to set-to. And on which occasion

ALL THE FIRST-RATE PUGILISTS

Of the Day will exhibit in a variety of Scientific Combats. A. BELASCO will exert himself, therefore, to produce Lots of Amusement. *Caper-sauce* and *Bunches* of *Fives* may be had gratis; *Claret* free o, expense; and nothing charged for *Electricity*. *The*

Advertisement for a sparring benefit at the Fives Court inviting patrons from both the West End and the East End to attend. From Egan, *Boxiana*, vol. 3.

The barrage of insults against Belasco and his family placed him in a difficult situation. Vilified by the major sporting newspapers, he could not find backing for a boxing match by the end of 1822.[54] Facing this predicament Belasco went on the offensive, using his Jewish identity to help revive his career. In January 1823, Sampson challenged him to a fight for £100. Sampson hoped to erase the stain of his earlier defeat by insisting on high stakes and then proclaiming Belasco a coward when he inevitably could not raise them. To make sure the strategy would work, his public challenge included a stipulation that the stake money could not come from any Jewish sources. Seizing on Sampson's casual anti–Semitism, Belasco wrote a passionate letter to the *Weekly Dispatch* in which he cast himself as a defender of the Jews. He declared that he considered "it no disgrace to belong to a community which can boast of Mendoza and Dutch Sam." Further, he wrote that the Jewish community "ranks among Its members … gentlemen … remarkablē for their honourable and gentlemenlike conduct." He wondered if Sampson actually had the courage to fight or if the exchange was simply "idle boasting and vulgar insolence."[55] Belasco's passionate defense of the Jewish community resonated particularly with wealthier Jews, who were becoming more publicly and politically assertive in the 1820s.[56]

Although Belasco could not immediately raise the funds to fight Sampson, his strong stand against anti–Semitism helped to rescue his family's fortunes. When his brother Israel fought Birmingham boxer Arthur Matthewson in March 1823, *Bell's Life in London* commented on the large number of Jewish spectators. Strong betting on the part of Jewish gamblers drove the odds to five to four in Belasco's favor.[57] The enthusiasm also helped Abraham make a match with Irish boxer Pat Halton in April. While in January Halton had complained that "the friends of A. Belasco" did not come forward to back Belasco, in April Belasco arrived for the match in a stylish coach and, according to Pierce Egan, was well supported by "swell *Sheenies*."[58] In the riot that followed the disputed conclusion to the match, Jewish supporters of Belasco fought Irish spectators. Jews were also involved in brawls that were prompted by arguments about the outcome of the match on the following day.[59]

Jewish enthusiasm for Abraham Belasco continued through the rest of the year. When he finally fought Sampson in August, Belasco presented himself to the crowd as a defender of Jews. Before the match began, he carried a yellow handkerchief, increasingly customary as a way for Jewish boxers to identify with Jewish spectators in the 1820s.[60] There were many Jewish spectators in attendance; the *Morning Chronicle* perhaps exaggerated when it estimated that they outnumbered Christians by three to one but it is clear that a strong contingent made the journey from London. Before the fourteenth round, Sampson told Belasco that he would defeat him and "drive your Jew brother out of Birmingham." Belasco coolly responded, "You can do neither, but you are an illiberal fellow." Jewish spectators encouraged him to "remember the honour of your brethren." Although Belasco lost this match, his strategy proved effective. A week later, his Jewish backers held a benefit for him at Howard's Coffee House, in Houndsditch. A crowd of nearly two hundred paid five shillings each for entry and Belasco received most of the proceeds.[61]

Belasco's performances as a representative and defender of the Jewish community in Britain were largely responsible for his success in 1823. The *Weekly Dispatch*, however, noted that his August benefit, the culmination of his achievements, was also "a 'John Bull' sort of thing." After dinner the Chairman of the event, the well-known singer John Isaacs, gave a toast to "the King, and God bless him!" Glasses were then raised for the Duke of York and the rest of the royal family and Isaacs led the company in a song praising the British navy. The night concluded with a "Hebrew Glee," sung by Nathan Mayer Rothschild and others, and with Isaacs performing "Scotland's 'Rob Roy.'" The sentiment at the benefit prompted the *Weekly Dispatch* to remark that the "*Sheenies* are all loyal to a man."[62]

Belasco's dinner benefit illustrated some of the most important aspects of the relationship between Jews and boxing in the post-war period. Held at a coffee house in Houndsditch and attended by many important members of the Jewish community, the benefit celebrated Belasco as a symbol of the Jews in Britain. Although he represented the Jewish community, however, the company toasted the royal family and sang celebrations of British armed might. While Belasco relied on his Jewishness in order to further his career, he did so in a sport permeated with loyalist sentiments.

The proximity of Ireland to Britain put Irish boxers in a much different situation than Jewish pugilists; they enjoyed a more supportive environment in Ireland than Jewish boxers might hope for anywhere in the United Kingdom. Prizefighting had existed in Ireland nearly as long as in England and had also been revitalized in the 1780s and 1790s. As we have seen, Mendoza performed at Astley's theater in the early 1790s and a prizefighting scene was maintained in Dublin and elsewhere in the subsequent decades. Young Irish peers, such as Howe Browne, the Marquess of Sligo from 1809, patronized the sport. The Marquess was a contemporary of Byron's at Cambridge and would have been familiar with the fighting culture that shaped Byron there. He and others like him brought their interest in training and watching boxing matches to Ireland.

The enthusiasm of Sligo and his like-minded fellows provided opportunities for enterprising boxers. Veteran Irish fighter Dan Dogherty sought to capitalize in the early 1810s. As we have seen Dogherty enjoyed a moderately successful career in London between 1806 and 1811, punctuated by his receiving Byron's patronage for his fight with Tom Belcher in 1808. In 1812, he traveled to Dublin and opened a successful boxing school there.[63] Shortly thereafter, Belcher and Tom Hall (another former opponent of Dogherty) came to Dublin and opened a rival school. Belcher was well known in the Irish capital and so many of Dogherty's patrons shifted their allegiance to the two Englishmen. In an attempt to restore his fortunes, Dogherty challenged Belcher to a fight.[64] The two men met in a small valley at the Curragh in County Kildare on April 23, 1813, for a £100 prize collected by a group of Irish sporting gentlemen. The ring was made at the base of the valley and spectators sat on the sloped hillsides. Belcher arrived first, before all of the spectators had assembled, but returned to his coach to undress for the fight. While he was gone, Dogherty entered the now enclosed valley, threw his hat in the air, and shouted "Ireland forever!" The crowd answered his cry and cheered. When Belcher returned and heard what Dogherty had done, he asked one of the Irish gentlemen present to tell the crowd that he had said nothing against Ireland.[65]

The fight began after these preliminaries, with Andrew Gamble as Dogherty's second and Hall for Belcher. Belcher dominated, bludgeoning Dogherty for thirty-five minutes until his nearly lifeless body had to be carried from the ring. Belcher was uninjured and did a somersault in the ring to celebrate his victory. Despite the beating he received, all was not lost for Dogherty. The Marquess of Sligo started a subscription for him and nearly £80 was soon collected.[66] His colorful entrance to the ring underscored the fact that he was an Irish fighter facing an Englishman and encouraged the crowd to see him as representing Ireland. It surely helped him realize a windfall despite his dismal performance.

The match between Belcher and Dogherty was the first major prizefight between an English and an Irish boxer in Ireland. Other enterprising gentlemen soon sought to repeat it. Racehorse owner and celebrated bagpiper "Sporting" Captain William Kelly resided at Maddenstown House on the Curragh and was almost certainly involved in the organization of the Dogherty and Belcher bout. Kelly supposedly learned of a new fighter—an untrained Dublin carpenter named Dan Donnelly—when he saw Donnelly knock out three other men with one punch each.[67] Whatever the actual circumstances of his acquaintance with Donnelly, he soon became the carpenter's patron. Kelly formed a partnership with the brother of the famous Scottish sportsman Captain Barclay (the trainer of Tom Cribb) to train him. Barclay schooled Donnelly for several months at the residence of Kelly's brother in Calverstown. Finally, in the summer of 1814, Donnelly issued a public challenge to Tom Hall, who was still touring Ireland with Belcher. While it was not uncommon for touring boxers to face local fighters, these locals were usually untrained and always easily defeated. Indeed, odds went heavily against Donnelly before the match. Once the match was arranged, Donnelly entered into three weeks of intensive training with Barclay.[68]

The fight between Donnelly and Hall took place in September 1814 on the same spot where Belcher had defeated Dogherty the year before and forty thousand people traveled to the Curragh in coaches, on horseback, or on foot to see it. The event revealed an astonishing level of support for Donnelly in Ireland. On his appearance, the huge crowd greeted Donnelly "with thunders of applause."[69] Donnelly had the better of the more experienced Hall throughout the match, only receiving a "trifling cut on his lip." Hall fell to the ground in the fifteenth round and then walked out of the ring, claiming that Donnelly had struck a foul blow while he was down. Donnelly's supporters countered that Hall had deliberately fallen. Without a clear winner, neither man received the £200 stakes. Despite the inconclusive result, the Irish crowds interpreted the result of the fight as a victory for Donnelly. Huge celebrations testified to their support for him. Bonfires were lit in Donnelly's honor in several Dublin streets and villagers from the surrounding communities continued the festivities for days. From London the *Star* compared the atmosphere to the aftermath of a great military victory.[70]

Portrait of Dan Donnelly. The Irish Champion fought two famous matches at the Curragh in 1814 and 1815. He came to England in 1819 and defeated leading English pugilist Tom Oliver. From Egan, *Boxiana*, vol. 3.

The success of the Donnelly and Hall match prompted Kelly and Barclay to arrange a fight on November 9, 1815, between Donnelly and English boxer George Cooper, who claimed to be champion of England. The two patrons again invested a great deal of time and money training Donnelly and another large crowd traveled to the Curragh to witness the bout. A popular ballad imagined Kelly's sister stepping in the ring and telling Donnelly "Dan, my boy, what do you mean, Hibernia's son? … My coach and horse I have bet on you, Dan Donnelly."[71] When Donnelly knocked Cooper down in the first round, a shout "not unlike a fire of artillery," Pierce Egan later claimed, came from the crowd. Cooper failed to make it to the scratch after the eleventh round, ending the match. The crowd celebrated and shouts of "Victory and Ireland for ever!" were heard.[72] Donnelly's supporters preserved the footprints he made on his path to the ring. These and an obelisk erected later can be seen in "Donnelly's Hollow" today. Commentators disagreed about the extent to which the crowd's support contributed to Donnelly's victory. Both Pierce Egan and John Badcock concurred that the crowd put Cooper at a disadvantage—Egan noted that a spectator had hit Cooper's second with a rock—but only Badcock suggested that the crowd helped to determine the outcome of the match.[73] In any case, the hostility of the spectators dissuaded many English boxers from coming to Ireland. No important English boxer fought an Irish boxer in Ireland for the next ten years.

While the absence of English fighters in Ireland prevented Donnelly from again playing the role of the conquering hero in Ireland, residual support from his victory provided the former carpenter a comfortable existence for

Donnelly's Hollow at the Curragh, west of Dublin. The monument, erected with money raised through a public subscription, marks the spot where Donnelly defeated George Cooper in 1815. Author's collection.

A closer view of the monument in Donnelly's Hollow also shows the footsteps of Donnelly preserved on the hillside. Author's collection.

the next several years. Shortly after his victory over Cooper, a wealthy Irish timber merchant acquired a liquor license for Donnelly and presented him with £150 worth of wine, spirits, and porter.[74] Donnelly's fame assured that his pub was a successful venture; Dubliners came to meet and drink with the "Irish Champion" at his pub for several years after his bout against Cooper. He also periodically held well-attended exhibitions at the Olympic Theatre in Dublin.[75] Still, no English boxers would come to Ireland to fight him and he was unwilling to go to England. *The Weekly Dispatch* reported in June 1817, that Donnelly would be matched against championship claimant Jack Carter for £300 but this match never materialized.[76]

The landscape for Irish boxers in England was different than Donnelly might have imagined, however. A cohort of Irish boxers, who offered one another aid, training, and patronage, had developed after the war. Their actions shaped popular perceptions about Irish boxers and opened new possibilities. Captain Robert Barton, described by *Bell's Weekly Messenger* as "the great patron of … the Hibernian *millers*," was an important agent of this change.[77] Barton was a career officer from Tipperary whose ancestor had won a grant of land in Ireland fighting with the Earl of Essex's army in the Nine Years' War. Born in 1770, he was in Bordeaux when the French Revolution broke out and volunteered for the National Guard in 1790. He joined the British army when war was declared with France and fought against the Revolutionary armies in the Low Countries in the 1790s. He led one of the units that attempted to quell the Burdett riots in April 1810, prompted by the government's arrest of radical Sir Francis Burdett, earning him and his regiment deep unpopularity. In 1812, he led the 2nd Life Guards in the Peninsular Campaign.[78] After the war he became involved in boxing and was the leading patron of Irish boxers until at least the mid–1820s. Irish fighters in London such as Tom Reynolds and Jack Randall were his clients and, through their connection to him and to other Irish boxers, seem to have considered themselves part of a cohort of Irish pugilists in the metropolis.

Barton's protége Jack Randall became one of the best-known figures in the sport in the 1820s. Born in St. Giles of Irish parents in November 1794, Randall became a leading prizefighter after the war. Barton was his chief patron; Pierce Egan even later claimed that Barton discovered him. When Randall took ownership of the Hole in the Wall pub in 1819, Barton paid for a lavish dinner to celebrate the occasion. Randall was too small—he was about 66 inches tall and less than 150 pounds—to fight for the championship but he defeated the best boxers of his size and retired undefeated in 1821.[79] Although some later writers denied his Irish heritage, Randall emphasized it throughout his career. He often used green as his color, for example.[80] After his retirement, Randall held a benefit on St. Patrick's Day, a common practice for Irish boxers after the war.[81] These actions shaped public opinion; after Randall's most famous match, a December 1818 victory over Welsh boxer Ned Turner, the *Star* commented that "the Welsh and Irish people

Portrait of Jack Randall. The English-born Irish boxer retired undefeated and assisted other Irish fighters in the 1820s. From Miles, *Pugilistica*, vol. 1.

were at issue, and they supported their opinions strongly by their purses." The two men fought for £200 and thousands more in wagers depended on the outcome of the fight. The *Star* claimed that "hundreds were waiting at the turnpike gates along the road" for the result. The size of the crowds made authorities anxious of a riot.[82]

Even before Randall's retirement in 1821, he was an important figure in the boxing scene. His Hole in the Wall pub was one of the chief meeting places for sporting journalists, boxers, and sporting gentlemen. In 1822, he founded the "Nonpareil Club" to promote "pugilistic harmony out of the ring." Randall was also an important trainer and patron of Irish boxers. In September 1818, an "Irish lad under the patronage of Jack Randall" fought a match. Two years later, the *Weekly Dispatch* identified an Irish boxer named O'Leary as "Randall's man." In October 1820, the same newspaper announced that Randall had "a *big* and a little *Paddy*, who are ready and willing to *accommodate* any English *gemmen*." In 1822, the *Sporting Magazine* noted that a match was to be made involving an Irish boxer named Johnson, who was "under the patronage of the *Non-pareil*."[83] Randall was thus a critical figure in the transformation of boxing in the postwar period. While the patronage of Captain Barton and others like him was still important to the sport, the "professionals" like Jack Randall now took a leading role in the organization and (the attempts at) regulation of boxing.

Because of the actions of Randall and others, the landscape for Irish fighters in England was quite different when Dan Donnelly finally decided to cross the Irish Sea in 1819 than it had been when Dan Dogherty left England in 1812. Donnelly and his wife made the crossing in January 1819 and Donnelly commenced what would be a lucrative tour of England. Quickly understanding the value of explicit displays of Irish identity in England, Donnelly presented himself as a symbol of Irishness. He arrived first in Liverpool—already a center of Irish settlement in England—where he sparred with Carter in two benefits before large crowds. The two then moved on to Manchester, where they held sparring exhibitions at the Emporium Rooms. In both places, they advertised their performances with a placard announcing Donnelly as the "champion of Ireland" and Carter as the "champion of England." The advertisement was effective and "an overflowing audience was the result."

Even beyond the Irish immigrant hubs of Liverpool and Manchester, Donnelly's arrival caused a sensation. News that the Irish Champion might come to London raised anticipation to a fever pitch. Rumors spread that another boxer was impersonating him and betting on their veracity surged. Finally, after spending about a very successful month in Liverpool and Manchester, Carter and Donnelly finished their lucrative sparring exhibitions and departed for the metropolis. Journalist George Kent remarked that "Bonaparte, amongst his *vassals*, was never more courted." Donnelly received cards from many leading supporters of the London Prize Ring and was besieged by invitations.

He arrived in London on March 11 and was introduced to "the *Commander-in-Chief* of the milling forces," John Jackson, and to leading fighters, including "his phenomenal countryman" Jack Randall.[84] On March 19, he sparred at the Peacock on Gray's Inn Road before a packed house of spectators paying a three-shilling admission fee. The *Weekly Dispatch* reported that Donnelly received thunders of applause. In the following weeks, excitement continued unabated in London. A benefit for Jack Scroggins at the Fives' Court overflowed with more than one thousand spectators when rumor spread that Donnelly was scheduled to perform. Unfortunately for the packed house, he did not appear on stage, "to avoid being too public."[85] Nevertheless, Donnelly's decision to present himself as the Champion of Ireland was both strategic and highly successful. Although he had only contested two prizefights in his career and had not fought in more than three years, he was a celebrity in London.

While initially excited at the mere prospect of seeing the Irish Champion, Irish and English spectators in London quickly began to demand that Donnelly fight an English boxer. A large crowd packed the Minor Theater in March for a benefit exhibition for him. Unsatisfied after the sparring ended, the numerous spectators grew restive and demanded that Donnelly face Tom Cribb, the retired former champion who had not fought in over seven years. Even though Cribb was not in attendance, the crowd hissed as Donnelly left the stage.[86] To placate their customers, the managers of the Minor Theater promised a sparring match between Donnelly and Cribb the following week. Unfortunately Donnelly could not spar, having hurt his arm in a fall from a coach. When told the unfortunate news, the crowd booed loudly and the nervous managers, fearing a riot, forced Donnelly to appear. After he left the stage, Bill Richmond addressed the crowd on his behalf and explained that Donnelly did not intend to engage in a prizefight in England. In response, someone from the crowd shouted: "What! only to have a few benefits!" When Donnelly told the crowd that he would have to consult his backers in England and Ireland, the audience hissed. Some openly questioned his courage.[87]

The accusations of cowardice threatened to derail Donnelly's lucrative tour. His popularity among English and Irish people rested on his claim, as Champion of Ireland, to be a symbol of Ireland. The events at the Minor Theater demonstrated how tenuous his position was. If he refused to contest a prizefight, he risked losing the support he had received in the preceding months. But he could not fight just any boxer and hope to maintain his position. Black boxer Harry Sutton had challenged him to a match for £50 but, if Donnelly agreed to fight Sutton, he risked undermining his elevated status. In response to this predicament, Donnelly issued "The Irish Champion's Manifesto to the Milling World" at the beginning of April, in which he offered to fight any man in England for between one hundred and five hundred guineas.[88] The size of this public challenge restored Donnelly's credibility and saved him from having to fight the unpopular Sutton, who could never hope to receive backing for that amount. By casting doubts upon his courage, the audience at the Minor Theater threatened the image cultivated by Donnelly as the symbol of Ireland. In order to maintain his lucrative career, he needed to fight a match against a top-tier English boxer, who, it went without saying, needed to be a white Christian.

For several weeks in April, Donnelly and his backer, Captain Barton, looked for a match against a prominent English boxer to restore his reputation. Finally, he received a challenge from English boxer Tom Oliver. In order to highlight Donnelly's connection to the London Irish, Barton arranged for Jack Randall to accept the challenge on Donnelly's behalf.[89] The London sporting newspapers, which stood to benefit from a symbolic contest between Ireland and England did their part to promote the match. *Bell's Life in London* noted that the "fight excited much interest by way of nationality."[90] Similarly, the *Weekly Dispatch* remarked that the bout would be "an interesting contest—more especially as it is a national one."[91] Such characterizations of the match as a battle between England and Ireland succeeded in generating excitement among the London Irish, a number of whom opened a "subscription bank" at a public house in St. Catherine's Dock to bet in support of Donnelly. Although many of the London gamblers continued to back Oliver, Irish betting drove the odds in Donnelly's favor.[92]

On July 21, 1819, Donnelly and Oliver played out the symbolic contest between Ireland and England. Despite rain on Crawley Common, a large crowd gathered to watch the match, including a number of people who had crossed the Irish Sea. Gamblers wagered nearly one hundred thousand pounds on the outcome.[93] Entering the ring, according to the *Weekly Dispatch*, Donnelly carried "the *green colour* for Ireland," while Oliver had "the *blue* for England."[94] Jack Randall was Donnelly's second, while the English Champion, Tom Cribb, performed the same role for Oliver. This symbolism increased the partisanship among the spectators. George Kent reported that "the prejudice in favour of Oliver on Wednesday in the London ring, was such as in Ireland would not be countenanced."[95] Despite this disadvantage Donnelly defeated Oliver in little more than an hour.

The result of the match prompted great celebration among Irish people in London and in Ireland, indicating the extent to which they embraced the idea that Donnelly was a symbol of Ireland and his victory a triumph for his country. Donnelly's Irish supporters, many of whom had won considerable sums of money wagering on him, gathered to fête him at Phil Dignam's public house the evening following the fight. The crowd at Dignam's, George Kent noted, was as "thorough bred Irish as any that ever dropped down the Liffey."[96] A large crowd of Irish supporters filled the main room, "anxious to see and to congratulate him on his recent victory." According to Pierce Egan Dignam asked Donnelly to walk through the room but Donnelly resisted, angrily asking Dignam, "*Do they take me for a* BASTE, *that is to be made a* SHOW *of?*" Nevertheless, Donnelly's companions convinced him to greet his supporters—performance out of the ring could be just as important as a good show within the ropes.[97] In Ireland, Dubliners anxiously awaited news of the bout and celebrated when Donnelly won. The *Dublin Evening Post* printed a notice of his victory received by express shortly after the match, while numerous handbills touted Donnelly's win.[98]

Donnelly's triumph over Oliver and, more generally, his success in presenting himself as a symbol of Ireland provided him opportunities in England and Ireland. In August, he received two challenges to fight English pugilists, the first of which offered him £100 to fight any one of nine English boxers. Donnelly refused these challenges, however, and decided to return to Ireland. When he arrived, an Irish crowd greeted him with great fanfare and even provided him a horse to ride back to Dublin.[99] At the beginning of September, Donnelly and two English pugilists he had brought with him set up a booth at the Donnybrook Fair. Their exhibitions, restaging the great Irish victory over England for paying customers, generated a great deal of interest. A popular ballad at the Fair, for example, concluded with the lines "Where was their fun and sport? Where was the gay resort? Where Donnelly held his Court—Donnybrook Fair."[100]

Only months later, Donnelly died suddenly.[101] His tragic death once again revealed the extent to which many people in Ireland accepted him as a symbol of Ireland. His funeral in Dublin was an enormous public event at which, according to the *Weekly Dispatch*, more than eight thousand mourners paid their respects. Moving through the streets of Dublin from the deceased Irish fighter's residence to the burial ground at Bully's Acre in Kilmainham, the funeral procession included an "immense number of people, some in carriages, and some on horseback, moving in slow and measured pace." Boxing gloves sat on the front of a horse-drawn hearse.[102] The crowd grew larger as the procession traveled through the principal streets of Dublin. The Dublin-based newspaper, *Saunders's News-letter*, noted that it was "the most numerous assemblage we ever beheld."[103] A committee formed by Dublin publicans raised a subscription for a table-shaped tomb enclosed by railings. In two months, the committee raised £2,327. A local notable named Halliday contributed an epitaph to be inscribed on the tomb, which included the lines "Erin lament; bear in record his name; Lament the man who fought to crown your fame."[104] The *Dublin Journal* printed a eulogy ending with the lines "Oh! Erin's daughters, come and shed your tears on your Champion's grave, who loved you many years. To Erin's sons this day's a day of sorrow, who have we now that will defend our Curragh?" Donnelly's fame among Irish people continued to follow him after his death. Shortly after his burial, grave robbers raided his grave and removed his body.[105] Public outcry only subsided when the body was found in the home of a Dublin surgeon, who returned the body on the condition that he keep the great fighter's arm. A pub near the Curragh kept the arm on display until the 1990s and, more recently, it toured the United States with an exhibition about the history of Irish boxing.[106]

Dan Donnelly's successful career reinforced the commercial potential of the performance of Irish identity. Irish boxers recognized the value of presenting themselves as symbols of Ireland, especially by fighting matches against English pugilists. In March 1822, Donnelly's protégé Pat Halton defeated an English boxer named Johnson in front of tens of thousands of spectators outside Dublin.[107] After this fight, Halton announced that he was "open to fight any Englishman of his weight for 500 guineas."[108] Like Donnelly, however, Halton found that he had to travel to England and, in January 1823, he did so. Once there his patron William Kelly announced that he would back his client "for £500 against any man of his weight, barring a *Patlander*."[109]

Halton also presented himself as a symbol of Ireland in other ways, performing an Irish identity in order to win the support of Irish spectators. He had his first match in England against Abraham Belasco on April 8, 1823. Before the fight, he entered the ring "arm-in-arm" with Kelly and followed by his second, Jack Randall. Like Donnelly, Halton wore a green handkerchief to highlight his connection to Ireland. The Irish in attendance responded to these gestures. According to *Bell's Life in London*, the Irish spectators "took off their hats, shouted, and greeted welcome."[110] When the fight ended with a questionable blow from Belasco, the onlookers demonstrated their identification with the boxers more vividly. The umpires declared the match over, but Randall protested and a riot ensued. A group of Irishmen armed with shillelahs attacked any Jewish spectator who would not declare Halton the winner. At the same time, a group of Jewish men attacked an Irishman, took his stick, and beat him. Elite spectators, wary of the escalating riot, fled the scene.[111] While the violence did not help Halton's cause directly, he and Irish boxers like him relied on the enthusiasm that provoked it to attract paying crowds to lucrative benefits or to public houses.

The spirit of change that swept the United Kingdom after the end of the long war with France shaped the world of bare-knuckle prizefighting. Journalists like Pierce Egan and boxers such as Aby Belasco and Jack Randall increasingly replaced landed elites as the leading organizers and shapers of public perceptions of the sport. The sport that they fashioned was about identity: British, English, Irish, black, white, Jewish, and Christian. As prizefighting became more commercially oriented, and thus less dependent on the funds and whims of gentlemen, it relied on building and maintaining excitement among the public. This enthusiasm guaranteed readership for newspapers and other publications, paying customers at pubs and at sparring exhibitions, and spectators at fights. Emphasizing contests between men of different identities was a critical means to accomplish this.

The sport also remained a bastion of popular loyalism amidst a rising tide of radicalism and reform, however. The toast given by John Jackson at a benefit for Jack Randall in 1818, in which the "Commander-in-Chief" proclaimed that boxing combatted the effeminacy that was "degenerating the true character of Englishmen," reflected the sport's ongoing investment in a conservative vision of the nation.[112] Central to the commercial appeal of bare-knuckle prizefighting in the postwar period was a vision of the United Kingdom in which people of different backgrounds competed with one another within the bounds of fair play and other essential British values. As we shall see, this vision of unity in difference played a critical role in the two matches in 1824 between Irishman Jack Langan and Tom Spring—two of the most famous matches of the era.

Chapter Six

The Career of Jack Langan, Ethnic Entrepreneur

Retired pugilist Jack Langan was one of the most prominent Catholic Irishmen in the north of England in the 1830s and 1840s. One account later recalled him striding through the Liverpool Exchange "conspicuous by his white hat [and] shoulder[ing] aside the 'merchant princes' that were in his way." His base was a "palatial" inn near the Clarence Dock, a newly opened facility where most steamers crossing from Ireland now made port. A large effigy of St. Patrick high on the wall of the inn was visible from the dock and Langan kept a spacious room on the ground floor to accommodate new arrivals from Ireland. This room included "a vast fire-place, with oven, boiler, and cooking apparatus of every kind."[1] He was a "strong supporter of creed and country" and appeared onstage with Daniel O'Connell at the Adelphi Theater when the Liberator visited Liverpool in 1843.[2] Later that year, Langan led a deputation that would have represented Manchester and Liverpool at O'Connell's cancelled Clontarf mass meeting.[3] Not surprisingly, Dublin Castle suspected that his house was the center of subversive activities in Liverpool, but local authorities determined that he was "too wealthy and too prudent" to be an underground nationalist.[4] Near the end of his life Langan retired to stately Thornton Hall, which he had purchased in 1844 for £9,000.[5]

All of this was made possible by two prizefights with English Champion Tom Spring in 1824. Langan lost both matches, but many Irish people nevertheless saw him as a hero because he had fought for and nearly won the Championship of England. To win his shot at the title required Langan to be a talented self-promoter as well as a skillful pugilist. After a relatively undistinguished career in Ireland, he arrived in England in late spring 1823. With the help of his trainer and mentor Tom Reynolds and Reynolds's patron Captain Robert Barton, Langan was cast as the "Irish Champion" and both Irish and English people were encouraged to view him as a symbol of Ireland. This proved an effective strategy and, by the fall of 1823, he was matched against the English Champion. The two fights between Spring and Langan, billed as a showdown between England and Ireland, captivated the boxing world and cemented the legacy of both men.

The tense environment in Ireland in the mid–1820s contributed to the success of the two bouts. In a time of great political disquiet, as Daniel O'Connell was galvanizing a movement for Catholic Emancipation in Ireland, Langan's reputation as a defiant Catholic Irishman struck a chord with Irish Catholics. After decades of publicity for the sport in Britain and Ireland, many Irish accepted the premise that a prizefight could offer a test of one people against another. They believed that the boxing ring offered a fairer fight between the English and the Irish and that the Irish Champion would prove Irish mettle, even in defeat. Langan was also a compelling, and even comforting, figure to many in England. Sporting journalists—particularly Pierce Egan—portrayed him as a proud but loyal Irishman, who embodied what Ireland could be if only agitators would accept the beneficence of British rule. They continually underscored Langan's pride in his Irish identity while distancing him from nationalist politics. This image presented Langan as a model for political and social order at home and even a basis for Britain's preeminent position in the world. For journalists, Langan was an Irish exemplar of martial manhood and British spirit and thereby an embodiment of their loyalist ideals and the success of the Act of Union. Against the backdrop of violence in Ireland, Langan was a barrier against the forces of chaos and disorder.

This chapter examines the life and career of Jack Langan as a case study of the ways that the ways that identity was used to advance the career of a boxer, to sell publications, and to popularize the sport of bare-knuckle pugilism. The patronage of gentlemen was quite important to his success and their intervention often critical but Langan's achievement was in large measure a product of his uses of identity and, as important, the ways that others in the boxing community used Irishness and Britishness as well. Surprisingly little has been written about Langan despite his participation in two of the most famous bouts of the era and his importance in the Irish community of England after his retirement.[6] This chapter therefore also aims to describe the life of one of the most remarkable Irishmen of his generation and one that, as a minority prizefighter in England, stands beside Daniel Mendoza and Tom Molineaux.

Jack Langan's career coincided with the strongest challenge to Protestant British rule in Ireland since the 1790s. From 1821 to 1824, agrarian disorders disrupted much of Munster and parts of the other three provinces of Ireland. Agricultural prices dropped dramatically in 1818 and continued downward for the next few years, causing widespread hunger and misery. Violence, much of it done in the name of the fictional "Captain Rock," exploded in the autumn of 1821. The following February, the government passed an insurrection act, which imposed curfews and other emergency measures.[7] The disturbances often had a sectarian inflection. The prophecies of eighteenth-century English Catholic bishop Charles Walmsley (writing under the pseudonym Signor Pastorini) foretelling the violent fall of Protestantism in 1825 gained currency with many Catholic Irish in the 1820s, especially among those living in the areas of south and west Ireland most threatened by the agricultural crisis of the early 1820s. By the end of 1824, Protestant fears reached a fever pitch. Many refused even to attend church on Christmas.[8] In 1825, both houses of Parliament created committees to determine the causes of the disorder. Popular discontent in Ireland was more serious and widespread in 1823 and 1824 than at any time since the great rebellion of 1798.

It was the achievement of Daniel O'Connell to shape this profound discontent into a campaign for Catholic Emancipation. By the middle of the decade, much of the energy behind the agrarian violence was being "funneled into an open, nonviolent crusade for political rights."[9] In January 1824, O'Connell vastly expanded membership in the Catholic Association, becoming the "undisputed leader of militant Catholicism" and galvanizing a national movement that would ultimately deliver Catholic Emancipation.[10] His success owed much to his larger-than-life personality and his reputation as a defiant and unapologetic Catholic. The tremendous support for Jack Langan in 1823 and 1824 drew from the same spring. In this highly charged political environment, his challenge to the English Champion carried powerful symbolic weight. Indeed, both Langan and O'Connell's success in the 1820s can be seen as embodying the appeal of Catholic assertiveness in the face of Protestant and English oppression.

Like O'Connell, Langan the man cannot be wholly separated from Langan the symbol. In stark contrast to the Liberator, however, little can be known with certainty about the life of the Irish Champion. Nearly all that can be established about him before his arrival in England comes from one source: an extended memoir written by Pierce Egan on the occasion of Langan's first fight with Tom Spring. Egan knew Langan well and so likely learned about his early life directly. Still, Egan told the story of his early years as a parable about the congruity between self-conscious but loyal Irishness and the values that Egan argued were central to Britishness. In short, Egan's life of Langan served a pedagogical purpose: to show readers how Irishmen could be good Britons. With the great rebellion of 1798 still in living memory, violent agrarian disturbances and sectarianism unsettling the present, and O'Connell inspiring a new movement for Catholic Emancipation, this was no small matter.

Langan was born in Clondalkin in May 1798, in the midst of the great rebellion of that year.[11] According to Egan's account, a group of United Irishmen tried "to get possession of a powder-mill, within fifty yards of his daddy's edifice" shortly after the future boxer's birth. This may be true—there was fighting near Clondalkin in May 1798—but Egan avoided any further potentially uncomfortable discussion of the rebellion by focusing instead on the figure of Langan's nurse, a stereotypical old Irishwoman named Judy O'Shaughnessy. O'Shaughnessy, Egan wrote, simply considered the commotion a bad omen that Jack "was born to make a great noise in the world." Egan then described how the young Langan sought out O'Shaughnessy in her cabin, where she would amuse him with humorous stories and dispense folksy wisdom. In this way Egan connected Langan with a comical and apolitical Irishness, a comforting caricature familiar from literature and the London stage.[12] Later in Langan's childhood, the family moved to the poor Dublin suburb of Ballybough and the future boxer spent his youth there learning to fight in brawls with the young men of "Mud Island." His parents were grocers and earned enough money to bring up a number of children "respectably."[13]

After establishing Langan's loyal Irish credentials, Egan's account shifted to show the ways in which the young Irishman embodied British heroism. In 1811, at a critical juncture of the campaign in Portugal and Spain, Langan "persuaded his father" to let him join a merchant ship bound for Lisbon. When he arrived in the Portuguese capital, two local men attacked him with a stiletto. Langan "made the cowards run before him" and, though he was wounded, "his courage ... did not desert him for an instant." As we have seen, William Cobbett and other proponents of boxing frequently contrasted the image of cowardly stiletto-wielding southern Europeans with courageous Britons. Even as he gave the unfortunate Portuguese a dose of British manliness, however, Langan remained a proud Irishman. On the return trip, he fought a messmate named Dunn who had insulted Ireland. After soundly beating Dunn, Egan told his readers, Langan shouted "Erin go Bragh" and began to sing the closing stanza from the popular song "Murdock Delany's Birth."[14] This song borrowed the name of the stage Irish character in William MacCready's popular 1793 play *The Irishman in London; or, the Happy African*, which, like others of its time, offered a whimsical comparison of Irish and African servants.[15] Egan's invention of this bit of color again connected Langan to non-threatening stage Irishness.

Langan soon decided to leave the merchant navy and return to Ballybough. There he became a sawyer's apprentice and started to pursue prizefighting more seriously. By the end of the war, he had defeated his rivals from Mud Island and had begun to face the best Dublin boxers. In his account of these matches, Egan emphasized Langan's courage and honor. One of the first important bouts was against a well-known Dubliner named Norman. According to Egan, Langan and Norman had agreed to fight on a Thursday. Norman, the owner of a jaunting car business, dishonestly announced that the fight was scheduled for the preceding Sunday and made a tidy profit when his cars carried hundreds of people to the scene of the match on that day. Norman then feigned surprise when Langan did not appear. After hearing of this attack on his honor, Langan found Norman at a tavern and "with more courage than propriety [and] without hesitation," publicly accused him of the swindle. Norman, his brothers, and his father together fell upon Langan and nearly killed him. Nevertheless, when Thursday arrived, Langan defeated Norman despite not being able to use his right arm. In another episode, Langan even challenged the great Dan Donnelly to a fight, "with more courage than prudence," after a dispute over the stakes for a match with Donnelly's protégé Pat Halton.[16] In Egan's telling, Langan repeatedly defended his honor without regard to the risk of bodily harm. The idea of incautious courage as a critical manly trait had a long pedigree, especially in accounts of the exploits of military heroes from General Wolfe to Admiral Nelson.[17]

Langan continued to advance his fighting career in 1818 and 1819, defeating several boxers before large crowds at different locations to the west and south of Dublin. In May 1819, he won a match against Owen McGowran of Donnybrook at the Curragh in the spot made famous by Donnelly a few years before. A story printed in the *Dublin Journal* described large crowds coming down to the Curragh from Dublin "in vehicles of every kind" and from other parts of Kildare and Wicklow on foot to watch the fight.[18] With his victory over McGowran, Langan was acknowledged as one of the leading pugilists in Ireland. He then confronted the same issue as Dan Donnelly in 1815: he could not make a match in Ireland and did not wish to travel to England.

Faced with this problem, Langan decided to leave Ireland again. Rather than cross the Irish Sea, however, he and his brother joined a legion raised by Irish adventurer John Devereux in 1819 to fight with rebels in Venezuela. Devereux, a Wexford native who played a small role in the 1798 rebellion and then became a Baltimore-based coffee merchant and blockade-runner, met Símon Bolívar in Cartagena as Devereux was delivering arms to rebels in Columbia. He told Bolívar that he had been a leader of the 1798 rebellion and offered to raise a legion in Ireland for his cause. He was promised $175 for each soldier brought to South America. After returning to Ireland, he posed as a companion of Bolívar and received substantial support, including from

Daniel O'Connell.[19] Thousands of volunteers joined Devereux's legion, most of them war veterans enticed by rumors of available land in South America. Langan and his brother joined a rifle regiment led by Colonel Meade and began the crossing in summer 1819 with one thousand other Irishmen on board the *Charlotte Gambier*. At the end of September, the regiment arrived on the island of Margarita, where they joined a disease-riddled English squadron with which they had to compete for provisions. Devereux did not accompany his troops, arrange supplies for them at Margarita, or even bother to tell the military leaders in Venezuela that they were coming. As a result, the troops suffered tremendously—disorder, disease, hunger, and a Spanish attack ravaged the men before the survivors were evacuated across the Atlantic. Infamous in Europe, Devereux ended his days living on a Venezuelan pension in the United States.[20]

For Egan, Langan's role in this ill-fated expedition was evidence of the pugilist's honor, courage, and perseverance. He joined it because Devereux and his agents "roused in his breast … a sympathy for the American sons of Liberty." Langan desired to fight for the cause of freedom rather than for a promise of material gain and so endured a difficult Atlantic crossing "without a murmur," unlike his greedy and grumbly shipmates. Even the tragic death of Langan's brother at Trinidad was grist for Egan's mill. He claimed that the brother had been part of the crew on Admiral Nelson's flagship HMS Victory, linking Langan (through his brother) to the touchstone of Napoleonic-era heroism: Nelson's martyrdom at Trafalgar.[21]

When the *Charlotte Gambier* arrived at Margarita, the crew discovered that food was in short supply and disease was rampant. While many other men died, Langan miraculously "defied all the horrors by which he was surrounded, and never enjoyed a better state of health." Not content to simply survive, the pugilist and two companions selflessly snuck into the hostile interior of the island to steal a pig for their crew to eat. The squealing pig aroused the residents of the neighborhood, however, who came out to confront the thieves. Langan's two companions fled, but "*running away* from the scene of action was so contrary to the feelings of our hero" that he did not follow. Instead he hid in a thicket, while his pursuers thrust bayonets into the brush. One of these blows plunged a bayonet into Langan's thigh. At this point, Egan asked his readers to "judge of the feelings of Langan." Langan's "*game* was put to the test. To *cry* out would have cost him his life." Of course, the courageous Langan managed to keep quiet and eventually hobbled back to join the rest of the crew.[22] As when Egan described Langan confronting Norman in Dublin, this story demonstrated a reckless neglect for his own safety that connected Langan with courageous British heroes of the past.

In Egan's account, the Irishman Langan was also an ambassador of British values among the "natives" of Margarita. Meade, Langan's commanding officer, knew that he was a prizefighter and arranged with the admiral of another ship for the Irish boxer to fight that ship's boatswain, a man named Jack Power. In the match Langan pummeled Power, undoubtedly winning money for Meade. For Egan, however, the bout had a far more important purpose: demonstrating British courage for the natives. He approvingly noted that the inhabitants of Margarita "appeared highly pleased with the above manly exhibition" and that they "profited by such a display of TRUE COURAGE, over the *stiletto* and the knife; the treacherous weapons generally used amongst the natives."[23] This fanciful description of Langan's fight with Power is contradicted by other accounts of Margarita, which depict drunken men roaming the streets and unruly crowds turning up for disorganized duels and brawls in the days and months after the arrival of the Irish legion.[24] Egan was not interested in precise realism, of course; as elsewhere in his description of Langan's life, his purpose was to demonstrate that the Irish pugilist embodied core British values. In this case, the critical idea was the way in which the values supposedly embodied by boxers might "civilize" natives. Writing in 1824, as British merchants and statesmen were preparing to exploit opportunities in a number of newly independent South American nations, this account would have been particularly relevant to his readers.

The appalling conditions on Margarita prompted Langan—like many others in the Irish legion—to desert his unit. He made his way to Trinidad and found work on a ship belonging to a merchant named Mr. Jewell. From his labors for Jewell and at least one other prizefight, he earned enough money for passage to Cork, where he arrived some time in 1821. He ultimately returned to Dublin and became a publican at a house in North King Street that bore the motto "Quiet when stroked, fierce when provoked."[25] Langan did not return to prizefighting immediately but, when a soldier from Wicklow named Robert Hanlon issued a public challenge to "any man in England or elsewhere ... except his own countrymen" for 300 guineas, he responded. Disingenuously claiming to be "a young man of humble habits, never professing the art or science of pugilism," he offered to fight Hanlon or any other man.[26] Hanlon does not seem to have answered the challenge, however, and Langan did not have a match in 1822.

Enterprising Irish fighters like Hanlon understood the money to be made from a match with an English boxer but, after Donnelly's victories in 1815, most English pugilists would not fight in Ireland. Fame and wealth as a prizefighter therefore meant crossing the Irish Sea. Langan finally did so in 1823, but not in circumstances entirely of his own choosing. On February 15 of that year, he appeared in the Court of Common Pleas in Dublin to answer charges brought by a dairyman named Flynn, who demanded £500 for the seduction of his daughter Catherine. He claimed that Langan had seduced Catherine with a promise of marriage and then deserted her to wed another woman. Langan's sister Cecilia testified for the defense. She admitted that the affair had occurred but explained that her brother was too ashamed of his life as a prizefighter to follow through on his promise to Catherine. She also claimed that Catherine knew Langan was betrothed, implying that she was a cynical opportunist rather than a victim of seduction. A priest's testimony that he had officiated at Langan's wedding and that the fighter had sworn that he was not promised to another woman seems to have been decisive, however, and, after considering the sordid affair, the jury awarded Mr. Flynn £100 and court costs.[27]

Not surprisingly, Egan's account of this episode differed from the testimony in court. In cheekily suggestive language, he claimed that the dairyman's daughter offered the "cream of her dairy … as a present to our hero to embellish his tea tackle … and frequently ALONE!" She pursued the charming fighter until he could not resist; Langan, Egan wrote, "was the seduced" in the relationship. No mention was made of Langan's marriage and his possible deception of Flynn. Unfortunately for the humble boxer, the jury awarded the plaintiff £100, which "induced Jack once more to quit Ould Ireland and try his luck in 'Merry England.'"[28] Once again, Egan highlighted the happy and timeless simplicity of the Irish, turning Catherine Flynn's misfortune and Jack Langan's alleged duplicity into a light-hearted tale of misguided young lovers. His emphasis on Langan's disappointment at the "treachery of a perfidious friend" provided a convenient explanation for the boxer's first journey to England, a voyage that, in reality, was likely motivated by his need to raise money for the substantial fine assessed by the jury.

Langan's exodus may have also been instigated in part by members of the growing network of Irish boxers and patrons in England. Once there, he certainly profited from their assistance. He arrived in Liverpool soon after the conclusion of the Flynn trial and lingered in Lancashire, staying at Irish fighter Peter Crawley's house in Manchester. While there he also renewed a connection with Irish pugilist Tom Reynolds, who would play a critical role in Langan's meteoric rise to fame. Langan had met and trained with Reynolds the previous year in Ennis, County Clare.[29] In England, Reynolds quickly became a manager of sorts for Langan, writing letters, making connections, and arranging fights. Reynolds understood the opportunities available for an Irish boxer in England; he had contested several prizefights since 1817 and was a protégé of the "the great patron of … the Hibernian *millers*," Robert

Barton.[30] In a letter written several months later to *Pierce Egan's Life in London*, Reynolds described how he began to train Langan and "introduced him to some Gentlemen Patrons of my own, and begged they would extend their patronage to him." These patrons almost certainly included Barton, who agreed to support Langan, provided Reynolds would "teach him to fight a little better."[31] Reynolds and Langan accomplished this and raised Langan's profile among the Lancashire Irish by engaging in a number of sparring exhibitions in Liverpool and Manchester.

Soon Reynolds arranged a fight between Langan and local boxer Matt Vipond.[32] The large and slow Vipond was understood to be an inferior boxer who Langan could easily defeat. Vipond's patron, a Manchester publican, apparently even told Reynolds that he knew his man would be beaten, but that excitement about the match would assure large crowds at his house.[33] The two fighters met on Wednesday, April 30 in a natural amphitheater in what is now the Peak District National Park. Five thousand spectators, many of them probably having made the thirty-mile journey from Manchester, turned up to watch the match. Egan wrote that the crowd was "the greatest body ever collected at one time for such a purpose in that part of the kingdom."[34] The *Manchester Guardian* agreed, claiming that the "fight excited more interest in Lancashire and the surrounding counties, than any thing of the kind that has happened in the recollection of the oldest man." More importantly for Reynolds and Langan, observers noted that the match was "a kind of war between England and Ireland." The Manchester Irish attended in large numbers to support Langan and wagered heavily on him, while many English supported Vipond. Langan won easily, laughing and interacting with the crowd throughout the match while the Irish spectators cheered and threw their hats in the air. After the fight, Langan "was exultingly carried by the Boys of Shillelah on their shoulders to his carriage."[35]

The enthusiastic support of the Lancashire Irish and Langan's performance against Vipond convinced he and Reynolds to aim higher. While Langan was in Dublin to settle his debts, Reynolds wrote a cordial challenge to Tom Spring in Langan's name. The English Champion ignored it.[36] In September, Reynolds sent a letter to the *Weekly Dispatch* announcing that Langan had financial backing to fight Bob Burn, Tom Oliver, Dick Acton, or Philip Sampson. The letter requested that, if any of these fighters were interested, they send a reply to retired fighter Bob Gregson's house in Liverpool.[37] None of the four pugilists bothered to answer the polite entreaty. Even a reprise of his match with Vipond fell through.[38] At the end of the summer of 1823, then, Langan and Reynolds were at an impasse. Langan certainly had the support of the Lancashire Irish and he probably had a promise of financial backing from Barton as well. Yet he could not get a match with a leading English boxer.

While Langan and Reynolds were in this predicament in early autumn, an opportunity for a different strategy appeared. In August and September Spring was on a sparring tour in the north of England with Tom Cribb and was engaged by the manager of the Manchester Theater to perform in his venue. To promote the event, the theater posted placards describing Spring as the Champion of England and announcing that he "was ready to fight any man in the world."[39] Seizing this opportunity, Langan and Reynolds responded. A letter signed by Langan began provocatively: "As you have taken on yourself, the title of Champion of England," implying that Spring's title had not been earned. Spring took the bait and replied. In a sharply worded letter, he referred to the earlier challenge and noted that Langan did not "understand what silant [sic] contempte means." He then charged that Langan had no intention of fighting but only wished to brag that the Champion of England was afraid to meet him. These were the tactics of a "sholl [school] boy," Spring wrote. He closed by agreeing to a match for the huge sum of £1,000 midway between Manchester and London.

A long response signed by Langan upped the ante. Claiming that Spring was an unworthy successor to the "manly Cribb," the letter attacked his prizefighting career, including Spring's loss to "the one-armed cripple Ned Painter" and his "great girl fight" with Jack Carter. Further, the letter argued that Spring was only interested in money and suggested that his demand for £1,000 stakes proved it. The letter positioned Langan, in contrast, as a humble Irishman without the resources to raise £500, noting that "money with me is the least consideration … only name the place and you will find me your humble ser-

Portrait of Tom Spring. The English Champion in the early 1820s, Spring reached the pinnacle of his career with two victories over Irishman Jack Langan in 1824. From Egan, *Boxiana*, vol. 3.

vant."[40] Langan, who had rapidly risen to prominence by appealing to the Irish of Manchester, now claimed the right to judge the Champion by the standards of British manhood.

Langan and Reynolds's audacious strategy worked. The three letters were made public on October 6 and, though Spring later claimed that his note had been altered, it was clear that Langan had won the public relations contest. Sporting journalist John Badcock later wrote that the "manly manner" in which Langan challenged Spring "cannot but claim the admiration of all the lovers of true courage."[41] On October 10, four days after the publication of their correspondence, Spring and Langan signed a contract to fight for £600 between Manchester and London.[42] Langan only managed to raise £200 in Manchester and so, while Spring began training for the match, he returned to Dublin to raise the final £100. To do so, he again cast himself as a symbol of his country, promising "a feast for the honour of Ireland" in the match. He found a receptive audience in Dublin; most of the £100 was collected before he arrived. The *Dublin Journal* also reported that Langan would be handsomely rewarded on his planned return to the Irish capital for St. Patrick's Day.[43] Irish enthusiasm for the fight was matched in England. According to *Bell's Life in London*, the bout "excited a greater degree of interest in the Sporting World, than any previous contest since the memorable engagement between Cribb and Molineaux."[44]

All of this excitement came at a good time for the sport. Corruption and scandal in the early 1820s had created a public image problem and an opening for bare-knuckle prizefighting's many critics. In October 1822, future champion Jem Ward deliberately lost a high-profile match against Bill Abbott. A few weeks later, a controversy involving the stakes for another match prompted John Jackson to say that he would never act as stakeholder again. The following August, two months before Langan and Spring agreed to a match, the "Commander-in-Chief" announced that he would no longer act as a master of ceremonies at prizefights. As Dennis Brailsford has shown, Jackson never fully absented himself from the sport, but nevertheless its image was tarnished.[45]

Potentially even more damaging to boxing was the case of Jack Thurtell. Thurtell, the son of a prominent merchant and mayor of Norwich, had come to London in 1819. In the metropolis he became a notorious gambler. A familiar face at prizefights, he was known to have attempted to fix a number of matches. The failure of these and a number of other schemes threatened him with ruin by 1823.[46] Frustrated and desperate, Thurtell and two accomplices brutally shot, bludgeoned, and slit the throat of a man named William Weare, who allegedly had cheated him of £300 in a game of cards, near Watford.[47]

Soon after the murder, two laborers found the weapons used to commit the crime. After a short investigation, magistrates captured Thurtell and his accomplices.

When news of the murder and of Thurtell's involvement reached London, it caused a sensation. The brutality of the crime and the fact that Thurtell was the son of a prominent businessman—Egan wrote that he "was viewed as a young man of integrity" when he first arrived in London—prompted public debate about the negative influence of London sporting culture on young gentlemen.[48] The Thurtell scandal seemed to demonstrate that, far from teaching men the values of courage and fortitude, prizefighting culture corrupted young men. In the last months of 1823, London newspapers were filled with information about the investigation and trial. Opponents of boxing used Thurtell's association with the sport as a means to attack it.[49] The *Times* harshly criticized "that infamous crew in the metropolis who compose what is termed 'the Fancy.'" They lacked "any moral tie of principal" and were a "desperate and marauding" confederacy.[50] A letter that appeared the following day applauded the *Times*'s strong stance against boxing and gambling, noting that "working men" made up the vast majority of crowds at prize-fights. They deprived "their families of their support" by attending boxing matches and were on "the high road (as recent circumstances have proved) to ruin."[51] These sentiments, suggesting that boxing made men less apt to perform their proper roles, repeated those of evangelical critics in the first decade of the century.

Thurtell was found guilty and executed on January 9, 1824. His hanging in Hereford was a huge public spectacle attended by some 15,000 people.[52] The *Times* used the occasion to resume its attack on boxing, blaming Thurtell's criminality on "his predilection for prize-fighting."[53] This direct link between pugilism and murder prompted a lengthy response in the *Weekly Dispatch*. In the same issue as an account of the fight between Spring and Langan, a column expounded on the benefits of boxing and especially the importance of the sport in fostering peace in Ireland. Pugilism was not a haven for criminals, but a model of manly behavior for the Irish, many of whom were very interested in the fight between Spring and Langan. In Ireland, it was claimed the manner of resolving differences "was for many years as irrational and savage as it was possible to conceive any thing to be." Many Irish men engaged in pistol duels, settling their disputes "in that *honourable* way," while Irish peasants after "getting drunk at fairs and other public meetings … recollect some old grudge which their ancestors entertained for each other" and then beat one another with cudgels. The article concluded with the hope that demonstration of the "most manly of our national customs" at the Spring and Langan fight would have a positive impact on Irish spectators.[54]

Depiction of the first match between Spring and Langan, at Worcester racecourse in January 1824. The grandstand and the masts of ships on the nearby River Severn are visible. The date on the print is inaccurate—the fight was actually contested on January 6—as is the image of the stage. Spring and Langan fought on the ground and the crowd broke the ring early in the match. From Miles, *Pugilistica*, vol. 2.

The public debate about boxing occasioned by the Thurtell scandal had little direct impact on the match between Jack Langan and Tom Spring, preparations for which had began in late 1823. The Pugilistic Club, with Egan and John Jackson (still active behind the scenes) in the lead, looked for a suitable location to stage what they hoped would be a huge spectacle somewhere between London and Manchester. They negotiated with representatives of a number of communities in the Midlands but, by the end of the year, had failed "to complete the contract upon suitable terms." This was because Jackson and Egan looked not only for a guarantee that local authorities would not stop the match but also for a substantial cash payment for the right to host it. A number of communities were considered but they could not meet both conditions. The Pugilistic Club negotiated with Melton Mowbray, for example, but magisterial interference seemed likely. Warwick was a safer choice but the town representatives only offered £40 and their "shabby proposition" was rejected. Egan and Jackson also turned down a few other "more liberal" proposals before settling on the Worcester racecourse. A group of

Worcester publicans agreed to pay the club £200 and, though the local magistrates circulated a handbill announcing that they would swear in special constables to prevent the match, Lord Deerhurst convinced them to reconsider.[55]

Since the justices of Worcestershire had agreed to permit the fight, enterprising locals made elaborate advance preparations. Mr. Share, the clerk of the Worcester racecourse, hired workers to build an additional grandstand. He posted a handbill around the city advertising tickets in the permanent grandstand for half a guinea and seats in two temporary structures on either side of it for ten shillings. He ultimately sold five thousand. In the middle of a larger "outer ring" there was a twenty-four-foot square fighting ring that was raised two feet above the turf. Workers placed six inches of sod on top of the planks and then covered it with sawdust. Spectators unwilling or unable to pay Share's prices watched the fight in deep, muddy slush beyond the outer ring. Ships moored in the adjacent River Severn also filled with spectators, who climbed their masts in an attempt to see the match. Temporary stands were erected on the top of wagons to provide a view for others. The racecourse filled so completely by ten o'clock in the morning that no spot could be had at any price. The inns of Worcester also did a brisk business, accommodating spectators arriving from London and, in some cases, from Ireland. Not surprisingly, innkeepers charged exorbitant sums for those beds that were available.[56]

Expectations of an economic windfall were not disappointed and crowds as large as those at any other prizefight of the period descended on Worcester. Egan reported that thirty thousand spectators attended on the raw and rainy Tuesday in early January. Other sources claimed that fifty thousand spectators were at the match that would "decide to whom the enviable distinction of 'Champion of England,' and of 'Ireland,' was to belong." Nobility and gentry from around the Kingdom were at the Worcester racecourse as well. The preparations and the huge crowds made for a festival atmosphere; Worcester was alive with the sound of blowing horns and ringing bells while flags were hung on the masts and ribbons on the sails of the vessels in the Severn. At half past twelve, Spring arrived and threw his hat in the air amidst loud cheers. He wore a fashionable blue dress coat, a brown overcoat, and jockey boots. Lord Deerhurst, an MP and the future Earl of Coventry, was his referee. Sir Henry Goodricke, a leading patron of horseracing who was soon to inherit a massive estate in Ireland, was Langan's referee and William Berkeley, the illegitimate first son of the 5th Earl of Berkeley and a well-known (and, to some, notorious) sportsman, was the umpire. All of these men and the massive crowd waited impatiently for Langan to arrive.

Langan's appearance was delayed by disaster. At ten minutes past one, as Spring and his attendants stood in the ring, the hastily constructed temporary stands to the right of the permanent grandstand collapsed. Nearly two thousand spectators (including a "Noble Lord") fell as much as twenty feet to the ground.[57] A great many people suffered scrapes and broken bones and a London livery stable-keeper and singer named James Treby later died from his injuries. Langan, who had arrived shortly after the collapse, was unable to make his way through the crowd until boxer Harry Holt called for the spectators to part. Another row of benches, holding at least one thousand more spectators, fell shortly after the match began but luckily no one was seriously injured. In its report of the fight, *Bell's Life in London* offered a withering criticism of Mr. Share. Without mentioning him by name, the paper poured scorn on "the person or persons, who, for their own exorbitant profits, admitted four thousand people on a temporary scaffolding without looking to its proper stability."[58]

Langan finally made his appearance and threw his hat in the air nearly one hour after Spring's arrival. As was customary, each second tied his fighter's colors to one of the stakes forming the ring. Spring used blue to represent Bristol, while Langan had black rather than the green more typical of Irish boxers. As we shall see, Egan claimed that Langan declined to use green because he believed that he was not important enough to represent Ireland. Nevertheless, *Bell's Life in London* assumed that the color was a dark green, "emblematical of the 'brightest gem of the western wave.'"[59] The two men then shook hands, stripped off their clothes, and appeared at the scratch twenty minutes before 2 o'clock.

Once the fighting began the two boxers seemed evenly matched. The overcrowded and makeshift venue affected the outcome of the fight, however, when partisan spectators in the muddy slush beyond the outer ring interfered. As was typical at large matches, boxers who were members of the Pugilistic Club were stationed outside the fighting ring with horsewhips and cudgels to keep the crowd at bay. Since stages were rarely erected in the nineteenth century, this helped keep spectators from influencing the result of a prizefight. At the Worcester racecourse, however, the tightly packed crowd quickly broke the outer ring and, beginning in the sixth round, overwhelmed the whip-wielding pugilists and surged into the inner ring. By the seventeenth round, few spectators could see the fight.[60] After an hour, the melee had reduced the ring to a space of several yards and the boxers were barely able to separate from the crowd. Although there is no direct evidence that the chaos gave an advantage to Spring, some in the crowd thought that Langan was being cheated of a possible victory. *The Sporting Magazine* reported, for example, that an Irishman hit Lord Deerhurst with a shillelagh and, when told that he had hit a nobleman, replied "Devil may care! All I want is fair play for Jack Langan!"[61]

The match continued for two and a half hours during which Spring steadily gained an advantage even after shattering bones in both hands. By the final rounds, very little space remained for the two boxers to move. Berkeley announced that he would no longer be responsible for the match and left the ring. In the midst of confusion after the final round, boxer Josh Hudson—who was Langan's second along with Reynolds—conveyed to Lord Deerhurst that Langan could fight no more. Langan, sitting on Reynolds's knee, said that he could continue. The appeal went to Deerhurst, who was the only authority remaining. He ruled that Langan had not appeared at the scratch in time and had therefore lost the match. Spring left the ring to "Thunders of applause" and jumped over the ropes of the outer ring before departing the racecourse in Deerhurst's coach. Langan was left behind, shouting "I am not beaten!"[62]

Immediately after the fight, Langan and Reynolds began to campaign for a rematch. Like Mendoza and Molineaux before him, Langan claimed that a partisan crowd had treated him unfairly. A number of newspapers published a letter from Langan arguing that he had been treated "in a manner that will throw disgrace on the English ring." He claimed that English spectators kicked and punched him while he was down and that "Molineux's treatment was fair play in comparison."[63] Reynolds followed this with a long letter in his own name "To the Sporting World" that expanded on these themes. He repeated the charge that the crowd had attacked Langan but added that, in the chaos, Spring's seconds and the prizefighters of the Pugilistic Club had also acted unfairly, saving Spring from falling and even striking Langan. In contrast, when "a poor Irishman … attempted to fan Langan with his hat," one of the fighters threatened to punch him. Reynolds also accused Langan's second Josh Hudson of betting against Langan. All of this happened, Reynolds argued, because Langan was Irish. He claimed it was widely known before the fight that the ring would be broken and that "the Irishman would not be allowed to win." Provocatively, he suggested that the vaunted fair play and equality of boxing—a key part of the argument for the importance of the sport—had been found wanting at the Worcester racecourse. He compared Langan to Molineaux, adding that Langan was "not a black, but unfortunately he is an Irishman; and that is a fault which has decided the battle against him." Spring was obligated to fight Langan on a stage as Cribb had done in his second fight with Molineaux, Reynolds concluded.[64] Whereas Langan and Reynolds had used Langan's Irish identity to build a following for Langan in England in 1823, they now drew on the ideals of prizefighting to win a rematch.

Spring and his supporters responded immediately, attempting to refute Reynolds's charge that Langan had been defeated because he was Irish. In a public letter, Spring claimed that Reynolds's invocation of identity only perpetuated "this invidious distinction between Englishmen and Irishmen." "Are we not all countrymen?" he asked.[65] Similarly, a letter to the *Weekly Dispatch* from "One of the Old School" argued that Reynolds's letter "stigmatises the character of Englishmen, and attempts to keep up an invidious distinction between [English people and] the inhabitants of the Sister Kingdom." The letter writer contended that Langan had had his opportunity and had lost. A letter from J.D. in the same edition of the *Weekly Dispatch* also argued that Spring had won fairly and had proven that he was Champion regardless of whether he was English or Irish.[66] The three letters defended the impartial fairness of boxing and attempted to shift the blame of partisanship from the crowd at the Worcester racecourse to Reynolds. Langan and Reynolds were unhappy with the result, they implicitly claimed, and so resorted to spurious claims of unfair treatment.

Despite this support for his position, it was becoming clear that Spring would fight Langan again. Indeed, Langan and Reynolds had begun negotiating with Spring and his supporters to arrange a second bout by the beginning of February. In Cheltenham, where he had traveled after recuperating in Worcester, Langan met with his patrons, including Robert Barton and John O'Neill of Antrim, another army officer, an MP, and a future Viscount. These men and others presented him with £50 and agreed to stake the £500 the Spring had demanded to fight again.[67] Reynolds traveled to London on February 2 with a £50 deposit to try to reach an agreement with Spring but the Champion initially refused the challenge. Langan then arrived on February 6 and, the following Monday, the two Irishmen went to Tom Belcher's Castle Tavern pub to meet Spring. Although Spring agreed to fight for £1,000, he refused to do so on a stage. Langan responded by again equating himself with Molineaux and the two left without having reached an agreement.[68]

Protracted negotiations continued in the following weeks, the main point of disagreement being whether the two would fight on a stage. Gentlemen amateurs continued to play an important role—the stake money for both men came from wealthy landed elites—but boxers and the newspaper press were central to the making of the second match. Reynolds continued his campaign in the press throughout the month. On February 17, he wrote a letter again making the argument that a partisan crowd helped defeat Langan. The Irish fighter, Reynolds argued, was "in the same situation that Molineaux was" and so needed to fight the Champion on the stage to assure that "it will be fair for one as for the other." Reynolds's letter was addressed from the Tom Belcher's Castle Tavern, where the backers of Langan and Spring had held another inconclusive meeting.[69] Reynolds again sought to break the impasse by appealing to a sense of fairness. Reynolds and Langan kept up the pressure for the rest of the month. At a sparring exhibition, for example, Langan addressed a large crowd and, placing his hand on his heart, promised "on the honour of an Irishman" to make a good showing against Spring if the Champion would consent to fight him on a stage.[70] Spring finally relented at the end of February, announcing that he could "bear the bullying of this Langan no longer" and that he would fight on a stage for £500.[71]

Langan and Reynolds profited handsomely from the publicity surrounding these negotiations. The two men commenced a very successful three-day run at the Surrey Theatre on February 13. *The Weekly Dispatch* noted that they were greeted with "thunders of applause (chiefly from their warm hearted countrymen)" and that the "sons and the daughters of 'the green Isle of Erin,' who were present, appeared in rapture with [Langan's] appearance." The newspaper also reported a probably fictional conversation between an Irishman named Dennis, who claimed that Langan would "bate any thing alive in the shape of a man" and an Englishman, who defended Spring.[72] A benefit exhibition at the Tennis Court the following week generated a windfall for Langan and Reynolds. Before the boxers arrived, "an immense crowd of the humbler classes of pugilistic amateurs" gathered in anticipation of his arrival, forming "an avenue along the pavement through which those approaching the Court had to pass." More than eight hundred people crowded inside to watch Langan and others spar. On St. Patrick's Day, Reynolds and Langan held another benefit exhibition at the Fives Court. A large number of Irishmen turned up for the event, "whose hats were decorated with the 'Chosen leaf of bard and chief, Old Erin's native shamrock.'"[73] The two likely shared over £100 from each benefit and many hundreds more from gifts and other performances since the match.[74]

Langan and Reynolds continued to profit from sparring exhibitions in March and April, including a lucrative trip to Manchester and Liverpool. On April 12 Langan arrived in Dublin, where crowds greeted him in the streets.[75] He told the audience at a benefit at the Fishamble Street Theatre on April 22 that he would "support the honour of his country while he lived." The crowd responded with exclamations of "may the lord love the Irish!"[76] By the time of this performance, however, Reynolds's name no longer appeared with Langan's; the two boxers had fallen out over money in early April. In a letter "To the Sporting World" explaining his conduct, Reynolds claimed that Langan had become "a different man to what he was when he had not three-pence. Gold was now his god." He contended that Langan wanted to force him out so that he could find a sparring partner with whom he would not have to split money.[77] The extraordinarily successful partnership that had brought Langan and Reynolds to national attention was a victim of its own success. Langan was now a bankable commodity and felt he did not need a partner to achieve his ends. After returning from Ireland, he went to rest by the sea for a few days and then began to train at Cheltenham, where he was treated as a celebrity.[78]

With both boxers in training in early May attention turned to the match, which was planned for Tuesday, June 8. John Jackson and Pierce Egan were again enlisted to find a suitable location. As in January, a monetary reward and the promise of no magisterial interference were key factors in the decision. Jackson received letters from around the country. The best of these came from a group of publicans in Warwick, which dispatched a messenger to offer £250 to Spring and Langan. Preparations began in that place, but a local magistrate announced that he would prevent the fight. The local group contested the magistrate's decision, arguing that they stood to lose a great deal of money, and the magistrate relented.[79] In the meantime, however, an entrepreneurial publican named Hewlings offered £200 for the match to be held in Chichester, near the south coast of England. Jackson accepted this proposal by letter the Saturday before the match.[80] Hewlings had heard that the match was to be held in Warwick and considered the letter a hoax so Egan was dispatched to Chichester to confirm the agreement. The "most extraordinary sensations were produced" by his arrival on Sunday evening as the news that the fight would take place in the vicinity spread through the town. Crowds of people swarmed to the Swan, Hewlings's pub, to see Egan. In the course of the evening, Hewlings and Egan determined the site of the match and summoned builders to begin constructing a stage.[81]

Hewlings undertook elaborate preparations to meet the specifications of the agreement between Spring and Langan and to capitalize on the great anticipation of the second match between the English and Irish Champions. These preparations also occasioned controversy, as competing groups attempted to benefit from the event. The site Hewlings chose for the match was three miles south of the city in a field adjacent to the recently opened Chichester Canal. He selected it primarily so that spectators could be forced to pay a toll to cross the bridge and see the fight.[82] Beginning the morning before the match, Hewlings superintended the work to prepare the field. He accepted an offer from local farmers of fifty-three large wagons to form an outer ring and workers constructed seating on them. Hewlings also had a grandstand carted nearly fifty miles from Epsom racecourse to provide extra seating. He charged a guinea for seating in this grandstand and five shillings for the wagons.[83] On the same day, work began on the construction of the stage. Workmen, many of whom were local residents volunteering their time, brought three-inch-thick deal planks to the site and raised a twenty-four square foot stage that stood six feet above the crowd. They also put up a number of posts surrounding the ring with boards attached horizontally, to prevent the men from falling off.[84] Finally, the workmen built two smaller stands for "the accommodation of the tip-top persons of society."[85]

These elaborate preparations brought Hewlings into conflict with established interests in the sport. He planned to use money collected from spectators crossing the bridge and sitting on his wagons to pay the £200 he had promised the fighters. By tradition, however, prizefighters collected money from spectators. On the day of the match, they claimed this right and threatened Hewlings's men. Supported by several other local notables, the publican threatened to call in the magistrate and tear down the stage. The standoff finally ended when he permitted three boxers to borrow wagons for their own profit in exchange for helping set up the field.[86] The episode demonstrated the immense difficulties involved in staging a prizefight of this size even when authorities agreed not to intervene.

As preparations continued at the site of the fight, the last-minute shift to a location far removed from Warwick—and from Langan's core of support in the Midlands—had important effects on the match. News that the fight would be held in Chichester spread rather slowly and thousands who had set out on foot for Warwick on Monday and Tuesday were unable to attend. Many who had come from Ireland also did not make it to Chichester.[87] As a result, the crowd was far smaller, wealthier, and almost certainly less Irish than that at the Worcester racecourse. The late change of location made the days before the fight rather chaotic for Langan as well. On Saturday morning, he left Slough for Leamington, a spa town outside Warwick. When he arrived, Langan found a letter from John O'Neill telling him to return to Slough. O'Neill also went to Leamington to retrieve him. The two men reached Slough at two o'clock Monday morning, the day before the fight, and Langan took a few hours of restless sleep before rising for his customary walk at five o'clock. Later that morning they left for Chichester, arriving around eight o'clock Monday evening. In the three days before the match, Langan had traveled nearly two hundred miles.[88]

While the change of location disrupted many plans, opportunities for celebration and for profit abounded. As soon as the site of the bout was made known in London, a great scramble to secure transportation to Chichester ensued. Coaches traveling anywhere close to the town were booked full on Sunday and Monday, even though drivers doubled their fares. Vehicles traveling south from London crowded the roads both days, as a great concourse of people made the journey to see the match.[89] All of the inns in Chichester and the surrounding communities were crowded to capacity, despite charging at least a guinea for a bed. Indeed the *Weekly Dispatch* complained about the determination of local innkeepers to "make *hay while the sun shines*."[90] As visitors poured into Chichester on Whit Monday, a festival atmosphere reigned. Coincidentally, recruits of the Irish 98th regiment were stationed in the area preparing to depart for India and the unit marched through the city in their dress uniforms.[91] When Langan arrived the men of this unit, who were all Irish, gave him three cheers. Spring arrived in the evening and was immediately recognized and cheered by the townspeople.[92]

Langan had benefited greatly from the support of Irish crowds since his arrival in England, but an incident that was widely reported in Irish and English newspapers reinforced the narrative that Langan was a symbol of non-threatening Irishness. According to the story, the wife of Lieutenant-Colonel Lucius O'Brien—a prominent East India Company officer who was in England after he had been controversially denied an important position in the Hyderabad residency—approached Langan at the Dolphin Inn.[93] Mrs. O'Brien wished him well and offered a green handkerchief for him to wear "in compliment to his country." Langan refused, however, not wanting "to make his humble efforts a matter of national consideration." Still, he assured Mrs. O'Brien that he "would do his best to deserve her favourable opinion and that of his countrymen."[94] This romantic story underscored the image of Langan sketched by Egan: a humble Catholic Irishman, proud of his identity but apolitical. The parts played by Colonel and Mrs. O'Brien, members of a prominent Protestant Irish family who had recently been at Court for the King's birthday (details of Colonel O'Brien's failed appointment were not yet widely known), also suggested that pride in Irish identity was not incompatible with loyalty to the Crown.[95] This was a comforting image for many English and Irish newspaper readers at a time when Ireland was increasingly volatile and O'Connell's movement for Catholic Emancipation seemed to threaten a massive Catholic rising.

By Tuesday morning, a crowd of between 10,000 and 20,000 began to gather at the scene of the match. While Hewlings hoped to charge a toll to cross the bridge over the Chichester Canal, many spectators simply traveled a few miles to go around it. Soon all attempts to force spectators to pay ceased. Once on the ground, hundreds of people mounted the stage "to say they had been there." Despite this somewhat disorganized start and failure of some efforts to profit, the preparations overseen by Hewlings, Jackson, and Egan assured that the scene at Worcester racecourse would not be repeated. Before the boxers arrived, the surface of the stage was chalked to prevent any slippage. Jackson then mounted the stage and appealed to the crowd not to interfere with the judgments of the umpires, who sat in purpose-built boxes on the edge of the ring with an unobstructed view of the fight. After the two combatants mounted the stage, Langan asked Spring to take off his belt to show that he was not hiding anything that might give him an advantage. Journalist John Badcock later commented that a "better formed ring, or a more orderly assemblage were, perhaps, never witnessed."[96] Efforts to regularize admission had been frustrated but attempts to create an impression of fairness had not.

Despite the tremendous build-up for another contest between England and Ireland, the fight was somewhat anticlimactic. Langan fought valiantly—Cribb called him "as brave a man as ever stepped in leather"—but was no match for the English Champion. In the early rounds, the Irishman tried to wrestle with Spring but failed to cause much damage. Spring moved skillfully and parried Langan's punches. He pummeled Langan so badly that, by the nineteenth round, he broken his own left hand. After an hour, Langan fought on but his blows had little effect on his opponent. By the fifty-third round, he was "almost blind" and Spring's hands were "both dreadfully swollen." Spring could no longer close his fist and so threw Langan to the ground to conclude most of the later rounds. The crowd began to agitate for an end to the match but Langan's second, Tom Belcher, refused. Finally, in the seventy-sixth round, Spring pushed the nearly-insensible Langan to the ground and all concerned agreed to end the fight. After nearly two hours, the great event was over.[97]

Spring left the stage immediately and returned to Hewlings's house, where he had stayed Monday night. He began his journey back to the metropolis the following day, accompanied by "the shouts of the populous all along the road; and the ladies waving their handkerchiefs."[98] He traveled first to Reigate, where he had trained for the match. Enthusiastic crowds received him there with great fanfare. A local draper supplied the men of the town with blue favors to put in their hats and many women waved blue handkerchiefs from windows as the Champion passed. When Spring left Reigate on Thursday, the town treated him like a military hero. Residents unhitched his horses and pulled his carriage out of town in a parade adorned with flags and laurel. A band played "See the conquering hero comes" to complete the scene.[99] The people of Reigate left little doubt that they considered Spring's victory over the Irishman Langan a national triumph.

Langan was dejected after his defeat; accounts of the match noted that he was "more wounded in spirit than in body."[100] Not only had he failed to win the Championship but he had also lost £200 of his own money. His bruised pride and lightened purse soon recovered, however. Jackson and Egan collected fifty guineas from the spectators before Langan left the site of the match. The officers of the Irish 98th regiment took up a subscription for him as well and the regimental band played several Irish songs below his window as he recuperated. Egan claimed that another guest at the Dolphin Inn leaned out his window and proposed a toast to "England and Ireland for ever!" By the time Langan left Chichester he had recovered most of his £200, benefiting from the perception that he had fought bravely in defeat on behalf of Ireland.[101] The result of the match, and the story of the toast, provided more than comfort to Langan. They also reassured readers that Ireland's representative had been treated fairly and honorably in his quest to win the Championship. That he had been defeated decisively seemed to confirm the ultimate superiority of English manhood.

Both Langan and Spring were back in the metropolis by June 11 and appeared at a benefit for Irish fighter Jack Randall. Spring appeared much more injured than reports of the fight suggested. Besides his broken hands, his eyes were both black and his arm was in a sling. His opponent still showed many signs of the hard-fought bout as well. Nevertheless, Langan appeared at boxing events frequently in the following weeks. Spring had announced that he was retired and so Langan issued an open challenge to any leading English boxer "in the humble hope that he might be able to unite in his own person the Championship of England and Ireland." This challenge, made at a benefit exhibition for Tom Oliver, was met with loud cheers from the spectators.[102] Langan had his own benefit at the Fives Court on July 1. When the exhibition began, the venue was so crowded that some people had to leave. Langan reiterated his open challenge, telling the audience that he did not appear "in any thing like a national point of view," though he was proud to be Irish. His only ambition, he claimed, was to "show as a man amongst pugilists, and contend for the Championship of England."[103] He thus sought a match by drawing on the narrative that he was a loyal Irishman seeking to advance in the meritorious British world of prizefighting.

In the summer and fall of 1824, several attempts to make matches for Langan failed. He had fallen out with Tom Belcher, who had become an important organizer and patron of the sport.[104] Jem Ward, the future Champion, offered to fight Langan for £200 but was refused.[105] More protracted negotiations with Thomas Shelton ultimately failed as well. In the meantime, he returned to Ireland in July to attend to his father, who had been attacked in Ballybough and had his leg broken by a group of men who had suspected the younger Langan of throwing the fight at Chichester. Crowds at Waterford took a different view and the boxer was greeted "amidst cheers from the persons assembled on the Pier" before proceeding to Dublin.[106] The following month, Langan was in Liverpool exhibiting with Irish boxer Peter Crawley "to very respectable audiences."[107] On this sparring tour Langan suffered a shoulder injury, effectively ending any chance he had of fighting again in 1824.[108] The following year, a match with Jem Ward was nearly arranged before ultimately falling through. Langan occasionally appeared at boxing events but was gradually becoming less involved. After his father and sister died in a fever outbreak in Dublin in 1826, he moved to Liverpool and opened his inn near the soon-to-be-completed Clarence Dock.[109]

Although Langan never fought in the prize ring again, the tremendous popularity of his two matches contributed to his lasting fame. Langan's inn did a brisk business with Irish immigrants in Liverpool, many of whom knew him as a famous boxer who had once contended for the Championship of England. Pierce Egan noted that Langan's house was a success because he was "quite a *star* amongst his warm-hearted country-men."[110] Langan returned the affections of his countrymen as well. His inn was a popular meeting place for the Irish of Liverpool and he offered a bed for two nights to any Irishman that needed one, provided they left their weapons at the door.[111] Langan's standing in the Irish community of Liverpool brought him considerable influence and wealth. Not only did he share a stage with Daniel O'Connell, but he also purchased Thornton Hall near Chester in 1844 for the enormous sum of £9,000. *The Times* noted that Langan earned most of his money from his business as an innkeeper and from the sale of distilled liquors. After he purchased Thornton Hall, he forwarded fifty guineas to temperance crusader Father Theobold Mathew in Ireland. When Langan died two years later, his estate was valued at £20,000.[112]

Jack Langan ended his life in Liverpool a wealthy and influential man. Much of his success was built on the reputation he earned as a courageous Irish man who audaciously challenged and then nearly defeated the Champion of England. Many Irish people supported Langan, wagered money on him, attended his sparring exhibitions, and viewed him as a representative of Ireland. As Catholics struggled for rights in the tumultuous 1820s, he was a symbol of defiant Irish Catholicism. The portrayal of Langan as a *loyal* Irishman also had a broad appeal for many in England and Ireland. While agrarian violence, millenarianism, and the popular campaign for Catholic Emancipation provided the sternest challenge to Protestant British rule in Ireland since the 1790s, the sport of boxing seemed to provide an antidote to nationalist politics, channeling ethnic loyalty into an innocuous (though not unimportant) conflict in the prize-ring.

Despite the great attraction of a battle pitting Ireland against England, the Langan and Spring matches were the last great ethnic spectacle of the bare-knuckle era in England. National, religious, and racial difference remained important in the culture of prizefighting, but changes in the sport and in English society made them less prominent than before. By the time of Langan's death in 1848, one had to travel to the United States or Australia to see Ireland matched against England in the ring.

Chapter Seven

Emphasizing Englishness in the Age of Reform, 1825–1833

The decade after the fights between Jack Langan and Tom Spring was a paradoxical moment for bare-knuckle prizefighting. As Victorian sporting journalist Henry Downes Miles later recalled, it was marked by "the more copious, accurate, and systematic reports" of matches. Coverage of prizefights in newspapers expanded and talented pugilists continued to appear.[1] At the same time, this was also a period of crisis for the sport. Several notorious cases of match fixing led a number of leading figures to retire from the sport. The departure of many patrons and amateurs and the hard economic times of the late 1820s meant lower stakes for most matches and more corruption. Political upheaval in Ireland and England encouraged authorities to act aggressively to stop matches, including the novel threat of legal action against upper-class patrons, because of fears of large assemblies of people. Finally, changing sensibilities and the spread of an ideal of humanitarianism undermined support in many influential quarters for an activity increasingly deemed a cruel and demoralizing spectacle.[2]

Journalists and other supporters of the sport responded to the problems that plagued bare-knuckle prizefighting in the late 1820s and 1830s by again emphasizing its timeless English pedigree. Whereas in the past this had provided opportunities for prizefighters from minority groups, now many viewed them as a source of the sport's troubles and sought to drive them out. Black boxers were often treated as ridiculous sideshow acts that were a distraction from the serious business of boxing. Some had success on sparring tours in the north of England and Scotland but were nevertheless rarely able to make lucrative matches. Attitudes toward Jewish fighters became more hostile as well and they and the Jewish community were repeatedly blamed for the corruption that bedeviled the sport. Many Jewish patrons abandoned bare-knuckle boxing, leaving the remaining Jewish boxers frequently unable to find sufficient stake money and vulnerable to hostile crowds. Irish-born pugilists fared somewhat better, though they and their supporters tended to be associated with unruly crowd behavior. Despite these hostile attitudes toward minority fighters, some of the leading prizefighters of the period were English-born Irishman. They and those who wrote about them used both their Irish and English identities strategically, though their Irishness was never totally invisible. When second-generation Irish fighters enjoyed great success, however, references to their Irish identities was minimized. Particularly in this time of trouble, it was believed, the sport could not have an Irish standard-bearer.

This chapter argues that, as the problems of bare-knuckle prizefighting multiplied in the second half of the 1820s, minority boxers and identities became less visible in the sport. Journalists—who were more influential than ever before—doubled down on arguments about the timeless Englishness of the sport and often blamed black, Jewish, and Irish-born fighters for its troubles. This helped to push many Jewish, black, and Irish-born boxers out. It also led to an emphasis on the Englishness of English-born Irish fighters. To defend the propriety and Englishness of boxing, the association with minority groups had to be minimized.

The late 1820s were a time of economic crisis and political turmoil in Britain and Ireland. The banking and market crash of December 1825 created panic in London and beyond. Riots erupted in a number of industrial areas as money shortages prevented the payment of wages. Several years later another wave of rioting swept through Britain.[3] Economic problems were linked to multifaceted popular campaigns for political reform, which were gathering strength at the same time. In both Britain and Ireland, political action drew on the energy of popular discontent and carried the implicit threat of violence.[4] The economic crisis and the accelerating political campaigns created problems for boxing; the economic downturn meant that less money was available for matches, while the threat of revolution made large gatherings at matches more suspicious to authorities.

These crises were not the sole source of boxing's problems, however. The sport had weathered previous periods of economic downturn and social disorder, but now political and ideological changes coupled with them to constitute a more profound threat. The successful political campaigns of the 1820s unleashed a reforming zeal culminating in a series of Acts of Parliament in the 1830s and 1840s that sought to remedy a variety of social ills.[5] As Boyd Hilton has argued, the progressive philosophy of governance that motivated these reforms began to supplant the liberal Tory ideology that had defended the status quo since the 1790s.[6] Related to this shift was a change in ideas about masculinity. As the war receded further into memory and the demands of a market economy became more pressing, a "bourgeois masculinity" that emphasized domesticity and avoidance of physical violence was widely accepted.[7] These ideological shifts weakened support for the combination of Tory loyalism and martial manhood that had underscored the importance of boxing since the turn of the century.[8]

Despite such ominous signs, newspapers continued to expand their coverage of bare-knuckle prizefighting and journalists played an ever-larger role in organizing, publicizing, and defining it. Pierce Egan remained one of the sport's most important figures for the remainder of the decade, often chairing meetings and holding stakes for matches. He also published the final two volumes of the popular anthology *Boxiana* in 1828 and 1829. Egan's rival Vincent Dowling was heavily involved in the organization of the sport in this period as well. He frequently acted as a referee, addressed spectators, and held stakes for matches.[9] In 1841, Dowling penned a history and defense of boxing called *Fistiana*. After his death, Henry Downes Miles remembered him as the "Oracle of the Ring."[10]

Dowling's career in many ways mirrored Egan's path. Like Egan, Dowling was a member of a Patriot Anglo-Irish family and, also like his rival, discovered boxing through an early career in journalism. Born in London in 1785, Dowling spent his childhood in Dublin, where his father was a publisher and journalist. The elder Dowling was an opponent of the Union and returned his family to the metropolis after its passage in 1800.[11] The son began work as a journalist at the *Star* in 1804 before beginning a long and lucrative association with the publisher William Clement at the *Observer*. The *Star* and the *Observer* were leading sources of boxing news in the first two decades of the century and, like Egan, Dowling became involved in the sport through his work as a journalist. He reported extensively on matches at the *Observer* and, when Clement purchased *Bell's Life in London* from Robert Bell in 1824, he brought Dowling with him as editor. *Bell's Life in London* offered expansive coverage of sporting news, providing more details about boxing and other sports than any other newspaper of its day. Although the paper increasingly covered horseracing from the 1830s, boxing news continued to attract readers until Dowling's death in 1852.[12]

Dowling also followed Egan in his loyalism, his promotion of martial masculinity, and his claim that a key virtue of boxing was its encouragement of the natural courageous manhood of British men. He worked as a government spy in the 1810s (the *Observer* received payments from the government during this period), admitting in court to passing information about a radical meeting to authorities.[13] This provoked a public feud in 1818 with the flamboyant radical leader Henry Hunt.[14] Hunt denounced Dowling in front of the headquarters of the *Observer* in June. Dowling then sought out Hunt and publicly horsewhipped him. Several months later Hunt came to the offices of the *Observer* and demanded that Dowling come outside "to prove yourself a man." Dowling offered to fight a duel instead, but Hunt declined.[15] The public confrontations between the two men were symbolic contests between radical and loyalist manhood as much as a political dispute.

Dowling more often demonstrated his ideas of manhood with his pen than with his whip. In *Fistiana*, he wrote that one of the great virtues of boxing was that its supporters "would have men, men; and women, women." This was part of a broader defense of the sport in that work, which echoed similar language from earlier in the century. He wrote, for example, that pugilism was the "sign and measure of English valour; and its professors may be considered the representatives of the courage of the nation." It continued to be necessary in the 1840s because "ultra-refinement and effeminacy are so much upon the increase, that some such stimulus is absolutely necessary to maintain an average degree of manliness amongst the rising generation."[16] While more defensive in tone than earlier species of the same argument, Dowling's words repeated themes that would have been familiar half a century before.

Dowling was more defensive than earlier writers because prizefighting had begun to encounter problems that seemed to threaten its existence. Several high-profile examples of match fixing and disputes about stakes had prompted John Jackson to retire from his "master of ceremonies" duties even before the Spring and Langan fight. The Pugilistic Club, which had brought organization and an air of respectability to the sport since 1814, was dissolved in December 1825 after several years of decline. Spectators more frequently broke the ring, seconds regularly interfered in fights, and several prominent examples of match fixing or disputed stakes occurred in the second half of the decade.

These problems were at least partly an unintended consequence of the sport's broad popularity and the growing influence of journalists and boxers, who had helped bring it to a wider audience. While the protection and money of gentry and aristocratic amateurs of the "Fancy" continued to be important (and often indispensible), writers and fighters relied ever more on generating publicity to attract readers and paying customers at pubs and benefit exhibitions. Such strategies stoked the passions of spectators, many of whom had less time for the genteel scene preferred by the amateurs of old, and made money a more prominent and visible part of the sport. These factors left gentlemen amateurs feeling that they had lost control. This, along with fears of large and unruly crowds, prompted many of them to discontinue their patronage. The evaporation of their support doomed the Pugilistic Club, which was dependent on elite sponsorship, and with it both the funds to pay boxers to keep order at fights and the mechanism used to solve disputes. An attempt was made to rebuild an organization with boxers, journalists, and publicans in the lead with the establishment of the Fair Play Club in 1828 but it did not succeed.[17] The sport thus remained popular but was troubled from the middle of the 1820s.

Several leading pugilists in this unsettled period were Irish. This is perhaps surprising given that the Irish in England faced greater hostility than ever before and that the troubled state of the sport led many writers to stress its English pedigree.[18] Unlike prominent Irish fighters in earlier years, however, these boxers had been born in England. As a result, they had more fluid identities than their Irish-born counterparts since they could emphasize their Englishness or their Irishness when and if it suited them. This was a critical advantage in generating publicity and winning popular support and patronage in a period when these things could be hard to secure. English-born Irish pugilists could turn to the Irish community for backing when necessary while avoiding some of the challenges faced by Irish-born fighters, especially the difficulty in making matches against leading boxers. Whereas Irish-born pugilists were believed to be limited to a narrow band of highly partisan and unruly supporters, English-born Irish boxers had a much broader appeal.

Jack Randall was among the most well known second-generation London Irish of the 1820s. As we saw in Chapter Five, Randall was a leading figure in boxing after the war and the most important client of Captain Robert Barton, the chief patron of Irish boxers in those years. For most of his relatively short fighting career, journalists consistently identified him as Irish. After one of his early matches in 1817, for example, the *Weekly Dispatch* referred to him as "the *Irishman*" and a "son of Hibernia."[19] The following year, *Bell's Weekly Messenger* remarked that Randall was "esteemed the best Irishman that has appeared in the ring since the days of Ryan."[20] In 1821, the *Sporting Magazine* noted that Randall was "a worthy scion of the shamrock."[21] After Randall retired in1821, however, writers increasingly omitted references to his Irish heritage. For those keen to hold him up as a symbol of the sport, his Irishness was inconvenient. Two separate defenses of boxing published in the *Sporting Magazine* in 1823 and 1824, for example, used Randall as evidence of the merits of the sport and made no mention of his Irish background. In a sport as steeped in identity politics as boxing, such an omission was not accidental.[22] Some went further and simply denied that Randall's parents had been Irish. John Badcock, for example, contended in 1826 that Randall learned to fight because he was born an Englishman among the Irish.[23] For his part,

Randall used his Irish identity strategically. He used green as his color, held several benefit exhibitions on St. Patrick's Day, and trained a number of Irish boxers.

The career of Ned Neale, like Randall's, demonstrates the plasticity of second-generation Irish identity. Born to Irish parents in Streatham on March 22, 1804, Neale had his first prizefight in 1822. Accounts of his earliest bouts used his nickname, "the Streatham Youth," and made little reference to his Irish heritage. This changed by the summer of 1823, when newspapers began to add an O to his name, possibly at Neale's instigation. Pierce Egan used the name O'Neale for the first time in the August 10, 1823, edition of the *Weekly Dispatch*, as did *Bell's Life in London* the same day (still owned by Robert Bell in 1823). Nicholas Byrne's *Morning Post* noted that "Neale, or O'Neil, is of Irish extraction" in September.[24] The articles for Neale's first major fight with David Hudson in September referred to him as "Edward O'Neal" and the same was true for a match the following month against Abraham Belasco.[25] Around the same time, Egan noted parenthetically in the *Weekly Dispatch* that Neale was "*vulgarly* called the Streatham Youth."[26] This change likely reflected an effort by both Neale and the sporting journalists who wrote about him to capitalize on the excitement surrounding Jack Langan in the autumn of 1823.

Unlike Irish-born fighters, however, Neale could (and was often willing to) exploit both his English and his Irish identities. At most matches Neale used blue bird's eye—also the standard of prominent English boxers such as "Gas Man" Thomas Hickman and Tom Spring—as his color rather than the green preferred by other Irish-born boxers.[27] He also emphasized his connection to England even when appearing before Irish crowds. When he crossed the Irish Sea for a set of performances at the Fishamble Theater in Dublin in the late spring 1825, an advertisement billed him as "NED NEAL—the *Streatham Youth*." Not only did this notice drop the O that Neale typically used in England, it also employed the nickname that connected him with his leafy birthplace outside London. At the same time, the advertisement left no doubt about Neale's Irish identity, noting that he was "soliciting the patronage of his countrymen" in Dublin and that, in all of his matches, he had "not been the cause of a stigma on his country."[28] Journalists also highlighted Neale's hybrid identity. In 1824, journalist George Kent wrote in the *Weekly Dispatch* that Neale inherited "all the fire and hardy-daring of the Irish character" as well as "that untiring game so peculiar to the conduct of John Bull." The same account even suggested that the young Neale beat up English children in his neighborhood.[29]

Neale's sojourn in Dublin was lucrative. When he returned to England in June, he was prepared to stake £200 of his own money for a possible championship fight against Tom Cannon.[30] Plans for this match fell through, but Neale used the profits from his Irish tour to establish himself as a fixture of the Irish sporting scene in the metropolis. He married a woman named Ellen Baldwin (who soon died in childbirth) and became a publican at the Bull in Cow Cross Lane, near Smithfield Market. Pierce Egan claimed that Neale had "the greatest encouragement and support from the warm-hearted Patlanders" at the Bull.[31] Like many enterprising pugilist-publicans, he soon was involved in organizing boxing matches that his customers were keen to see. In October, he helped arrange a bout in Streatham for £25 between a Munster fighter named Donovan and an English boxer called Hill. Although officers from the Union Street police office—one of the twenty-four offices in the metropolis established by the Police Act of 1792—prevented the match, it attracted the interest of large numbers of London Irish.[32] His interests also extended to other pursuits favored by metropolitan publicans, such as dog fighting.[33] Neale thrived in his new role: he enjoyed enough food and drink that Dowling pronounced him "too heavy for active operations" in late 1825.[34]

As Neale's profile continued to rise in the boxing scene and he became more important to the image of the sport, some journalists began to minimize his association with Ireland. When he finally entered the ring again in December 1826, facing veteran boxer Phillip Sampson, the match occasioned great fanfare. The £400 stakes were the largest seen in eighteen months and the crowd was the biggest since the first fight between Langan and Spring at Worcester racecourse in January 1824. Hopes were also raised that the match would "re-instate the Ring in all its purity of honour and manliness."[35] Such optimism was frustrated, however. The huge stream of spectators that collected at a cold and rainy field in South Mimms (after magistrates prevented the match twenty miles to the north in Dunstable) witnessed a farcical spectacle that almost certainly involved match fixing.[36] Perhaps eager to avoid encouraging the impression that corrupt ethnic partisans were overrunning the sport, most journalists omitted any reference to Neale's Irishness or to his Irish supporters. Vincent Dowling's long description of the preparations, the fight, and its aftermath made no mention of either Neale's Irishness or of his Irish supporters.[37] Several different accounts of his victory over Tom Cannon for £100 in February also omitted any reference to Irish spectators.[38] In sharp contrast, Pierce Egan's stories about both fights referred repeatedly to Neale's Irish supporters chanting, singing, and cheering.[39] Later writers have tended to charge Egan with exaggerating or even inventing an Irish connection for pugilists like Neale—Henry Downes Miles, one of Dowling's successors at *Bell's Life in London*, even claimed that Egan made up Neale's Irish parentage—but, given his well-documented Irish connections, it seems much more likely that many journalists simply chose to omit reference to his Irishness.[40]

Whatever the attitudes of journalists, Neale continued his involvement with the Irish community in 1827. In the spring of that year, he trained and offered patronage to Irish-born Michael Larkins, who he likely met on his tour in Dublin in 1825. In May, he and his fellow publican (and dog fight promoter) Josh Hudson arranged a match between Larkins and Hudson's brother David. Larkins arrived with Neale in a coach "heavily laden with Emeralders" and easily defeated Hudson.[41] Clearly the support of the Irish community was still important to Neale and his business.

Soon, however, he began to downplay his own Irishness and to drop the O from his name, perhaps in response to the anti–Irish (and anti–Catholic) sentiment that was growing in the 1820s. Dowling began to call him Ned Neal in October and the following month the *Weekly Dispatch* noted that Neale "sometimes drops the big O."[42] By the time of his next match, in which he easily defeated Jem Burn for £100, the O had completely disappeared. The only reference to Neale's Irish connection in Dowling's detailed story was a mention of "loud shouts from the Potatoe Boys" after he scored an early knockdown. Neale clearly had Irish partisans—Egan's story of the match again included numerous references to the vocal support of "the Patlanders"—but they were largely invisible in Dowling's account.[43] Dowling was not averse to describing Irish spectators; a few weeks later, his account of a match between Philip Sampson and Irishman Paul Spencer (who had been trained and backed by Neale) highlighted and mocked Irish spectators' blind support for Spencer. Elsewhere in the story he implicitly contrasted Irish spectators with "those classes which may be said to comprise the *sinew* of John Bull."[44] There was still a role for Irish boxers and spectators in the sport but it was not to be as a standard-bearer of British pugilism.

It was clear by the beginning of 1828 that Neale had become one of the most important symbols of the sport. In January at a dinner to celebrate his victory over Burn, Egan announced a subscription fund to purchase a silver cup to honor Neale's achievements in the ring and "his hitherto brave, manly, and upright conduct." He presented the cup to Neale (spelled Neal) at a benefit exhibition in July. It was topped by the figure of a boxer and covered in wreaths interwoven with rose, thistles, and shamrocks.[45] The symbolism was clear: boxing brought the nations of the United Kingdom together. In his presentation speech, Egan said that he hoped that the gift to Neale "would stimulate other members of the Ring to *follow in his wake, and do likewise*." The cup was then filled with nine bottles of port wine and drunk to the bottom.[46]

This ceremony came at an important moment for the sport. Neale had recently lost his first match to Ned Baldwin and there were rumors that he had done so deliberately. In response to these rumors, Dowling (who had been the stakeholder for the bout) gave a speech about the "national principles" of boxing in which he referenced the support the King had shown for the sport in the past.[47] The same year, leading boxers formed the "Fair Play Club" in an attempt to control the epidemic of match fixing. Neale was thus presented as a symbol at the moment when leading figures were attempting to revive it. This was a critical reason that the earlier emphasis on his Irish heritage and his Irish supporters disappeared. The Irish were obviously a part of the sport but when "national principles" were concerned an Irishman could not be the standard-bearer for it.

As successful as he was, Neale was never the Champion. For much of this period, that distinction belonged to another "English-bred Irishman." Unlike Neale and Randall, however, James "Jem" Ward chose not to identify himself as an Irish boxer. Jem, the eldest son of the Protestant Irish immigrant Nicholas Ward, was born on December 26, 1800, in London's East End.[48] His father left Ireland as a young man and settled on the Ratcliffe Highway which, by the early nineteenth century, had become an important center of Irish settlement in the metropolis. Indeed, many of the immigrants who settled there were Irish speakers.[49] Nicholas Ward probably owned a butcher shop on the Highway during his eldest son's boyhood and sent young Jem to a school in Chadwell Heath. Unfortunately, Nicholas was forced to close his shop sometime near the end of the war.[50] To support his wife and seven children he had to find work on the Thames as a ballast-heaver, an arduous occupation that employed many Irish immigrants in London.[51] Jem left school at the age of twelve and went to work on the Thames as a coal whipper. This occupation was similar to his father's in that it was back-breaking labor often performed by Irish immigrants.[52] The future boxer spent much of his early life immersed in the Irish immigrant community of the East End, but his Protestantism ultimately set him apart from many of them.

Ward began boxing before his father lost his butcher shop, but became more seriously involved in the sport after commencing work on the Thames, where he honed his fighting skills. He first attracted public notice at a sparring club in Bromley New Town, which catered to aspiring fighters from the East End. At this club, he acquired both the nickname "Black Diamond"—a slang term for a coal heaver—and his first patron.[53] Ward was a talented young pugilist but, after a promising debut in the summer of 1822, his career was nearly derailed when he threw a match against Bill Abbot at Moulsey Hurst for a promise of £100.[54] Patrons shunned him at first but, after he won a few matches in the provinces using the name "Sawney Wilson," Ward found his way back into the London ring. He won the Championship less than three years after his notorious loss to Abbot.[55] Through the vicissitudes of his early career, Ward does not seem to have sought or received support from the Irish community; Pierce Egan wrote that the Irish "hailed him ... as their hero, and stuck to him like glue," but there is little evidence of the kind of partisan support on which Ned Neale relied.[56] In stark contrast to Randall and Neale, Ward (and the journalists who wrote about him) seems to have made no use of his Irish identity.

While Ward was not identified publicly with his Irish heritage, journalists and other boxing supporters increasingly considered him an apt representative of British manhood. When he fought Tom Cannon for the title on July 19, 1825, for £1,000 on a stage outside of Warwick, an article in the *Sporting Magazine* identified the date as "the day on which native courage was to be triumphant" and connected the contest for the championship to the exploits of Admiral Horatio Nelson and his martyrdom at Trafalgar. Ward entered the ring wearing a large straw hat that "gave him more the appearance of a West India planter than of a British boxer."[57] In a scorching July heat, Ward defeated Cannon in ten exhausting minutes. Three days later, a large crowd gathered at the Fives' Court in London to welcome the two combatants back to the metropolis. The highlight of the event was prizefighter Harry Holt's presentation to Ward of a tiger skin belt "in commemoration of his scientific and manly conquest of Thomas Cannon." Ward's blue and Cannon's color red ran around the middle of the belt, with blue outermost. An engraving on the belt announced that his victory had entitled Ward "to the high and distinguished appellation of the British Champion."[58] The symbolism surrounding Jem Ward's greatest triumph was clear: for supporters, the bout underscored the connection between martial manhood, the nation, and the sport of boxing. At the same time, the championship belt demonstrated the evolution of the national idea. The use of the term "British" in place of "English" (all previous champions had been "English Champion") and the use of tiger skin, with its evocation of India, were innovations.

The fanfare surrounding Ward's victory over Cannon seemed to herald a new age of respectability for the sport, but it proved to be a false dawn. Ward did not defend his championship for eighteen months. During that time, corruption continued to plague the ring and an economic downturn drove down stakes. When Ward fought again, in early January 1827 against Peter Crawley, he did so for £200—a far cry from the £1,000 stakes in his match against Cannon. Despite this, after Crawley defeated Ward in an honest and exciting bout, sporting journalists took the opportunity to forecast the revival of the ring. *The Sporting Magazine* opined that the match received the highest praise "from the admirers of true courage and manhood" and that patronage would surely return to the sport as a result.[59] The Fair Play Club was formed the following year to try and improve the organization of matches, the enforcement of rules, and control of crowds. Unfortunately, Ward—who had reclaimed the championship after Crawley announced his retirement—helped undermine such efforts with the notorious "Leicester Hoax," in which he likely accepted a bribe to cancel a long-planned fight against Irishman Simon Byrne in 1829.[60]

Ward and Byrne finally fought on July 12, 1831, near Stratford-upon-Avon in what was the final match of Ward's career. The fight demonstrated the extent to which Ward had come to be seen as a symbol of British manhood. Vincent Dowling wrote that the bout would "give a new impetus to manly sports & the good old fashioned school of British boxing." Despite Ward's Irish heritage (which Dowling acknowledged in his account), the bout was widely considered to pit England against Ireland. Ward's supporters, in fact, were rabidly anti–Irish. In the third round one of them shouted "we want no Irishman for champion" and in the seventh another called for Byrne to "go back to Ireland & raffle for pigs and potatoes." Ward won a hard-fought match and, two days later, was presented a champion's belt at a ceremony at the Tennis Court. The belt was made of purple velvet and had a wreath made of a rose, thistle, and shamrock surrounding a crown beneath which was a "British lion."[61] Jem Ward, the son of Irish immigrants who was born and bred among the poor Irish of London's East End, was thus lauded as the symbol of Britain. The fact that he was Protestant surely played a role in this shift, but Ward's unwillingness to actively court the Irish community in England (as had Randall and Neale) was critical in making him an emblem of Britishness as well.

If Ward came to represent Britain, his opponent Simon Byrne was unambiguously Irish. Born in Dublin, Byrne fought his early matches in Ireland before forging a partnership with Tom Reynolds and following the well-worn path of Irish boxers across the Irish Sea. The two men spent much of the late 1820s performing for the growing Irish immigrant communities of Scotland and northern England. Byrne also contested several matches in Scotland in these years. In August 1826, he fought Bristol champion Robert Avery for £100 near Kilmacolm. A huge crowd choked the roads from Glasgow and Byrne clearly identified with the many Irish people among them. He used green as his color, a choice that resonated with his supporters, who wore green and carried green flags to the match. One coach of Byrne's partisans, for example, returned to Glasgow after his victory carrying a green flag and green boughs. When news reached the Irish district of Bridgegate, there were celebrations in the streets.[62]

Byrne's matches in Scotland brought him fame and, as we have seen, a planned match against Jem Ward in 1829. The "Leicester Hoax" prevented this fight, but the Irishman affirmed his status as a rising star by defeating veteran Philip Sampson later in the year. In the wake of this bout, a number of wealthy patrons decided to stage a rematch between Byrne and Scottish boxer Alexander MacKay, who Byrne had defeated near Glasgow in 1827. An ethnic spectacle pitting the "Irish Champion" against the "Scottish Champion" would, some hoped, breathe new life into the sport. The two most prominent Scottish sporting figures of the early nineteenth century, Squire Osbaldestone and Robert Barclay Allardice, agreed to back Mackay. Mackay traveled to Barclay's family seat in Ury (where Cribb had prepared for his second match with Molineaux) for training, while Byrne went with Reynolds to Brighton. The Fair Play Club made preparations to identify a suitable location for the match and contracted with several boxers to keep order in the ring.[63]

The symbolic contest between Scotland and Ireland—a match that Dowling billed as "The Shamrock and the Thistle, or Ireland v. Scotland"—had broader resonance as well.[64] Workmen wagered large sums on the fight and animosity between the Scottish and Irish Glaswegians "often proceeds to blows; and … many Irishmen were knocked down." Great crowds assembled for two nights at the railway crossing, waiting for news about the match to arrive from England. A writer at the *Glasgow Chronicle* was reminded of the groups that waited for news of the Duke of Wellington's victories during the war.[65] At the site of the match near Hanslope in Buckinghamshire, the fighters used symbols to reflect their connection with their supporters. Mackay wore a "broad Kilmarnock cap, ornamented with an eagle's feather and orange tassel" into the ring, while Byrne tied his color green to the stakes. Each boxer's partisans displayed their colors in the crowd as well. Once the fight began, Byrne beat Mackay badly and the Scot ultimately died of his wounds. Back in Glasgow, riots broke out when news was received that Byrne had won and that Mackay had perished.[66] In many instances rioters formed rings for local Irish and Scottish fighters to face one another. In two days, the Glasgow authorities detained over one hundred and forty people. *The Glasgow Chronicle* reported that almost all of these cases "had their origin in the disputes … about the 'Grand Fight' between the Champions of Ireland and Scotland."[67]

Rioting in Glasgow was not the only worrying result for supporters of prizefighting. The death of Mackay prompted authorities to seek the arrest of Simon Byrne. He and Reynolds tried to escape to Ireland but were apprehended in Liverpool, where an informant had alerted local officials. Byrne was detained in Kirkdale prison while a jury assembled by the Buckinghamshire coroner committed him to trial during the summer assizes for having "feloniously killed and slain one Alexander Mac Kay."[68] Even worse for boxing supporters, as Byrne awaited trial the *Times* named the backers of Mackay—long a taboo in major publications—and called for their prosecution.[69] Rumors then began to spread that "individuals of distinction" would also be indicted if Byrne were convicted.[70] Luckily for men like Allardice and Osbaldeston, expert testimony at Byrne's trial suggested that Mackay's death could have been caused by a fall and Byrne was found not guilty.[71] For his part, Allardice was undaunted by the threat of prosecution. After his cousin rebuked him, Allardice sent a letter arguing that boxing, like soldiering, was necessary "to impress the lower orders with a feeling of mercy & fair-play to a fallen foe."[72] Even still, Allardice's need to defend his support for prizefighting to his cousin illustrated the disastrous consequences of this attempt to rehabilitate the sport.

While Irishness was either minimized or associated with rioting and disorder, black boxers faced greater hostility than in the past. This had not been the case for much of the 1810s. Capitalizing on the wild popularity of the Molineaux and Cribb matches, a number of African American men became prizefighters in that decade. Bill Richmond, a still popular figure whose pub was an important gathering place for those connected with the sport, aided these aspiring pugilists, providing training and patronage when possible. The newcomers included New Yorker Samuel Robinson and Baltimore native Harry Sutton, who each received some support from Richmond and vied to claim the mantel of the next Molineaux. Both men had their most financial success in sparring tours in Scotland and Ireland—as had Molineaux before them—where a highly skilled black pugilist was much more of a novelty than in London. Both also struggled to find patronage, however, and could not make the high stakes matches that enabled other prizefighters to buy public houses or to seek some financial security in other ways.[73] This had tragic consequences for Harry Sutton, the best black boxer of the postwar period. Soon after Sutton returned from a sparring tour in Ireland in 1822, he began to suffer from a respiratory illness. Richmond started a collection for the dying Sutton at the Fives Court but only received £7. When he held a benefit exhibition for Sutton's wife and children after the young fighter's death, Richmond barely collected enough money to cover the costs of the event.[74]

Even at the high point of black pugilism in the London prize ring, black boxers were dependent on white audiences that were condescending at best and hostile at worst. Richmond's popularity derived in large part from his reputation as the "facetious hero of the ring." When he rented a large and elegant room at the Tennis Court to teach "the Art of Self Defense" in December 1819, the *Weekly Dispatch* assured its readers that Richmond's "facetious qualities" and his "fund of milling anecdotes" would make the venture a great success.[75] Richmond's flamboyance and high profile were also met with hostility. When the proprietor of the Tennis Court sued the *Weekly Dispatch* (in connection with attacks on the Belasco family described in Chapter Five), one of the newspaper's solicitors attempted to inflame the feelings of the jury by raising the question of women's attendance at the Tennis Court. The solicitor imagined a father looking for his daughter: "when [he asks] where is Jenny? the answer is, she is gone to see the Black."[76]

A St. Kitts-born fighter named John Kendrick was even more dependent on the whims of whites than the veteran Richmond. In May 1819, Kendrick walked 100 miles from London to a sporting dinner at a country house. He gained entry by offering to fight any of the boxers who were there. After much discussion and laughter, George Cooper agreed to fight Kendrick for a small sum collected from the dinner guests. The *Weekly Dispatch* commented that Kendrick "grinned with delight" when the match was made. When he lost to the experienced Cooper, he was given four guineas for his trouble and sent on his way. On Christmas Eve, Kendrick turned up at a fight at Blindlow Heath "to get a bit of roast beef, for Christmas Day." One of the scheduled boxers did not show up and so Kendrick fought Harry Sutton. Although he lost, the spectators subscribed a small sum of money for him.[77] Kendrick was considered a talented pugilist—Pierce Egan claimed that he would have been successful if he had had a patron—but the white spectators on whom he relied tended to regard him as a ludicrous sideshow rather than a serious boxer.[78]

By the late 1820s, with Molineaux's matches against Cribb further in the past, opportunities for black fighters were greatly diminished. Richmond last publicly supported a black fighter in 1826 and died three years later. The rising tide of anti-slavery sentiment, with its characterization of slaves as the victims of rapacious slave-owners, surely played a role in the declining prospects for black boxers; although abolitionists had long been opposed to pugilism in general, abolitionist imagery influenced a much wider population and probably helped make the prospect of a powerful black challenge to white British manhood less enticing to spectators. Finally, given the increasing publicity of the sport, potential black pugilists must have known about the realities facing black fighters.

The brief career of the last prominent black boxer of the decade demonstrates the landscape for black pugilists in those years. American-born

Thomas Morgan was part of the crew of the East Indiaman Carn Brae in the 1820s and apparently won bouts in ports around the world. He had heard of the exploits of Molineaux and so saw an opportunity to earn some money with his fists in London. The captain of his ship encouraged him to go to the metropolis and even provided a letter of introduction to Josh Hudson, the former fighter turned publican and patron. Morgan met with Hudson, who offered him room and board at his Half-Moon Tap pub in exchange for controlling Morgan's boxing career.[79] On June 4, 1827, Hudson held a benefit exhibition at the Tennis Court and took the opportunity to introduce Morgan as "young Molineux."[80] Following Hudson's lead, the *Weekly Dispatch* also connected Morgan to Molineaux, announcing that, "truly, in point of strength and determination, this tyro bids fair to emulate the deeds of that renowned sable chieftain." Hudson tightly control Morgan's introduction to the sport. When another fighter challenged him at a benefit exhibition, for example, Hudson would not allow it. Instead he declared that Morgan "shall fight any man in England, big or little, for a purse at Ascot races!"[81]

Hudson cannily brought Morgan to important boxing meetings throughout June and early July, allowing interest and curiosity to grow. The strategy showed signs of working. At a benefit exhibition in July for Thomas Brown, then in the midst of negotiations with Jem Ward to fight for the championship, the crowd clamored for Brown to spar with Morgan and then jeered lustily when Brown refused.[82] When a spectator defended Brown by arguing that "the *Black* was not worthy to wipe Brown's shoes," John Jackson delivered an impassioned speech in which he declared that "true courage never refused country, colour, size, weight, length, youth, nor years." Jackson's enlightened rhetoric notwithstanding, there were other signs that attitudes toward black fighters had changed. At a boxing meeting at the Half-Moon Tap, Morgan commended his patron, yelling (in Pierce Egan's rendering), "Me tank you, Massa, you be very good to fighting men!" In response, another member of the audience barked, "Silence you black Rascal!" The insult went unchallenged.[83]

As important, Hudson was unable to make a match for Morgan even though the newcomer had shown some potential in sparring exhibitions.[84] Finally, Morgan agreed to fight a little-known boxer named Abbinet on July 3 at Ranscombe Range for £10 collected among the spectators. In the first round, the nervous and inexperienced Morgan rushed at Abbinet and picked him up. Unsure what to do next, he "laid him down as tenderly as if his adversary had been a lady." As he did, his pants ripped open in the back. At this sight, "the spectators were convulsed with roars of laughter … and even *Blacky* blushed *blue* at the circumstance." After this inauspicious start, Morgan easily dispatched Abbinet in eleven minutes. Despite his victory and positive reviews of his performance, Morgan decided to discontinue his boxing career and returned to his ship, promising to "have another try, when next he arrived in England." In the end, Morgan perhaps unsurprisingly decided that the costs for—and the ridicule faced by—black fighters far outweighed the benefits. No other black prizefighters appeared in the 1820s.[85]

Jewish boxers faced a different set of problems in the 1820s. While black pugilists were usually treated with contempt and not taken seriously, Jewish fighters and patrons came to be associated with the corruption plaguing the sport. An alleged fixed bout involving prominent Jewish fighter Barney Aaron in 1824 sparked a public discussion of Jewish honor that deployed many anti-Semitic stereotypes. As a result of this public debate, the perception that greedy and disloyal Jews were responsible for the scourge of match-fixing gained credence.

Barney Aaron, nicknamed "The Star of the East," was born in Aldgate on November 21, 1800, and gained attention in his youth fighting fellow Jews in the East End. His first prizefight was for a subscription purse following a match between Peter Crawley and Dick Acton in Surrey in May 1823.[86] Early in his career, journalists commended Aaron for his exemplary behavior. After he defeated a boxer named Lenney, Aaron claimed that he had been offered £30 to lose, but had refused it. Egan offered great praise "to the Jew, for not throwing his 'own people' over the bridge." As Aaron continued to win matches, he became more popular among Jewish boxing supporters. When he defeated Frank Redman in January 1824, he "returned to town in first rate style" and went to Howard's Coffee Shop, a center of activity for Jewish boxers and patrons. A large crowd assembled to celebrate his victory.[87] Egan claimed that Aaron's supporters sung "Vat a nishe boy, To give the Jews joy—O Barney's a second DUTCH SAM" at the match.[88]

As quickly as Barney Aaron rose to prominence, his career took a dramatic turn. After unluckily losing a fight, he was involved with an allegedly fixed match. On June 21, 1824, he faced Arthur Matthewson, who had defeated Israel Belasco in a closely fought bout the preceding year. A large crowd turned up to watch the fight. Jewish spectators were supposedly "the majority of the persons on the ground" and surrounded the ring with their carriages. Before the match began, one of Aaron's patrons tied a yellow handkerchief to the stakes for him, as was increasingly customary for Jewish boxers in the 1820s. Aaron dominated the match and the excited spectators broke the ring in some places. When some men on horseback attempted to clear it, "the Jews were in solid phalanx, and were proof to the charge." After more than an hour of fighting and fifty-six rounds, Matthewson could barely reach the scratch. Unfortunately for Aaron and his Jewish supporters, however, Matthewson landed a lucky blow on Aaron's throat, knocking him unconscious. The "losses of the Jews," according to the *Sporting Magazine*, were "immense, as they backed their man to the last at the highest odds." Aaron sent a letter to the *Weekly Dispatch* arguing that the men employed to keep the ring clear purposely whipped him, but his position failed to gain traction.[89]

Despite his unfortunate loss to Matthewson, Jewish patrons backed Aaron for a fight against Dick Curtis in November. The bout was to be fought on a stage outside Warwick following another match between Josh Hudson and Tom Cannon. In the week before the bout, betting odds began to favor Aaron over Curtis and, on the morning of the fight, word spread that it was cancelled.[90] In the midst of confusion, Aaron's backers took him to London. After they left, Curtis and Tom Belcher mounted the stage and called for Aaron. When he did not appear, they proclaimed victory. Later, Aaron's patrons claimed that their man had left the scene because Curtis's supporters had attempted to fix the match. In contrast, Curtis's partisans argued that Aaron's Jewish patrons forced him to leave because their attempts to bribe Curtis had failed and they were sure that Aaron could not win.[91]

Journalists and followers of the sport responded rapidly, initiating a debate that helped to strengthen the specious claim that Jewish people were responsible for the corruption that led to the decline of the sport in the 1820s. The November issue of the *Sporting Magazine* offered an interpretation of the events that unequivocally blamed Jews for the attempted fix. After his loss to Matthewson, an article in the magazine argued that "there was no true confidence in Barney" and, as a result, "the Jews" spent thousands in an effort to get Curtis to throw the fight. Curtis, however, "was incorruptible to all the bribes and temptations of the Jews" and stayed "true to his pledge and his character." Since "the Jews" had wagered considerable sums on Aaron, they decided not to let him fight. The article concluded by deriding the Jewish community for having "not even the manliness to declare a forfeit."[92]

One of Aaron's patrons wrote a letter to the *Weekly Dispatch* responding to the charges against Aaron and "the Jews." J. Alexander contended that Curtis's backers set up the intended fix and that he, upon hearing of it, took Aaron back to London. Alexander also denounced the anti–Semitism that accompanied the charges of match fixing. After Aaron's principal supporters left Warwick, he claimed, Curtis and Belcher mounted the stage and shouted, "Where are your Jews now?" In response, Alexander asked the "Christian fighting men … to remember the Jews that have fought with honour" and to recall that the vast majority of fixed matches involved Christians. He also decried the "illiberality" of the press "towards the Jews" during the controversy. In conclusion, Alexander asked all of those concerned with the sport to recall that "there are as good men among the Jews as any other class of men."[93]

Two letters to the *Weekly Dispatch* in subsequent weeks responded to Alexander and took up the charge of Jewish honor and manliness. A letter from "Investigator" began by announcing that its author was a "strong advocate for the manly art of boxing." As long as the "national mode of deciding quarrels" remained, "the introduction of the stiletto need not be feared." Because of this, "Investigator" contended, he "could not ... help feeling extreme regret" upon reading Alexander's letter. His regret stemmed not from the anti–Semitic attacks on Aaron and his patrons, but rather from Alexander's denial of their match fixing. In contrast to Alexander, "Investigator" assumed that Jews were behind the fix because, though "there are honourable Jews, it is pretty generally conceived that persons of that persuasion are not *very squeamish* or particular in what way benefits are conferred upon them, so [long] as they ... receive [benefits]."[94] For "Investigator," the sport of boxing was being undermined not just by corruption but the relentless pursuit of money at any cost that he associated with Jews.

A letter answered "Investigator" the following week. The letter writer, identified as "Fair Play," attempted to reassert the egalitarian rhetoric of the sport. "Fair Play" began by noting that he did "not like the indiscriminate abuse of the JEWS." In fact, the letter argued, the anger directed at Jewish people was completely misplaced because Aaron's backers "were, *or professed to be*, Christians." Further, supporters of the sport should not be angered when Jewish people supported one of their own because "it is the real *esprit de corps*, that ought to be encouraged; it is the same feeling that induces.... Irishmen to back Jack Langan." For "Fair Play," the fact that Jewish people supported Jewish boxers was a critical issue. This natural impulse was a central pillar of the sport's popularity and, therefore, should be encouraged. Corruption was the problem, not partisanship. Although this letter ended the debate in the *Weekly Dispatch* on a positive note, the values championed by "Fair Play" were undermined in other publications. Journalist John Badcock claimed that "the system of pugilism we term the Israelitish or Hebrew School" degraded the sport because it inaugurated the practice of "each side hoisting up the stakes to unexampled sums."[95]

The controversy did not deter Aaron, and he continued to seek a match with Curtis throughout 1825. Jewish patrons were wary of supporting him, however. In May Vincent Dowling argued that "some [Jewish patrons] are pushing Barney Aaron and Belasco forward; others are waddling off like lame ducks."[96] In late September, Curtis wrote a letter to *Bell's Life in London* complaining that a fight had not been made between the two because Aaron did not have enough money for the stakes.[97] In January 1826, "One of the People" wrote a letter to the *Weekly Dispatch* complaining that Jewish patrons would not support Barney Aaron, who had been "literally shut out of the ring." The author of this letter considered this a poor reward for a "brave and honest lad."[98] Finally, in March 1826, Aaron fought again, entering the ring with veteran fighter Dick Ayres for half the money Curtis had demanded. Dowling claimed that Aaron was backed by Jewish patrons and remarked on the large number of Jewish spectators present. Aaron won the match easily and was rewarded the following month with a successful benefit exhibition at Howard's Coffee House.[99] When he resumed efforts to make a match with Curtis, however, patronage was not immediately forthcoming.[100] After much discussion, a bout between Curtis and Aaron was agreed and the two men fought for £100 on a stage in Andover in February 1827, over two years after the aborted first contest. Curtis defeated Aaron in a compelling match.[101]

While the controversy and the expressions of anti–Semitism surrounding Barney Aaron certainly had an effect on Jewish spectatorship and patronage, it did not entirely drive Jewish people from the sport. Aaron received patronage for several other bouts and was supported at benefits after Curtis defeated him. He remained active in the sport after his retirement as well, as a fish vendor supplying fight-goers.[102] There were other signs that Jewish involvement in the sport continued as well. Howard's Coffee Shop debuted a room with a roped ring in late 1826, when the terms of the fight between Aaron and Curtis were being negotiated.[103] The flamboyant Jewish fighter Samuel Evans also had a successful career in this period. The son of "Dutch" Sam Elias, Evans was known as "Young Dutch Sam." Like Jem Ward, Evans drew his support from outside the Jewish community. Some writers even doubted that Evans was Sam Elias's son or that he was Jewish. He also kept the company of debauched young aristocrats and, after winning several high-profile bouts, fell in with a notorious crowd of rakes and died in the early 1840s.[104]

By 1833, the ethnic spectacles that had been a critical element of the popularity of boxing since Mendoza's matches against Humphries were on the wane. Some of the best fighters of this era—Ned Neale, Jem Ward, and Samuel Evans—were less willing to present themselves as champions of a narrow community (or, in the case of Neale, became less willing to do so). Jewish, black, and Irish-born boxers remained part of the sport but came to be associated with disorder, corruption, and ridiculous spectacle. As we have seen, this was partly a consequence of changes in the sport. More matches were fought and were more widely reported than ever before but, increasingly, the greater visibility of bare-knuckle prizefighting exposed it to the prejudices of popular opinion. The self-confident minority identities on display in the ring (and amplified by the press) provoked strong reactions from the white, Protestant, and English majority. The spectacle of two men determining the worth of their ethnic communities in a bloody combat also seemed positively primitive to many in the age of reform. Increasingly, these reformers were willing to call the enablers of the sport to account, as the organizers of the Byrne and Mackay bout found.

Despite these troubled times, the sport endured. After Jem Ward defeated Simon Byrne in 1831 it was not clear that he would fight again and so another second-generation Irishman, James "Deaf" Burke, claimed the Championship. Byrne, who had retired to Ireland, returned to England to fight him near St. Alban's in May 1833. The scene was much changed from even a few years earlier. The Fair Play Club was moribund and very few fighters appeared to clear the ring and keep order. Before the fight began, Burke played to the crowd, making faces, smoking a cigar, and jokingly taking Byrne's arm. Byrne supposedly questioned Burke's sanity. After the fight began, spectators breached the ring and interfered with the fight, which Dowling called "most disgusting and disgraceful." Despite the interference, Burke finally defeated Byrne in the ninety-third round. The unfortunate Byrne died as a consequence of injuries suffered in the fight.[105]

English-born of Irish parents, James Burke was champion in the 1830s. From Miles, *Pugilistica*, vol. 3.

"Deaf" Burke, like Byrne before him, was able to avoid prosecution for Byrne's death. He was unable, however, to make a match for the next several years. As a consequence, he made an important decision that pointed the way toward the future of the sport: he traveled to the United States. Boxing was also illegal in the United States, but the size of the country made it easier to evade authorities. Ethnic spectacles also made the sport very popular in the young country. After arriving in the U.S.—which Burke called "Yankeeshire"—he made a match with Irish immigrant Sam O'Rourke. The two fought outside New Orleans on May 9, 1837. New Orleans had a large Irish population, which "adopted O'Rourke as a hero." These partisans interrupted the fight, chased Burke away, and carried O'Rourke back to town in a wagon.[106] The sport of bare-knuckle boxing, with ethnic conflict at its core, had arrived in America.

Chapter Eight

The Spread and Transformation of Bare-Knuckle Boxing in the Victorian World, 1834–1867

Many of the troubles that bedeviled bare-knuckle prizefighting between 1825 and 1833 endured for the next several decades. Match fixing and crowd control were always a concern and the new professional police forces that appeared in these years made fights difficult and dangerous to stage. The sport was also less popular among the upper class than at any point since the 1770s and many considered it an atavistic remnant of Old Corruption in an age of attacks on slavery, child labor, and cruelty to animals.[1] A series of underwhelming champions in the 1830s and 1840s deprived boxing of a symbol to rival the fabled titleholders of the past. Such a champion might have helped sporting journalists bolster their claims about the national importance of the sport. As it was, Vincent Dowling and his colleagues frequently lamented its decline and feared that effeminacy was on the march.

The gloom of Dowling and others masks a great deal of innovation and growth, however, much of it building on innovations from the postwar period. Newspaper coverage of matches continued to increase, many more fights were contested around the country and beyond, and some embryonic organizational structures confronted long-standing problems of corruption and order at bouts. Steam-powered transportation created opportunities for profit as specially chartered trains and steamboats took small groups of paying customers to matches and helped them evade authorities. The trend toward democratizing the sport continued as well. Gentlemen amateurs receded further into the background while journalists and publicans (many of them former boxers) made matches, posted stakes for fighters, and publicized the sport. One consequence of this was that those involved in the sport sought creative ways to profit from the prizefighting and, in the process, helped to transform it. Black, Jewish, and Irish boxers were at the forefront of these changes.

This chapter will show that, despite endemic corruption and the repeated efforts of authorities to stamp it out, bare-knuckle prizefighting was marked by innovation and expansion in the period from the 1830s to the 1850s. A number of provincial cities challenged the prizefighting dominance of London and the sport also expanded around the world to the United States and Australia. Newspapers reported on matches in all of these places, helping to make British boxing a world sport. Entrepreneurial prizefighters and publicans experimented with other paths to profit as well. These blended pugilism with emerging forms of urban amusement and helped make theatricality and performance even more important to the sport. The chapter will examine the career of several boxers in order to show that, though leading figures in the sport were more hostile to them than ever before black, Jewish, and Irish boxers were a critical part of these developments. Their contributions to the development of the sport have often been forgotten, however, because of the dismissive attitudes of many writers toward them.

When Vincent Dowling was diagnosing the problems of boxing in 1841, he highlighted the lack of "big men" who were likely to "live in story" after retirement. The best pugilists were small, while a series of underwhelming and unsavory fighters claimed the Championship.[2] The perception was that the sport lacked a title-holder who could be cast as the quintessence of British manhood and be the standard-bearer of the sport. As we have seen, second-generation Irishman James "Deaf" Burke claimed the Championship after defeating Simon Byrne in 1833. Former champion Jem Ward disputed Burke's title, however, and then continued to increase the amount for which he was willing to fight Burke. Finally, in 1835, a group of boxing supporters met and announced that the champion must meet a challenge for £200 or more. Ward conceded and Burke had the title. Never particularly popular, Burke held it until losing to the unscrupulous William Thompson (known as "Bendigo") in 1839. Bendigo, in turn, suffered a career-threatening injury while clowning after a steeplechase, leaving the title open to others. Hulking and slow-moving Ben Caunt fought and defeated Jem Ward's brother Nick in May 1841 for £100 a side and claimed the title for the next four years. In 1845, the rehabilitated Bendigo recaptured it by defeating Caunt with questionable tactics (including falling without being struck) in front of a rowdy crowd. Dowling proclaimed the match the most "disgraceful and disgusting exhibition" in the "annals of British boxing." Nevertheless, Bendigo was considered the champion for the remainder of the decade.[3] Throughout the 1830s and 1840s, then, the championship was mired in controversy, corruption, and mediocrity.

This did not keep the promoters of the sport from making determined efforts to present unpalatable title-holders as representatives of British manhood. The champion's belt was an important means to do so. Jem Ward gave his belt (which he had received for defeating Byrne in 1831) to Bendigo after that fighter's triumph over "Deaf" Burke in 1839. As we have seen, this belt had a wreath of rose, thistle, and shamrock above a British lion. Wearing this symbol, the champion was believed to represent the United Kingdom. When Caunt won the title in 1841, he received a belt that was quite similar to Ward's, including its prominent intertwined rose, thistle, and shamrock. This was a transferable prize that bore the names of all holders of the title and would be carried by each new champion.[4] Journalists also reminded readers of the important role played by the champion. As Dowling denounced the Bendigo and Caunt match in 1845, he reminded his readers that the title "Champion of England" was a "high distinction." It was presumed that the champion was a man of "humanity and honourable bearing," who was respected and admired by "all classes of his countrymen."[5] If Bendigo and Caunt did not demonstrate these qualities, Dowling argued, it reflected their shortcomings and not a failure of the ideals of the sport.

Journalists also continued to rehearse the old arguments about the connection between boxing and the superiority of English manhood. Despite the British symbolism of the Champion's belt, this increasingly meant a heightened emphasis on white, Protestant, English manhood. These ideas were most fully formed in Vincent Dowling's *Fistiana, or Oracle of the Ring* published by *Bell's Life in London* owner William Clement in 1841. In this work Dowling argued that a critical advantage of boxing was that it placed on display, unalloyed, the manhood of the peoples of the earth. Stepping in the ring laid bare "the headlong impetuosity of the Irishman—the caution of the wary Jew, risking no more than is absolutely necessary," and "the short-lived fury of the … negro … commonly bottomless, and yielding to opposition." In contrast, "the genuine John Bull, armed at all points by a courage equally active and passive" was "the safest man to back in the universe." Dowling also looked outward to a world where British naval and economic might were increasingly dominant, asking "pusillanimous inhabitants of finer climes than ours" to look at "what courage has done for us!" Answering his own question, he triumphantly proclaimed that "we have conquered ye, we have seized upon your countries, explore and cultivate them for our advantage, and made ye our vassals!" A scourge of effeminacy was infecting the world, he argued, and solid John Bull manhood—best represented in the boxing ring—was the cure.[6] Proponents of Rugby football made similar arguments about their sport in the 1850s and 1860s as well.[7]

Such attitudes contrasted with the views of Pierce Egan. Egan, as we have seen, strongly believed in a connection between boxing and British greatness but favored an expansive notion of Britishness in which Irish, Jewish, and black boxers might be included. He had been one of the leading figures in the sport for much of the 1810s and 1820s, but his style and sensibility seemed outmoded and he was largely absent from the prizefighting world for the last two decades of his life. He had some success in the 1830s building on his earlier fame with *The Book of Sports*, *Life in Dublin* and *Life in Liverpool*, but struggled financially. In 1842, he wrote a letter to Sir Robert Peel to ask for help. Citing the fact that he had "afforded … considerable amusement to the Public" and providing a list of his many publications, Egan requested assistance "in any manner you have the power to grant." Peel declined.[8] This poignant postscript to Egan's illustrious career illustrated not only the difficult financial position that Egan faced by the 1840s, but also the position in society he at one time enjoyed, one which enabled him to apply to the soon-to-be Prime Minister for financial assistance. By his death in 1849, his "flash" style and jocularly inclusive sensibility seemed to belong to a different age.

Around the time of Egan's departure further attempts were made to combat some of the sport's most serious problems, especially disruptive crowds and match fixing. As we have seen, leading boxers, journalists, and sporting gentlemen formed the Fair Play Club in 1828. This was meant to provide a rudimentary organizational structure that would pay pugilists to maintain crowd order at fights and also organize collections for losing fighters. It did not last long, however, and, in 1832, the club's official ropes and stakes were entrusted to ex-pugilist Tom Oliver, who had assumed John Jackson's role as master of ceremonies.[9] More enduring changes occurred as well. In June 1838, *Bell's Life in London* called for a meeting to revise and expand Broughton's sparse seven rules. A modified code was written and some pugilists began to use it by the end of the year.[10] The new rules standardized many customary practices, such as the twenty-four-foot ring and the tying of colors to the stakes. They also explicitly prevented kicking and gouging, addressed issues of crowd control, and regularized the payment of bets. By 1853, after further reforms, the twenty-nine rules were "intensely detailed and legalistic."[11] Although often flouted, the new code defined the sport more explicitly than ever before, making clear what was a legitimate prizefight and what was not.[12]

The transformation of transportation and law enforcement in the second third of the nineteenth century were perhaps even more consequential to the development of bare-knuckle prizefighting. The rapid spread of railway lines in the 1830s and 1840s had an immediate effect on the way that spectators traveled to matches. The motley collection of pedestrians, animals, and vehicles crowding the roads to important matches—famously described in William Hazlitt's essay "The Fight"—were increasingly supplanted by trains or steamships, though spectators still had to travel long distances to the fight from the nearest station. The convenience of this novel form of travel was balanced by the dependence of spectators on rigid train schedules. Special chartered excursion trains or steamboats, not specifically banned until 1868, were an alternative.[13] The evasion of hostile authorities, a part of the sport since the shift to outdoor venues in 1760s, became much more challenging in consequence of a series of reforms beginning in 1829, which led local governments to set up their own paid police forces. The new forces aggressively sought intelligence about where fights would be held and much more frequently intervened to prevent matches.[14]

Advances in transportation and communication technologies also helped boxing become a more truly national sport, as prizefighting became entrenched in the midlands and the north and local organizations challenged the preeminence of London. Provincial "Prize Rings," such as the "Liverpool Prize Ring" and the "Birmingham Prize Ring," were associations of boxing supporters that owned ropes and stakes, organized prizefights, and kept order at them.[15] Provincial tours, a staple of the sport since Mendoza in the late eighteenth century, also became more important than ever. The rapid growth of urban industrial areas in the midlands and north of England and in Scotland created large potential audiences, who could spend a few shillings at a theater or pub in the evening but found it much more difficult to walk to a remote rural location on a weekday for a prizefight. Many pugilists recognized this shift and learned to become better showman, especially as they had to compete with the burgeoning entertainments of Victorian Britain. The tactics used by Mendoza, Molineaux, and many others—behaving outlandishly to gain a response from the crowd, dressing and acting flamboyantly, and defeating overconfident local toughs—became ever more important for many pugilists.

Fighters from minority groups were at the forefront of these innovations, despite the increasing hostility they faced from the likes of Dowling and other journalists. Moroccan-born James Wharton, among the most talented and popular fighters of the period, was important to the growth of boxing outside of London, for example. Wharton, born in Tangiers in 1813, worked on a British merchant vessel carrying goods from Cairo to London as a teenager and gained a reputation as a boxer on board. On one voyage, Major George Broadfoot—on furlough from India and soon to make his reputation in the First Anglo-Afghan War—noticed Wharton's fighting skill and convinced him to go to Jem Burn's Queen's Head Tavern. The ex-pugilist Burn was a prominent patron and, as Dowling later wrote, "not particular to a shade."[16] Burn matched Wharton in several fights between 1833 and 1836, and "the

Moroccan Prince" (as he came to be called) won them all. During this time, he began to tour with "Deaf" Burke and Bob Cootes in the midlands and north. He also began to be associated with the Liverpool Prize Ring, which organized two prizefights involving Wharton: a November 1835 victory over Bill Fisher and a controversial draw with Tom Britton the following February. Both matches were contested near Newcastle-under-Lyme. Although he faced hostile crowds in many of his early fights, newspaper accounts attributed this to pride of place rather than racial feeling.[17]

After his match with Britton, Wharton moved north to Liverpool and continued to tour. He was now well known in Liverpool, Manchester, and Birmingham and was the main attraction in a group of touring exhibitors associated with Lancashire boxing. In 1837, he made a match with undefeated Harry Preston of Birmingham for £100 a side. The highly anticipated bout, fought under the auspices of the Birmingham Prize Ring, brought together boxing supporters from around the country. Tom Oliver, the successor to John Jackson as "Commander-in-Chief" of the London Prize Ring, brought ropes and stakes from the Birmingham Prize Ring to the site of the contest. *Bell's Life in London* reported that thousands came from Birmingham, Manchester, and Liverpool and many more than expected from London. The paper commented that the "desire to witness a 'mill' was equal to that evinced in the most palmy days" of the sport.[18]

The match did not disappoint expectations. A violent contest throughout, it was decided by Wharton's superior wrestling; Preston was unresponsive and feared dead after Wharton threw him on his head to end the bout. Preston survived but Wharton's fame reached new heights after his impressive performance. He went to London and was welcomed there by supporters of the ring. Later, he was "loudly cheered" when introduced to the crowd before the match between Bendigo and Bill Looney in Derbyshire.[19] Wharton also returned to his sparring tour. He and his partner dramatized the Preston fight for spectators and interspersed the action with jokes and songs. Like Daniel Mendoza, Wharton dressed in finery and made a show of his sophistication.[20] Not surprisingly, he received a number of challenges on tour, some more serious than others. In Scotland, he pummeled a local tough who heckled him during a performance and, during, a visit to Newcastle-upon-Tyne, when Wharton and his partners were exhibiting at the Newcastle Theater, Wharton was challenged by local wrestler William Renwick. Renwick was large and experienced but Wharton nevertheless defeated him with relative ease.[21]

Wharton's final fight came against undefeated John Lane of Birmingham on June 9, 1840. Known as "Hammer Lane," the Birmingham boxer challenged

Wharton to fight for £100 a side and Wharton accepted.[22] Like Wharton's match against Harry Preston, his fight with Hammer Lane prompted excitement around the country. *Bell's Life in London* noted that no match since the championship bout between Bendigo and "Deaf" Burke had "created so extraordinary a sensation among the followers of the ring." A large body of spectators from Liverpool, Birmingham, and London descended on a field outside Worksop, Nottinghamshire while representatives of the Birmingham Prize Ring set up the ring with their ropes and stakes. A few young noblemen even attended. The large assemblage witnessed an exciting fight in which Wharton was nearly defeated when Lane choked him against the ropes. He soon recovered, however, and slammed his opponent to the ground. The fight continued but the damage was done. Wharton won and *Bell's Life in London* showered him with praise, noting that "his science is beautiful, but his skill, foresight, and generalship is preeminent."[23] This was quite different than the "short lived fury of the negro," which Dowling claimed the ring revealed in *Fistiana* published the following year.

Despite such glowing reviews of his skill, Wharton never fought for the title. At less than seventy inches and around 150 pounds, he was smaller than any champion. He nearly made a match with Bendigo but negotiations broke down on the issue of weight. When Bendigo was injured, the opportunity was lost. Wharton retired undefeated and remained involved in the sport as a trainer, a second, and a publican in Manchester and Liverpool (where he took over Jem Ward's pub) before dying in Liverpool of consumption in 1856.[24] Although he was one of the most successful and influential pugilists of the 1830s and 1840s, Wharton received very little acclaim after his death. *Bell's Life in London* lamented that he died poor and left a destitute widow. A promised sketch of his career never appeared, however.[25] Henry Downes Miles, one of Dowling's successors at *Bell's Life in London*, only mentioned him briefly in his three-volume history of the sport. In contrast, Miles devoted twenty-eight pages to describing the career of Nick Ward, a far inferior fighter mostly known for being Jem Ward's brother. When he did write about Wharton, Miles minimized his importance by noting that he was "the talk of the provincial fancy."[26]

Other black boxers were active in the 1830s and 1840s as well, often freely mixing entertainment with pugilism. Among the most prosperous of these was African American immigrant Thomas Sutton, who enjoyed a successful career as an entertainer and boxer in the late 1830s. Born in the United States in about 1816, Sutton first came to public notice as part of a wrestling exhibition held at the Pantheon Theater in the Strand in late December 1835. After some wrestlers and a Highland dancer appeared, Sutton came on stage and performed the act for which he would be best known: singing and dancing on his head. Impressed audience members threw coins on stage.[27] Ultimately, his act came to include a routine that capitalized on the "Jim Crow" mania during the second half of 1836, which was prompted by American T.D. Rice's run of minstrel performances at the Surrey Theatre.[28] Sutton gained a reputation for singing "Jim Crow Jump" and dancing at benefit exhibitions and after matches. By 1837, newspapers even began to refer to Sutton as "Jim Crow."[29] In 1839, he performed that song and others at the London Theater and, later, toured with "Deaf" Burke in a combination of sparring and Shakespeare's Othello.[30]

In the course of his early performances, Sutton came in contact with pugilists and began to spar at exhibitions. Wharton's former collaborator Jem Burn trained and promoted him and, after a Friday evening cockfight, matched Sutton against Nick Ward for £5. The fight, which was arranged as a test for Ward, resulted in Ward walking out of the ring after being punched once by Sutton. Sutton celebrated by dancing on his head while his supporters laughed and clapped.[31] Burn, also buoyed by Sutton's success in sparring exhibitions, then began promoting him around the country in an attempt, according to *Bell's Life in London*, to reassert the superiority of the London Prize Ring and "to keep alive the olden spirit of British boxing." Finally, Harry Preston of Birmingham challenged Sutton for £50 a side.[32] On the day of the fight, December 20, a large entourage from Birmingham arrived in an omnibus drawn by four horses as a bugler played "See the Conquering Hero Comes." To the delight of his supporters, Preston easily defeated Sutton. *Bell's Life in London* noted that the match demonstrated the "triumph of 'the Brums' over the fast-fading" London Prize Ring.[33]

With the exception of an interrupted rematch with Nick Ward in 1837, Sutton did not have another prizefight for more than five years. By 1840, he was using the profits from his various acts to put his finances on a firmer footing. He met Isabella Pearce at the Burlington Arcade (where she worked in a jewelry shop) and married her at St. Martin's Church later in the year. The couple opened a cigar shop in Drury Lane and lived near Soho Square. Sutton continued to perform and to teaching boxing to wealthy young men for extra income. He was particularly popular with the undergraduates of Cambridge and, in May 1842, he and Isabella moved to the Black Bear Inn in Cambridge while Sutton tried to establish himself as a wine merchant.[34] The report of one of his last matches in *Bell's Life in London* provides a glimpse of Sutton in this period. The paper reported that he "displayed his person in fashionably cut togs," which often included white kid gloves. A curled imperial mustache accented his fine clothes. Clearly, Sutton considered it important to look the part of a gentleman for his well-heeled clientele.[35]

Sutton finally entered the ring again in October 1842, for a fight against the Australian John Gorrick (known as Bungaree), who had been brought to Britain by George Humphrey, an aged Tory printer and former associate of the famous illustrator George Cruickshank. Gorrick had performed poorly in his first match, but Humphrey seems to have hoped that a fight with Sutton would resurrect interest in his man. *Bell's Life in London* claimed that Sutton agreed to enter the ring again because Humphrey had made racist remarks to him, but it is far more likely that he sought money to help him set up as a wine merchant in Cambridge. The fight took place near Royston, about ten miles southwest of Cambridge, for £100 a side. Large numbers of well-heeled spectators took the train north from London and many more came down from Cambridge to see the match. When the boxers arrived, Bungaree made clear that he represented Australia. He tied to the stake a white standard with a blue border and emblazoned with the national colonial flag and the word "Australia." Sutton did not appear as the champion of England, but there was some suggestion that he represented black Britons. *Bell's Life in London* wrote that he was a member of the "ebony brotherhood" and Jem Wharton came from Liverpool to act as his second. His color was cream with a black spot. After the fight began, it was clear that Sutton had underestimated his opponent, having declined intensive training or even trimming his hair. Bungaree beat him rather easily.[36]

Sutton's last bout was a rematch with Bungaree in March 1843. The two signed articles shortly after the conclusion of their first fight; Sutton still needed money to set up as a wine merchant and Humphrey was eager to realize another profit. In order to do so, he chartered a steamboat that carried a small and wealthy crowd to the site of the match. Building on the narrative of the first bout, *Bell's Life in London* characterized the match as a contest between an Australian and a black man. A story headlined "Rouge et Noir" (Bungaree used crimson as his color for the second bout) began with a poem purportedly written by Sutton. The poem included the line "A white feather shouldn't belong to a black" and asked if "Bungaree, the Australian, or black Sambo Sutton" would win. Whatever he thought of this interpretation of the battle, Sutton trained seriously and outfought his opponent. Bungaree was far less motivated and may even have been forced to fight as he abruptly left the ring after the ninth round and declared that he would not speak to Humphrey again. He soon returned to Australia. Sutton's victory prompted *Bell's Life in London* to include a gloating poem called "The Lament of Australia," noting that Bungaree and his backers would find their flag emblazoned with "Australia, retreat."[37]

Sutton's victory over Bungaree was his final prizefight. Unfortunately, his attempts to become a wine merchant and boxing trainer in Cambridge were frustrated when his wife left him for a local bricklayer named Samuel Preston.[38] After a failed legal action against Preston in 1844, Sutton returned to London and threw himself into the boxing and entertainment scene for the next several years. He held two benefit exhibitions in 1845 and was matched to fight Nobby Clarke for £50 a side. When this match failed to materialize, he tried (without success) to find another opponent in August.[39] In January 1846, he was the opening performer of the season in the sparring room at the Black Lion in Drury Lane and even agreed to sing "some of his negro melodies."[40] The following month, he began a tour of Ireland with future champion William Perry (known as "the Tipton Slasher") and, in the fall, he was back in London to hold a costume ball at the Parthenon Assembly rooms in St. Martin's Lane.[41] He continued this mix of sparring and entertainment in London and around the kingdom for the rest of the decade. In 1850, Jem Ward asked him to manage his new Gymnasium for Gladiatorial Exercises in Liverpool.[42] The frenetic activity—especially the late hours and drinking necessitated by his occupation—took their toll, however, and Sutton died at thirty-seven in July 1852.[43] Despite his nearly two decades of success, he died penniless.

Along with black boxers, Jewish pugilists continued to play a critical role in the sport in the 1830s and 1840s. The most successful Jewish fighter of these years was Israel Lazarus. Like Wharton and Sutton, Lazarus was involved in the changes in the sport and, more broadly, in urban entertainment. Like Wharton, Lazarus was a key part of the growth of boxing in the midlands and north in the 1830s and 1840s and, ultimately, in the United States in the 1850s. His pubs were important centers for the making of matches, the posting of stakes, and for gathering before and after fights. At the same time, like Sutton, he was a part of the transformation of urban entertainment in mid–Victorian England. His houses were known for so-called "Free-and-Easies," predecessors to music halls that involved drinking and singing in a large group, led by a celebrity guest.

Lazarus was born on February 9, 1812, in Whitechapel and became a successful prizefighter by his early twenties. He grew up surrounded by the thriving London Jewish boxing culture of the early nineteenth century, which was led by Daniel Mendoza and the Belasco family. Like many aspiring pugilists, he first gained notoriety in bouts with young men in his neighborhood. Sources disagree about his first prizefight, but his first verifiable encounter was against "Young Brinson" near Newport Pagnell in March 1834. *Bell's Life in London* wrote simply that the fight "was won by the Jew."[44] At age twenty-two, Lazarus began to rise in the estimation of the supporters of the sport. He had already begun managing former champion Peter Crawley's sparring rooms—and tutoring his paying clients—when he defeated Brinson. After his victory, he was matched against Bill Atkinson, who had just lost to Owen Swift, for £10.[45]

Like Jewish boxers before him, Lazarus faced aggressively hostile crowds when traveling far from London. After he agreed to meet Atkinson twelve miles or nearer to that pugilist's home city of Nottingham, *Bell's Life in London* expressed anxiety about whether "the *Sheeney* will have fair play" and feared that the Nottingham men would break the ring to prevent the defeat of Atkinson, if necessary.[46] While Atkinson's partisans did not interrupt the match, Lazarus complained of suffering from foul play; he was disqualified after he struck a blow when Atkinson was falling, even though Atkinson had done the same to him several times earlier in the match. *Bell's Life in London* saw this as confirmation of its concern, noting that "the Jew was in the hands of the Philistines, and we did not anticipate that he would have had a fair chance."[47] Lazarus disputed the outcome of the match publicly but was unable to generate any support for his position. Atkinson offered to fight him again but the match never came off.

A critical reason that Lazarus lost his match against Atkinson was that he lacked support among the crowd. Minority fighters had long known the hazards of facing a hostile audience and Jewish spectators do not seem to have made the journey north to Nottingham for the match. In contrast, when aging Jewish pugilist Barney Aaron fought Tom Smith around the same time, Jewish supporters predominated in the crowd. Even though Smith won easily, Aaron's backers organized a benefit for him at the Pavilion Theater in Whitechapel.[48] This was partly because Aaron's match was much nearer London. More importantly, though, it was also because Aaron had long deliberately cultivated the support of the Jewish community. He was based in Whitechapel and held benefits at Howard's Coffee Shop in Aldgate. Lazarus, in contrast, worked at Peter Crawley's for much of the 1830s and was generally associated with boxing in the West End. As a result, few Jewish spectators seem to have attended his next match, an easy victory over a fighter named Allen just outside the metropolis in February 1836.[49] As a result of his failure to cultivate Jewish supporters, when Lazarus tried to make a match against Tom Smith for £25 a side in 1836, he could not find any Jewish backers.[50]

The same trend continued through Lazarus's next two fights. He was matched against Londoner Tom Maley in August 1836 for the paltry sum of £15. A small crowd gathered at Colney Heath to see Lazarus defeat the smaller Maley in a difficult, thirty-five-minute fight. Once again, few Jewish spectators seem to have made the twenty-mile journey from the metropolis to support

Lazarus, though Barney Aaron served as his second.[51] The following March, Lazarus fought the unimpressively named "Surrender" Lane of Birmingham for £25 after a match involving Lane's more celebrated relation "Hammer" Lane. A sizeable crowd, coming mostly from Birmingham, assembled in a field near Woodstock to see the two fights. The reporter for *Bell's Life in London* noticed that Lazarus "seemed a little down on his luck" because he was alone and "uncheered by the presence of his backers" until Peter Crawley and others arrived. Seconded again by Barney Aaron, Lazarus won easily.[52]

Lazarus's final prizefight, against Owen Swift near Royston in June 1837, was also his most lucrative. The notorious Marquess of Waterford, who was Swift's patron, arranged the match and organized money for training and stakes. According to *Bell's Life in London*, he and his associates did so to promote "that manly bearing and 'fair play' which the example of the sports of the Ring are calculated to produce on the minds of the lower orders."[53] Rumors also circulated that Waterford had paid Lazarus £300 to lose the match in order to take advantage of heavy Jewish betting on him.[54] Whatever the merit of the rumor about Waterford, accounts of the fight confirm that Jewish spectators came out in force to support Lazarus. He used yellow as his color and once again had Barney Aaron—now joined by Samuel Evans—as a second. *Bell's Life in London* also reported cheers of support from Jewish spectators and the vigorous efforts of Aaron, who "seemed to make the case his own." A week later, the newspaper published a poem titled "The Lament of the Children of Israel for the Defeat of Izzy Lazarus," which imagined Jewish supporters calling Lazarus "our Hebrew Pet" and comparing him to great Jewish fighters of the past. Still, Lazarus was reluctant to fully embrace the mantel of Champion of the Jews. He arrived at the scene of the fight with a party of "Corinthian" amateurs, all wearing his yellow color. His supporters thus undermined the symbolism of his color, which usually suggested a connection with Jewishness.[55]

Supporters of Lazarus, whatever their background, were disappointed in the result of the match, which Lazarus lost after breaking his collarbone in a fall. Although he was considered to be one of the best pugilists in London and was only twenty-five when Swift defeated him, Lazarus never contested another prizefight. Instead, he embarked on a career as a publican, a fight promoter, and an entertainment entrepreneur. Unlike celebrated Jewish fighters before him, Lazarus left the East End and lived in the north of England and, ultimately, the United States. Apart from a brief return to London in the late 1840s, he lived away from the place of his birth for the rest of his life. His pubs became gathering places for the boxing community and helped pioneer new forms of entertainment. In the process, he made a critical contribution to the spread and transformation of the sport.

As a prizefighter, Lazarus had traveled widely outside London and seen the opportunities available. A few months before his fight with Swift, for example, he had been part of a sparring exhibition at the Queen's Theatre in Liverpool.[56] Only a few months after losing, he moved to Sheffield, where he ran the Castle Tap. His reputation as a noted London boxer helped Lazarus carry on "a roaring trade" by the end of 1837.[57] He was part of a thriving boxing scene in rapidly growing Sheffield—in October 1838, "Deaf" Burke and Bendigo performed at the Sheffield Theatre—and his Castle Tap was where most matches were made.[58] Lazarus apparently did well in Sheffield: *Bell's Life in London* commented in 1839 that he had gained a tremendous amount of weight.[59] In that year, he handed the Castle Tap to his old rival Bill Atkinson and took over The King William. There, he continued to help make matches and train new fighters.[60] By the end of the decade, Lazarus was acknowledged as one of the leaders of the "provincial fancy."

With the Sheffield boxing scene flourishing in the early 1840s, Lazarus moved further north to Newcastle-upon-Tyne in the spring of 1841. For the next six years under the sign of the Golden Anchor and, later, the Angel Inn, Lazarus became a significant figure in the advance of boxing in the north of England. The Golden Anchor quickly became an important site for the making of matches in the region. At the same time, Lazarus also maintained relations with the London Prize Ring. In late spring 1842, he welcomed champion Ben Caunt at the Golden Anchor. The following year, he sent money to a benefit in London for the widow of retired boxer Dick Curtis and hosted the Australian Bungaree. The relationship worked both ways: he contributed accounts of matches to *Bell's Life in London*, keeping Londoners apprized of the state of the sport in the north of England.[61] Such activities were certainly self-serving—Lazarus regularly appealed to wealthy sporting men from London to visit his house in Newcastle—but nevertheless helped shape a national boxing culture in which communities outside London created and maintained their own prizefighting organizations rather than simply seeing the sport as an exotic import from the metropolis.

In addition to his involvement in training fighters, making matches, and reporting results, Lazarus also was an innovative entrepreneur and, as such, was part of a change in the culture of sporting public houses, with important implications for the rest of the century. Like many pugilists since the days of James Figg, Lazarus was a trainer. By the beginning of 1843, he had opened a sparring school at the Angel Inn on Akenside Hill, which he later called by the grandiose title "assembly rooms and theatre of arts and science."[62] He had also found new ways to profit from interest in sport. In December 1844, he helped organize a rowing match "between Coombes, the Champion of the Thames, and Clasper, the Champion of the Tyne" and hired a "fast and commodious" steamer called the Cygnet, promising "ample provision" so that spectators could have a close view of the race in comfort.[63] Lazarus offered other kinds of amusement in Newcastle as well, advertising entertainments "musical and fistical" at the Golden Anchor.[64] By the time he operated the Angel Inn, he hosted a "free and easy" on Tuesdays. These events, involving drinking and group singing hosted by professional entertainers in a pub, were important forerunners of the music hall.[65] On Wednesdays, he offered public boxing instruction.[66] In sport and musical entertainment, Lazarus was part of the gradual commercialization of urban leisure activities that reached full fruition in the second half of the century.

Despite the diversification of his interests, Lazarus's main business continued to involve boxing matches. By the mid–1840s, his Angel Inn was an organizational hub for prizefighting in the northeast of England. Lazurus's high profile and his efforts to promote Newcastle pugilism in London ultimately led to the end of his career there, however. In March 1846, he attended a fight between Michael Reilly and William Gleghorn, taking notes outside the ring in order to write an account for *Bell's Life in London*. When the match resulted in the death of Reilly, Lazarus and others were arrested as accessories. Although the case against him was ultimately thrown out, he was held in Morpeth Gaol for two months.[67] Following his release, Lazarus decided to have a benefit in the metropolis to defray the expenses he had incurred while incarcerated. The venue was the Pavilion Theatre in Whitechapel, the typical customers of which were local and often Jewish.[68] Barney Aaron had held benefit exhibitions in the Pavilion in the past as well. It seems clear then that Lazarus hoped that Jewish crowds would help him recover financially. The gamble was a success and the benefit proved a lucrative night for Lazarus.

Lazarus briefly returned to Newcastle but his experience with the authorities there convinced him to relocate to London. He took over the management of the Kean's Head in Drury Lane and brought with him the same mixture of sparring lessons and free-and-easies—advertised by the late 1840s as harmonic meetings—for which the Angel Inn had been known. Well-known fighters as well as musicians often sat in the chair at these meetings.[69] Lazarus's house seems to have been a success but, by the following January, he had returned to the north of England, this time to Carlisle. He followed the formula of harmonic meetings and sparring lessons here as well.[70] He also kept up the connection with London, advertising regularly in *Bell's Life in London* and sending £10 for the memorial erected for Tom Cribb.[71] Lazarus remained in Carlisle for the remainder of the decade but, by 1850, he and his family left that city and began touring in the north of England and in France. By this time, his two young sons, Harry and John, participated in his sparring exhibitions.[72] Later in the year, the Lazarus family settled in Liverpool and Israel, Harry, and John regularly performed at Jem Ward's gymnasium. Lazarus also began to manage the Crown and Anchor on Great Charlotte Street, where he advertised boxing lessons for children given by his sons.[73] Finally, in 1852, the peripatetic Lazarus, following a trail blazed by a number of other British boxers, took his sons across the Atlantic to take advantage of burgeoning opportunities in the United States.

Like Jewish and black pugilists, Irish boxers continued to be important to the sport in the 1830s and 1840s. Still, after the death of Simon Byrne, no Irish boxer captured the public imagination as had Byrne, Jack Langan, Dan Donnelly, or Andrew Gamble. Significantly, the only match pitting an Irish champion against a British champion after Byrne's death—between "Deaf" Burke and Sam O'Rourke—happened in the United States. In Britain, decades of increasing immigration had swelled the numbers of Irish people in urban areas and made Irish boxers much less a novelty. *Fistiana*, Vincent Dowling's reference book that had gone through more than ten editions since its first publication in 1841, had stopped identifying most fighters with Irish names as Irish by the 1860s. Second-generation Irish pugilists, including Jem Ward and "Deaf" Burke, were considered unambiguously British.[74]

While second-generation Irishman were some of the best prizefighters of this period, fewer Irish-born boxers were successful. This can be seen in the fate of the title "Irish Champion" in these years. After the retirement of Jack Langan, Simon Byrne claimed the title, which had always been nominal and was most often claimed to pique interest for a particular bout. Still, it had great utility if a fighter could make a plausible claim to it. As we have seen, Byrne used it to great effect for his fight against Alexander MacKay (himself claiming to be the Scottish Champion). After his victory over MacKay, despite having a relatively unimpressive resume, he used the title to gain a match against the Champion of England, Jem Ward, as Jack Langan had done several years earlier.[75] Byrne died in June 1833, following his last bout with "Deaf" Burke. At the end of July, Irish-American Sam O'Rourke—a former pupil of Byrne and Tom Reynolds who had returned to Ireland—challenged Burke to fight him at the Curragh.[76] Burke was unwilling to come to Ireland, however, and ignored O'Rourke's challenge. In response, the Irish-American scheduled a match with Fanning, "the Athlone Champion." O'Rourke easily defeated his opponent and, thereafter, began to claim the title "Irish Champion."[77]

Claiming to be the Irish Champion strengthened O'Rourke's hand in trying to make a match with Burke. Negotiations proceeded in the first few months of 1834 but the location of the proposed match could not be agreed; Burke would not go to Ireland and O'Rourke would not fight in England. Scotland was proposed as a neutral ground but the pugilists rejected the proposition.[78] In May, O'Rourke announced that he was returning to the United States, where he claimed to have had a lucrative career as a prizefighter. Passing through London before his Atlantic crossing, he showed off a number of gold chains and watches given to him in the United States.[79] As he was preparing to leave the country, Jem Ward answered O'Rourke's challenge to any man in the world and agreed to fight him at the Curragh. O'Rourke continued his journey, however, and the fight did not occur.[80]

After O'Rourke's departure, Ward continued to frustrate Burke's attempts to make a match for the championship. Finally, in 1835, a meeting of boxing supporters declared that, if Ward would not fight him, the championship belonged to Burke.[81] Burke could still find no suitable opponents, however, and in April 1836, he left for the United States.[82] He sparred in New York and in other cities along the east coast. Eventually, he encountered O'Rourke and the two toured together, benefitting from the fact that the nascent American Prize Ring had imported ethnic rivalry along with the rules and culture of boxing. As Elliott Gorn has argued, the replication "in microcosm [of] the long-standing enmity between Irish and English" was a particularly important characteristic of early American boxing. Finally, Burke and O'Rourke agreed to a prizefight. They chose to meet in New Orleans, a city with a large Irish population that O'Rourke had adopted as a base. O'Rourke's Irish partisans broke the ring during the third round and Burke had to make an escape using a Bowie knife and a fast horse. He returned to New York and, after winning a much more orderly bout against another Irish immigrant, he returned to England in June 1838.[83] O'Rourke stayed in North America and was ultimately killed in 1845 near Grenville, Quebec by a man named Brady.[84]

With O'Rourke in North America, other boxers appropriated the title Irish Champion in an effort to raise their profiles. In early 1842, Mick Haydon claimed to be the Irish Champion when he arrived in Liverpool to prepare for a fight against Simon Byrne's brother Jem.[85] In England and Scotland, relatively high stakes matches quickly became available. John Gould of Glasgow, the "Scotch Champion," challenged him for £50 a side and the two champions met near Salter's Brook, just across the Yorkshire border, in August.[86] Haydon, using green as his color and supported by a number of wealthy backers from Dublin, won easily.[87] Haydon did not sustain his success, however. He claimed to have only received £10 from his winnings and, after being charged with deserting his family, he died of brain fever just over a year later.[88] Other boxers tried to follow Haydon's success and made brief claims to be the Irish Champion. A fighter identified only as "the Irish Champion" defeated a pugilist named Triggs for £5 near Greenhithe in September 1845.[89] In 1847, a fighter named Finn claimed to be the Irish Champion at a wrestling exhibition near Bristol.[90] Neither of these men achieved any lasting success.

Unlike these aspiring Irish champions, the most accomplished Irish pugilist of the period did not identify professionally as Irish. He was William Gill, the "champion of the lightweights" in the 1840s. Gill was probably born in Dublin around 1819 and came with his parents to Coventry shortly thereafter. Although he was known as "Paddy," he always associated himself with Coventry rather than Ireland.[91] Gill made his name in several matches organized by the Birmingham Prize Ring in 1842–43, defeating two Coventry men, the first at Atterton in February 1842 for £20 and the second at Stoke Green in July. In November, he beat Hubbard of Leicester near Caldecotte.[92] On June 6, 1843, he triumphed over Edward Moseley of Derby for £25 outside Tamworth. After these successes, Gill began to look beyond Coventry and Birmingham. *Bell's Life in London* reported after his victory over Hubbard that he wanted a "suitable adversary" at his weight "for a cool fifty or above it."[93] Two months later, he made his first trip to the metropolis to spar at Jem Burn's house.[94]

During his stay in London, Gill made a match for £50 a side with George Norley of Manchester that was organized by the London Prize Ring. Preparations included a steamboat to convey spectators to the match. Gill received £10 to come to London and depart with the convoy to the scene of the match, east of London on the Thames near Northfleet and Gravesend. With the proceeds from tickets sold for the steamer, fine accommodations were made. Benches were arranged for aristocratic spectators and straw laid out for the comfort of others. An orderly crowd watched Gill gain an early advantage before hurting his shin against one of the stakes. Unable to put weight on his left leg, Gill was at a distinct disadvantage and lost in about two hours.[95] As the injury was widely believed to be the reason for his defeat, Gill's Coventry patrons continued to support him.[96]

After his unlucky loss to Norley on the Thames, Gill returned to the more familiar territory of the Birmingham Prize Ring and was matched against Birmingham pugilist Jack Bethell for £50 a side in June 1844. The two fighters met about fifteen miles outside Birmingham using ropes and stakes from nearby Nuneanton. As he did in every fight, Gill displayed his "well known" banner with a white spot on a blue field on the stakes rather than the green favored by most Irish pugilists. A large crowd, including many spectators from Coventry, witnessed Gill defeat Bethell in an hour and twenty minutes. His partisans were ecstatic about the victory; he returned to his home city that evening "with flying colours" and the locals were "uproarious on the occasion."[97] In October, Gill met George Holden of Walsall for £50 a side near Tamworth, where several thousand assembled to see Gill win easily in thirty minutes. To demonstrate his fitness after the fight, he danced a polka. As was his custom, Gill held a benefit exhibition at the Sword and Mace in Coventry shortly after the bout.[98]

Gill's successful return to the Birmingham and Coventry boxing scene positioned him for greater things. His principal patron, the wine merchant John Gadsby, and other boxing supporters in Coventry agreed to stake £100 for a match against the London boxer and Owen Swift protégé William Reed. As Reed was considered the best lightweight in London and Gill among the top smaller fighters outside the metropolis, the match was promoted as a contest to determine whether London or provincial pugilism was superior. Large numbers of spectators came to Oxford from Birmingham and Coventry and an excursion train brought more from London. From there, the assemblage traveled to Eynsham to see the match. To the Londoners great surprise, Gill—the representative of Coventry and Birmingham—easily defeated Reed. Apart from a brief note about Gill's Irish birth in *Bell's Life in London*, no mention was made of Gill's Irishness or of Irish spectators in various accounts of the fight.[99]

Gill's Coventry connection continued to be lucrative after his victory over Reed. In May 1846, his Coventry patrons staked £250 for a match against George Norley, the only pugilist to defeat him. Three excursion trains again brought Londoners to Oxfordshire for the fight and many more spectators came down from Coventry. They witnessed an extraordinary contest in which the two men fought 160 rounds in more than four hours before Gill finally defeated Norley. *Bell's Life in London* pronounced the fight "a specimen of British bravery and patient endurance ... seldom, if ever, exceeded in the annals of British pugilism."[100] Gill had reached the pinnacle of fame and, after another victory over Liverpool fighter Tommy Davies in 1847, announced his retirement. He took over management of the Lamb and Flag on Spor Street in Coventry and began to train and patronize other fighters. Gill fought three more times—including a match involving the death of his opponent—but increasingly transitioned to the life of a local sporting publican. He died in 1869 after spending the last three months of his life in the Hatton Lunatic Asylum.[101]

Apart from his nickname, Paddy Gill made little effort to identify himself professionally with his Irish heritage. He represented Coventry and the boxing enthusiasts in that city loyally supported him. Second-generation Irish immigrants, especially those from cities with large Irish populations, identified more with their Irishness than did the Irish-born Gill. Ned Donnelly of Glasgow, for example, used green as his color for a match against Angus McKay in 1847.[102] Still, Donnelly did not court Irish support as actively as other fighters. When he faced fellow second-generation immigrant and London East-Ender Mike Madden near Gravesend in December 1852, Irish spectators cheered loudly for Madden and even tried to break the ring on his behalf. In its report of the match, *Bell's Life in London* referred to Donnelly as a Scot.[103] Some boxers continued to cultivate an Irish following but this was now the exception. English supporters of the sport now tended to view Ireland not as a cradle for fighters but as a source of pity, as when boxers held a series of benefits for Famine victims in 1847 called "Fistic Tournament for the Benefit of the Irish and Scotch."[104]

By the 1850s, the geography, organization, and culture of bare-knuckle prizefighting had been significantly altered and pugilists from minority groups were at the forefront of these changes. The development of the sport outside London—in which James Wharton, Israel Lazarus, and Paddy Gill had played critical roles—had made Birmingham, Liverpool, and Glasgow formidable rivals to London as boxing centers. Journalists and sporting publicans helped provide a nascent organization to the sport and, as Lazarus's experience in Newcastle showed, authorities began to recognize this as well. As sporting public houses (often run by former fighters) increasingly became organizational hubs for the sport, they began to diversify their entertainment, offering music and dancing and arranging contests in other sports. Many boxers were as adept (or, as in the case of Thomas Sutton even more skilled) at entertaining crowds as they were at fighting. All of these developments and the outbreak of war in 1853 helped usher in a brief period of renewal for the sport.[105]

As boxing experienced a period of reform and revival in the 1850s, it also began to become a global phenomenon. As Elliott Gorn has shown, "scores of fights were taking place annually" in the United States by the middle of the decade. Newcomers from Ireland and Britain were a critical reason for the growth of the sport. Much more than in Britain, matches often turned on ethnic enmity and Irish immigrants, who were becoming increasingly numerous during and after the Famine years in the 1840s, were at the forefront. Following in the wake of Sam O'Rourke, the notorious "Yankee" Sullivan of Cork came to the United States after defeating Hammer Lane in England. He quickly became a symbol of "the encroachments of the Green Flag of the Emerald Isle" for American nativists in the 1840s. Sullivan's popularity spawned many imitators and boxing became "one of the most important expressive forms of a flourishing plebeian culture."[106]

Irish-Americans played a critical role in the growth of boxing in the United States but other immigrants from Britain were important as well. The remarkable Israel Lazarus who, as we have seen, helped nurture the development of bare-knuckle boxing in the north of England, migrated to the United States with his sons Harry and John in 1852 and became an important part of the organization of boxing in the state of New York. After the three toured California, Israel established a sporting saloon in Buffalo. As he had done in England, Lazarus used his house to organize matches, give lessons, arrange transportation to fights, and offer musical entertainments. It was the base for three major fights in 1857, two pitting Irish immigrants against one another (including a Catholic and a Protestant in one match) and the other involving his son Harry.[107] When his saloon burned down in 1859, Israel and Harry Lazarus returned to New York City. As his father aged, Harry took the reins of the family business. In 1865, he was brutally murdered by a rival in a notorious incident that helped lead to a decline in prizefighting in the United States. The aging Israel, now very obese and moving with great difficulty, testified at the trial. He died two years later of heart disease.[108]

Boxing developed somewhat more slowly in Australia than in the United States but it had become an important center of the sport by the second half of the century. As in the United States, Irish immigrants played an important role in the development of boxing there. Matthew Schownir has documented a number of fights involving Irish immigrants in the 1840s and 1850s. In one match between an Irish and an English immigrant, the Irishman's second waved an Irish flag in his corner.[109] Black boxers were also a significant part of early Australian prizefighting. John "Black" Perry, the Irish-born son of an African American father and an Afro-Caribbean mother, was trained by Jem Ward in Liverpool and fought successfully in Australia in the 1840s.[110] Despite the efforts of these pugilists, boxing in the antipodes only became important globally after the arrival of English pugilist Jem Mace in the 1870s. Thereafter, Australia produced some of the leading fighters in the world, including Afro-Caribbean immigrant Peter Jackson and Irish immigrant (via Cornwall) Bob Fitzsimmons.[111]

The global spread of boxing and the culture of identity in the sport came together in the first fight for the "Championship of the World," between Londoner Tom Sayers and Irish-American John C. Heenan in 1860. Sayers had emerged as champion in the late 1850s, a few years after the foundation of the Pugilistic Benevolent Association had provided some order to title fights. When Bendigo retired in 1850, the aging William Perry (known as "the Tipton

Slasher") claimed the title. He promptly lost to Bristol's Harry Broome—an important ally of Paddy Gill—but then became champion again when Broome retired. Finally, in June 1857, the thirty-eight-year-old Perry faced Sayers. Sayers had developed a reputation as a clean and talented fighter that made him very popular. The increased use of excursion trains or steamboats and the development of the Pugilistic Benevolent Association had led many to believe the sport was reviving; the excursion trains and boats assured more regular earnings and the Pugilistic Benevolent Association helped keep order at matches. Both helped control the corruption and rough crowds that had been a feature of the sport since the 1820s. When Sayers defeated Perry, then, he became a "popular hero."[112]

John C. Heenan was, like many of the best boxers in England after the mid–1820s, the child of Irish immigrants and was best known for a loss to American Champion John Morrissey in October 1857. Israel Lazarus played an important role in organizing the Heenan and Morrissey match, fought just across the border from Buffalo in Canada. Similar to early fights in England, nativists considered the second-generation Irish-American Heenan

Depiction of the bout between Tom Sayers and American John C. Heenan in 1860. The last great bout of the bare-knuckle era, it was billed as a contest for the "Championship of the World." From Miles, *Pugilistica*, vol. 3.

their champion, while many Irish identified with the immigrant Morrissey. Heenan underscored his connection to the United States by using the stars and stripes as his banner. Morrissey won the battle, in part because of an injury Heenan sustained in the early stages of the match. Morrissey retired after the match, however, and Heenan claimed the title. In a bold stroke, he then challenged Sayers to fight.[113]

The match between Sayers and Heenan for the "Championship of the World" generated great interest on both sides of the Atlantic. In the United States, the fight "drew more public attention than any other athletic event during the fifty years straddling mid-century." American newspapers published all the details of Heenan's training and his trip across the ocean. More importantly, newspapers and popular prints depicted the bout as a contest between the two nations. An American print depicted George Washington and Heenan side-by-side as "The Two Champions" and American newspapers used the occasion of the fight to comment on "John Bull's effete decadence." For their part, British newspapers noted that the "Anglo-Saxon stock [had] degenerated in the Yankee Republic."[114] Even the *Times*, a long-time opponent of boxing, offered Sayers grudging support, wryly remarking that, though "all decent people disliked the idea of two fine men beating each other half to death, as somebody was to be beaten, it might be the American."[115] The boxers both strongly supported the symbolism. Sayers used red and buff with a British lion for his colors, while Heenan used red, white, and blue with an eagle. Sayers wrote a letter to the *Times* declaring that no foreigner would have the belt "or the buckle of it, from Old England while my arm and heart are capable of defending it."[116]

The fight revived the old spirit of rivalry and identity that had been a critical part of the sport's popularity since the early 1700s, but it also demonstrated critical changes in bare-knuckle boxing. The new forms of transportation played a prominent role in the Sayers and Heenan fight. Two trains left from London Bridge station at four o'clock in the morning, carrying around one thousand spectators to the site of the match in the Hampshire countryside.[117] The intense publicity surrounding the match had the metropolitan police and their provincial counterparts on the alert, however. Whereas in earlier decades local authorities were often unable or unwilling to interfere with matches, now armed policemen with swords drawn lined the railway line.[118] Prompted by the vigor of the metropolitan police, a group of Hampshire constables arrived to stop the match after two hours of bloody fighting. The constables fought through the crowd, forcing spectators into the ring. In the melee, referee Francis Dowling, the son of Vincent Dowling and the editor of *Bell's Life in London*, declared the fight drawn. Dowling and his

Print placing Tom Sayers with Tom Cribb and Tom Spring as three great "Toms" of British prizefighting. Significantly, each achieved his greatest fame with a victory over a non-English opponent. "A Trio of Champions—the Three Toms," from Miles, *Pugilistica*, vol. 3.

American counterpart George Wilkes of the *Spirit of the Times* announced that Sayers and Heenan were joint champions and presented each of them with belts.[119] A subscription of more than £3,000 was raised for Sayers, with contributions even coming from the Stock Exchange and Parliament.[120] The fight had been interrupted but boxing seemed on the cusp of becoming a global phenomenon.

Despite the popularity of the Sayers and Heenan bout, and the brief return of the old rivalries, professional bare-knuckle boxing began a rapid descent to obscurity in the 1860s. Sayers retired and uncertainty again surrounded the championship. The police interfered with matches more aggressively than ever before and criminal elements began to infiltrate excursion trains. Jem Mace, the champion for much of this period, barely avoided arrest in Ireland in 1864 and was frequently monitored by agents of the London Metropolitan Police. After being detained before a fight with Ned O'Baldwin in 1867, he left England for the United States and, ultimately, for Australia, where he would play a critical role in the development of the sport there.[121]

Bare-knuckle prizefighting continued in England after Mace's departure but its days were clearly numbered. In 1867, the Marquess of Queensberry lent his name to a new set of rules that mandated the use of gloves, established timed rounds, and forbade the few wrestling moves still permitted in bare-knuckle boxing. These rules were first used for amateur bouts at public schools and elsewhere. Gloved and timed bouts became more popular among professional boxers as well. Prize-fighting at the Derby, a part of the rowdy

Funeral monument for Tom Sayers.

world of race meetings for nearly a century, ended after 1875, when police arrested two bare-knuckle boxers and, in conjunction with the Jockey Club, stamped out the practice of bare-knuckle boxing. In its place, timed contests with gloves appeared. Even pubs began to feature such matches by the last quarter of the century. By the end of the 1880s, one journalist noted that bare-knuckle prizefights were "few and far between." Finally, in 1891, a group of merchants, bookmakers, and sporting aristocrats under the leadership of the Earl of Londsdale formed the National Sporting Club in order to regularize professional boxing under the Queensberry rules. In 1909, the group introduced the Londsdale belt to recognize a national champion. In dramatic contrast to the raucous world of the early nineteenth century, members of the National Sporting Club wore dinner jackets to matches and, more importantly, were expected to remain silent during fights.[122]

Although the sport of boxing continued, the ideals of manliness, especially those of restraint and decorum, with which reformers attacked boxing and other "blood sport" in the early nineteenth century, had conquered the sporting fraternity by the end of the century. Nevertheless, the notions of manly courage and honor did not disappear; the connection between martial manhood, sport, and Britishness reappeared in the Victorian public school. In 1872, for example, one commentator noted that a "nation of effeminate, enfeebled bookworms scarcely forms the most effective bulwark of a nation's liberties."[123] Such words clearly echoed the ideas of Pierce Egan and many other supporters of bare-knuckle boxing.

As these ideas about manhood and nation became a part of English public school culture, those journalists who still wrote about bare-knuckle boxing took an even harder line against boxers who were not white, Christian, and English, rewriting the history of the sport in the process. Henry Downes Miles published the first volume of his influential history of bare-knuckle prizefighting, which he called *Pugilistica*, in 1866 and, in 1881, produced an expanded version, with two additional volumes, which were reprinted in 1906. Miles' work, like earlier histories of boxing, was replete with nationalist rhetoric. Unlike them, however, *Pugilistica* reflected the new ideas about race emerging around Europe in the final third of the nineteenth century.[124] While earlier constructions of Britishness, as we have seen, permitted the inclusion of minority groups, notions of an "Anglo-Saxon" nation excluded these groups by definition. These new ideas about race were evident in Miles's introduction to the 1881 edition of *Pugilistica*, in which he remarked that "to England and her Anglo-Saxon race is due this fairest and least dangerous of all forms of the duel." Miles's discussion of the famous black boxer Tom Molineaux betrayed a much more hostile attitude toward black people than that held by his early nineteenth-century predecessors. He noted that Molineaux was "the descendant of an African race, remarkable for insensibility to pain, a low cerebral development, and immense muscular powers."[125] For Miles, the idea that Irish, Jewish, or black boxers might demonstrate their Britishness in the boxing ring was absurd.

Miles was hardly sympathetic to Jewish or black boxers, but his work especially reflected the increasing anti–Irishness of his age. As new ideas of race gained ground and post–Famine Irish immigration to Britain dramatically expanded the Irish population in Britain, popular magazines, such as *Punch*, produced a string of virulently anti–Irish cartoons.[126] In addition, Miles wrote and published the second edition of his work during the divisive Irish Land War, in which Irish people used extraordinary methods to resist the oppressive tactics of landlords in Ireland. In *Pugilistica*, Miles continually derided the ability of Irish boxers. In his discussion of English boxer Tom Belcher's trip to Ireland, for example, Miles remarked that Belcher was "teaching the natives the advantages of" boxing. Unfortunately for the "natives," the art was "never properly understood or appreciated by Irishmen." Elsewhere, Miles disparaged early nineteenth-century Irish boxer Andrew Gamble, calling him a "hard-hitting, clumsy, knock-kneed Hibernian."[127]

Miles attributed the undeniable notoriety achieved by Irish boxers to the work of Irish-born Pierce Egan. Throughout *Pugilistica* Miles ridiculed Egan—who he at one point called a Dublin "gossoon"—despite relying heavily on Egan's work and frequently lifting entire passages from *Boxiana*. More importantly, Miles claimed that Egan pretended Irish boxers were more accomplished than they actually were and that truly successful English boxers were actually Irish. Miles mocked, for example, "the absurd penchant of 'the historian' (as Pierce was wont to style himself) to Hibernicise and appropriate to Ireland the names and deeds of fistic heroes" as well as his "thousand and one claims of 'Irish descent' for most of his heroes." Miles also derided Egan's "ludicrous magniloquence in the case of several Irish roughs in 'Boxiana,' on whom he has expended his slang panegyric."[128]

By the end of the century, the sport of bare-knuckle prizefighting had practically disappeared. More effective policing and the hostility of many Victorians led to its demise. Some elements of the sport endured, however. The Queensberry Rules ultimately gave amateur and professional boxing new life, though in a quite altered form: gloves, timed rounds, and the controlled behavior of the gentlemen supporters all made it very different from the brutal contests of the bare-knuckle era. Irish-American champion John L. Sullivan was only the most famous pugilist to make the transition from the modified Broughtonian system to the new Queensbury rules. The ideas of martial manhood and Britishness that had justified bare-knuckle prizefighting in the early nineteenth century (and, indeed, helped to make it extraordinarily popular) lived on as well, becoming part of the English public school ethos in the Victorian period and, ultimately, contributing to late nineteenth century imperial attitudes.[129]

As the sport of boxing was tamed and its martial values transplanted to the public school and to the empire, Victorian writers carefully diminished the role of Irish, Jewish, and black boxers earlier in the century. If, as many believed, sport was crucial to the maintenance of the British Empire, then Irish, Jewish, and black people would have no significant part in it. The Victorian rewriting of the history of bare-knuckle prizefighting has shaped our understanding of this influential sport down to the present and obscured the important role played by minority boxers in the evolution of bare-knuckle prizefighting in the first half of Victoria's reign.

Conclusion

This book has sought to show how ideas about identity in Britain and Ireland between the early eighteenth century and the late nineteenth century shaped the immensely popular sport of bare-knuckle prizefighting. Even before bare-knuckle prizefighting emerged as a distinct sport, fighters used national identity to promote their performances. The dramatic advertisements for early eighteenth century bear gardens, which associated bloody combats with a timeless Englishness, provided a template exploited by the entrepreneurial fighters James Figg, George Taylor, and Jack Broughton. By 1750, the promoters of bare-knuckle prizefighting regularly claimed that their sport fostered native strength and courage. This link between boxing and the nation was a critical part of the sport's phenomenal resurgence in the aftermath of the loss of the American colonies. It was made even more vehemently, especially in response to the efforts of reformers to suppress it, during the long war with revolutionary and Napoleonic France. Journalists and pugilists brought this language to an ever-expanding audience as elite patrons deserted the sport from the 1820s. The association between sport and national strength endured even after the dramatic decline of bare-knuckle prizefighting in the final third of the century.

The relatively disproportionate involvement of minority fighters in the sport was a direct consequence of the increased emphasis on English or British identity. For much of boxing's history, promoters tried to generate interest in bouts and other activities by claiming that Irish (and, later, Jewish and black) fighters offered a test of white, Christian, English manhood. Because of this, a large number of bare-knuckle boxers were Irish, Jewish, or black. No passive symbols, these pugilists used their identities strategically to cultivate support in their own communities. As a result, prizefighting increasingly became a vehicle for the expression of minority identities. Some boxing supporters welcomed this development and saw it as demonstrating the unique tapestry of the United Kingdom. Many others, however, considered the assertiveness of minority boxers and their communities as indicative of the degeneration of the sport and the dilution of its essential Englishness.

From the late 1820s, leading journalists began to take a more hostile attitude toward the involvement of minorities in bare-knuckle prizefighting. This was partly the result of social and political developments: the growth of poor Irish and Jewish communities in major English cities and the increasing demands for political rights by Irish and Jewish leaders made both groups seem more threatening to many English Protestants. Around the same time, the abolition of slavery and its aftermath helped shift attitudes toward people of African descent.

The more antagonist views of minorities in bare-knuckle prizefighting may also have had to do, however, with Britain's changing position in the world. For the last sixty years of the nineteenth century, with the exception of the Crimean War in the 1850s, Britain largely stood aloof from continental politics while engaging in conflicts around the world. Rivalry with European powers remained important, of course, but Britain's soldiers fought Indians, Afghans, or Zulus much more often than Europeans. In the eighteenth and early nineteenth centuries, with France as an antagonist, minority prizefighters in Britain were often seen as proxies for the enemy across the Channel. The absence of the French threat after 1815 limited the popular taste for prizefights as tests of English manhood. As their focus shifted to the wider world, most Britons refused to see Asian or African peoples as similarly worthy antagonists of sturdy John Bull.

Decolonization and immigration of former colonial peoples to Britain in the twentieth century renewed debate about the long-simmering question of race and British identity. Sport remained an important vehicle for the expression of identity and, therefore, a flashpoint. As black players began to join football clubs in the 1970s, some fans reacted in a number of notorious instances of racism. In 1995, writer Robert Henderson pointedly asked if "mixed groups" of cricketers would play together as well as "eleven unequivocal Englishmen." Henderson also tellingly linked his question to "the problem … facing England as a nation."[1]

As we have seen, the belief that certain sports embody a pure national character has a long history, as does the notion that the inclusion of "outsiders" will adulterate that character. The homogenous or "pure" heritage for which some long is largely mythical, however, and their calls to return to it say more about the present than the past.

The story of bare-knuckle prizefighting reminds us that this impulse to romanticize and simplify the history of nations and sports was as alive in the eighteenth and nineteenth century as it is today. As I have tried to show, it was a critical reason for the popularity of the sport and the participation of minority prizefighters.

Boxing was never a quintessentially English sport. Indeed, it would not have thrived without the non–English, non–Protestant, and non-white people who competed in, watched, or read about matches. Its Englishness was only "unequivocal" in its diversity.

Chapter Notes

Introduction

1. In some cases, most notably the modern Olympics, nationalism was part of the motivation to organize events in the first place. Allan Guttman, *The Olympics: A History of the Modern Game*, 2d ed. (Champaign: University of Illinois Press, 2002), 2.

2. Linda Colley, *Britons: Forging the Nation, 1707–1837*, 2d ed. (New Haven: Yale University Press, 2005). Supporters of bareknuckle prize-fighting used the terms "English" and "British" interchangeably throughout this period. I have tried, as far as possible, to follow their usage. Kumar has discussed the problems associated with the conflation of the two words in Krishan Kumar, *The Making of English National Identity* (Cambridge: Cambridge University Press, 2003), 1–17.

3. Kathleen Wilson, "The good, the bad, and the impotent: Imperialism and the politics of identity in Georgian England," in *The Consumption of Culture, 1600–1800: Image, Object, Text*, eds. Ann Bermingham and John Brewer (London: Routledge, 1995), 255.

4. The term "minority" is famously difficult to define. I use it here in the sense suggested by Franceso Caportorti's 1977 definition for the United Nations: "A group numerically inferior to the rest of the population of a State, in a non-dominant position, whose members—being nationals of the State—possess religious or linguistic characteristics differing from those of the rest of the population and show, if only implicitly, a sense of solidarity, directed toward preserving their culture, traditions, religion, or language." Cited in Athanasia Spiliopoulou Åkermark, *Justifications of Minority Protection in International Law* (London: Kluwer Law International, 1996), 89. I use the term for the Irish in Britain but not, of course, in Ireland.

5. For example, Michael de Nie, *The Eternal Paddy: Irish Identity and the British Press* (Madison: University of Wisconsin Press, 2004), 24. Todd M. Endelman, *The Jews of Britain, 1656–2000* (Berkeley: University of California Press, 2002), 76.

6. Dana Rabin, "The Jew Bill of 1753: Masculinity, Virility, and the Nation," *Eighteenth-Century Studies* 39. No. 2 (Winter 2006): 157–171. Nicholas Rogers has complicated interpretations of the Gordon riots, linking them to anti-government sentiments in the late stages of the American war. Nicholas Rogers, "The Gordon riots and the politics of war," in Ian Haywood and John Seed, eds., *The Gordon Riots: Politics, Culture and Insurrection in Late Eighteenth-Century Britain* (Cambridge: Cambridge University Press, 2012), 24–25.

7. In the case of the "Hottentot Venus," both condescension and ridicule were in evidence. Clifton Crais and Pamela Scully, *Sara Baartman and the Hottentot Venus: A Ghost Story and a Biography* (Princeton: Princeton University Press, 2009).

8. Michael Ragussis, *Theatrical Nation: Jews and Other Outlandish Englishmen in Georgian Britain* (Philadelphia: University of Pennsylvania Press, 2010), 1–3. John Belchem, "Comment: Whiteness and the Liverpool Irish," *Journal of British Studies* 44, no. 1 (January 2005): 146–152. Belchem argues that Irish people used minstrelsy shows in Liverpool to combat the negative image of the "stage Irishman."

9. A number of scholars in the past two decades, while not rejecting Colley's approach, have qualified it by pointing to the proliferation and contesting of identities in Britain and Ireland. For example, Murray G.H. Pittock, *Inventing and Resisting Britain: Cultural Identities in Britain and Ireland, 1685–1789* (New York: St. Martin's Press, 1997) and Laurence Brockliss and David Eastwood, "Introduction," in Laurence Brockliss and David Brockliss, eds., *A Union of Multiple Identities: The British Isles, c. 1750–c.1850* (Manchester: Manchester University Press, 1997), 2–3.

10. Malissa Smith, *A History of Women's Boxing* (Lanham, MD: Rowman and Littlefield, 2014), 1–10.

11. Wilson, "Imperialism and the politics of identity in Georgian Britain," 255.

12. Kasia Boddy, *Boxing: A Cultural History* (London: Reaktion Books, 2008), 32.

13. Kathleen Wilson, "Nelson and the People: Manliness, Patriotism and Body Politics," in *Admiral Lord Nelson: Context and Legacy*, ed. David Cannadine (Houndmills, Hampshire: Palgrave Macmillan 2005), 50. See also, Kathleen Wilson, *The Island Race: Englishness, Empire, and Gender in the Eighteenth Century* (London: Routledge, 2003).

14. Tillman W. Nechtman, *Nabobs: Empire and Identity in Eighteenth-Century Britain* (Cambridge: Cambridge University Press, 2013). J.R. Ward, "The British West Indies in the Age of Abolition," in *The Oxford History of the British Empire, Volume II: The Eighteenth Century*, eds. P.J. Marshall and Alaine Low (Oxford: Oxford University Press, 1998), 415–439. Dror Wahrman has identified this period as a time of "gender panic." Dror Wahrman, "*Percy's* Prologue: From Gender Play to Gender Panic in Eighteenth-Century England," *Past and Present* 159 (May 1998): 113–160.

15. J.E. Cookson, *The British Armed Nation, 1793–1815* (Oxford: Clarendon Press, 1997), 81–83.

16. John Tosh, "Masculinities in an Industrializing Society: Britain, 1800–1914," *Journal of British Studies* 44, no. 2 (April 2005): 331. See also Dror Wahrman, *Imagining the Middle Class: The Political Representation of Class in Britain, c. 1780–1840* (Cambridge: Cambridge University Press, 1995), 298–376. Anna Clark, *The Struggle for the Breaches: Gender and the Making of the British Working Class* (Berkeley: University of California Press, 1995), 220–247.

17. See Rhonda A. Semple, "Missionary Manhood: Professionalism, Belief and Masculinity in the Nineteenth-Century British Imperial Field," *The Journal of Imperial and Commonwealth History* 36, no. 3 (September 2008): 397–398.

18. Richard Holt, *Sport and the British: A Modern History* (Oxford: Clarendon Press, 1990), 74–134.

19. Boddy, *Boxing: A Cultural History* is an important recent example. One exception to this is Elliot J. Gorn, *The Manly Art: Bare-Knuckle Prize-fighting in America* (Ithaca: Cornell University Press, 1986), which describes these strategies at length but is focused on the United States.

20. Dennis Brailsford, *Bareknuckles: A Social History of Prize-Fighting* (Cambridge: Lutterworth Press, 1988).

Chapter One

1. I use the phrase "bareknuckle prizefighting" to denote the form of paid fighting that is the subject of this book. Although the sport evolved over its two centuries of existence, it was united by a common set of rules (from the 1740s and revised in the 1830s and 1850s) and the sense of contemporaries that it was an ongoing phenomenon with a history that stretched back to the early eighteenth century. They often called it the London Prize Ring or, simply, the Prize Ring.

2. For much of the early modern period, bull-baiting was believed to improve the quality of meat and was therefore required to be performed before butchering. Many cities and towns maintained bull-rings for this purpose. Emma Griffin, *England's Revelry: A History of Popular Sports and Pastimes 1660–1830* (Oxford: Oxford University Press, 2005), 42–43, 59–74. Benjamin Litherland, "The Field and the Stage: Pugilism, Combat Performance and Professional Wrestling in England, 1700–1980" (PhD diss., University of Sussex, 2014), 39–40.

3. Henri Misson de Valbourg, François Maximilien Misson, *Mémoires et observations faites par un voyageur en Angleterre* (Van Bulderen, 1698), 252.

4. William B. Boulton, *The Amusements of Old London: Being a Survey of the Sports and Pastimes, Tea Gardens and Parks, Playhouses and Other Diversions of the People of London from the 17th to the Beginning of the 19th Century* (London: John C. Nimmo, 1901), 1–18. Pead was a well-known Anglican clergyman who published sermons on many subjects of the day.

5. Walter Scott, *The British Drama; Comprehending the Best Plays in the English Language* (London: William Miller, 1804), 47.

6. Brailsford, *Bareknuckles*, 4.

7. Quoted in Boddy, *Boxing: A Cultural History*, 28.

8. Brailsford, *Bareknuckles*, 4.

9. "History of Boxing," *Sporting Magazine* 1, no. 2 (November 1792): 79.

10. Peter Borsay, "Urban Life and Culture," in *A Companion to Eighteenth Century Britain*, ed. H.T. Dickinson (Blackwell, 2002), 204.

11. Brailsford, *Bareknuckles*, 4.

12. Wilson, *The Island Race*, 5.

13. Wilson, "Imperialism and the politics of identity in Georgian England," 238.

14. Captain John Godfrey, *A Treatise on the Useful Science of Defense* (London: Robert Milton,1747), 58.

15. Quoted in Litherland, "The Field and the Stage," 47.

16. Godfrey, *A Treatise on the Useful Science of Defense*, 60.

17. David O'Shaugnessy, "'Tolerably Numerous': Recovering the London Irish of the Eighteenth Century," *Eighteenth-Century Life* 30, no.1 (January 2015): 1–13. John Bergin, "Irish Catholics and their Networks in Eighteenth-Century London," *Eighteenth-Century Life* 30, no.1 (January 2015): 66–102.

18. John Nichols, George Steevens, and Thomas Phillips, *The Genuine Works of William Hogarth:*

Illustrated with Biographical Anecdotes, a Chronological Catalogue and Commentary, volume 3 (London: Longman, Hurst, Rees and Orme, 1808), 108–109.

19. *Sporting Magazine* 13 no. 4 (January 1799): 207.

20. Boulton, *Amusements of Old London*, 30.

21. *Parker's Penny Post*, August 20, 1733.

22. Boulton, *Amusements of Old London*, 30.

23. Boddy, *Boxing: A Cultural History*, 28–30.

24. Brailsford, *Bareknuckles*, 6.

25. *The Gentlemen's and London Magazine: or Monthly Chronologer* (May 1788), 247.

26. Reprinted in "A Chronological History of Boxing," *Sporting Magazine* (June 1797): 139–140.

27. O'Shaughnessy, "Recovering the London Irish," 5.

28. Henley fought and was defeated by Thomas Smallwood at the Great Booth on February 19, 1740. *The Political State of Great Britain*, volume 59 (February 1740), 144.

29. Reprinted in "History of Boxing," *Sporting Magazine*, 79–80.

30. H.V. Bowen, *War and British Society*, 1688–1815 (Cambridge: Cambridge University Press, 1998), 3.

31. Colin Haydon, "'I love my King and my Country, but a Roman catholic I hate': anti-catholicism, xenophobia, and national identity in eighteenth-century England," in *Protestantism and National Identity: Britain and Ireland, c. 1650–c. 1850* (Cambridge: Cambridge University Press, 1999), 44. See also Kathleen Wilson, "Empire, Trade, and Popular Politics in Mid-Hanoverian Britain: The Case of Admiral Vernon." *Past and Present* 121, no. 1 (November 1988): 74–109.

32. Alexander Hamilton, *A New Account of the East Indies: Giving an Exact and Copious Description of the Situation, Product, Manufactures, Laws, Customs, Religion, Trade, &c. of All the Countries and Islands, which Lie Between the Cape of Good Hope and the Island of Japon* (London: C. Hitch, 1744), 272.

33. Captain John Godfrey, *A Treatise on the Useful Science of Defense* (London: Robinson and Milton's, 1747)

34. Brailsford, *Bareknuckles*, 4–6.

35. *Sporting Magazine* 1, no. 2 (November 1792): 80.

36. Pierce Egan, *Boxiana, Or, Sketches of Antient and Modern Pugilism*, vol. 1 (London: G. Smeeton, 1812), volume 1, 51.

37. Advertisement in the *Daily Advertiser*, February 1, 1747, reprinted in Henry Wilson, *Wonderful Characters*, vol. 3 (London: Robins & Albion Press, 1822), 448.

38. Boddy, *Boxing: A Cultural History*, 30.

39. Godfrey, dedication in *A Treatise on the Useful Science of Defense*.

40. The text of Broughton's rules can be found in many places. The above is summarized from *The Sporting Magazine* 1, no. 2 (November 1792): 81–82.

41. Wilson, *Wonderful Characters*, 449.

42. Egan, *Boxiana*, vol. 1, 57.

43. *The Gentleman's Magazine and Historical Chronicle* 20 (April 1750): 184.

44. Broughton left £7000 at his death in 1789. Brailsford, *Bareknuckles*, 11.

45. Pierce Egan among many others claimed that "the interference of the Legislature" led to the closing of Broughton's amphitheatre and preventing the opening of others. Egan, *Boxiana*, volume 1, 59.

46. Brailsford, *Bareknuckles*, 10.

47. *London Chronicle: or, Universal Evening Post*, June 20–23, 1761.

48. "Theatrical Licenses," *Fraser's Magazine* 75 (January 1867): 94. Emma Griffin connects growing hostility toward these amusements to attempts by elites to assert greater control over public spaces. Griffin, *England's Revelry*, 82–83.

49. *The Country Journal, or the Craftsman*, May 11, 1751.

50. *Gentlemen's Magazine and Historical Chronicle*, volume 22 (May 1752): 238.

51. Contemporary newspaper account reprinted in *The Connoisseur* 1, no. 30 (August 22, 1754): 231–232.

52. Emma Griffin shows that walking long distances to see a sporting contest was not unique to prizefighting in the eighteenth century. Griffin, *England's Revelry*, 52–54.

53. *Whitehall Evening Post*, February 8–11, 1755 and March 8–11, 1755.

54. William Oxberry, *Pancratia, or, A history of pugilism: containing a full account of every battle of note from the time of Broughton and Slack down to the present day* (London: W. Oxberry, 1812), 50–53.

55. *Ibid.*, 54.

56. *London Chronicle*, March 3, 1761. Oxberry, *Pancratia*, 55.

57. *London Chronicle*, June 20–23, 1761.

58. Brailsford, *Bareknuckles*, 13–15.

59. *The Complete Art of Boxing According to the Modern Method ... by an Amateur of Eminence*, new ed. (London: M. Follingsby and M.Smith, 1788), 39, 41.

60. James Kelly, *Sport in Ireland, 1600–1840* (Dublin: Four Courts Press, 2014), 287.

61. Michael Ragussis highlights this phenomenon in the theater in the same period. Michael Ragussis, *Theatrical Nation*, 1.

Chapter Two

1. *London Evening Post*, October 15, 1771.

2. See, for example, Egan, *Boxiana*, vol. 1, 77–78.

3. Oxberry, *Pancratia*, 69.

4. Brailsford, *Bareknuckles*, 17, makes this critical point.

5. See, for example, Peter M. Briggs, "Daniel Mendoza and sporting celebrity: a case study," in *Romanticism and Celebrity Culture, 1750–1850,* ed. Tom Mole (Cambridge: Cambridge University Press, 2009), 103–119 and John Whale, "Daniel Mendoza's Contests of Identity: Masculinity, Ethnicity, and Nation," *Romanticism* 14, no. 3 (October 2008): 259–271.

6. *Hoey's Dublin Mercury*, August 10–13, 1771.

7. Toby Barnard, "The Irish in London and the London Irish, ca. 1660–1780," *Eighteenth-Century Life* 39, no. 1 (January 2015): 29–30.

8. Donald M. MacRaild, *Irish Migrants in Modern Britain, 1750–1922* (New York: St. Martin's Press, 1999), 1.

9. A special edition of *Eighteenth-Century Life* in January 2015 was focused on elite and middling Irish in London. Craig Bailey, *Irish London: Middle-Class Migration in the Global Eighteenth Century* (Liverpool: Liverpool University Press, 2013) is a critical addition to this scholarship.

10. "Sketch of the Life and Character of Dennis O'Kelly, Esq.," *Edinburgh Review, or Literary Miscellany* 7, no. 2 (February 1788): 105–106.

11. *Complete Art of Boxing*, 41.

12. *Ibid.*, 42.

13. Egan, *Boxiana*, vol. 1, 82–84. Corcoran's early years are shrouded in some mystery. Egan claimed that he was born at Athoye in County Carlow, but there is no such place. It is more likely that he was a native of Athy in Kildare, as many suggest, where some Corcorans continue to reside.

14. Vincent Dowling, *Fistiana; or, Oracle of the Ring* (London: William Clement, jr., 1841), 265.

15. William Oxberry's claim that Darts obvious threw the match was representative of most other nineteenth-century opinion. Oxberry, *Pancratia*, 60. Pierce Egan, in contrast, contended that Corcoran was the simply better man and won fairly. Egan, *Boxiana*, vol. 1, 85. Nat Fleischer identified Corcoran as "the first Irish-born pugilist to win a British championship." Nat Fleischer and Sam Andre, *An Illustrated History of Boxing*, rev. ed. (New York: Citadel Press, 2001), 15.

16. Egan, *Boxiana*, vol. 1, 84.

17. *The Craftsman; or Say's Weekly Journal*, September 17, 1774.

18. Dowling, *Fistiana*, 266,

19. The hostile account in *The Craftsman* referred to them as "thieves, pickpockets, and sharpers, of all denominations."

20. *The General Evening Post*, June 19, 1776. The story of the fight was reproduced in a number of other newspapers around England and Ireland. Later sources incorrectly date the fight to October 1776.

21. Egan, *Boxiana*, vol. 1, 87.

22. Oxberry, *Pancratia*, 60.

23. Warwick William Wroth and Arthur Edgar Wroth, *The London Pleasure Gardens of the Eighteenth Century* (London: MacMillan & Co., 1896), 149–151. These efforts did not save the Three Hats, however, and it shifted to a tea garden after magistrates stopped another boxing match in 1773.

24. *General Evening Post*, April 8–10, 1773. In *Pancratia*, William Oxberry wrongly identified the date of this match as July 13, 1770.

25. Oxberry, *Pancratia*, 61.

26. Egan, *Boxiana*, vol. 1, 88.

27. "Corcoran, the boxing hero," in J. W. von Archenholtz, ed., *The British Mercury, or Annals of History, Politics, Manners, Literature, Arts, etc., of the British Empire*, vol. 3 (Hamburg, BC Hoffman, 1787), 314. Feirns name is given by Archenholtz as Duggan. Other sources render his name as Jack Feirns or Duggan Feirns. Whatever his name, Feirns defeated Sellers in 1779.

28. Kelly, *Sport in Ireland*, 297.

29. Todd M. Endelman, *The Jews of Britain, 1656–2000* (Berkeley: University of California Press, 2002), 41 and Todd M. Endelman, *The Jews of Georgian England, 1714–1830: Tradition and Change in a Liberal Society* (Philadelphia: The Jewish Publication Society of America, 1979), 19, 31–32.

30. Endelman, *The Jews of Britain*, 6. Rabin, "The Jew Bill of 1753," 157–171. Alan Howard Singer, "Aliens and Citizens: Jews and Protestant Naturalization in the Making of the Modern British Nation, 1689–1753" (PhD diss., University of Missouri–Columbia, 1999).

31. Rabin, "The Jew Bill of 1753," 160.

32. Endelman, *The Jews of Georgian Britain*, 200–201.

33. Egan, *Boxiana*, vol. 1, 78.

34. *London Evening Post*, June 24, 1766 and *Public Advertiser*, August 6, 1766.

35. *Public Advertiser*, January 6, 1772.

36. *The Craftsman; Or Say's Weekly Journal*, October 2, 1773.

37. *Memoirs of the Life of Daniel Mendoza* (London: G. Hayden, 1816), 7–11.

38. Mr. Beach, "Life of Mr. Tattersall," *Sporting Magazine* 6, no. 1 (April 1795): 4–5.

39. Wilson, *The Island Race*, 51–52.

40. *Public Advertiser*, April 12, 1786.

41. Dana Rabin, "Imperial disruptions: city, nation, and empire in the Gordon riots," in Ian Haywood and John Seed, eds., *The Gordon Riots: Politics, Culture and Insurrection in Late-Eighteenth Century Britain* (Cambridge: Cambridge University Press, 2012), 95.

42. Michèle Cohen, "Manliness, Effeminacy, and the French: Gender and the Construction of National Character in Eighteenth-Century England," in Tim Hitchcock and Michèle Cohen, eds., *English Masculinities, 1660–1800* (London: Longman, 1999), 50.

43. William Leman Rede, *The Royal Rake, and the Adventures of Alfred Chesterton* (London: Chapman and Elcoate, 1842), 66. Hanger retired from the army in 1780 after contracting an illness and convalescing in the Caribbean. His income was a relatively modest £1,100 per annum. Derek Birley, *Sport and the Making of Britain* (Manchester: Manchester University Press, 1993), 145.

44. *Public Advertiser*, April 12, 1786 and April 28, 1786.

45. *Morning Post and Daily Advertiser*, May 5, 1786 is perhaps the most complete contemporary account of the match.

46. John Bee (pseud.) [John Badcock], *Fancy-Ana; or, A History of Pugilism, From Figg and Broughton's Time to Spring and Langan's; Including Every Transaction in the Prize-Ring, And Every Incident Worthy Notice (Whether of Spree, Turn-up, Boxing-Match, or Prize-Fight,) From 1719 to 1824 Inclusive* (London: W. Lewis, 1824), 10.

47. *Morning Post and Daily Advertiser*, May 5, 1786. The account of the match with this closing remark appeared in other contemporary newspapers as well.

48. *Cambridge Chronicle*, January 5, 1787. The *Chronicle* was generally politically neutral. According to Bob Clarke, the paper supported the Americans in their war for independence but was otherwise bipartisan. It adopted an ardently loyalist position after the French Revolution. Bob Clarke, *From Grub Street to Fleet Street: An Illustrated History of English Newspapers to 1899* (Aldershot, Hants: Ashgate, 2004), 135.

49. Birley, *Sport and the Making of Britain*, 145. Brailsford, *Bareknuckles*, 24.

50. "Boxing Made Easy or Humphries Giving a Lesson to a *Lover of the Polite Arts*." Printed for John Smith, No. 35, Cheapside, Feb. 16, 1788, catalog no. 0901.379, British Museum Print Room. *The Art of Boxing, or Science of Manual Defence, Clearly Displayed on Rational Principles, Whereby Every Person may easily make themselves Masters of that Manly Acquirement, So as to ensure Success both in Attack & Defence. To Which is Added, Memoirs and Delineations of the Most Celebrated Pugilists, And an Account of some of their Principal Battles* (London: W. Mason, 1815), 16.

51. *The Morning Post, and Daily Advertiser*, June 4, 1788. *Sporting Magazine* 13, no. 4 (January 1799), 236.

52. J.W. von Archenholtz, ed.,*The English Lyceum, or, Choice of Pieces in Prose and in Verse, Selected from the Best Periodical Papers, Magazins, Pamphlets and other British Publications* (Hamburg: Mr. Bohn, 1787), 284–285.

53. Egan, *Boxiana*, vol. 1, 110.

54. *The World and Fashionable Advertiser*, April 19, 1787 noted that Bradyll was Mendoza's patron and that the two had sparred the day before the match. Bradyll was a large landowner in Lancashire. The word "amateur" in this context denoted a man of means who sparred with prizefighters in padded gloves and who offered patronage and other support to prizefighters.

55. Mendoza, *Life of Mendoza*, 61.

56. *The World and Fashionable Advertiser*, April 18. 1787.

57. *The World and Fashionable Advertiser*, April 19, 1787. Mendoza, *Life of Mendoza*, 59.

58. Michael Ragussis, *Theatrical Nation: Jews and Other Outlandish Englishmen in Georgian Britain* (Philadelphia: University of Pennsylvania Press, 2010), 6.

59. Mendoza, *Life of Mendoza*, 52, 60, 71.

60. *The World and Fashionable Advertiser*, September 14, 1787.

61. *The World and Fashionable Advertiser*, October 13, 1787.

62. *The World and Fashionable Advertiser*, October 15, 1787.

63. *Whitehall Evening Post*, December 6, 1787.

64. *Scots Magazine* 50, no. 1 (January 1788): 46.

65. *Cambridge Chronicle*, January 19, 1788.

66. *London Chronicle*, January 10, 1788. *Scots Magazine* 50, no. 1 (January 1788): 46.

67. *Morning Post*, January 7, 1788. Ruti Ungar, "The Boxing Discourse in Late Georgian Britain, 1780–1820: A Study in Civic Humanism, Class, and Race" (PhD diss., Humboldt University of Berlin, 2012), 96, makes the important point that portraits of pugilists demonstrate a subtle bias against "shifting," which was considered unmanly.

68. *Morning Post*, January 12, 1788 and January 15, 1788.

69. *Morning Post*, January 21, 1788.

70. E.g. Peter M. Briggs, "Daniel Mendoza and sporting celebrity: a case study," in *Romanticism and Celebrity Culture, 1750–1850*, ed. Tom Mole (Cambridge: Cambridge University Press, 2009), 103–119. Alan Palmer, *The East End: Four Centuries of London Life*, rev. ed. (New Brunswick: Rutgers University Press, 2000), 34.

71. *Morning Post and Daily Advertiser*, January 11, 1788.

72. *Public Advertiser*, January 15, 1788.

73. *Public Advertiser*, January 16, 1788.

74. *Morning Post and Daily Advertiser*, January 21, 1788.

75. *Public Advertiser*, January 23, 1788.

76. *Public Advertiser*, January 25, 1788.

77. *Public Advertiser*, January 28, 1788.

78. *London Chronicle*, July 5, 1788.

79. *Public Advertiser*, August 11, 1788.

80. *London Chronicle*, November 15, 1788.

81. *The World*, January 6, 1789.

82. *Morning Post, and Daily Advertiser*, April 29, 1789.

83. The estimate of £300 is calculated from a report that the builder received "half a crown in every half guinea" and that something like 2500 spectators paid the half guinea entry fee. *The World*, May 8, 1789.

84. *Whitehall Evening Post*, May 5–7, 1789; *Public Advertiser*, May 8, 1789; *Morning Post, and Daily Advertiser*, May 8, 1789. Unfortunately for the *Morning Post*, their report did not arrive in time for publication. *The World*, May 8, 1789 reported that two thirds of the admission fee went to the winner and one third to the loser.

85. *Whitehall Evening Post*, May 5–7, 1789. *Morning Star*, May 8, 1789 reported that a gentleman in attendance had counted forty-two times that Humphries fell to the ground. *The World* recorded sixteen falls for Humphries.

86. In this context the word "amateur" was meant to distinguish between those who fought for money and those who did not. It did not carry the more recent connotation of a dilettante and, in fact, many eighteenth-century amateurs were very serious about their boxing prowess.

87. Michael Ragussis, *Theatrical Nation*, 6.

88. *Public Advertiser*, May 8, 1789.

89. *Morning Post, and Daily Advertiser*, May 14, 1789.

90. *The Whitehall Evening Post*, May 16, 1789.

91. *The St. James's Chronicle, or British Evening Post*, May 21, 1789. The Priestley-Levi debates of the 1780s resulted from the Priestley's attempts to win Jewish converts to Christianity.

92. *The Whitehall Evening Post*, May 16, 1789. Mendoza, *Life of Mendoza*, 167.

93. *The Diary; or, Woodfall's Regiter*, June 22, 1789. This newspaper defended Mendoza, claiming that he had been given the shirt as a present and that it would have been an insult for Mendoza not to wear it. Others took a less charitable view of Mendoza's sartorial choice.

94. *The St. James's Chronicle, or British Evening Post*, June 13, 1789.

95. *The Oracle. Bell's New World*, June 25, 1789.

96. *The Oracle. Bell's New World*, August 26, 1789.

97. *The Oracle. Bell's New World*, November 27, 1789.

98. *The St. James's Chronicle, or British Evening Post*, September 30, 1789.

99. *The Argus*, October 5, 1790. The account of the fight was completed in the October 6 edition.

100. *Public Advertiser*, April 19, 1788.

101. *The Morning Post, and Daily Advertiser*, June 10, 1788.

102. *The Morning Post, and Daily Advertiser*, August 21, 1789.

103. Kelly, *Sport in Ireland*, 290–300. Egan, *Boxiana*, vol. 1, 225. "History of Boxing," *Sporting Magazine* 1, no. 5 (February 1793): 289, claimed that Ryan had "that pleasantry and humour which so often characterise the lower order of the Irish." The phrase "lower order of the Irish" was typically reserved for Catholics.

104. *Morning Post, and Daily Advertiser*, August 29, 1786. Dunn gave in after a foul blow from Ryan. The *Morning Post* implied that the match was fixed. *The World and Fashionable Advertiser*, September 27, 1787 mentions that Ryan had fought Fry. Unfortunately, no date for the match was given.

105. Several newspapers reported after the match that it had been made while Ryan was in Ireland. *Cambridge Chronicle*, December 29, 1787. *The World*, December 26, 1787 made note of the fact that Ryan's patron was the Captain of his ship.

106. *Whitehall Evening Post*, December 6, 1787.

107. *Whitehall Evening Post*, December 20, 1787. *The World*, December 20, 1787. *The World*, December 22, 1787.

108. *The World*, December 22, 1789.

109. *The World*, December 27, 1789. *The Morning Post, and Daily Advertiser*, January 2, 1788.

110. *Morning Post, and Daily Advertiser*, June 4, 1788. *Bristol Journal*, November 8, 1788.

111. *The London Chronicle*, November 4–6, 1788. *Morning Post, and Daily Advertiser*, December 3, 1788. *Star and Evening Advertiser*, February 6, 1789.

112. The stage was initially built in the yard of the Bell Inn and many of the spectators paid their admission fee but, when the magistrates threatened to intervene, the stage was moved to Whitfield's property. *Morning Post*, February 12, 1789. *The World*, February 12, 1789. The Rev. Robert Bayne, *Historical Sketch of Rickmansworth and the Surrounding Parishes* (London: Watson & Hazell, 1870), 14. Bayne claimed that Whitfield, who had been high sheriff of Hertfordshire in 1762, "considerably reduced the estate by his style of living" before his death in 1813.

113. Egan, *Boxiana*, vol. 1, 96.

114. *Morning Post and Daily Advertiser*, February 19. 1789.

115. Oxberry, *Pancratia*, 83.

116. "Account of Johnson, the Boxer," *Sporting Magazine* 9, no. 6 (March 1797), 315.

117. *Morning Post*, February 12, 1789; Egan, *Boxiana*, vol. 1, 226.

Chapter Three

1. *Lloyd's Evening Post*, June 24, 1791.

2. George III, following a royal precedent, issued the proclamation after his coronation. While this was a formality observed by newly crowned monarchs since Elizabeth I, Wilberforce and his supporters wanted it reissued so that it would be taken more seriously. David J. Cox, Kim Stevenson, Candida Harris, and Judith Rowbotham, *Public Indecency in England, 1857–1960: 'A Serious and Growing Evil'* (London: Routledge, 2015), 19. John Pollock, *Wilberforce* (London: Constable, 1977), 58–62.

3. Edward Barry, *A Letter on the Practice of Boxing* (London: A. Grant, 1789), 8, 17, 21, 32.

4. Mary Thale, "London Debating Societies in the 1790s," *Historical Journal* 32, no. 1 (1989): 59.

5. *The Complete Art of Boxing*, 24.

6. *Public Advertiser*, February 5, 1790.

7. Amanda Goodrich, *Debating England's Aristocracy: Pamphlets, Polemics, and Political Ideas* (London: Royal Historical Society, 2005), 5–8.

8. *A Dialogue in the Shades, between Mercury, a Nobleman, and a Mechanic* (London: J.S. Jordan, 1794), vi, 21.

9. *Morning Post, and Daily Advertiser*, November 30, 1791 and August 11, 1791.

10. *Lloyd's Evening Post*, June 24, 1791

11. William Windham, *The Diary of the Right Hon. William Windham, 1784–1810*, ed. Mrs. Henry Baring (London: Longmans, Green, and Co., 1866), 81.

12. William Windham letter to James Boswell, October 26, 1792, in *Correspondence of James Boswell*, ed. Fifer, 378.

13. Martial qualities were most associated with Scottish Highland soldiers in the eighteenth century. As Rosalind Carr has shown, in the half century after the Jacobite rebellion, views of Highland troops began to shift "towards an image of courageous and loyal soldiers fighting for the British Empire." Rosalind Carr, *Gender and Enlightenment Culture in Eighteenth-Century Scotland* (Edinburgh: Edinburgh University Press, 2014), 154. The image of Highland soldiers ultimately "functioned as an inspirational tool, an image of ideal masculinity and racial superiority." Heather Streets, *Martial Races: The Military, Race and Masculinity in British Imperial Culture, 1857–1914* (Manchester: Manchester University Press, 2004), 4. Especially after 1857, British purveyors of "martial races theory" began to deploy the idea that certain groups were particularly martial in the service of imperialism.

14. Charles Burney to William Windham, September 9, 1794, British Library, Windham Papers, vol. 73, Add. 37914, fol. 105.

15. Cookson, *British Armed Nation*, 34, 207.

16. Hannah Barker, *Newspapers, Politics, and Public Opinion in Late Eighteenth Century England* (London: Clarendon Press, 1998), 2–4. Adrian Harvey, *The Beginnings of a Commercial Sporting Culture in Britain*, 1793–1850 (Burlington, VT.: Ashgate, 2004), 32–33.

17. *The Morning Post* continued to be owned by Richard Tattersall until 1795. John Wolcot (using his pseudonym Peter Pindar) was the main writer in this era. The circulation of the paper shrunk to 350 when Tattersall sold it to Daniel Stuart in 1795. H. R. Fox Bourne, *English Newspapers: Chapters in the History of Journalism*, vol. 1 (London: Chatto & Windus, 1887), 271–273.

18. Bob Clarke, *From Grub Street to Fleet Street*, 97–102. Kalman A. Burnim and Philip H. Highfill, Jr., *John Bell: Patron of British Theatrical Portraiture: A Catalog of the Theatrical Portraits in his Editions of* Bell's Shakespeare *and* Bell's British Theatre (Carbondale: Southern Illinois University Press, 1998), 3–9. The *Oracle* was partly financed by a £200 bribe to publish stories favorable to the government.

19. In July, Wheble was advertising a publication with all of the correspondence. *Lloyd's Evening Post*, July 13–16, 1770. The Duke—a younger brother of the King—had been sued by Lord Grosvenor.

20. *London Evening Post*, March 21–23, 1771.

21. John Nichols, "Memoir of John Wheble, Esq.," *Gentleman's Magazine* 128 (November 1820): 471–473. *Public Advertiser*, December 21, 1772. *Morning Post, and Daily Advertiser*, May 22, 1776.

22. Nichols, "Memoir of John Wheble," 473.

23. Advertisement in *The World*, December 15, 1787.

24. Nichols, "Memoir of John Wheble," 473.

25. John B. Nichols, *Illustrations of the Literary History of the Eighteenth Century*, vol. 6 (Westminster: J.B. Nichols & Son, 1831), 244.

26. Harvey, *The Beginnings of a Commmerical Sporting Culture*, 32–33.

27. Mendoza, *Life of Mendoza*, 176–179.

28. Kelly, *Sport in Ireland*, 297.

29. *St. James's Chronicle; or British Evening Post*, February 18, 1792.

30. Mendoza, *Life of Mendoza*, 175–197. John C. Greene, *Theatre in Dublin, 1745–1820: A Calendar of Performances* (Bethlehem: Lehigh University Press, 2011), 2698, 2722. Greene does not list Mendoza on the 1790–91 calendar, but he does appear for the 1791–92 season.

31. For example, he appeared at a benefit for Thomas Johnson. *The World*, January 26, 1791. *The World*, May 4, 1791. *Times*, July 14, 1791

32. *Evening Mail*, June 6, 1791

33. The poem, "Peter's Pension," was widely printed in the early 1790s, for example in *The Phoenix; Or, Weekly Miscellany Improved*, August 21, 1793.

34. Quoted in M. Dorothy George, *London Life in the Eighteenth Century*, reprint (London: Penguin Books 1976), 137–138.

35. *Morning Post, and Daily Advertiser*, July 4, 1791

36. Mendoza, *Life of Mendoza*, 225–237.

37. *Lloyd's Evening Post*, January 6–8, 1794, November 12–14, 1794.

38. Brailsford, *Bareknuckles*, 68. Jackson's father owned a business that was involved in the arching of Fleet Ditch. *Morning Chronicle*, April 17, 1795.

39. "Boxing," *Sporting Magazine* 6, no. 1 (April 1795): 55–56.

40. *Morning Chronicle*, April 17, 1795.
41. Egan, *Boxiana*, vol. 1, 290.
42. Mendoza made this claimed in his December 1801 challenge to Jackson, which Jackson refused. Oxberry, *Pancratia*, 147.
43. Mendoza, *Life of Mendoza*, 240.
44. *The St. James's Chronicle, or, British Evening-Post*, April 21–23, 1795
45. *Sporting Magazine*, Volume 2, no. 5 (August 1793): 316.
46. *Sporting Magazine* 6, No. 4 (July 1795): 163.
47. *Sporting Magazine* 7, No. 5 (Feb 1796): and *Sporting Magazine* 14, no. 6 (September 1799):
48. *Sporting Magazine*, Volume 2, no. 5 (August 1793): 316.
49. "On the Decline of Pugilism," *Sporting Magazine* 13, no. 6 (March 1799): 336. The author used the terms "English" and "British" interchangeably.
50. Bob Boxer (pseud.), "Retrospect of Royal Boxers," *Sporting Magazine* 15, no. 5 (February 1800): 239–240.
51. Egan, *Boxiana*, vol. 1, 239.
52. *The St. James's Chronicle, or British Evening Post*, October 9–11, 1792 and *The Evening Mail*, October 8–10, 1792. *The Evening Mail* described the skill of the fighters in the match and provided details of Gamble's life, claiming that Gamble had won eighteen matches by 1800.
53. The match was widely reported in London and Dublin newspapers. For example, *The Observer*, July 6, 1800, *Sun*, July 3, 1800, *The Star*, July 3, 1800, *Dublin Journal*, July 10, 1800. "Boxing Matches," *Sporting Magazine* 16, no. 4 (July 1800): 184–185.
54. *Star*, July 3, 1800, reported that gamblers wagered £5000 on the outcome of the match. This sum was not particularly large by contemporary gambling standards. In fact, in the same issue, the *Star* reported that gamblers won £6400 on a cricket match in Woolwich the day before the fight between Jones and Gamble.
55. *Whitehall Evening Post*, July 3, 1800. "Boxing Matches," 184.
56. *Star*, December 23, 1800.
57. Peter Radford, *The Celebrated Captain Barclay: Sport, Money and Fame in Regency Britain* (London: Headline Books, 2001), 77. *Bell's Weekly Messenger* claimed that the Prince of Wales and the Duke of York (referred to as "two great personages") won £8000. Dr. John Moore, the Duke of Hamilton's physician, was Belcher's patron for this match. Benjamin Cullington, a dealer and victualler in Tottenham Court Road, was the stakeholder. *Bell's Weekly Messenger*, December 28, 1800.
58. *Sun*, December 23, 1800
59. *Times*, December 27, 1800. Chairmen were those who carried sedan chairs. Many of them were Irish.
60. *Star*, December 23, 1800
61. *Star*, December 25, 1800. According to *Bell's Weekly Messenger*, December 28, 1800, Gamble trained Kelly.
62. *Morning Post and Gazetteer*, December 23, 1800. Patrick Myler, *The Fighting Irish: Ireland's Role in World Boxing History* (Dingle, Ireland: Brandon Book Publishers, 1987), 23.
63. *Times*, December 23, 1800.
64. *Morning Post and Gazetteer*, December 23, 1800.
65. *Star*, December 25, 1800.
66. Egan, *Boxiana*, vol. 1, 131.
67. *Evening Mail*, January 1, 1803.
68. "Boxing and Sparring," *Sporting Magazine* 21, no. 1 (October 1802): 15–17.
69. *Evening Mail*, November 17, 1802, *Courier and Evening Gazette*, November 16, 1802.
70. *Courier and Evening Gazette*, November 16, 1802.
71. *Evening Mail*, November 17, 1802.
72. *Courier and Evening Gazette*, November 16, 1802.
73. Wilberforce letter to Hannah More, quoted in Robert Isaac Wilberforce and Samuel Wilberforce, *The Life of William Wilberforce*, vol. 2 (London: John Murray, 1838), 366.
74. *Hansard's Parliamentary Debates*, Commons, vol. 35 (1800), col. 202. Pulteney told the Commons that he introduced the bill because several gentlemen had come to London wishing Parliament to "put a stop to the evil" of bull-baiting. It is unclear who these gentlemen were. Pultenay, one of the wealthiest men in Britain, did not have any clear connection to the Clapham Sect and, in fact, inherited a plantation and slaves at the death of his elder brother in 1794. M. J. Rowe and W. H. McBryde, "Pulteney, Sir William, fifth baronet (1729–1805)," in *Oxford Dictionary of National Biography, ed. H. C. G. Matthew and Brian Harrison* (Oxford: Oxford University Press, 2004), http://www.oxforddnb.com/view/article/56208 (accessed January 15, 2017). The *Times* suggested that Pulteney acted because of the "great dissoluteness and riot among the lower orders" caused by bull-baiting. *Times*, April 2, 1800.
75. *Hansard's Parliamentary Debates*, Commons, vol. 35 (1800), col. 205–206.
76. *Sporting Magazine* 26, no. 1 (April 1800): 35. Because the issues raised in this debate concerned its readers, the monthly periodical the *Sporting Magazine* reported parts of the debate (including Windham's remarks) more extensively than Hansard.
77. *A letter to the Right Hon. William Windham, on his late opposition to the bill to prevent bull-baiting: by an old Member of Parliament. To which are annexed, some letters and extracts on the same subject. Also some verses on hunting*, 2d ed., rev. and cor., with additions (London: W. Stratford, 1800) [http://galenet.galegroup.com.

proxy.bc.edu/servlet/ECCO, accessed June 6, 2006], 11.

78. Quoted in Robert Isaac Wilberforce and Samuel Wilberforce, *The Life of William Wilberforce*, vol. 2 (London: John Murray, 1838), 366.

79. Piers Mackesy, *War without Victory: The Downfall of Pitt*, 1799–1802 (Oxford: Clarendon Press, 1984), 209.

80. *Edinburgh Advertiser*, April 23, 1802.

81. John Dent introduced the measure to ban bull-baiting on May 4, 1802. *Times*, May 5, 1802. Like Pulteney, Dent was no evangelical reformer. One possible reason for Dent's introducing the bill was his hatred of aggressive dogs. Only a few years earlier, he had proposed a tax on dogs and "vehemently denounced" them. The dogs bred and kept for bull-baiting were often aggressive and violent. D. R. Fisher, "Dent, John (*b.* in or after 1761, *d.* 1826)," in *Oxford Dictionary of National Biography*, ed. H. C. G. Matthew and Brian Harrison (Oxford: Oxford University Press, 2004), http://www.oxforddnb.com/view/article/65137 (accessed January 15, 2017). *Morning Chronicle*, April 29, 1802.

82. *Times*, May 25, 1802.

83. *Hansard's Parliamentary Debates*, Commons, vol. 36 (1801–1803), col. 829–830. *Times*, May 25, 1802.

84. *Hansard's Parliamentary Debates*, Commons, vol. 36 (1801–1803), col. 847.

85. Frankland was the sixth baronet of a prominent Yorkshire family with imperial connections. His grandfather was an East India Company servant and governor of Bengal in the 1730s. His father, the fifth baronet, had a long and successful career as a naval commander as well as a long career in Parliament in the pocket borough of Thirsk, Yorkshire. Frankland succeeded his father in Parliament but had a less distinguished career, notable in part for a minor treatise about hunting safety, which he had authored shortly before this debate, Sir Thomas Frankland, *Cautions to Young Sportsmen* (London: J. Smeeton, 1801). A. W. H. Pearsall, "Frankland, Sir Thomas, fifth baronet (1718–1784)," in *Oxford Dictionary of National Biography*, ed. H. C. G. Matthew and Brian Harrison (Oxford: OUP, 2004), http://www.oxforddnb.com/view/article/10087 (accessed January 15, 2017). *Hansard's Parliamentary Debates*, Commons, vol. 36 (1801–1803), col. 849.

86. *Times*, May 25, 1802. Windham claimed that he "would not disparage that amusement [boxing] by comparing it with horse-racing," before implicitly doing so.

87. *Times*, May 25, 1802.

88. Plan for inscription on Windham Monument in Felbrigh Church, Norfolk. British Library, William Dale Farr Papers, vol. 2, Add. 37061, fol. 35.

89. *Hansard's Parliamentary Debates*, Commons, vol. 36 (1801–1803), col. 839–840.

Chapter Four

1. "The Battle of Tom Blake and Jack Holmes," *Sporting Magazine* 23, no. 6 (March 1804): 350.

2. Colley, *Britons*, 283–320.

3. The Volunteer forces increased from 146,000 in 1801 to 380,000 in 1804. Boyd Hilton, *A Mad, Bad, and Dangerous People?: England 1783–1846* (Oxford: Oxford University Press, 2006), 98–102. Cookson, *The British Armed Nation*, 207. See also, Charles John Fedorak, "In Defense of Great Britain: Henry Addington, the Duke of York and Military Preparations against Invasion by Napoleonic France, 1803–1804," in Mark Philip, ed., *Resisting Napoleon: The British Response to the Threat of Invasion, 1797–1815* (Aldershot, Hants: Ashgate, 2004), 91–110.

4. Cookson, *The British Armed Nation*, 18, 34, 66–67. *The Letters of Richard Brinsley Sheridan*, vol. 2, ed. Cecil Price (Oxford: Clarendon Press, 1966), 201–202. Hilton, *A Mad, Bad, and Dangerous People?*,103.

5. William Cobbett to William Windham, 23 November, 1803, British Library, Windham Papers, vol. 12, Add. 37853, fol. 103.

6. William Cobbett to William Windham, 2 May, 1804, British Library, Windham Papers, vol. 12, Add. 37853, fol. 119. Emphasis in original.

7. *Times*, May 25, 1802.

8. John Derry, ed., *Cobbett's England: A Selection from the Writings of William Cobbett with Engravings by James Gillray* (London: The Folio Society, 1968) 174–178.

9. "The Battle of Tom Blake and Jack Holmes," *Sporting Magazine* 23, no. 6 (March 1804): 350.

10. John Francis, *Annals, Anecdotes, and Legends: A Chronicle of Life Assurance* (London: Longman, Brown, Green, and Longmans, 1853), 243.

11. Captain Barber, *Considerations Upon the Best Means of Ensuring the Internal Defence of Great Britain* (London: C. Rosworth, 1805), 4, 7. Emphasis in original.

12. *Morning Chronicle*, April 10, 1806. *Morning Chronicle*, April 17, 1806.

13. [William P. Russel], *Arguments upon Boxing or Pugilism; which will always be proper for perusal, so long as the brutal practice of boxing shall continue; but more especially applicable now, as the subject has just been discussed at the British Forum, No. 22 Piccadilly, By a Friend to Rational Debate* (London: William P. Russel, 1806), 9.

14. *Ibid.*, 12–14, 17, 19.

15. Quintilius, "On the Effects of Boxing Matches on the Lower Classes," *Sporting Magazine* 28, no. 6 (August 1806): 261.

16. Discriminator, "Dr. Bardsley and Mr. J. Lawrence on Popular Sports and Pugilism," *Sporting Magazine* 28, no. 6 (August 1806): 263.

17. J.F. Hughes, *Memoirs of His Royal Highness, the Prince of Wales* (London: B. Clark, 1808), 4–5.

18. Dowling, *Fistiana*, 15.

19. *Daily Advertiser, Oracle, and True Briton*, June 6, 1804.

20. Derry, *Cobbett's England*, 165, 171. Italics in original.

21. *Sporting Magazine* 21, no. 1 (October 1802): 41.

22. "Female Pugilism," *Sporting Magazine* 26, no. 3 (June 1805): 167.

23. *Sporting Magazine* 12, no. 6 (September 1798): 317–318

24. Oxberry, *Pancratia*, 143.

25. In 1807, Pearce supposedly saved one woman from a fire and, a few months later, another from the clutches of three threatening men. Brailsford, *Bareknuckles*, 37.

26. Robert Bell was no relation to John Bell but used his name in the new publication's title to take advantage of John Bell's notoriety. The *Weekly Dispatch* was a "bitter rival" of *Bell's Weekly Messenger* in the 1800s and 1810s partly as a consequence of this. Harvey, *The Beginnings of a Commercial Sporting Culture*, 9, 43.

27. Brailsford, *Bareknuckles*, 45–52.

28. Quoted in Harold Felix Baker Wheeler and Alexander Meyrick Broadley, *Napoleon and the Invasion of Britain: The Story of the Great Terror*, vol. 2 (London: The John Lane Company, 1908), 251.

29. Michael Ragussis, *Figures of Conversion: "The Jewish Question" and English National Identity* (Durham: Duke University Press, 1995), 4. As Ragussis shows, many English millenarians thought that Britain should be the one to return Jews to their homeland.

30. "George Maddox and Pitton the Jew," *Sporting Magazine* 21, no. 3 (December 1802): 148–149.

31. *British Press*, July 16, 1804.

32. *Courier*, July 17, 1804. *Morning Post*, July 17, 1804. The *Morning Post* did not mention the hostility of the crowd to Pitton.

33. *Sporting Magazine* 23, no. 4 (January 1804): 216.

34. *Morning Post*, November 30, 1804. Bourke had fought, and been defeated by, both Jem Belcher and Pearce.

35. *Sun*, April 29, 1805.

36. Ragussis, *Theatrical Nation*. Michael Ragussis, "Jews and Other 'Outlandish Englishmen': Ethnic Performance and the Invention of British Identity under the Georges," *Critical Inquiry* 26, no. 4 (Summer 2000): 773–797. V.E. Chancellor, "Anti-Racialism or Censorship? The 1802 Jewish Riots at Covent Garden Opera and the Career of Thomas John Dibdin," *The Opera Quarterly* 18, no. 1 (Winter 2002): 18–25.

37. *Star*, July 14, 1801.

38. "Boxing," *Sporting Magazine* 18, no. 4 (July 1801): 172.

39. "Boxing, Caleb Baldwin and Dutch Sam," *Sporting Magazine* 24, no. 5 (August 1804): 263. *The Courier*, August 8, 1804.

40. *Sun*, April 29, 1805. This commentary also appeared in the *Sporting Magazine*. "Pugilism," *Sporting Magazine* 26, no. 1 (April 1805): 56.

41. For example, "Boxing, Samuels, alias Dutch Sam, and Tom Belcher," *Sporting Magazine* 27, no. 5 (February 1806): 243–245.

42. Letters from Mendoza and Lee summarizing their positions in the dispute are reprinted in Egan, *Boxiana*, vol. 1, 271–276.

43. *Morning Chronicle*, March 22, 1806.

44. For example, *Morning Post*, April 29, 1805. An article in the *Sporting Magazine* describing Elias' first match with Tom Belcher remarked on Mendoza's influence on Elias: "Sam fought very much in the Mendoza style, and it was no inconsiderable advantage to have him at his elbow." "Boxing, Samuels, alias Dutch Sam, and Tom Belcher," *Sporting Magazine* 27, no. 5 (February 1806): 245.

45. Pierce Egan, *Boxiana, Or, Sketches of Antient and Modern Pugilism*, vol. 2 (London: Sherwood, Neely, and Jones, 1818), 87–88.

46. "Sparring," *Sporting Magazine* 28 no. 3 (June 1806): 147. *Morning Post*, June 24, 1806. *Morning Chronicle*, June 24, 1806.

47. *St. James's Chronicle or British Evening Post*, July 28, 1807.

48. *Star*, August 21, 1807. *St. James's Chronicle or British Evening Post*, August 20, 1807. *The British Press*, August 21, 1807.

49. John Bee (pseud.) [John Badcock], *The Fancy; or True Sportsman's Guide: Being Authentic Memoirs of the Lives, Actions, Prowess, and Battles of the Leading Pugilists, From the Days of Figg and Broughton ot the Championship of Ward, by an Operator*, vol. 1 (London: J. McGowan and Son, 1826), 348.

50. *Morning Post*, July 29, 1807. *Bell's Weekly Messenger*, August 2, 1807.

51. "Boxing," *Sporting Magazine* 30, no. 4 (July 1807): 193.

52. Endelman, *The Jews of Georgian England*, 220. Elias's principal patron was a man named Ephraim Jacobs. Little is known about Jacobs, but he was probably a member of the growing Jewish middle class. He sued another patron to recover £200 he used to back Elias in a match against Bill Nosworthy, arguing that the match was fixed. "An Original Memoir of the late Bill Nosworthy, the Conqueror of the Pugilistic Phenomenon, Dutch Sam, Communicated by an Amateur," *Sporting Magazine* 49, no. 5 (February 1817): 229.

53. [Badcock], *The Fancy*, vol. 1, 351–352.

54. George Cruikshank, "The Baker kneeding Sammy's Dough," (London: G. Knight, December 1816), British Museum Print Room.

55. [Badcock], *The Fancy*, vol. 1, 352.

56. Endelman, *Jews of Georgian England*, 220.

57. "Caleb Baldwin & O'Donnel," *Sporting*

Magazine 23, no. 1 (October 1803): 6–7. Egan, *Boxiana*, vol. 1, 307–309, 317.

58. *Sporting Magazine* 23, no. 2 (November 1803): 96.

59. Tom Belcher was Jem Belcher's younger brother. For example, *Morning Post*, April 29, 1805 and *The Courier*, April 29, 1805.

60. "Boxing: O'Donnel and Emery," *Sporting Magazine* 27, no. 3 (December 1805): 125.

61. "Boxing: O'Donnell and Wasdell," *Sporting Magazine* 28, no. 4 (June 1806): 133. *Morning Post*, May 28, 1806.

62. "O'Donnell and Smith," *Sporting Magazine* 28, no. 4 (June 1806): 136. The report simply stated that the fight "afforded no diversion" and offered no further details.

63. *Old Bailey Proceedings Online* (www.oldbaileyonline.org, version 7.2, 26 September 2015), 17 September 1806, trial of John O'Donnell, Samuel Carter, and John Gore (t18060917–69).

64. *The Morning Post*, September 23, 1806.

65. *Old Bailey Proceedings Online* (www.old baileyonline.org, version 7.2, 26 September, 2015), 17 September 1806, trial of John O'Donnell (t18060917–83).

66. *Morning Post*, November 30, 1804.

67. *Bell's Weekly Messenger*, June 9, 1805. Shepperton is a little more than 15 miles from central London.

68. *Morning Post*, August 7, 1805.

69. Egan, *Boxiana*, vol. 1, 464.

70. Egan, *Boxiana*, vol. 1, 478 Egan refers to Dogherty's opponent only as "a Jew."

71. *Westminster Journal and Old British Spy*, June 21, 1806

72. *Star*, August 21, 1807.

73. *Morning Post*, August 21, 1807.

74. *Star*, August 21, 1807.

75. Byron to Mr. Murray, November 12, 1820. *Letters and Journals of Lord Byron*, ed. Thomas Moore (London: John Murray, 1839), 61.

76. *Sun*, April 15, 1808.

77. *Morning Post*, June 13, 1808.

78. *Evening Mail*, May 7, 1810.

79. *The Bristol Gazette and Public Advertiser*, January 17, 1811. *Bell's Weekly Messenger*, November 17, 1811

80. Egan, *Boxiana*, vol. 1, 479–480.

81. Oxberry, *Pancratia*, 103. The *Morning Post* recorded virtually no information about the bout except to note that evidence that magistrates needed to stop boxing "was upon record in *black and white!*" *Morning Post, and Daily Advertiser*, June 20, 1791.

82. Kevin R. Smith, *Black Genesis: The History of the Black Prizefighter, 1760–1870* (New York: iUniverse, Inc., 2003), 12–17.

83. Sancho and Equiano were both deceased by the time that Richmond was active. Cugoano's thoughts about Richmond, if any, are not recorded. Norma Myers, *Reconstructing the Black Past: Blacks in Britain c. 1780–1830* (London: Frank Cass, 1996), 27–28, 56–57, 67. James Walvin, *Black and White: the Negro and English Society, 1555–1945* (London: Allen Lane, 1973), argues for the importance of abolitionism in uniting black people.

84. Egan, *Boxiana*, vol. 1, 440–449.

85. "Boxiana, no. VIII: The Sable School of Pugilism," *Blackwood's Magazine* 8, no. 1 (October 1820): 65.

86. *Star*, January 24, 1804.

87. *Courier*, May 22, 1805.

88. Reid had been one of Daniel Mendoza's backers as well. *Morning Post*, May 22, 1805. *Star*, May 22, 1805.

89. *Star*, July 9, 1805.

90. *Star*, October 10, 1805. Luke Williams speculates that this period of inactivity coincided with and was a reaction to the illness and death of one of Richmond's children. Luke G. Williams, *Richmond Unchained: The Biography of the World's First Black Superstar* (Gloucestershire: Amberley, 2015).

91. Oxberry, *Pancratia*, 245.

92. *Star*, April 15, 1808. "Boxiana, no. VIII: The Sable School of Pugilism," *Blackwood's Magazine* 8, no. 1 (October 1820): 68. *Morning Post*, April 15, 1808.

93. Colorful legends about Molineaux's early life abound but, unfortunately, there is very little evidence to support them. Elliott Gorn describes what is known about Molineaux's life in the United States. Gorn, *The Manly Art*, 34–36. See also, W. Jeffrey Bolster, *Black Jacks: African Americans in the Age of Sail* (Cambridge: Harvard University Press, 1997), 118. Most information about Molineaux's life is derived from Egan, *Boxiana*, vol. 1, 360–361.

94. *Westminster Journal and Old British Spy*, July 21, 1810. *Sun*, July 26, 1810.

95. *Westminster Journal and Old British Spy*, August 11, 1810. *Morning Chronicle*, August 23, 1810.

96. *St. James's Chronicle and Evening Post*, August 18, 1810. *Kentish Chronicle*, August 24, 1810.

97. *Bell's Weekly Messenger*, August 26, 1810.

98. *Morning Post*, May 22, 1805.

99. *Morning Post*, April 9, 1807.

100. *The Art of Boxing, or Science of Manual Defence, Clearly Displayed on Rational Principles, Whereby Every Person may easily make themselves Masters of that Manly Acquirement, So as to ensure Success both in Attack & Defence. To Which is Added, Memoirs and Delineations of the Most Celebrated Pugilists, And an Account of some of their Principal Battles. By Thomas Belcher* (London: W. Mason, 1815), 13. The author of this pamphlet notes that "Some have censured Shifting as an unmanly custom."

101. *Morning Post*, October 26, 1808.

102. Rory Muir, *Britain and the Defeat of Napoleon, 1807–1815* (New Haven: Yale University Press, 1996), 59, 77.

103. Clark, *Scandal*, 148, 155.

104. Muir, *Britain and the Defeat of Napoleon*, 113–137.

105. Egan, *Boxiana*, vol. 1, 401.

106. *Morning Post*, December 19, 1810.

107. None of the London newspapers claimed that the crowd action resulted in Molineaux's defeat. *The Courier*, December 24, 1810, published a two-column account written by "an amateur." The account mentioned "a little national prejudice against the Black" but claimed it was "passive" and that Molineaux was shown fair play throughout. Journalist Pierce Egan, however, claimed that "if justice hold the scales ... his *colour* alone prevented him from becoming the hero of that fight." Egan, *Boxiana*, vol. 1, 493. The debate continues today. Carl B. Cone compiled all of the contemporary accounts of the fight to argue that the actions of the crowd deprived Molineaux of victory. Carl B. Cone, "The Molineaux-Cribb Fight, 1810: Wuz Tom Molineaux Robbed?" *Journal of Sport History* 9 (Winter, 1982): 83–91. In contrast, Dennis Brailsford contends that Molineaux was only cheated of victory by later standards of "fair play," not by those of the day. Dennis Brailsford, "Morals and Maulers: the Ethics of Early Pugilism," *Journal of Sport History* 12, no. 2 (Summer 1985): 126–142, 127.

108. The letter was likely written by Richmond as Molineaux was almost certainly illiterate. *Morning Post*, December 24, 1810.

109. Muir, *Britain and the Defeat of Napoleon*, 135.

110. *Bell's Weekly Messenger*, December 23, 1810.

111. Quoted in Paul Edwards, "Black Personalities in Georgian Britain," *History Today* 31, no. 9 (September 1981): 43.

112. Bill Gibbons, cited in Egan, *Boxiana*, vol. 1, 493.

113. *A Treatise on the Art and Practice of Self-Defence; or, Instructions how to obtain a scientific mode of boxing... To which are added, descriptions of pugilistic attitudes, etc. By a celebrated Pugilist* (London: 1826), 17.

114. The term "pedestrian" referred to running and walking. Barclay was best known for accomplishing the incredible feat of walking one mile every hour for one thousand hours in 1809. *Glasgow Herald*, July 19, 1811.

115. [John Badcock], *The Fancy*, vol. 2, 730–731. Cribb was a coal porter before achieving success as a boxer.

116. In addition to extensive reporting in London newspapers, the match received considerable attention in newspapers around England and Scotland, including, for example, *Bristol Gazette and Public Advertiser*, *Manchester Mercury*, and *Glasgow Herald*.

117. *Bristol Gazette and Public Advertiser*, October 3, 1811.

118. *Manchester Mercury*, October 1, 1811.

119. *Evening Star*, September 30, 1811. *The Bristol Gazette and Public Advertiser*, October 3, 1811.

120. *Bell's Weekly Messenger*, October 6, 1811.

121. *Bell's Weekly Messenger*, October 13, 1811.

Chapter Five

1. This narrative runs counter to many general histories of sport in Britain, which emphasize a sharp decline in traditional sports from the second half of the eighteenth century due to the intensifying attempts of the commercial classes to curtail traditional leisure practices. Richard Holt, "Historians and the history of sport: An interdisciplinary and critical survey," in Pascal Delheye, ed., *Making Sport History: Disciplines, identities, and the historiography of sport* (Abingdon, Oxon: Routledge, 2014), 46. Robert Malcomson, *Popular Recreations in English Society, 1700–1850* (Cambridge: Cambridge University Press, 1973). Malcomson's core argument is summarized in Adrian Harvey, *Football: The First 100 Years: The Untold Story* (London: Routledge, 2005), 2–4. Harvey challenges the orthodoxy in a number of publications. Especially Harvey, *The Beginnings of a Commercial Sporting Culture*.

2. Dennis Brailsford uses the phrase "boxing's professionals" to describe the pugilists and publicans who handled "all the arrangements on the ground" at prizefights. Brailsford, *Bareknuckles*, 67. I add journalists as they played a critical organizational role as well.

3. A similar dynamic happened in other literary realms, as authors such as Sydney Owenson and Walter Scott tried to "recuperate minority ethnic identity" and thus counteract the ethnic stereotypes of the eighteenth-century stage. Ragussis, *Theatrical Nation*, 140.

4. This apt term comes from the subtitle of John Ford's *Prizefighting: The Age of Regency Boximania* (Newton Abbot: David & Charles, 1971).

5. Boddy, *Boxing*, 55–66. Boddy uses the *OED* to show that the term "flash" combined an older meaning of "dashing, ostentatious, swaggering" and a newer definition specifically highlighting a connection with the prize ring. Flash style also included a slang language that marked one as inside or outside the prizefighting scene. Gregory Dart has suggested the cross-class possibilities of this language. Gregory Dart, "'Flash Style': Pierce Egan and Literary London 1820–28," *History Workshop Journal* 51, no. 1 (Spring 2001): 180–205.

6. John Gibson Lockhart and an "old college friend" cited in Edward Tuckerman Mason, *Per-*

sonal Traits of British Authors (New York: C. Scribner's Sons, 1885), 175, 190, 199–200.

7. *London Review and Literary Journal* 60, no. 3 (September 1811), 211. *Star*, August 27, 1811.

8. *Oxberry's Dramatic Biography and Histrionic Anecdotes* (London: George Virtue, 1825), 25. The line continues "and scarcely ever finishing anything." Dennis Brailsford describes Oxberry as a "part-time sporting journalist." Brailsford, *Bareknuckles*, 165.

9. Harvey, *The Beginnings of a Commercial Sporting Culture*, 32.

10. Oxberry, *Pancratia*, 3.

11. *The Monthly Magazine*, April 1, 1812.

12. Brailsford, *Bareknuckles*, 165. W. P. Courtney, "Badcock, John (fl. 1810–1830)," rev. Dennis Brailsford, in *Oxford Dictionary of National Biography*, ed. H. C. G. Matthew and Brian Harrison (Oxford: OUP, 2004), http://www.oxforddnb.com/view/article/1014 (accessed December 1, 2015).

13. Badcock was declared bankrupt twice. The first bankruptcy was proclaimed on October 3, 1805. *London Gazette*, October 5, 1805 issue 15849, 1263–1263. The second bankruptcy was proclaimed on November 30, 1813. *London Gazette*, May 3, 1814, issue 16894, 946. The last public notice appeared on November 28, 1815. *London Gazette*, November 28, 1815, issue 17085, 2391. Most sources identify 1816–1830 as his period of active publishing.

14. Oxberry, *Pancratia*, 7, 25–26.

15. *Morning Post*, August 30, 1815.

16. J.C. Reid, *Bucks and Bruisers: Pierce Egan and Regency England* (London: Routledge & Kegan Paul, 1971), 2.

17. Charles Phillips, esq., *Recollections of Curran and some of his contemporaries* (London, 1818), 95.

18. The account of Egan's ancestry and early life comes from Reid, *Bucks and Bruisers*, 2–6.

19. *Sporting Magazine* 26, no. 1 (April 1800): 35.

20. Dennis Brailsford, "Egan, Pierce (1772–1849)," in *Oxford Dictionary of National Biography*, ed. H. C. G. Matthew and Brian Harrison (Oxford: OUP, 2004), http://www.oxforddnb.com/view/article/8577 (accessed January 5, 2017). For further discussion of Egan's career and, especially, his uses of Irishness and Britishness, see Adam Chill, "Ireland Forever! Irish Boxers and Britishness in the early Nineteenth Century,'" *Journal for the Study of British Cultures* 18, no. 1 (January 2011): 15–26.

21. Boddy, *Boxing*, 57. Dart, "Pierce Egan and Literary London," 180–205.

22. Egan, *Boxiana*, vol. 1, iv–v.

23. *Star*, April 28, 1813. *The Star*, June 29, 1813.

24. *Courier*, September 2, 1813.

25. "The Pugilistic Club," *Sporting Magazine* 49, no. 2 (November 1816): 83. Egan, *Boxiana*, vol. 2, 24–28. It is a strong possibility that Egan was also the "correspondent" who wrote "The Pugilistic Club" for the *Sporting Magazine* as this essay is nearly identical to the account of the club included in *Boxiana*.

26. *Star*, May 4, 1814.

27. Brailsford, *Bareknuckles*, 67–72.

28. Pierce Egan, *Boxiana: or Sketches of antient and modern pugilism*, vol. 4 (London: G. Virtue, 1828), 444–445.

29. *Bethell's Life in London* reprinted in *Weekly Dispatch*, August 6, 1826.

30. *Morning Chronicle*, September 8, 1814.

31. *St. James's Chronicle, and London Evening Post*, April 3, 1817.

32. *Weekly Dispatch*, March 23, 1817, *Weekly Dispatch*, September 14, 1817

33. *Weekly Dispatch*, January 7, 1821.

34. Sporting journalists were part of a larger effort by writers in the non–English parts of the United Kingdom "to remind England that although it was the dominant power, the other component of the kingdom had contributed to England's greatness and continued to excel England in some respects." Linda E. Connors and Mary Lu MacDonald, *National Identity in Great Britain and British North America, 1815–1851, the Role of Nineteenth-Century Periodicals* (Farnham, Surrey: Ashgate, 2011), 191.

35. Egan, *Boxiana*, vol. 1, 111, 265, 447. Richmond was born in the American colonies, though he spent nearly his entire life in England.

36. *Weekly Dispatch*, October 5, 1817.

37. Egan, *Boxiana*, vol. 4, 77.

38. [Badcock], *The Fancy*, vol. 1, 112.

39. *Ibid.*, 153–154, 200, 300, 325–326.

40. After indoor boxing in London ended in the 1760s, boxers continued to train and to spar with gloves in public houses, clubs, and other facilities. While some complained about the "evil effects of dramatizing a Boxing Match," sparring exhibitions seem to have always been tolerated by authorities. *Morning Post*, January 21, 1788.

41. The *Sporting Magazine* mentioned a benefit at the Fives Court in June 1806 and noted that this meeting was the "monthly exhibition of pugilistic science." "Sparring," *Sporting Magazine* 28 no. 3 (June 1806): 147. The Fives Court was demolished in the 1820s to help make room for Trafalgar Square. Dowling, *Fistiana*, 48.

42. An account in the *New Monthly Magazine*, for example, noted that "the company … put an end" to the performance of particular fighters by shouting at them. "Jonathan Kentucky's Journal, no. VI" *New Monthly Magazine and Literary Journal* 2, no. 12 (December 1821): 556.

43. According to the *Weekly Dispatch*, two men named Owen and Lancaster managed the Minerva Rooms. *Weekly Dispatch*, February 16, 1817. *Weekly Dispatch*, April 26, 1817. *Weekly Dispatch*, May 3, 1818. *Weekly Dispatch*, November 19, 1820.

44. The *Weekly Dispatch* noted that he stood "very high among his own tribe, the Jews." *Weekly Dispatch*, July 13, 1817.

45. *Weekly Dispatch*, July 27, 1817. Egan, *Boxiana*, vol. 2, 275–277. *Weekly Dispatch*, October 26, 1817.

46. *Weekly Dispatch*, December 8, 1818. Emphasis in original.

47. Pierce Egan, *Boxiana; or, Sketches of ancient and modern pugilism*, vol. 3 (London: Sherwood, Neely, and Jones, 1821), 512.

48. For further discussion of these events see Adam Chill, "The Performance and Marketing of Minority Identity in Late-Georgian Boxing," in *Fighting Back? Jewish and Black Boxers in Britain*, ed. Michael Berkowitz and Ruti Ungar (London: University College London, 2007), 33–49.

49. *The Devil Among the Fancy; or, the Pugilistic Courts in an Uproar: To which is added, A Whimsical Dialogue between Dickey Martin, M.P. and Charley Eastup, W.P. (Or, of the Westminster-Pit) on the subject of Bears, Badgers, Bull-dogs, and the famous monkey, Jacco Maccacco; Showing the comparative Humanity of the Sports pursued in High Life and Low Life. By a member of the Pugilisitic Club* (London: John Fairburn, 1822), 5, *Weekly Dispatch*, December 9, 1821.

50. *Weekly Dispatch*, January 6, 1822.

51. *Weekly Dispatch*, January 20, 1822.

52. *The Devil Among the Fancy*, 5–6.

53. *Bell's Life in London*, May 5, 1822. May 12, 1822.

54. Irish boxer Pat Halton claimed that he had tried to make a match with Belasco at the end of 1822, but Belasco had no backing. *Weekly Dispatch*, January 26, 1823.

55. Abraham Belasco letter to the *Weekly Dispatch*, January 19, 1823. Daniel Mendoza and Samuel "Dutch Sam" Elias were the most famous Anglo-Jewish boxers of the era.

56. Most Jews remained politically quietist, however. See Endelman, *The Jews of Georgian England*, 280–281.

57. *Bell's Life in London*, March 23, 1823. Emphasis in original.

58. *Weekly Dispatch*, January 26, 1823. Egan, *Boxiana*, vol. 4, 145–146.

59. *Bell's Life in London*, April 13, 1823.

60. The *Weekly Dispatch* reported that many of those in attendance were Jewish. *Weekly Dispatch*, August 24, 1823. For example, Belasco used yellow in a match later the same year against Irish boxer Pat Halton. Pierce Egan, *Boxiana: or Sketches of antient and modern pugilism*, vol. 5 (London: G. Virtue, 1829), 142. Similarly, Jewish boxer Barney Aaron used yellow in his match against Arthur Matthewson. *The Weekly Dispatch*, June 27, 1824. Jews were often forced to wear the color yellow as a badge of their difference in many European countries from the late-medieval period.

61. *Morning Chronicle*, August 20, 1823. [Badcock], *The Fancy*, vol. 2, 376. *Morning Chronicle*, August 20, 1823. *Weekly Dispatch*, September 7, 1823.

62. *Weekly Dispatch*, September 7, 1823.

63. Egan, *Boxiana*, vol. 1, 480.

64. *Morning Chronicle*, April 29, 1813.

65. "Belcher and Dogherty," *Sporting Magazine* 42, no. 2 (May 1813): 66.

66. *Hibernian Journal*, reprinted in *Saunder's News-Letter and Daily Advertiser*, April 26, 1813.

67. Capt. Francis O'Neill, *Irish Minstrels and Musicians, with Numerous Dissertations on Related Subjects* (Chicago: Regan Printing House, 1913), 184.

68. [Badcock], *The Fancy*, vol. 1, 371. Badcock reported that the odds were 60 to 40 on Hall in the weeks leading up to the fight and 25 to 20 immediately before the match. Patrick Myler, *Regency Rogue: Dan Donnelly, His Life and Legends* (Dublin: O'Brien, 1976), 31–38.

69. The *Star*, September 20, 1814, citing a Dublin newspaper, claimed that not less than 40,000 people were in attendance. Pierce Egan later claimed that "not less than 40,000 spectators were present." Egan, *Boxiana*, vol. 2, 383. John Badcock cited the same figure in his description of the match, noting also that Dublin was emptied of people on the day of the bout. [Badcock], *The Fancy*, vol. 1, 370.

70. Egan, *Boxiana*, vol. 2, 383. *Star*, September 20, 1814.

71. O'Neill, *Irish Minstrels and Musicians*, 186.

72. Egan, *Boxiana*, vol. 2, 385. *St. James's Chronicle and Evening Post*, November 16, 1815 noted that "the air resounded with shots from the spectators" after the knockdown. *Star*, November 17, 1815.

73. [Badcock], *The Fancy*, vol. 2, 371, claimed that the "many disadvantages arising from the prejudice against him" hindered Cooper's performance. Egan, *Boxiana*, vol. 2, 387, while acknowledging these disadvantages, argued that "It is not meant to be urged that [Cooper] could have won the battle."

74. Myler, *Regency Rogue*, 67–68.

75. Egan, *Boxiana*, vol. 2, 388.

76. *Weekly Dispatch*, June 22, 1817. The newspaper opined that, in case Donnelly would not fight, "it is said to be the intention of the FANCY, to send immediately out to America for a shipload of Blacks."

77. *Bell's Weekly Messenger*, July 25, 1819.

78. Sir Bernard Burke, *History of the Landed Gentry of Great Britain and Ireland*, vol. 1 (London: Harrison and Sons, 1894), 99. *Gentleman's Magazine* 39, no. 5 (May 1853): 544. H. M. Chichester, "Barton, Sir Robert (1770–1853)," rev. David Gates, in *Oxford Dictionary of National Biography*, ed. H. C. G. Matthew and Brian Harrison (Oxford: OUP, 2004), http://www.oxforddnb.com/view/article/1603 (accessed January 15, 2017).

79. Egan, *Boxiana*, vol. 3, 160, 262, 620. In a poem, Egan wrote "Then in General Barton's praise, I could sing all my days, For he found out this *gem* in the darkey, O! He's the friend of Erin's sons, And a *pal* of Wellington's; Health to him and the Nonpareil, Jack Randall, O!"

80. *Bell's Life in London*, April 13, 1823, noted that an Irish boxer used green "*(a la Randall)*." Emphasis in original. John Badcock argued that Randall learned to fight because he grew up English amongst the Irish of St. Giles. [Badcock], *The Fancy*, vol. 1, 249–250. This interpretation of Randall's parentage is repeated in contemporary scholarship as well. Tom Sawyer, *A Noble Art: An Artistic and Literary Celebration of the Old English Prize-Ring* (London: Unwin Hyman Limited, 1989), 64, claims (with no supporting evidence) that a number of writers fell "into the Hibernian habit, introduced by Egan and the Dowlings, of ascribing Irish parentage to Jack Randall, who always strongly denied the assertion." The story may derive from the virulently anti–Irish journalist Henry Downes Miles, writing at the end of the nineteenth century in very different times. Miles claimed that "Jack, who was always called by Pierce Egan and Co., the 'prime Irish lad,' himself laughed, when primed with gin—he would not touch whisky—at his imputed Irish descent" Henry Downes Miles, *Pugilistica: The History of British Boxing, containing lives of the most celebrated pugilists; full reports of their battles from contemporary newspapers, with authentic portraits, personal anecdotes, and sketches of the principal patrons of the prize ring, forming a complete history of the ring from Fig and Broughton, 1719–40, to the last championship battle between King and Heenan, in December 1863*, vol. 1 (London: Weldon, 1880–1881; reprint, Edinburgh: John Grant, 1906), 328.

81. *Sporting Magazine* 67, no. 6 (April 1826): 412.

82. *Star*, December 7, 1818.

83. Randall's nickname was "The Nonpareil." *Weekly Dispatch*, September 22, 1822. *Weekly Dispatch*, September 20, 1818. *Weekly Dispatch*, September 3, 1820. *Weekly Dispatch*, October 8, 1820. *Sporting Magazine* 60, no. 5 (August 1822): 267.

84. *Morning Chronicle*, March 13, 1819.

85. *Kent's Weekly Dispatch*, March 14, 1819; *Weekly Dispatch*, February 14, 1819; *Weekly Dispatch*, February 28, 1819; *Weekly Dispatch*, March 21, 1819. *Morning Post*, March 24, 1819.

86. *Weekly Dispatch*, March 28, 1819. Egan, *Boxiana*, vol. 3, 73.

87. *Morning Chronicle*, April 2, 1819; Kent's *Weekly Dispatch*, April 4, 1819.

88. *Weekly Dispatch*, April 4, 1819.

89. Egan, *Boxiana*, vol. 3, 80.

90. *Bell's Weekly Messenger*, July 25, 1819.

91. *Weekly Dispatch*, May 30, 1819.

92. *Weekly Dispatch*, June 13, 1819.

93. Egan, *Boxiana*, vol. 3, 81–82.

94. *Weekly Dispatch*, July 25, 1819.

95. *Kent's Weekly Dispatch*, July 25, 1819.

96. *Kent's Weekly Dispatch*, July 25, 1819.

97. Egan, *Boxiana*, vol. 3, 123–124.

98. *Dublin Evening Post*, July 24, 1819.

99. *Weekly Dispatch*, August 1, 1819. Egan, *Boxiana*, vol. 3, 99. Egan claimed that "Thousands of persons assembled on the beach" to greet Donnelly, but this may be an exaggeration.

100. *Carrick's Evening Post*, August 27, 1819, reprinted in Egan, *Boxiana*, vol. 3, 101.

101. The cause of Donnelly's death is not entirely clear. The *Dublin Journal* reported that "an inflammation of the lungs" after being "overheated" following a game of rackets caused his demise. *Dublin Journal*, February 21, 1820. John Badcock added that he had drunk a "draught of cold water in a state of perspiration." [Badcock], *The Fancy*, vol. 1, 376.

102. *Weekly Dispatch*, March 16, 1820. *Dublin Journal*, February 25, 1820.

103. *Saunders's News-letter and Daily Advertiser*, February 21, 1820.

104. Myler, *Regency Rogue*, 130–131; letter to the *Dublin Journal* announcing the creation of the committee, February 25, 1820.

105. *Dublin Journal*, February 25, 1820.

106. The arm was dipped in red lead for preservation and appeared at a medical college in Edinburgh and a traveling circus in Ireland before ending up at the Hideout Pub in Kilcullen in the mid-twentieth century. An exhibit called "Fighting Irishmen: A Celebration of the Celtic Warrior," which featured Donnelly's mummified arm among other artifacts, toured the United States in 2007.

107. *Freeman's Journal* reprinted in the *Bell's Life in London*, April 7, 1822. The *Freeman's Journal* claimed that the crowd "did not fall short of Fifty Thousand."

108. [Badcock], *The Fancy*, vol. 1, 449.

109. Badcock identified Halton's backer as "a captain in the army, from the Sister Kingdom." This was almost certainly William Kelly, to whom contemporary sources referred as Captain Kelly. [Badcock], *The Fancy*, vol. 2, 111, *Weekly Dispatch*, January 5, 1823.

110. *Bell's Life in London*, April 13, 1823.

111. *Weekly Dispatch*, April 13, 1823.

112. *Weekly Dispatch*, December 20, 1818. Bareknuckle boxing was therefore one site of the "political contests between popular traditions of radicalism and conservatism" that took place "particularly among the lower classes" in the nineteenth century. Jörg Neuheiser, *Crown, Church and Constitution: Popular Conservatism in England, 1815–1867*, trans. Jennifer Walcoff Neuheiser (New York and Oxford: Berghahn Books, 2016), 2.

Chapter Six

1. Edwin F. Roberts, "Something Further Anent Dockside; or Liverpool Twenty-Five Years Ago," *Colburn's United Service Magazine and Naval and Military Journal*, part 3 (September 1855): 222.

2. John Denvir, *Life Story of an Old Rebel* (Dublin: Sealy, Bryers, and Walker, 1910), 4, 52.

3. *Observer*, October 9, 1843.

4. John Belchem, *Merseypride: Essays in Liverpool Exceptionalism* (Liverpool: Liverpool University Press, 2000), 90.

5. *Morning Post*, November 5, 1844.

6. John Belchem mentions Langan's pub and his influence in Liverpool. Belchem, *Merseypride*, 90. There are a number of brief biographical sketches of his life but these are drawn almost entirely from the memoir written by Pierce Egan, which is discussed below. For example, Frank Hopkins, *Rare Old Dublin: Heroes, Hawkers, and Hoors* (Dublin: Marino Books, 2002), 40–42.

7. S.J. Connolly, "Union government, 1812–23," in *Ireland under the Union, I, 1801–1870*, ed. W.E. Vaughan, A New History of Ireland, vol. 5 (Oxford: Clarendon Press, 1989), 70–71.

8. S.J. Connolly, "Mass politics and sectarian conflict, 1823–1830," in *A New History of Ireland*, vol. 5 (Oxford: Clarendon Press, 1989), 82.

9. James S. Donnelly, Jr., "Pastorini and Captain Rock: Millenarianism and Sectarianism in the Rockite Movement of 1821–4." In *Irish Peasants: Violence and Political Unrest, 1780–1914*, ed. Samuel Clark and James S. Donnelly, Jr. (MadisonI: University of Wisconsin Press, 1983), 135.

10. Connelly, "Mass Politics and Sectarian Conflict," 84, 87, 105.

11. Egan's memoir identifies the place as Clondalton, County Kildare but this was almost certainly a mistake.

12. Maureen Waters, *The Comic Irishman* (Albany: State University of New York Press, 1984), 41–57.

13. Egan, *Boxiana*, vol. 4, 336.

14. *Ibid.*, 337–338.

15. Ragussis, *Theatrical Nation*, 57.

16. Egan, *Boxiana*, vol. 4, 344–347.

17. General Wolfe was depicted, for example, "unconcerned by the wounds he had sustained" while he lay dying after the Battle of the Plains of Abraham. Nicholas Rogers, "Brave Wolfe: The Making of a Hero," in *A New Imperial History: Culture, Identity, and Modernity in Britain and the Empire, 1660–1840* (Cambridge: Cambridge University Press, 2003), 250.

18. *Dublin Journal*, May 14, 1819.

19. A notice in *Morning Chronicle*, October 12, 1819 describes Devereux (in Latin) as the "friend and companion in arms of Bolívar." The notice further explains that "the Friends of South American Liberty in Ireland" planned to present Devereux with a "splendid sword" in recognition of his efforts.

20. Edmundo Murray, "John Devereux," in James P. Byrne, Philip Coleman, and Jason King, eds., *Ireland and the Americas: Culture, Politics, and History, A Multidisciplinary Encyclopedia*, vol. 1 (Santa Barbara: ABC-CLIO, 2008), 250–251. See also Ben Hughes, *Conquer or Die! Wellington's Veterans and the Liberation of the New World* (Oxford: Osprey Publishing, 2012).

21. Egan claimed that Langan's brother was on board the *Victory* when Nelson perished at Aboukir Bay. Nelson died aboard the *Victory* at Trafalgar in August 1805. Aboukir Bay was part of the Battle of the Nile in August 1798.

22. Egan does not mention whether Langan's assailant noticed any blood on his bayonet. *Weekly Dispatch*, January 11, 1824. Egan, *Boxiana*, vol. 4, 354–357.

23. *Weekly Dispatch*, January 11, 1824. Egan, *Boxiana*, vol. 4, 358.

24. See Hughes, *Wellington's Veterans and the Liberation of the New World*, Chapter 22.

25. Egan, *Boxiana*, vol. 4, 359–360. A John Langan, listed as a grocer and spirit-dealer, continued to be a leaseholder at a similar address in North King Street in the 1830s and 1840s. This address was adjacent to Langan's public house and thus suggests that he or a close relative continued to have an interest in this district of Dublin long after his relocation to Liverpool. See *The Treble Almanac* (Dublin, 1832), 98 and *The Dublin Almanac and General Register for Ireland, for the Year of Our Lord, 1847* (Dublin: Pettigrew and Oulton, 1847), 526.

26. Langan's letter was published in the *Freeman's Journal* and reprinted in *British Press*, April 6, 1822.

27. *Statesman*, February 24, 1823.

28. Egan, *Boxiana*, vol. 4, 361.

29. Egan, *Boxiana*, vol. 4, 362. *Bell's Life in London*, January 11, 1824.

30. *Bell's Weekly Messenger*, July 25, 1819. An obituary for Reynolds in May 1832 noted that he "acted the part of [Langan's] secretary." *Bell's Life in London and Sporting Chronicle*, May 27, 1832.

31. Thomas Reynolds letter to *Egan's Life in London* reprinted in Egan, *Boxiana*, vol. 4, 370.

32. Vipond was often called "Matt Wheeping." The *Dublin Journal*, October 22, 1823, claimed that this confusion came from Vipond's nickname: "Wheeping Matt."

33. [John Badcock], *The Fancy*, vol. 2, 430.

34. Egan, *Boxiana*, vol. 4, 362.

35. *Manchester Guardian*, May 3, 1823. The same account appears in *Boxiana*, vol. 4, 365–366 and the *Weekly Dispatch*, May 4, 1823.

36. In a public answer to a later challenge, Spring referred to an earlier letter from Langan in June 1823. *Morning Post*, October 6, 1823.

37. *Weekly Dispatch*, September 7, 1823. Emphasis in original.

38. Egan, *Boxiana*, vol. 4, 366.

39. Egan, *Boxiana*, vol. 4, 367.

40. The three letters were reprinted in a number of newspapers, including *Morning Post*, October 6, 1823.

41. [Badcock], *The Fancy*, vol. 2, 427, 440.

42. *Morning Post*, October 11, 1823; *Morning Post*, October 14, 1823.

43. *Dublin Journal*, October 22, 1823. Langan had also made another match against Matt Vipond that was to occur after the Spring bout. The *Dublin Journal* printed the articles for this match.

44. *Bell's Life in London*, January 11, 1824.

45. Brailsford, *Bareknuckles*, 73.

46. The most immediate cause of Thurtell's financial difficulties was his unsuccessful attempt to collect £1900 after he and his brother burned down their own house. *The Fatal Effects of Gambling Exemplified in the Murder of Wm. Weare, and the Trial and Fate of John Thurtell, the Murderer, and His Accomplices* (London: Thomas Kelly, 1824), xii–xv, 21. The Middlesex Grand Jury started proceedings against Thurtell and his accomplices in this case on October 20. *Statesmen*, October 21, 1823.

47. Angus Fraser, "Thurtell, John (1794–1824)," in *Oxford Dictionary of National Biography*, ed. H. C. G. Matthew and Brian Harrison (Oxford: OUP, 2004), http://www.oxforddnb.com/view/article/27414 (accessed January 15, 2015), has suggested that Thurtell murdered Weare either to get revenge for being cheated or in hopes of stealing money from Weare.

48. Reid, *Bucks and Bruisers*, 105.

49. Angus Fraser has remarked that the "case was manna from heaven for the moralists of post–Regency England, who inveighed against the twin evils of gambling and pugilism." Fraser, "Thurtell, John (1794–1824)." The case was quickly immortalized in popular songs, in print, and on stage. One play was performed before the trial.

50. *Times*, November 11, 1823. "The Fancy" was the term that the followers of boxing and similar sports had applied to themselves since the late-eighteenth century.

51. *Times*, November 12, 1823.

52. Reid, *Bucks and Bruisers*, 109.

53. *Times*, January 10, 1824.

54. *Weekly Dispatch*, January 11, 1824. This spirited defense of boxing did not appear in *Boxiana* and is therefore probably not the work of Pierce Egan. *Weekly Dispatch*, January 18, 1824.

55. *Bell's Life in London*, January 11, 1824.

56. *Bell's Life in London*, January 11, 1824. *Weekly Dispatch*, January 11, 1824. "The Pugilistic Ring. Fight between Spring and Langan," *Sporting Magazine* 13, no. (1824): 201–202. The outer ring was constructed to keep spectators away from the inner ring, where Langan and Spring fought. Only members of the Pugilistic Club, boxers hired to keep the crowd away from the ring, and a few others were permitted within this outer ring.

57. *Weekly Dispatch*, January 11, 1824. The estimate of the number of spectators who fell is from *Bell's Life in London*, January 11, 1824.

58. *Bell's Life in London*, January 11, 1824. The newspaper claimed that twenty people were seriously injured and nine of these were in the Worcester infirmary with fractured bones. Treby died from complications resulting from a compound fracture of his thigh.

59. The outer ring was constructed to keep spectators away from the inner ring, where Langan and Spring fought. Only members of the Pugilistic Club, boxers hired to keep the crowd away from the ring, and a few others were permitted within this outer ring. *Bell's Life in London*, January 11, 1824.

60. [Badcock], *The Fancy*, vol. 2, 445.

61. "The Pugilistic Ring. Fight between Spring and Langan," *Sporting Magazine* 13, no. (1824): 205.

62. According to Broughton's rules, a fight was considered ended when a fighter failed to report to the scratch thirty seconds after the end of the previous round. The scratch was a square chalked in the center of the ring. *Bell's Life in London*, January 11, 1824. Egan, *Boxiana*, vol. 4, 304. "The Pugilistic Ring. Fight between Spring and Langan," *Sporting Magazine* 13, no. (1824): 206.

63. *St. James Chronicle and General Evening Post*, January 10, 1824. In 1810, Molineaux had charged that he was assaulted by spectators during his first match with Cribb. As a result, they fought another match on a stage in 1811.

64. *Morning Chronicle*, January 17, 1824.

65. Letter to *Bell's Weekly Dispatch* reprinted in *Sporting Magazine* 63, no. 4 (January 1824): 209.

66. *Weekly Dispatch*, January 25, 1824.

67. *Bell's Life in London*, January 25, 1824.

68. *Morning Post*, February 3, 1824. *Observer*, February 8, 1824. *St. James's Chronicle and General Evening Post*, February 10, 1824.

69. *St. James's Chronicle and General Evening Post*, February 17, 1824.

70. *Morning Chronicle*, February 20, 1824.

71. *St. James's Chronicle and General Evening Post*, February 28, 1824. The articles were signed on March 2 at Tom Cribb's house.

72. *Weekly Dispatch*, February 15, 1824.

73. *Weekly Dispatch*, March 21, 1824.

74. The usual admission price for a benefit was three shillings for "gentlemen" and five shillings for titled spectators. Even after the deduction of expenses for the court, Langan probably received over £100 from this benefit. Langan most likely received additional gifts that were not recorded.

75. *St. James's Chronicle and General Evening Post*, April 17, 1824.

76. *Dublin Journal*, April 22, 1824.

77. Egan, *Boxiana*, vol. 4, 370–371.

78. *Bell's Life in London*, May 9, 1824. He was an honored guest, for example, at a public house named the Duke of Wellington, owned by a man named Earl. According to the *Weekly Dispatch*, Earl was putting gloves on Langan and told Langan that Thurtell was the last man for whom he had put on gloves. Langan apparently replied, "then by Jasus you shall not tie those on mine."

79. *Weekly Dispatch*, June 13, 1824. *Freeman's Journal*, June 9, 1824. One innkeeper, for example, purchased one hundred extra blankets in anticipation of the crowd. The publicans and innkeepers of Warwick and the surrounding areas claimed that they collectively stood to lose one hundred thousand pounds as a result of the magistrate's interference.

80. *Bell's Life in London*, June 13, 1824.

81. *Dublin Evening Post*, June 12, 1824.

82. *Bell's Life in London*, June 13, 1824. The newspaper also noted that, "from the sums extracted from the passengers, it is now generally called the *double draw*-bridge."

83. *Freeman's Journal*, June 14, 1824.

84. *Bell's Life in London*, June 13, 1824.

85. Egan, *Boxiana*, vol. 4, 375.

86. *Dublin Evening Post*, June 12, 1824. *Freeman's Journal*, June 14, 1824.

87. *Bell's Life in London*, June 13, 1824.

88. *Freeman's Journal*, June 14, 1824.

89. *Bell's Life in London*, June 13, 1824.

90. *Weekly Dispatch*, June 13, 1824.

91. *Bell's Life in London*, June 13, 1824.

92. *Weekly Dispatch*, June 13, 1824.

93. Anthony Webster, *The Richest East India Merchant: The Life and Business of John Palmer of Calcutta, 1767–1836* (Woodbridge: The Boydell Press, 2007), 77. Webster shows that O'Brien's relationship with his patron Palmer was an important reason for his advancement in India and his ultimate fall. O'Brien returned to Europe, ostensibly for his health, at the end of 1823. J. Pattison to East India Company Board of Directors, October 29, 1823. *Papers Relative to Certain Pecuniary Transactions of Messrs. William Palmer and Co. with His Highness the Nizam* (London: J.L. Cox, 1824), 453–460.

94. *Freeman's Journal*, June 14, 1824. The story was also reported in *The Fancy*, *Pierce Egan's Life in London*, and *Bell's Life in London*, among others.

95. *Morning Post*, May 21, 1824.

96. *Weekly Dispatch*, June 13, 1824. Other sources estimated the crowd at sixteen thousand. In either case, however, the number of spectators was at least half that of the crowd at Worcester. *Freeman's Journal*, June 14, 1824. [Badcock], *The Fancy*, vol. 2, 526.

97. *St. James's Chronicle and General Evening Post*, June 8, 1824. *Freeman's Journal*, June 14, 1824. *Bell's Life in London* claimed that Spring's hands were "swollen to the size of large apple-dumplings." *Bell's Life in London*, June 13, 1824. *Bell's Life in London*, June 13, 1824 claimed that Langan put down only £100. The *Dublin Evening Post* maintained that Langan "put down at least £200 of his own money." *Dublin Evening Post*, June 12, 1824.

98. Egan, *Boxiana*, vol. 4, 391.

99. *Weekly Dispatch*, June 13, 1824. Spring used blue as his color.

100. *St. James's Chronicle and General Evening Post*, June 8, 1824.

101. *Weekly Dispatch*, June 13, 1824. *Bell's Life in London*, June 13, 1824. Egan, *Boxiana*, vol. 4, 397.

102. *Morning Chronicle*, June 25, 1824.

103. *Morning Post*, July 2, 1824.

104. Belcher offered to back any boxer for £300 for the Championship except Langan. The conflict had to do with Langan's failure to appear at a benefit. *Morning Post*, June 30, 1824.

105. *St. James's Chronicle and General Evening Post*, July 1, 1824.

106. *Weekly Dispatch*, July 25, 1824.

107. *Weekly Dispatch*, August 22, 1824.

108. Egan, *Boxiana*, vol. 4, 405. *Weekly Dispatch*, September 25, 1825.

109. *Weekly Dispatch*, September 12, 1826; May 20, 1827. Langan did not end his involvement with the prize ring altogether. He acted as stakeholder in 1828 for a match involving Dubliner Simon Byrne. A criminal and member of the Fancy called Clarke was apprehended at Langan's house in 1831. *Times*, November 14, 1831.

110. Egan, *Boxiana*, vol. 4, 406.

111. Brailsford, *Bareknuckles*, 85.

112. *Times*, November 4, 1844. Belchem, *Merseypride*, 90.

Chapter Seven

1. Miles, *Pugilistica*, vol. 2, 199.

2. This period has often been seen as the beginning of a decline for bareknuckle prizefighting from which the sport never recovered. See, for example, Reid, *Bucks and Bruisers*, 138. More recent reinterpretations of the Victorian "revolution in sport" have qualified earlier claims about the cataclysmic impact of urbanization and industrialization on early modern sport. Neil Tranter, *Sport, Economy, and Society in Britain 1750–1914* (Cambridge: Cambridge University Press, 1998), 13–15.

3. The most distressing of these to members of the government were the Swing Riots against people and property in rural areas. Hilton, *A Mad, Bad, and Dangerous People?*, 398, 416.

4. Although Parliament banned the Catholic Association (along with all other "unlawful societies" in Ireland) in March 1825, O'Connell's popular campaign continued. Connolly, "Mass Politics and Sectarian Conflict," 97.

5. Along with the most important actions undertaken by the reformed Parliament—the abolition of slavery, the factory acts, and the end of the Corn Laws—was the 1835 Cruelty to Animals Act, which finally banned bull baiting.

6. Hilton, *A Mad, Bad, and Dangerous People?*, 350–353.

7. Tosh, "Masculinities in an Industrializing Society," 331. Clark, *The Struggle for the Breeches*, 267. These shifting attitudes can also be seen in the greater emphasis on a more controlled and disciplined masculinity in Victorian public schools, which began to promote very different sporting ideals from mid-century. Holt, *Sport and the British*, 74–117. The connection between physical hardihood in men and the nation remained important for proponents of Rugby football until the 1860s, however. Timothy J.L. Chandler, "The Structuring of Manliness and of Rugby Football at the Public Schools and Oxbridge, 1830–1880," in *Making Men: Rugby and Masculine Identity*, ed. John Nauright and Timothy J.L. Chandler (London: Frank Cass & Co., 1996), 13–31.

8. By the first part of the nineteenth century, army officers were looking beyond the shores of Britain to find "other 'martial' societies in the Empire—particularly in India." Streets, *Martial Races*, 8.

9. In 1826, Liverpool-based *Bethell's Life in London* complained of Dowling's work as a referee. Reprinted in *The Weekly Dispatch*, August 6, 1826. Two days after a dispute at a May 1828 match for which he served as referee, Dowling appeared at a gathering of boxers and supporters of the sport to reassure the assembled audience that the match had not been fixed. Egan, *Boxiana*, vol. 5, 651–653.

10. Miles, *Pugilistica*, vol. 2, 199.

11. The elder Dowling published, for example, Henry Grattan's answer to his political opponents in 1798. *Mr. Grattan's Observations on the Certain Proceedings Against Him in Dublin* (Dublin: Vincent Dowling, 1798).

12. Tony Mason, "Dowling, Vincent George (1785–1852)," in *Oxford Dictionary of National Biography*, ed. H. C. G. Matthew and Brian Harrison (Oxford: OUP, 2004), http://www.oxforddnb.com/view/article/7970 (accessed January 15, 2017).

13. *Times*, July 4, 1818 alludes to this evidence given by Dowling at trial. In addition, one of the accused at this trial testified that Dowling told him that Dowling might receive a 500l. position with the government as a result the information he provided. *Times*, June 17, 1817. Dowling always publicly denied that he was a spy.

14. Anna Clark has described Hunt as the embodiment of "virile heterosexual radical manhood." Clark, *Struggle for the Breeches*, 155

15. Clark, *Struggle for the Breeches*, 155. *Times*, October 27, 1818.

16. Dowling, *Fistiana*, 9, 12, 15.

17. Brailsford, *Bareknuckles*, 89

18. The Irish-born population in the metropolis probably tripled between the end of the war and 1841. Lynn Hollen Lees, *Exiles of Erin: Irish Migrants in Victorian London* (Ithaca: Cornell University Press, 1979), 42, 45. Roger Swift, ed., *Irish Migrants in Britain, 1815–1914: A Documentary History* (Cork: Cork University Press, 2002), 27, 36–37. Graham Davis, *The Irish in Britain, 1815–1914* (Dublin: Gill and MacMillan, 1991), 5, 51. Ruth-Ann M. Harris, *The Nearest Place That Wasn't Ireland: Early Nineteenth-Century Irish Labor Migration* (Ames: Iowa State University Press, 1994) 16–17.

19. *Weekly Dispatch*, March 2, 1817.

20. *Bell's Weekly Messenger*, May 25, 1818. Michael Ryan was an Irish boxer who fought for the championship in 1788 and 1789.

21. *Sporting Magazine* 58, no. 6 (September 1821): 263.

22. Letter from "A Constant Reader," "On the Utility of Pugilism" to *Sporting Magazine* 62 no. 4 (July 1823): 192. Letter from "Your Constant Reader," "On the Decline of Boxing," to *Sporting Magazine* 63, no. 6 (March 1824): 312.

23. [Badcock], *The Fancy*, vol. 1, 249–250.

24. *Weekly Dispatch*, August 10, 1823; *Bell's Life in London*, August 10, 1823. *The Morning Post*, September 24, 1823.

25. [Badcock], *The Fancy*, vol. 1, 382. *Morning Advertiser*, October 17, 1823.

26. *Weekly Dispatch*, October 5, 1823.

27. For example, in his December 1824 fight against Jem Burn. *Morning Post*, December 22, 1824. Also, his fight against Tom Cannon in February 1827. *Morning Chronicle*, February 21, 1827.

28. Advertisement reprinted in Egan, *Boxiana*, vol. 5, 572–573.

29. *Weekly Dispatch*, May 2, 1824. The *Dispatch* ceased to employ Pierce Egan in January 1824. George Kent, another influential boxing journalist, then became the main sporting journalist at the paper.

30. *Bell's Life in London*, June 19, 1825.

31. Egan, *Boxiana*, volume 5, 575.

32. *Bell's Life in London*, October 9, 1825.

33. *Bell's Life in London*, September 24, 1826. This issue advertised a match between the dogs of O'Neale and Josh Hudson. As we have seen, Hudson was also a publican and boxing match organizer.

34. *Bell's Life in London*, November 1, 1825.

35. "Pugilism," *Sporting Magazine* 69, no. 3 (January 1827): 214.

36. "Pugilism," *Sporting Magazine* 69, no. 3 (January 1827): 214.

37. O'Neale hopped around the ring refusing to engage Sampson (who stood with his hands at his sides), until bets that Sampson would not lose in the first hour were decided. Then, O'Neale hit

Sampson with a series of punches and Sampson refused to continue, to the shock of his seconds. *Bell's Life in London*, December 17, 1826.

38. See stories in *Morning Chronicle*, February 21, 1827, *Morning Post*, February 21, 1827, and "Pugilism," *Sporting Magazine* 69, no. 5 (March 1827). The *Sporting Magazine* noted that much of the large crowd came from the vicinity of Windsor so it is likely that there were not many Irish spectators in attendance at this particular bout.

39. Egan, *Boxiana*, vol. 5, 585–600.

40. Miles claimed that O'Neale wrote a letter to *Bell's Life in London* in which "the young aspirant disclosed his parentage and place of birth, depriving 'ould' Pierce's rhodomontade of its applicability and point." Miles, however, provides no date for this letter and it could not be found in *Bell's Life* during the period in which O'Neale was active (1822–1831). Miles, *Pugilistica*, vol. 2, 291.

41. *Weekly Dispatch*, May 13, 1827.

42. *Bell's Life in London*, October 21, 1827; *Weekly Dispatch*, November 11, 1827.

43. *Bell's Life in London*, November 18, 1827. Egan, *Boxiana*, volume 5, 602–608.

44. *Bell's Life in London*, December 2, 1827.

45. Egan, *Boxiana*, vol. 5, 610. *Morning Advertiser*, July 22, 1828.

46. *Sporting Magazine* 73, no. 5 (March 1829): 368.

47. Egan, *Boxiana*, vol. 5, 651–652;

48. Ward's friend Edward Mingaud wrote that Ward's parents were married in St. George-in-the-East, an Anglican Church. Edward Mingaud, *The Life and Adventures of James Ward, Viewed as "The Champion" and "The Artist"* (London: W.S. Johnson, 1853), 14.

49. The Irish Society of London, an Anglican foundation intended to provide education in Irish, was established in 1822 on the Ratcliffe Highway. *Irish Society of London, for Promoting the Education of the Native Irish, through the Medium of Their [sic] Own Language* (London: J.Wilson, 1822).

50. Several accounts of Ward's early life from the 1820s record that Nicholas Ward was a butcher. See, for example, *Weekly Dispatch*, July 4, 1824. Ward's friend and biographer Edward Mingaud only noted that Nicholas was a "ballast-getter." He also mentions, however, that Jem attended school in Chadwell Heath, which would have been much more likely for the son of a butcher. Mingaud, *The Life and Adventures of James Ward*, 14.

51. Henry Mayhew described the difficult work of a ballast-heaver several decades later and included the account of an Irish ballast-heaver's wife, who complained that ballast-heavers were treated "worse than slaves in the West Indies." Henry Mayhew, *London Labour and the London Poor*, vol. 3 (London: Griffin, Bohn, and Company, 1861), 280.

52. Accounts of Ward's life written in the 1820s include Egan, *Boxiana*, vol. 4, 514–515; *Weekly Dispatch*, July 4, 1824, [Badcock], *The Fancy*, vol. 2, 581–582. Mingaud, *The Life and Adventures of James Ward*, 15.

53. *Weekly Dispatch*, July 4, 1824. Egan, *Boxiana*, vol. 4, 515–516.

54. *Bell's Life in London and Sporting Chronicle*, October 27, 1822 provides the most complete account of the match. Ward tearfully acknowledged the deception later at a meeting of boxers and patrons.

55. Egan, *Boxiana*, vol. 4, 539. Ward's assumption of the Championship was very controversial, considering his early involvement in match fixing. Letter from A.H., "State of the Ring—Anecdote of Jem Ward," *Sporting Magazine* 67, no. 4 (February 1826 Supplement): 197–198, Brailsford, *Bareknuckles*, 88.

56. Egan, *Boxiana*, vol. 4, 514. Writing for the *Weekly Dispatch*, Egan claimed that he used the color green for a November 1823 match against Josh Hudson. Other newspaper accounts of the match do not include this information, however. *Weekly Dispatch*, November 30, 1823.

57. Considering the very negative image of West Indian planters held by reformers and radicals in the 1820s, this neutral comment reminds us of the politics of this periodical. *Sporting Magazine* 66, no. 5 (August 1825): 309.

58. *Weekly Dispatch*, July 24, 1825. Vincent Dowling objected that a belt did not "entitle [Ward] to the rank of Champion" and argued that, to retain that rank, Ward had to meet any reasonable challenge. *Bell's Life in London*, July 24, 1825.

59. "The Championship," *Sporting Magazine* 69, no. 4 (February 1827): 260.

60. Brailsford, *Bareknuckles*, 88–89.

61. *Bell's Life in London and Sporting Chronicle*, July 17, 1831.

62. *Belfast Commercial Chronicle*, September 5, 1827.

63. *Bell's Life in London*, May 30, 1830; *Bell's Life in London*, June 6, 1830.

64. *Bell's Life in London*, June 6, 1830.

65. *Glasgow Chronicle*, June 4, 1830, reprinted in *Bell's Life in London*, June 6, 1830.

66. *Bell's Life in London*, June 6, 1830.

67. *Glasgow Chronicle*, reprinted in *Bell's Life in London*, June 13, 1830. *The Chronicle* reported that "there were not fewer than five hundred people in the green, formed into rings and witnessing pugilistic fights in various places."

68. *Bell's Life in London*, June 13, 1830. Coroner's Inquest, July 19, 1830, Buckinghamshire Summer Assizes, National Archives, ASSI 94/2079.

69. *Times*, June 5, 1830; *Times*, June 11, 1830.

70. *Bell's Life in London*, July 4, 1830. Dowling, *Fistiana*, 58.

71. *Squire Osbaldeston: His Autobiography*, ed. E.D. Cuming (London: John Lane, The Bodley Head, 1927), 262. Byrne faced seven charges, on all of which he was found not guility. Buckinghamshire County Assize, July 22, 1830, National Archives, ASSI 33/11.

72. Letter from Robert Barclay Allardice to Joseph John Gurney, reprinted in *Osbaldestone: His Autobiography*, 263.

73. As we have seen, Dan Donnelly successfully evaded a £100 challenge from Sutton shortly after his arrival in London.

74. *Weekly Dispatch*, February 23, 1817. *Weekly Dispatch*, Sunday, July 6, 1817. Egan, *Boxiana*, vol.2, 211. *Weekly Dispatch*, February 21, 1819. Egan, *Boxiana*, vol. 3, 518–519. *Weekly Dispatch*, December 12, 1819.

75. *Weekly Dispatch*, December 12, 1819.

76. *The Devil Among the Fancy*, 13–16.

77. *Weekly Dispatch*, May 16, 1819. *Weekly Dispatch*, December 26, 1819.

78. Egan, *Boxiana*, vol. 3, 12.

79. Smith, *Black Genesis*, 90. Pierce Egan, *Boxiana*, vol. 5, 212.

80. Writers often spelled Molineaux's name differently. *Ibid.*, vol. 4, 458.

81. *Weekly Dispatch*, June 10, 1827.

82. *Sporting Magazine* 70, no. 3 (July 1827): 245.

83. Egan, *Boxiana*, vol. 4, 461, 512.

84. Kevin Smith describes a benefit at the Tennis Court on June 21 in which Morgan got the best of the Oxford Champion and also a prizefighter known as "Young Gas." Smith, *Black Genesis*, 90–91. *The Sporting Magazine* reported that Morgan and Ward had sparred at Ward's benefit at the Tennis Court on June 17 and that Morgan had performed poorly. "Pugilism," *Sporting Magazine* 70, no. 4 (August 1827): 330.

85. Egan, *Boxiana*, vol. 5, 213–216. Kevin Smith shows that Morgan returned for another fight in 1829 but quickly left again. Smith, *Black Genesis*, 93. The *Birmingham Journal* reported that Morgan returned to the ring after his ship ran aground near the coast of Mottiston on the Isle of Wight. *Birmingham Journal*, July 18, 1829.

86. *Morning Chronicle* May 7, 1823.

87. Egan, *Boxiana*, vol. 5, 159, 163.

88. *Weekly Dispatch*, January 4, 1824.

89. *Sporting Magazine* 64 no. 3 (June 1824): 177–179. *Weekly Dispatch*, June 27, 1824.

90. *Morning Chronicle*, November 24, 1824.

91. For Aaron's perspective, see the letter from one of his backers, J. Alexander, to the *Weekly Dispatch*, December 5, 1824. For that of Curtis, see *Sporting Magazine* 65, no. 2 (November 1824): 116, 120. Also letters from "Investigator" and "Fair Play" to the *Weekly Dispatch*, December 12, 1824 and December 19, 1824.

92. *Sporting Magazine* 65, no. 2 (November 1824): 116, 120.

93. Letter from J. Alexander to *Weekly Dispatch*, December 5, 1824. A Jewish convert to Christianity named J. Alexander published a series of works on Jewish history in the 1860s and 1870s. It is possible that he was a patron of Jewish boxers in his youth and the writer of this letter. See *Jewish Herald, Conducted Under the Superintendence of the British Society for the Propagation of the Gospel Among the Jews* 13, no. 5 (May 1870): 72.

94. Letter from "Investigator" to *Weekly Dispatch*, December 12, 1824.

95. [Badcock], *The Fancy*, vol. 1, 153–154. As Todd Endelman writes, a host of writers disproportionately blamed Jewish people for the corruption plaguing the sport. Todd Endelman, *The Jews of Georgian England*, 223.

96. *Bell's Life in London*, May 29, 1825.

97. *Bell's Life in London*, September 25, 1825.

98. Letter from "One of the People" to *Weekly Dispatch*, January 1, 1826.

99. *Bell's Life in London*, April 23, 1826.

100. Dowling reported that two gentlemen had offered to post £30 of Aaron's stakes. *Bell's Life in London*, November 12, 1826.

101. *Bell's Life in London*, March 4, 1827.

102. Aaron defeated Frank Redman in 1827 and lost to the "Sailor Boy" in November 1828. After describing this defeat, the *Sporting Magazine* 73, no. 2 (December 1828): 184 remarked that "the *Shenies* on their return home appeared … groggified from the effects of the fog, and losing their *coriander seeds*." Henry Downes Miles claimed that he sold fish to spectators going to matches. Miles, *Pugilistica*, vol. 2, 515.

103. *Bell's Life in London*, December 3, 1826.

104. Miles, *Pugilistica*, vol. 2, 353, 397. See *Bell's Life in London*, October 28, 1827.

105. *Bell's Life in London and Sporting Chronicle*, June 2, 1833.

106. Gorn, *The Manly Art*, 41–42.

Chapter Eight

1. An ethic of humanitarianism dominated the political and social landscape of the 1830s and 1840s. Recent studies have emphasized the enduring influence of the humanitarian ethic beyond the 1840s. Kenton Scott Storey, "Colonial Humanitarian? Thomas Gore Browne and the Taranaki War, 1860–61," *Journal of British Studies* 53, no. 1 (January 2014): 112–113. See also, Richard Huzzey, *Freedom Burning: Anti-Slavery and Empire in Victorian Britain* (Ithaca: Cornell University Press, 2012).

2. Dowling, *Fistiana*, 61–62.

3. *Bell's Life in London and Sporting Chronicle*, September 14, 1845. Brailsford, *Bareknuckles*, 95–96.

4. *Bell's Life in London and Sporting Chronicle*, May 16, 1841.

5. *Bell's Life in London and Sporting Chronicle*, September 14, 1845.

6. Dowling, *Fistiana*, 16, 82–83, 88–89.

7. Chandler, "The Development of Rugby Football," 19–26.

8. Pierce Egan letter to Sir Robert Peel, December 5, 1842. British Library, Peel Papers, 3d Series, General Correspondence, Add. 40520, fol. 92. A nearly-illegible note scrawled in pencil on the front of the letter records Peel's sentiment that "it is not in my power to aid" Egan.

9. *Bell's Life in London and Sporting Chronicle*, September 28, 1828. In 1831, Dowling described a fictional auction to sell the Club's ropes and stakes "because the proprietors have no further occasion for its use" *Bell's Life in London and Sporting Chronicle*, August 21, 1831. Brailsford, *Bareknuckles*, 98.

10. *Bell's Life in London and Sporting Chronicle*, June 10, 1838. At the formation of the Fair Play Club, several members expressed their intention to revise Broughton's rules. *Sporting Magazine* 72, no. 6 (October 1828): 447.

11. The "new rules" are listed in Dowling, *Fistiana*, 65–66. Brailsford, "Morals and Maulers," 142. W. Russel Gray, "For Whom the Bell Tolled: The Decline of British Prize Fighting in the Victorian Era," *Journal of Popular Culture* 21, no. 2 (1987): 57.

12. Standardization and publication of rules was beginning to happen in other sports as well around the same time. Rules for the Rugby School version of football were published in the 1840s and the Football Association famously met in 1863 to standardize its form of football. Chandler, "The Development of Rugby Football,"18–24.

13. Brailsford, *Bareknuckles*, 101–102.

14. A series of reforms after 1829 dramatically altered metropolitan, borough, and county policing. These reforms created a professional and uniformed police force to replace the existing largely volunteer forces. See David Taylor, *The New Police in Nineteenth-Century England: Crime, Conflict and Control* (Manchester: Manchester University Press, 1997) and David Philips and Robert Storch, *Policing Provincial England, 1829–1856: The Politics of Reform* (London: Leicester Press, 1999).

15. The loose collection of boxing supporters in the metropolis, united mostly by a shared adherence to Broughton's rules, was long known as the London Prize Ring. Brailsford, *Bareknuckles*, 119.

16. *Bell's Life in London and Sporting Chronicle*, April 23, 1837.

17. *Bell's Life in London and Sporting Chronicle*, November 29, 1835. *Bell's Life in London and Sporting Chronicle*, February 14, 1836. Wharton was clearly winning his match against Britton when Britton's supporters intimidated his seconds and ultimately broke the ring. Smith, *Black Genesis*, 95–101.

18. *Bell's Life in London and Sporting Chronicle*, April 23, 1837.

19. *Bell's Life in London and Sporting Chronicle*, June 18, 1837.

20. Smith, *Black Genesis*, 103. *Bell's Life in London and Sporting Chronicle*, October 22, 1837.

21. *Bell's Life in London and Sporting Chronicle*, November 5, 1837.

22. *Bell's Life in London and Sporting Chronicle*, March 1, 1840.

23. *Bell's Life in London and Sporting Chronicle*, June 14, 1840.

24. Smith, *Black Genesis*, 105, 112–113.

25. *Bell's Life in London*, April 27 and May 4, 1856.

26. Miles, *Pugilistica*, vol. 3, 7.

27. *Bell's Life in London*, January 3, 1836.

28. *Bell's Life in London*, November 6, 1836. *Morning Advertiser*, July 29, 1836 carried an advance advertisement. Rice arrived from Philadelphia at the end of July.

29. *Bell's Life in London*, January 8, 1837.

30. Smith, *Black Genesis*, 113–114.

31. *Bell's Life in London*, May 29, 1836.

32. *Bell's Life in London*, October 16, 1836. December 25, 1836.

33. *Bell's Life in London*, December 25, 1836.

34. All of these details were reported in a Cambridge courtroom in 1843, when Sutton sued a local brick-maker named Samuel Preston for seducing and detaining his wife. Sutton lost the case. *Cambridge Chronicle and Journal*, July 20, 1844.

35. *Bell's Life in London*, October 30, 1842.

36. *Bell's Life in London*, October 30, 1842.

37. *Bell's Life in London*, March 26, 1843.

38. *Cambridge Chronicle and Journal*, July 20, 1844. Because of Sutton's fame, the case was reported around the country.

39. *Bell's Life in London*, March 30, 1845. *Era*, July 6, 1845. *Era*, July 13, 1845. *Era*, August 24, 1845.

40. *Bell's Life in London*, January 25, 1846.

41. *Bell's Life in London*, February 15, 1846. *The Era*, October 18, 1846.

42. *Era*, April 21, 1850.

43. *Bell's Life in London*, July 13, 1851.

44. *Bell's Life in London and Sporting Chronicle*, March 9, 1834. An obituary in the *New York Times* claimed that Lazarus's first prizefight was a victory against an Irishman named McCarty, "while quite a lad." *New York Times*, September 28, 1867. *Bell's Life in London* identified his first match as a draw against Jem Brown in May 1832. *Bell's Life in London*, October 19, 1867.

45. *Bell's Life in London and Sporting Chronicle*, March 16, 1834.

46. *Bell's Life in London and Sporting Chronicle*, March 23, 1834.

47. *Bell's Life in London and Sporting Chronicle*, March 30, 1834.

48. *Bell's Life in London and Sporting Chronicle*, April 6, 1834.

49. *Bell's Life in London and Sporting Chronicle*, February 21, 1836. Like the Jewish identity of boxers, accounts of matches almost always commented on the presence of Jewish spectators. This is not, of course, definitive evidence that Jewish spectators were not in attendance, but it is suggestive.

50. *Bell's Life in London and Sporting Chronicle*, March 27, 1836.

51. *Bell's Life in London and Sporting Chronicle*, September 4, 1836.

52. *Bell's Life in London and Sporting Chronicle*, March 12, 1837.

53. *Bell's Life in London and Sporting Chronicle*, June 4, 1837.

54. "My Young Days, By a Semi-Centenarian," in *Colburn's United Service Magazine and Naval and Military Journal* volume 147, no.1 (May 1878): 61–62. Another recollection from the same period followed *Bell's Life in London*'s line, arguing that Waterford organized the match "in order to promote sport." *Baily's Magazine of Sports & Pastimes*, vol. 34, no. 2 July 1879, 67.

55. A "Corinthian" suggested a well-heeled man of fashion. It was assumed that a Corinthian would not be a Jew. *Bell's Life in London*, June 4, 1837. *Bell's Life in London and Sporting Chronicle*, June 11, 1837.

56. *Bell's Life in London and Sporting Chronicle*, April 24, 1836.

57. *Bell's Life in London and Sporting Chronicle*, November 5, 1837.

58. *Bell's Life in London and Sporting Chronicle*, October 21, 1838.

59. *Bell's Life in London and Sporting Chronicle*, June 23, 1839.

60. *Bell's Life in London and Sporting Chronicle*, October 13, 1839.

61. *Bell's Life in London and Sporting Chronicle*, June 19, 1842. *Bell's Life in London and Sporting Chronicle*, February 5, 1843, *Bell's Life in London and Sporting Chronicle*, October 15, 1843, *Bell's Life in London*, July 19, 1846.

62. *Bell's Life in London and Sporting Chronicle*, April 9, 1843. *The Era*, November 5, 1843.

63. *Newcastle Journal*, December 14, 1844.

64. *Bell's Life in London and Sporting Chronicle*, May 22, 1842.

65. Susie L. Steinbach, *Understanding the Victorians: Politics, Culture and Society in Nineteenth-Century Britain* (London: Routledge, 2012), 190–193.

66. *Bell's Life in London and Sporting Chronicle*, January 26, 1845.

67. *Bell's Life in London and Sporting Chronicle*, March 22, 1846. *Bell's Life in London and Sporting Chronicle*, May 24, 1846. *Bell's Life in London and Sporting Chronicle*, July 19, 1846.

68. Jim Davis and Victor Emeljanow, *Reflecting the Audience: London Theatregoing, 1840–1880* (Iowa City: University of Iowa Press, 2001), 61–64.

69. *Bell's Life in London and Sporting Chronicle*, April 18, 1847.

70. *Bell's Life in London and Sporting Chronicle*, January 9, 1848. *Bell's Life in London and Sporting Chronicle*, August 6, 1848.

71. *Bell's Life in London and Sporting Chronicle*, June 18, 1848.

72. Henry was eleven and John nine when they sparred at the Chancellor Head in Newcastle in June 1850. *Bell's Life in London and Sporting Chronicle*, June 30, 1850.

73. *Bell's Life in London and Sporting Chronicle*, January 12, 1851. *Bell's Life in London and Sporting Chronicle*, December 21, 1851.

74. *Bell's Life in London and Sporting Chronicle*, October 2, 1836 notes that Burke's parents were Irish. Dowling, *Fistiana*, 47. *Bell's Life in London and Sporting Chronicle*, June 9, 1844.

75. Vincent Dowling's son and successor Frank wrote "What could have induced Byrne to fly at such high game as the champion, appears to have puzzled most of the knowing-ones. It was true he was the Champion of Ireland, and perhaps it was imagined … he might turn out a second Langan, but his performances in the P.R. were below mediocrity. Frank Dowling, *Fights for the Championship and Celebrated Prize Battles* (London: Bell's Life, 1855), 115.

76. O'Rourke's challenge noted that it would have been made earlier but that O'Rourke did not want to be embroiled in Burke's trial for the death of Byrne. *Bell's Life in London and Sporting Chronicle*, July 28, 1833.

77. *Dublin Observer*, December 21, 1833. *Dublin Observer*, March 8, 1834 referred to O'Rourke as the Irish Champion in a story about O'Rourke defeating a local in Dublin.

78. *Bell's Life in London and Sporting Chronicle*, April 13, 1834.

79. *Bell's Life in London and Sporting Chronicle*, May 11, 1834.

80. *Bell's Life in London and Sporting Chronicle*, May 18, 1834. Ward claimed that O'Rourke knew of the challenge before he left and deliberately avoided him because of cowardice. *Bell's Life in London and Sporting Chronicle*, June 1, 1834. O'Rourke responded from Canada with a different view. *Bell's Life in London and Sporting Chronicle*, August 31, 1834.

81. *Bell's Life in London and Sporting Chronicle*, October 11, 1835 declared Burke Champion of England.

82. *Leeds Times*, April 9, 1836.

83. Gorn, *The Manly Art*, 42–46.

84. [H.D. Miles], *Fistiana, or the Oracle of the Ring* (London: Bell's Life, 1868), 93.

85. *Bell's Life in London and Sporting Chronicle*, January 23, 1842.

86. In April, Jem Ward announced that he would back Jack Cain of Liverpool for £50 to fight Haydon but Haydon chose to fight Gould instead. *Bell's Life in London and Sporting Chronicle*, April 17, 1842. *Bell's Life in London and Sporting Chronicle*, May 15, 1842

87. *Bell's Life in London and Sporting Chronicle*, August 28, 1842

88. *Bell's Life in London and Sporting Chronicle*, October 2, 1842. *Bell's Life in London and Sporting Chronicle*, January 7, 1844.

89. *Era*, February 16, 1845.

90. *Bell's Life in London and Sporting Chronicle*, August 1, 1842.

91. Several accounts suggest that Gill was born in Dublin. For example, *The Era*, October 22, 1843. Gill's obituary gives his birthplace as Coventry. *Bell's Life in London and Sporting Chronicle*, October 23, 1869. Gill clearly always saw Coventry as his home and it seems more likely that he chose to forget his Dublin birth. Coventry had a very small Irish community until after the Second World War. Enda Delany, *The Irish in Postwar Britain* (Oxford: Oxford University Press, 2007), 103.

92. Young Foster was his opponent in February and Prichett in July. The fight with Hubbard began near Nuneaton but was interrupted by local authorities and renewed two weeks later near the country border. *Bell's Life in London and Sporting Chronicle*, February 27, 1842. *Era*, July 31, 1842. *Bell's Life in London and Sporting Chronicle*, November 27, 1842.

93. *Bell's Life in London and Sporting Chronicle*, June 25, 1843.

94. *Era*, August 20, 1843.

95. *Era*, October 22, 1843.

96. *Era*, November 5, 1843.

97. *Bell's Life in London and Sporting Chronicle*, June 9, 1844. *Era*, June 9, 1844.

98. *Bell's Life in London and Sporting Chronicle*, November 3, 1844. *Era*, November 3, 1844.

99. *Bell's Life in London and Sporting Chronicle*, July 27, 1845. *Era*, July 27, 1845.

100. *Bell's Life in London and Sporting Chronicle*, May 17, 1846.

101. *Bell's Life in London and Sporting Chronicle*, October 23, 1869.

102. *Bell's Life in London and Sporting Chronicle*, January 3, 1847.

103. *Bell's Life in London and Sporting Chronicle*, January 2, 1853.

104. *Bell's Life in London and Sporting Chronicle*, March 7, 1847.

105. Brailsford, *Bareknuckles*, 132–137.

106. Gorn, *The Manly Art*, 69–97.

107. Gorn, *The Manly Art*, 99, 113.

108. *New York Times*, September 28, 1867; *Bell's Life in London and Sporting Chronicle*, October 19, 1867.

109. Matthew Aaron Schownir, "Antipodean Identities: Violent Behaviors, Pugilism and Irish Immigrant Culture in New South Wales, 1830–1861," (M.A. Thesis, Purdue University, 2013) 43–47.

110. Grantlee Kieza, *Boxing in Australia* (Canberra: National Library of Australia, 2015), 14–15

111. Bob Petersen, "Boxing, Australia," in John Nauright and Charles Parrish, eds., *Sports around the World: History, Culture, and Practice*, vol. 1 (Santa Barbara: ABC-CLIO, 2012), 363.

112. Brailsford, *Bareknuckles*, 129–133. Brailsford makes clear that the original "pro-am" arranagement of the Pugilistic Benevolent Association did not work and it was only when real power was given to a committee of gentlemen that reforms took hold. There was dispute about whether Sayers was born of Irish parents. Strongly anti–Irish Henry Downes Miles emphatically claimed a few decades later that "Tom's pedigree is … indisputably that of an Englishman." Miles, *Pugilistica*, vol. 3, 360. *Bell's Life in London and Sporting Chronicle*, April 17, 1860, claimed that Sayers's parents came from Dingle, County Kerry.

113. Gorn, *The Manly Art*, 114–119, 148.

114. Gorn, *The Manly Art*, 148–152, 156.

115. *Times*, April 18, 1860.

116. *Times*, May 16, 1860.

117. Dennis Brailsford, *British Sport: A Social History* (Cambridge: Lutterworth Press, 1997), 85.

118. *Times*, April 18, 1860.

119. Gorn, *The Manly Art*, 154–155.

120. Brailsford, *Bareknuckles*, 129–130.

121. *Fifty Years a Fighter: The Life Story of Jem Mace (retired Champion of the World) Told By Himself* (London: C. Arthur Pearson, Ltd., 1908), 156–158, 187–193; Graham Gordon, *Master of the Ring: The Extraordinary Life of Jem Mace Father of Boxing and the First Worldwide Sports Star* (Wrea Green: Milo Books, 2007), 132–133, 172.

122. Holt, *Sport and the British*, 64–67, 149. Irish-American John L. Sullivan defeated Jim Corbett in the United States in 1892 to win the first heavyweight championship match fought under the Queensberry rules. Americans dominated the heavyweight division throughout the twentieth century, though, as Holt notes, British boxers (including many Jewish, Irish, and black boxers) had great success in the lighter weight classes.

123. Jeffrey Richards, "Introduction," in J.A. Mangan, *Athleticism in the Victorian and Edwardian Public School*, 2d ed. (London: Frank Cass, 2000), xxiv. Mangan highlights the importance of athleticism and codes of honor as a means to control behavior in the public schools, as they were invested with new importance in the Victorian period. See, esp. 22–28.

124. For evolving Victorian attitudes to race, see Christine Bolt, *Victorian Attitudes to Race* (London: Routledge & Kegan Paul, 1971) and Douglass Lorimer, *Colour, Class, and the Victorians:*

English attitudes toward the Negro in the mid-nineteenth century (Leicester: Leicester University Press, 1978). Catherine Hall, *Civilising Subjects: Metropole and Colony in the English Imagination, 1830–1867* (Chicago: University of Chicago Press, 2002) and Thomas C. Holt, *The Problem of Freedom: Race, Labor, and Politics in Jamaica and Britain, 1832–1938* (Baltimore: Johns Hopkins University Press, 1992) also demonstrate the hardening of attitudes toward race from the mid-nineteenth century. For an account of general European attitudes to race in this period, see Neil McMaster, *Racism in Europe* (New York and Basingstroke, Hampshire: Palgrave, 2001).

125. Miles, *Pugilistica*, vol. 1, v, 243.

126. L. Perry Curtis, *Apes and Angels: the Irishman in Victorian Caricature* (Washington: Smithsonian Institution Press, 1971). There is considerable debate about the importance of these caricatures. Roy Foster, "Paddy and Mr. Punch," in *Paddy and Mr. Punch: Connections in Irish and English History* (London: Penguin, 1993) is an example of those who oppose Curtis' position.

127. Miles, *Pugilistica*, vol. 1, 160, 219.

128. *Ibid.*, vol. 1, 49, 137.

129. Mangan, *Athleticism in the Public School*, 122–140. Mangan argues that many Victorians firmly believed that "there was an obvious link between the development of endurance, toughness and courage on English playing fields and pioneering in Australia, preaching in Africa and soldiering in Burma," 138.

Conclusion

1. Mike Marqusse, "In search of the unequivocal Englishman: The conundrum of race and nation in English cricket," in *'Race,' Sport, and British Society*, ed. Ben Carrington and Ian McDonald (London: Routledge, 2001), 123. This problem is unfortunately not in the past. A recent uptick of racism in football was the subject of a Parliamentary inquiry in 2012.

Bibliography

Manuscript Sources

British Library, London
William Dale Farr Papers
Robert Peel Papers
William Windham Papers
National Archives, London
Buckinghamshire Summer Assize
Buckinghamshire County Assize

Newspapers and Periodicals

London

Argus
Baily's Magazine of Sports & Pastimes
Bell's Life in London
Bell's Weekly Messenger
The British Mercury, or Annals of History, Politics, Manners, Literature, Arts, etc., of the British Empire
British Press
Colburn's United Service Magazine and Naval and Military Journal
The Country Journal, or the Craftsman
Courier
Courier and Evening Gazette
The Craftsman; or Say's Weekly Journal
Daily Advertiser, Oracle, and True Briton
The Diary; or, Woodfall's Register
Era
Evening Mail
Fraser's Magazine
General Evening Post
Gentleman's Magazine
Jewish Herald, Conducted Under the Superintendence of the British Society for the Propagation of the Gospel Among the Jews
Kent's Weekly Dispatch
Lloyd's Evening Post
London Chronicle
London Gazette
London Review and Literary Journal
Morning Advertiser
Morning Chronicle (London)
Morning Post, and Daily Advertiser (London)
New Monthly Magazine and Literary Journal
Observer
The Oracle. Bell's New World
Parker's Penny Post
The Phoenix; Or, Weekly Miscellany Improved
The Political State of Great Britain
Public Advertiser (London)
Sporting Magazine
St. James's Chronicle and Evening Post
Star (London)
Statesman
Sun (London)
Times (London)
Weekly Dispatch
Westminster Journal and Old British Spy
Whitehall Evening Post
World (London)

Dublin

Dublin Evening Mail
Dublin Evening Post
Dublin Journal
Dublin Observer
Freeman's Journal
Hoey's Dublin Mercury
Saunder's News-Letter and Daily Advertiser

Other British, Irish and International Newspapers and Periodicals

Belfast Commercial Chronicle
Birmingham Journal
Blackwood's Edinburgh Magazine
Bristol Gazette and Public Advertiser

Bristol Journal
Cambridge Chronicle
Edinburgh Review
Felix Farley's Bristol Journal
Glasgow Chronicle
Glasgow Herald
Kentish Chronicle
Leeds Times
Manchester Guardian
Manchester Mercury
Newcastle Journal
New York Times
Reading Mercury and Oxford Gazette
Scots Magazine

Published Pamphlets, Prints and Broadsides

The Art of Boxing, or Science of Manual Defense, Clearly Displayed on Rational Principles, Whereby Every Person may easily make themselves Masters of that Manly Acquirement, So as to ensure Success both in Attack & Defence. To Which is Added, Memoirs and Delineations of the Most Celebrated Pugilists, And an Account of some of their Principal Battles. By Thomas Belcher. London: W. Mason, 1815.

Battle between Simon Byrne and Deaf Burke. Edinburgh, 1833.

"Boxing Made Easy or Humphries Giving a Lesson to a Lover of the Polite Arts." Printed for John Smith, No. 35, Cheapside, Feb. 16, 1788, catalog no. 0901.379, British Museum Print Room.

The Complete Art of Boxing According to the Modern Method; Wherein the whole of that Manly Accomplishment is rendered so easy and intelligent that any Person may be an entire Master of the Science in a few Days, without any other Instruction than this book. To Which is Added the General History of Boxing, Containing an Account of the most eminent Professors of that noble Art, who have flourished from its Commencement to the present Time. By an Amateur of Eminence, new ed. London: M. Follingsby and M.Smith, 1788.

The Devil Among the Fancy; or, the Pugilistic Courts in an Uproar: To which is added, A Whimsical Dialogue between Dickey Martin, M.P. and Charley Eastup, W.P. (Or, of the Westminster-Pit) on the subject of Bears, Badgers, Bull-dogs, and the famous monkey, Jacco Maccacco; Showing the comparative Humanity of the Sports pursued in High Life and Low Life. By a member of the Pugilistic Club. London: John Fairburn, 1822.

A Dialogue in the Shades, between Mercury, a Nobleman, and a Mechanic. London: J.S. Jordan, 1794.

The Fatal Effects of Gambling Exemplified in the Murder of Wm. Weare, and the Trial and Fate of John Thurtell, the Murderer, and His Accomplices. London: Thomas Kelly, 1824.

Frankland, Sir Thomas. *Cautions to Young Sportsmen*. London: J. Smeeton, 1801.

The Genuine Memoirs of Dennis O'Kelly Esq. commonly called Count O'Kelly Containing many curious Anecdotes of that Celebrated Character, and his Coadjutors on the Turf and in the Field, with a Variety of authentic, singular, and entertaining Militia Manoeuvres, never before published. London: C. Stalker, 1788.

A Hit at the Tenth, In Three Cantos, By One of the Fancy. London: Sherwood, Jones, and Co., 1824.

A letter to the Right Hon. William Windham, on his late opposition to the bill to prevent bull-baiting: by an old Member of Parliament. To which are annexed, some letters and extracts on the same subject. Also some verses on hunting, 2d ed., rev. and cor., with additions. London: W. Stratford, 1800.

Moore, Thomas. *Memoirs of Captain Rock, the Celebrated Irish Chieftain With Some Account of His Ancestors*. Paris: A. and W. Galignani, 1824.

[Moore, Thomas]. *Tom Crib's Memorial to Congress with a Preface, Notes, and Appendix. By One of the Fancy*. London: William A. Mercein, 1819.

Russel, William P. *Arguments upon Boxing or Pugilism; which will always be proper for perusal, so long as the brutal practice of boxing shall continue; but more especially applicable now, as the subject has just been discussed at the British Forum, No. 22 Piccadilly, By a Friend to Rational Debat*. London: William P. Russel, 1806.

A Treatise on the Art and Practice of Self-Defence; or, Instructions how to obtain a scientific mode of boxing... To which are added, descriptions of pugilistic attitudes, etc. By a celebrated Pugilist. London: 1826.

Published Diaries, Letters, Memoirs and Collected Works

Andrew, Donna T., ed. *London Debating Societies, 1776–1799*. London: London Record Society, 1994.

Boswell, James. *The Correspondence of James Boswell with Certain Members of The Club including Oliver Goldsmith, Bishops Percy and Barnard, Sir Joshua Reynolds, Topham Beauclerk, and Bennet Langton*, ed. Charles N. Fifer, vol. 3. New York: McGraw-Hill Book Company, 1976.

Byron, George Gordon, Lord Byron. *Letters and Journals of Lord Byron*, ed. Thomas Moore. London: John Murray, 1839.

Clare, John. *John Clare: Selected Poems*, ed. Geoffrey Summerfeld. London: Penguin Books, 1990.

Denvir, John. *The Life Story of an Old Rebel*. Shannon: Irish University Press, 1972; 1st Edition, Dublin, 1910.

Derry, John, ed. *Cobbett's England: A Selection from the Writings of William Cobbett with Engravings by James Gillray*. London: The Folio Society, 1968.

Hughes, J.F. *Memoirs of His Royal Highness, the Prince of Wales*. London: B. Clark, 1808.

Mace, Jem. *Fifty Years a Fighter: The Life Story of Jem Mace (retired Champion of the World) Told By Himself*. London: C. Arthur Pearson, Ltd., 1908.

Maginn, William. *Miscellaneous Writings of the Late Dr. Maginn*, ed. Shelton Mackenzie, vol. 2. New York: Redfield, 1955.

Mendoza, Daniel. *The Memoirs of the Life of Daniel Mendoza*, ed. Paul Magriel. London: B.T. Batsford, Ltd., 1951.

Moore, Thomas. *Memoirs, Journal, and Correspondence of Thomas Moore*, ed. Lord John Russell. London and Boston: Longman, Brown, Green, and Longmans; and Little, Brown, & Co., 1853.

Osbaldeston, George. *Squire Osbaldeston: His Autobiography*, ed. E.D. Cuming. London: John Lane, The Bodley Head, 1927.

Phillips, Charles. *Recollections of Curran and some of his contemporaries*. London, 1818.

Sheridan, Richard Brinsley. *The Letters of Richard Brinsley Sheridan*, vol. 2, ed. Cecil Price. Oxford: Clarendon Press, 1966.

Wilberforce, Robert Isaac, and Samuel Wilberforce, *The Life of William Wilberforce*, vol. 2. London: John Murray, 1838.

Windham, William. *The Diary of the Right Hon. William Windham*, ed. Mrs. Henry Baring. London: Longmans, Green, and Co., 1866.

_____. *Speeches in Parliament of the Right Honourable William Windham*, vol. 1, ed. Thomas Amyot. London: Longman, Hurst, Rees, Orme, and Brown, 1812.

Other Published Primary Sources

Archenholtz, J.W. von, ed., *The English Lyceum, or, Choice of Pieces in Prose and in Verse, Selected from the Best Periodical Papers, Magazins, Pamphlets and other British Publications*. Hamburg: Mr. Bohn, 1787.

Barber, Captain. *Considerations Upon the Best Means of Ensuring the Internal Defence of Great Britain*. London: C. Rosworth, 1805.

Barry, Edward. *A Letter on the Practice of Boxing*. London: A. Grant, 1789.

Bayne, The Rev. Robert. *Historical Sketch of Rickmansworth and the Surrounding Parishes*. London: Watson & Hazell, 1870.

Bee, Jon (pseud.) [John Badcock]. *The Fancy; or True Sportsman's Guide: Being Authentic Memoirs of the Lives, Actions, Prowess, and Battles of the Leading Pugilists, From the Days of Figg and Broughton ot the Championship of Ward, by an Operator*, 2 vols. London: J. McGowan and Son, 1826.

_____. *Fancy-Ana; or, A History of Pugilism, From Figg and Broughton's Time to Spring and Langan's; Including Every Transaction in the Prize-Ring, And Every Incident Worthy Notice (Whether of Spree, Turn-up, Boxing-Match, or Prize-Fight,) From 1719 to 1824 Inclusive*. London: W. Lewis, 1824.

_____. *Slang, A Dictionary of the Turf, the Ring, the Chase, the Pit, of Bon-ton, and the Varieties of Life, Forming the Completest and Most Authentic Lexicon Balatronicum Hitherto Offered to the Notice of the Sporting World, for Elucidating Words and Phrases that are Necessarily, or Purposely, Cramp, Mutative, and Unintelligible, Outside their Respective Spheres*. London: T. Hughes, 1823.

Borrow, George. *Lavengro: The Scholar, the Gypsy, and the Priest*. London: J. Murray, 1851; reprint, London: J. Murray, 1907.

Boulton, William B. *The Amusements of Old London: Being a Survey of the Sports and Pastimes, Tea Gardens and Parks, Playhouses and Other Diversions of the People of London from the 17th to the Beginning of the 19th Century*. London: John C. Nimmo, 1901.

de Valbourg, François Maximilien Misson. *Mémoires et observations faites par un voyageur en Angleterre*. Van Bulderen, 1698.

Dowling, Frank. *Fights for the Championship and Celebrated Prize Battles*. London: Bell's Life, 1855.

Dowling, Vincent. *Fistiana; or, Oracle of the Ring*. London: William Clement, Jr., 1841.

The Dublin Almanac and General Register for Ireland, for the Year of Our Lord, 1847. Dublin: Pettigrew and Oulton, 1847.

Egan, Pierce. *Boxiana; or Sketches of ancient and modern pugilism: from the days of the renowned Broughton and Slack to the heroes of the present milling era!*, 5 vols. London: G. Smeeton, 1812; London: Sherwood, Neely, and Jones, 1818–1821; London: George Virtue, 1828–1829.

Francis, John. *Annals, Anecdotes, and Legends: A Chronicle of Life Assurance.* London: Longman, Brown, Green, and Longmans, 1853.

Gidney, W.T. *The History of the London Society for Promoting Christianity Amongst the Jews, From 1809 to 1908.* London: London Society for Promoting Christianity amongst the Jews, 1908.

Godfrey, Captain John. *A Treatise on the Useful Science of Defense.* London: Robinson and Milton's, 1747.

Grattan, Henry. *Mr. Grattan's Observations on the Certain Proceedings Against Him in Dublin.* Dublin: Vincent Dowling, 1798.

Great Britain. *Hansard Parliamentary Debates*, vol. 35 (1800), cols. 202–206.

Hamilton, Alexander. *A New Account of the East Indies: Giving an Exact and Copious Description of the Situation, Product, Manufactures, Laws, Customs, Religion, Trade, &c. of All the Countries and Islands, which Lie Between the Cape of Good Hope and the Island of Japon.* London: C. Hitch, 1744.

Hazlitt, William. "The Fight." In *The Collected Works of William Hazlitt*, ed. A.R. Waller and Arnold Glover. London: J.M. Dent & Co., 1904.

Irish Society of London, for Promoting the Education of the Native Irish, through the Medium of Their [sic] Own Language. London: J.Wilson, 1822.

Mason, Edward Tuckerman. *Personal Traits of British Authors.* New York: C. Scribner's Sons, 1885.

Mayhew, Henry. *London Labour and the London Poor*, vol. 3. London: Griffin, Bohn, and Company, 1861.

Miles, Henry Downes. *Pugilistica: The History of British Boxing, containing lives of the most celebrated pugilists; full reports of their battles from contemporary newspapers, with authentic portraits, personal anecdotes, and sketches of the principal patrons of the prize ring, forming a complete history of the ring from Fig and Broughton, 1719–40, to the last championship battle between King and Heenan, in December 1863*, 3 vols. London: Weldon, 1880–1881; reprint, Edinburgh: John Grant, 1906.

[Miles, H.D.]. *Fistiana, or the Oracle of the Ring.* London: Bell's Life, 1868.

Mingaud, Edward. *The Life and Adventures of James Ward, Viewed as "The Champion" and "The Artist."* London: W.S. Johnson, 1853.

Nichols, John, George Steevens, and Thomas Phillips. *The Genuine Works of William Hogarth: Illustrated with Biographical Anecdotes, a Chronological Catalogue and Commentary*, vol. 3. London: Longman, Hurst, Rees and Orme, 1808.

Nichols, John B. *Illustrations of the Literary History of the Eighteenth Century*, vol. 6. Westminster: J.B. Nichols & Son, 1831.

O'Neill, Capt. Francis. *Irish Minstrels and Musicians, with Numerous Dissertations on Related Subjects.* Chicago: Regan Printing House, 1913.

Oxberry, William. *Oxberry's Dramatic Biography and Histrionic Anecdotes.* London: George Virtue, 1825.

_____. *Pancratia, or, A history of pugilism: containing a full account of every battle of note from the time of Broughton and Slack down to the present day.* London: W. Oxberry, 1812.

Papers Relative to Certain Pecuniary Transactions of Messrs. William Palmer and Co. with His Highness the Nizam. London: J.L. Cox, 1824.

Rede, William Leman. *The Royal Rake, and the Adventures of Alfred Chesterton.* London: Chapman and Elcoate, 1842.

Scott, Walter. *The British Drama; Comprehending the Best Plays in the English Language.* London: William Miller, 1804.

Simond, Louis. *Journal of a Tour and Residence in Great Britain During the Years 1810 and 1811, by a French Traveller: with Remarks on the Country, its Arts, Literature, and Politics, and on the Manners and Customs of its Inhabitants.* Edinburgh: George Ramsay and Company, 1815.

The Spirit of the Public Journals for 1802, Being an Impartial Selection of the Most Exquisite Essays and Jeux D'Esprits, Principally Prose, that Appear in the Newspapers and other Publications, vol. 6. London: James Ridgway, 1803.

Strutt, Joseph. *The Sports and Pastimes of the People of England*, new ed. London: Methuen & co., 1903.

The Treble Almanac. Dublin, 1832.

United Kingdom. *Hansard Parliamentary Debates*, vol. 36 (1801–1803), cols. 829–849.

Wilson, Henry. *Wonderful Characters*, vol. 3. London: Robins & Albion Press, 1822.

Wroth, Warwick William, and Arthur Edgar Wroth. *The London Pleasure Gardens of the Eighteenth Century.* London: Macmillan & Co., 1896.

Online Records and Digital Archives

The British Newspaper Archive. http://www.britishnewspaperarchive.co.uk (last accessed August 1, 2016).

Hitchcock, Tim, Robert Shoemaker, Clive Emsley, Sharon Howard, and Jamie McLaughlin, et al. *The Old Bailey Proceedings Online*, 1674–1913 (www.oldbaileyonline.org, version 7.2, 26 September 2015).

Newspaper Archive. Newspaperarchive.com (last accessed April 1, 2016).

Published Secondary Sources

Åkermark, Athanasia Spiliopoulou. *Justifications of Minority Protection in International Law*. London: Kluwer Law International, 1996.

Bailey, Craig. *Irish London: Middle-Class Migration in the Global Eighteenth Century*. Liverpool: Liverpool University Press, 2013.

Barker, Hannah. *Newspapers, Politics, and Public Opinion in Late Eighteenth Century England*. London: Clarendon Press, 1998.

Barnard, Toby. "The Irish in London and the London Irish, ca. 1660–1780." *Eighteenth-Century Life* 39, no. 1 (January 2015), 14–40.

Belchem, John. "Comment: Whiteness and the Liverpool Irish." *Journal of British Studies* 44, no. 1 (January 2005), 146–152.

_____. *Merseypride: Essays in Liverpool Exceptionalism*. Liverpool: Liverpool University Press, 2000.

Bergin, John. "Irish Catholics and their Networks in Eighteenth-Century London." *Eighteenth-Century Life* 30, no.1 (January 2015), 66–102.

Birley, Derek. *Sport and the Making of Britain*. Manchester: Manchester University Press, 1993.

Boddy, Kasia. *Boxing: A Cultural History*. London: Reaktion Books, 2008.

Bolster, W. Jeffrey. *Black Jacks: African Americans in the Age of Sail*. Cambridge,: Harvard University Press, 1997.

Bolt, Christine. *Victorian Attitudes to Race*. London: Routledge & Kegan Paul, 1971.

Borsay, Peter. "Urban Life and Culture." In *A Companion to Eighteenth Century Britain*, ed. H.T. Dickinson. Malden, MA: Blackwell, 2002, 196–208.

Bourne, H. R. Fox *English Newspapers: Chapters in the History of Journalism*, vol. 1. London: Chatto & Windus, 1887.

Bowen, H.V. *War and British Society, 1688–1815*. Cambridge: Cambridge University Press, 1998.

Brailsford, Dennis. *Bareknuckles: A Social History of Prize-Fighting*. Cambridge: Lutterworth Press, 1988.

_____. *British Sport: A Social History*. Cambridge: Lutterworth, 1997.

_____. "Morals and Maulers: The Ethics of Early Pugilism." *Journal of Sport History* 12, no. 2 (Summer 1985): 126–142.

Briggs, Peter M. "Daniel Mendoza and Sporting Celebrity: A Case Study." In *Romanticism and Celebrity Culture, 1750–1850*, ed. Tom Mole. Cambridge: Cambridge University Press, 2009, 103–119.

Brockliss, L. W. B., and David Eastwood. "Introduction." In *A Union of Multiple Identities: The British Isles, C. 1750–c. 1850*. Manchester: Manchester University Press, 1997, 1–8.

Burke, Sir Bernard. *History of the Landed Gentry of Great Britain and Ireland*, vol. 1. London: Harrison and Sons, 1894.

Burnim Kalman, A., and Philip H. Highfill, Jr. *John Bell: Patron of British Theatrical Portraiture: A Catalog of the Theatrical Portraits in his Editions of Bell's Shakespeare and Bell's British Theatre*. Carbondale: Southern Illinois University Press, 1998.

Carr, Rosalind. *Gender and Enlightenment Culture in Eighteenth-century Scotland*. Edinburgh: Edinburgh University Press, 2014.

Chancellor, V.E. "Anti-Racialism or Censorship? The 1802 Jewish Riots at Covent Garden Opera and the Career of Thomas John Dibdin." *The Opera Quarterly* 18, no. 1 (Winter 2002), 18–25.

Chandler, Timothy J.L. "The Structuring of Manliness and of Rugby Football at the Public Schools and Oxbridge, 1830–1880." In *Making Men: Rugby and Masculine Identity*, ed. John Nauright and Timothy J.L. Chandler. London: Frank Cass & Co., 1996, 13–31.

Chill, Adam. "Ireland Forever! Irish Boxers and Britishness in the early Nineteenth Century." *Journal for the Study of British Cultures* 18, no. 1 (January 2011), 15–26.

_____. "The Performance and Marketing of Minority Identity in Late-Georgian Boxing." In *Fighting Back? Jewish and Black Boxers in Britain*, ed. Michael Berkowitz and Ruti Ungar. London: University College London, 2007, 33–49.

Clark, Anna. *Scandal: The Sexual Politics of the British Constitution*. Princeton: Princeton University Press, 2004.

_____. *The Struggle for the Breaches: Gender and the Making of the British Working Class*.

Berkeley: University of California Press, 1995.

Clarke, Bob. *From Grub Street to Fleet Street: An Illustrated History of English Newspapers to 1899*. Aldershot, Hants: Ashgate, 2004.

Cohen, Michèle. "Manliness, Effeminacy, and the French: Gender and the Construction of National Character in Eighteenth-Century England." In Tim Hitchcock and Michèle Cohen, ed., *English Masculinities, 1660–1800*. London: Longman, 1999.

Colley, Linda. *Britons: Forging the Nation, 1707–1837*. New Haven: Yale University Press, 1992.

Cone, Carl B. "The Molineaux-Cribb Fight, 1810: Wuz Tom Molineaux Robbed?" *Journal of Sport History* 9 (Winter 1982), 83–91

Connolly, S.J. "Mass Politics and Sectarian Conflict, 1823–1830." In *Ireland under the Union, I, 1801–1870*, ed. W.E. Vaughan, A New History of Ireland, vol. 5. Oxford: Clarendon Press, 1989, 74–107.

_____. "Union Government, 1812–23." In *Ireland under the Union, I, 1801–1870*, ed. W.E. Vaughan, A New History of Ireland, vol. 5. Oxford: Clarendon Press, 1989, 48–73.

Connors, Linda E., and Mary Lu MacDonald. *National Identity in Great Britain and British North America, 1815–1851, the Role of Nineteenth-Century Periodicals*. Farnham, Surrey: Ashgate, 2011.

Cookson, J.E. *The British Armed Nation, 1793–1815*. Oxford: Clarendon Press, 1997.

Cox, David J., Kim Stevenson, Candida Harris, and Judith Rowbotham, *Public Indecency in England, 1857–1960: 'A Serious and Growing Evil.'* London: Routledge, 2015.

Crais, Clifton C., and Pamela Scully. *Sara Baartman and the Hottentot Venus: A Ghost Story and a Biography*. Princeton: Princeton University Press, 2011.

Cronin, Richard. "Keats and the Politics of Cockney Style." *Studies in English Literature, 1500–1900* 36, no. 4 (Autumn 1996), 785–806.

Curtis, L. Perry. *Apes and Angels: the Irishman in Victorian Caricature*. Washington: Smithsonian Institution Press, 1971.

Dart, Gregory. "'Flash Style': Pierce Egan and Literary London 1820–28." *History Workshop Journal* 51, no. 1 (Spring 2001), 180–205.

Davis, Graham. *The Irish in Britain, 1815–1914*. Dublin: Gill and MacMillan, 1991.

Davis, Jim, and Victor Emeljanow. *Reflecting the Audience: London Theatregoing, 1840–1880*. Iowa City: University of Iowa Press, 2001.

Delany, Enda. *The Irish in Postwar Britain*. Oxford: Oxford University Press, 2007.

Delheye, Pascal, ed. *Making Sport History: Disciplines, Identities, and the Historiography of Sport*. Abingdon, Oxon: Routledge, 2014.

de Nie, Michael. *The Eternal Paddy: Irish Identity and the British Press*. Madison: University of Wisconsin Press, 2004.

Donnelly, James S., Jr. "Pastorini and Captain Rock: Millenarianism and Sectarianism in the Rockite Movement of 1821–4." In *Irish Peasants: Violence and Political Unrest, 1780–1914*, ed. Samuel Clark and James S. Donnelly, Jr. Madison: University of Wisconsin Press, 1983, 102–142.

Edwards, Paul. "Black Personalities in Georgian Britain" *History Today* 31, no. 9 (September 1981), 39–43.

Endelman, Todd M. *The Jews of Georgian England, 1714–1830: Tradition and Change in a Liberal Society*. Philadelphia: The Jewish Publication Society of America, 1979.

_____. *The Jews of Britain, 1656–2000*. Berkeley: University of California Press, 2002.

Fedorak, Charles John. "In Defense of Great Britain: Henry Addington, the Duke of York and Military Preparations against Invasion by Napoleonic France, 1803–1804." In Mark Philip, ed., *Resisting Napoleon: The British Response to the Threat of Invasion, 1797–1815*. Aldershot: Ashgate, 2004, 91–110.

Fleischer, Nat, and Sam Andre. *An Illustrated History of Boxing*. Rev. ed. New York: Citadel Press, 2001.

Ford, John. *Prizefighting: The Age of Regency Boximania*. Newton Abbot: David & Charles, 1971.

Foster, Roy. *Paddy and Mr. Punch: Connections in Irish and English History*. London: Penguin, 1993.

George, M. Dorothy. *London Life in the Eighteenth Century*. Reprint, London: Penguin Books, 1976.

Goodrich, Amanda. *Debating England's Aristocracy: Pamphlets, Polemics, and Political Ideas*. London: Royal Historical Society, 2005.

Gordon, Graham. *Master of the Ring: The Extraordinary Life of Jem Mace Father of Boxing and the First Worldwide Sports Star*. Wrea Green: Milo Books, 2007.

Gorn, Elliot J. *The Manly Art: Bare-Knuckle Prizefighting in America*. Ithaca: Cornell University Press, 1986.

Gray, W. Russel. "For Whom the Bell Tolled: The Decline of British Prize Fighting in the Victorian Era." *Journal of Popular Culture* 21, no. 2 (Fall 1987), 53–64.

Greene, John C. *Theatre in Dublin, 1745–1820: A Calendar of Performances*. Bethlehem: Lehigh University Press, 2011.

Griffin, Emma. *England's Revelry: A History of Popular Sports and Pastimes 1660–1830*. Oxford: Oxford University Press, 2005.

Guttmann, Allen. *The Olympics, a History of the Modern Games*. Urbana: University of Illinois Press, 2002.

Hall, Catherine. *Civilising Subjects: Metropole and Colony in the English Imagination, 1830–1867*. Chicago: University of Chicago Press, 2002.

Harris, Ruth-Ann M. *The Nearest Place That Wasn't Ireland: Early Nineteenth-Century Irish Labor Migration*. Ames: Iowa State University Press, 1994.

Harvey, Adrian. *The Beginnings of a Commercial Sporting Culture, 1793–1850*. Burlington, VT: Ashgate, 2004.

_____. *Football: The First 100 Years: The Untold Story*. London: Routledge, 2005.

Haydon, Colin. "'I love my King and my Country, but a Roman catholic I hate': Anticatholicism, Xenophobia, and National Identity in Eighteenth-Century England." In *Protestantism and National Identity: Britain and Ireland, c. 1650–c. 1850*. Cambridge: Cambridge University Press, 1999, 33–52.

Hilton, Boyd. *A Mad, Bad, and Dangerous People?: England 1783–1846*. Oxford: Oxford University Press, 2006.

Holt, Richard. *Sport and the British: A Modern History*. Oxford: Clarendon Press, 1990.

Holt, Thomas C. *The Problem of Freedom: Race, Labor, and Politics in Jamaica and Britain, 1832–1938*. Baltimore: Johns Hopkins University Press, 1992.

Hopkins, Frank. *Rare Old Dublin: Heroes, Hawkers, and Hoors*. Dublin: Marino Books, 2002.

Hughes, Ben. *Conquer or Die! Wellington's Veterans and the Liberation of the New World*. Oxford: Osprey Publishing, 2012.

Huzzey, Richard. *Freedom Burning: Anti-Slavery and Empire in Victorian Britain*. Ithaca: Cornell University Press, 2012.

Johnes, Martin. "Great Britain," *Routledge Companion to Sports History*. Abingdon, Oxon: Routledge, 2010, 444–460.

Kelly, James. *Sport in Ireland, 1600–1840*. Dublin: Four Courts Press, 2014.

Kieza, Grantlee. *Boxing in Australia*. Canberra: National Library of Australia, 2015.

Kumar, Krishan. *The Making of English National Identity*. Cambridge: Cambridge University Press, 2003.

Lees, Lynn Hollen. *Exiles of Erin: Irish Migrants in Victorian London*. Ithaca: Cornell University Press, 1979.

Litherfield, Benjamin. "The Field and the Stage: Pugilism, Combat Performance, and Professional Wrestling in England, 1700–1980." PhD diss., University of Sussex, 2014.

Lorimer, Douglass. *Colour, Class, and the Victorians: English attitudes toward the Negro in the mid-nineteenth century*. Leicester: Leicester University Press, 1978.

MacRaild, Donald M. *Irish Migrants in Modern Britain, 1750–1922*. New York: St. Martin's Press, 1999.

Mackesy, Piers. *War without Victory: The Downfall of Pitt, 1799–1802*. Oxford: Clarendon Press, 1984.

Malcomson, Robert. *Popular Recreations in English Society, 1700–1850*. Cambridge: Cambridge University Press, 1973.

Mangan, J.A. *Athleticism in the Victorian and Edwardian Public School*, 2d ed. London: Frank Cass, 2000.

Marqusse, Mike. "In Search of the Unequivocal Englishman: The Conundrum of Race and Nation in English Cricket." In *'Race,' Sport and British Society*, ed. Ben Carrington and Ian McDonald. London: Routledge, 2001, 121–132.

Matthew, H.C.G., and Brian Harrison, eds. *Oxford Dictionary of National Biography*. Oxford University Press, 2004. http://www.oxforddnb.com/ (last accessed January 15, 2017).

Muir, Rory. *Britain and the Defeat of Napoleon, 1807–1815*. New Haven: Yale University Press, 1996.

Murray, Edmundo. "John Devereux." In *Ireland and the Americas: Culture, Politics, and History, A Multidisciplinary Encyclopedia*, ed. James P. Byrne, Philip Coleman, and Jason King, vol. 1. Santa Barbara: ABC-CLIO, 2008, 250–251.

Myers, Norma *Reconstructing the Black Past: Blacks in Britain c. 1780–1830*. London: Frank Cass, 1996.

Myler, Patrick. *The Fighting Irish: Ireland's Role in World Boxing History*. Dingle, Ireland: Brandon Book Publishers, 1987.

_____. *Regency Rogue: Dan Donnelly his life and legends*. Dublin: The O'Brien Press, 1976.

Nechtman, Tillman W. *Nabobs: Empire and Identity in Eighteenth-Century Britain*. Cambridge: Cambridge University Press, 2013.

Neuheiser, Jörg. *Crown, Church and Constitution: Popular Conservatism in England, 1815–1867*. Trans. Jennifer Walcoff Neuheiser. Oxford: Berghahn Books, 2016.

O'Shaugnessy, David "'Tolerably Numerous': Recovering the London Irish of the Eighteenth Century," *Eighteenth-Century Life* 30, no.1 (January 2015), 1–13.

Palmer, Alan. *The East End: Four Centuries of London Life*, rev. ed. New Brunswick: Rutgers University Press, 2000.

Petersen, Bob. "Boxing, Australia." In *Sports around the World: History, Culture, and Practice*, vol. 1, ed. John Nauright and Charles Parrish. Santa Barbara: ABC-CLIO, 2012, 363–364.

Philips, David, and Robert Storch. *Policing Provincial England, 1829–1856: The Politics of Reform*. London: Leicester Press, 1999.

Pittock, Murray G. H. *Inventing and Resisting Britain: Cultural Identities in Britain and Ireland, 1685–1789*. Basingstoke: Macmillan, 1997.

Pollock, John. *Wilberforce*. London: Constable, 1977.

Rabin, Dana. "Imperial Disruptions: City, Nation, and Empire in the Gordon Fiots," in *The Gordon Riots: Politics, Culture and Insurrection in Late-Eighteenth Century Britain*, ed. Ian Haywood and John Seed. Cambridge: Cambridge University Press, 2012, 93–114.

_____. "The Jew Bill of 1753: Masculinity, Virility, and the Nation," *Eighteenth-Century Studies* 39, no. 2 (2006), 157–171.

Ragussis, Michael. *Figures of Conversion: "The Jewish Question" and English National Identity.* Durham: Duke University Press, 1995.

_____. "Jews and Other 'Outlandish Englishmen': Ethnic Performance and the Invention of British Identity under the Georges." *Critical Inquiry* 26, no. 4 (Summer 2000), 773–797.

_____. *Theatrical Nation: Jews and Other Outlandish Englishmen in Georgian Britain.* Philadelphia: University of Pennsylvania Press, 2010.

Radford, Peter. *The Celebrated Captain Barclay: Sport, Money and Fame in Regency Britain.* London: Headline Books, 2001.

Reid, J.C. *Bucks and Bruisers: Pierce Egan and Regency England.* London: Routledge & Kegan Paul, 1971.

Rogers, Nicholas. "Brave Wolfe: The Making of a Hero." In *A New Imperial History: Culture, Identity, and Modernity in Britain and the Empire, 1660–1840*, ed. Kathleen Wilson. Cambridge: Cambridge University Press, 2003, 239–259.

_____."The Gordon Riots and the Politics of War." In *The Gordon Riots: Politics, Culture and Insurrection in Late Eighteenth-century Britain*, ed. Ian Haywood and John Seed. Cambridge: Cambridge University Press, 2015, 21–45.

Sawyer, Tom. *A Noble Art: An Artistic and Literary Celebration of the Old English Prize-Ring.* London: Unwin Hyman Limited, 1989.

Schownir, Matthew Aaron. "Antipodean Identities: Violent Behaviors, Pugilism and Irish Immigrant Culture in New South Wales, 1830–1861" M.A. Thesis, Purdue University, 2013.

Semple, Rhonda A. "Missionary Manhood: Professionalism, Belief and Masculinity in the Nineteenth-Century British Imperial Field." *The Journal of Imperial and Commonwealth History* 36, no. 3 (2008): 397–415.

Shyllon, F.O. *Black Slaves in Britain.* London: Oxford University Press, 1974.

Singer, Alan Howard. "Aliens and Citizens: Jews and Protestant Naturalization in the Making of the Modern British Nation, 1689–1753" PhD diss., University of Missouri–Columbia, 1999.

Smith, Kevin R. *Black Genesis: The History of the Black Prizefighter, 1760–1870.* New York: iUniverse Press, 2003.

Smith, Malissa. *A History of Women's Boxing.* Lanham, MD: Rowman and Littlefield, 2014.

Steinbach, Susie. *Understanding the Victorians: Politics, Culture and Society in Nineteenth-Century Britain.* New York: Routledge, 2012.

Storey, Kenton Scott. "Colonial Humanitarian? Thomas Gore Browne and the Taranaki War, 1860–61." *Journal of British Studies* 53, no. 1 (January 2014), 111–135.

Streets, Heather. *Martial Races: The Military, Race and Masculinity in British Imperial Culture, 1857–1914.* Manchester: Manchester University Press, 2011.

Swift, Roger, ed. *Irish Migrants in Britain, 1815–1914: A Documentary History.* Cork: Cork University Press, 2002.

Taylor, David. *The New Police in Nineteenth-Century England: Crime, Conflict and Control.* Manchester: Manchester University Press, 1997.

Thale, Mary. "London Debating Societies in the 1790s," *Historical Journal* 32, no. 1 (1989), 57–86.

Tosh, John. "Masculinities in an Industrializing Society: Britain, 1800–1914." *The Journal of British Studies* 44, no. 2 (April 2005), 330–42.

Tranter, Neil. *Sport, Economy, and Society in Britain 1750–1914.* Cambridge: Cambridge University Press, 1998.

Ungar, Ruti. "The Boxing Discourse in Late Georgian Britain, 1780–1820: A Study in Civic Humanism, Class, and Race." PhD diss., Humboldt University of Berlin, 2012.

Wahrman, Dror. *Imagining the Middle Class: The Political Representation of Class in*

Britain, c. 1780–1840. Cambridge: Cambridge University Press, 1995.

_____. "*Percy*'s Prologue: From Gender Play to Gender Panic in Eighteenth-Century England." *Past and Present* 159 (May 1998), 113–160.

Walvin, James. *Black and White: The Negro and English Society, 1555–1945.* London: Allen Lane, 1973.

Ward, J.R. "The British West Indies in the Age of Abolition." In *The Oxford History of the British Empire, Volume II: The Eighteenth Century*, ed. P.J. Marshall and Alaine Low. Oxford: Oxford University Press, 1998, 415–439.

Waters, Maureen. *The Comic Irishman.* Albany: State University of New York Press, 1984.

Webster, Anthony. *The Richest East India Merchant: The Life and Business of John Palmer of Calcutta, 1767–1836.* Woodbridge: The Boydell Press, 2007.

Whale, John. "Daniel Mendoza's Contests of Identity: Masculinity, Ethnicity, and Nation." *Romanticism* 14, no. 3 (October 2008), 259–271

Wheeler, Harold Felix Baker, and Alexander Meyrick Broadley. *Napoleon and the Invasion of Britain: The Story of the Great Terror*, vol. 2. London: The John Lane Company, 1908.

Williams, Luke G. *Richmond Unchained: The Biography of the World's First Black Superstar.* Gloucestershire: Amberley, 2015.

Wilson, Kathleen. "Empire, Trade and Popular Politics in Mid–Hanoverian Britain: The Case of Admiral Vernon." *Past and Present* 121, no. 1 (November 1988), 74–109.

_____. "The Good, the Bad, and the Impotent: Imperialism and the Politics of Identity in Georgian England," in *The Consumption of Culture, 1600–1800: Image, Object, Text*, ed. Ann Bermingham and John Brewer. London: Routledge, 1995, 236–262.

_____. *The Island Race: Englishness, Empire, and Gender in the Eighteenth Century.* London: Routledge, 2003.

_____. "Nelson and the People: Manliness, Patriotism and Body Politics." In *Admiral Lord Nelson: Context and Legacy*, ed. David Cannadine. Houndmills, Hampshire: Palgrave Macmillan 2005, 49–66.

Index